CULTURAL HISTORIES OF CINEMA

This new book series examines the relationship between cinema and culture. It will feature interdisciplinary scholarship that focuses on the national and transnational trajectories of cinema as a network of institutions, representations, practices and technologies. Of primary concern is analysing cinema's expansive role in the complex social, economic and political dynamics of the twentieth and twenty-first centuries.

SERIES EDITORS
Lee Grieveson and Haidee Wasson

ALSO PUBLISHED
Empire and Film, *edited by Lee Grieveson and Colin MacCabe*
Film and the End of Empire, *edited by Lee Grieveson and Colin MacCabe*
Shadow Economies of Cinema: Mapping Informal Film Distribution, *Ramon Lobato*

Global Mexican Cinema: Its Golden Age

'el cine mexicano se impone'

Robert McKee Irwin and Maricruz Castro Ricalde

with Mónica Szurmuk, Inmaculada Álvarez and Dubravka Sužnjević

A BFI book published by Palgrave Macmillan

First published in 2013 by
PALGRAVE MACMILLAN

on behalf of the

BRITISH FILM INSTITUTE
21 Stephen Street, London W1T 1LN
www.bfi.org.uk

There's more to discover about film and television through the BFI.
Our world-renowned archive, cinemas, festivals, films, publications and learning resources are here
to inspire you.

Palgrave Macmillan in the UK is an imprint of Macmillan Publishers Limited, registered in
England, company number 785998, of Houndmills, Basingstoke, Hampshire RG21 6XS. Palgrave
Macmillan in the US is a division of St Martin's Press LLC, 175 Fifth Avenue, New York, NY 10010.
Palgrave Macmillan is the global academic imprint of the above companies and has companies and
representatives throughout the world. Palgrave® and Macmillan® are registered trademarks in the
United States, the United Kingdom, Europe and other countries.

Cover image: *La balandra Isabel llegó esta tarde* (100% Venezuelan production, 1950), image
courtesy of Productora Cinematográfica Bolívar Films, C.A.
Images on pp. 5, 29, 32, 39, 53, 62, 72, 92, 100, 126, 130, 137, 149, 171, 174, reproduced with
permission of Colección Filmoteca UNAM, Mexico; p. 74, reproduced with permission of
Fundación Patrimonio Fílmico Colombiano; p. 102, reproduced with permission of Productora
Cinematográfica Bolívar Films, C.A.
Designed by couch

Set by Cambrian Typesetters, Camberley, Surrey
Printed in China

This book is printed on paper suitable for recycling and made from fully managed and sustained
forest sources. Logging, pulping and manufacturing processes are expected to conform to the
environmental regulations of the country of origin.

British Library Cataloguing-in-Publication Data
A catalogue record for this book is available from the British Library
A catalog record for this book is available from the Library of Congress

ISBN 978–1–84457–532–9 (pb)
ISBN 978–1–84457–533–6 (hb)

Contents

Acknowledgments

Our collective writing process has been unusual for a humanities project, but, given the project's breadth, it was, in our opinion, necessary. Indeed, even with five of us deeply involved in its realisation, this book is the product of the work of a group much larger in number whose behind the scenes contributions have been invaluable. While two of us coordinated the process and participated either as authors, co-authors or translators of each chapter, and all five of us researched and wrote parts of the book, we owe a great deal to the many people who assisted us in one way or another with our research, which took us all over the Americas and into Europe.

University of California, Davis, undergraduates Tracey Ross and Dorisa González helped to carry out significant preliminary archival research, while graduate students Valentina Velázquez, Moisés Park, Jorge Andrade, Milagros Gómez, Tania Lizarazo and Sergio Díaz Luna all worked many hours in the archives, reviewing microfilms and interlibrary loan materials. At the Toluca campus of the Tecnológico de Monterrey, undergraduates Sandra Luz Núñez, Alma Jiménez, Besabé del Valle, César Méndez, Carlos Torres and Violeta Velasco, as well as graduate students Alejandra Sánchez and Carlos Zermeño, all worked many hours in the archives as well. The help of Jomar Díaz was indispensible for the exploration of materials archived in Havana.

It should also be mentioned that while Dubravka Sužnjević is credited with co-writing only one chapter, she contributed substantially to the archival research carried out for two other chapters in Colombia and Venezuela in addition. In the Balkans, where Sužnjević was in charge of the investigation, Jasna Novakov aided in obtaining materials both in Serbia and in Bosnia, and film aficionado Milomir Irković offered us access to materials from his sizable personal collection of film memorabilia.

We are greatly appreciative of the expertise, generosity and professionalism of colleagues in the many archives in which we worked, most especially Raúl Miranda and Abel Muñoz Hénonin of the Cineteca Nacional, Radoslav Zelenović of the Film Archive of the Republic of Serbia and Myra Appel of the University of California, Davis's Shields Library, along with wonderfully knowledgable librarians with whom we worked in the Museo del Cine Pablo Ducrós Hicken in Buenos Aires; the Biblioteca Nacional José Martí in Havana; the Biblioteca and Archivo de la Filmoteca Nacional in Madrid; the Biblioteca Luis Ángel Arango and the Patrimonio Fílmico Colombiano in Bogotá; the Biblioteca Nacional de Venezuela in Caracas; the Municipal Library, along with the archives of the newspapers *Politika* and *Borba* in Belgrade; the Biblioteca Nacional de Chile in Santiago; and the Biblioteca and Hemeroteca Nacionales de

México in Mexico City. This project would have taken years longer to research without the responsive and efficient interlibrary loan services of the University of California, Davis, and of Tecnológico de Monterrey, Toluca campus, some of whose employees will probably never forget the number of tomes of old journals and boxes of microfilms that were delivered for this project.

We are also indebted to the many colleagues who have offered us suggestions, critiques and encouragement over the past several years, most especially Ana López, Carlos Monsiváis, Francisco Peredo Castro, Eric Smoodin, Diana Palaversich, Héctor Fernández L'Hoeste, Seraina Rohrer, Valentina Velázquez, Rosa Beltrán, Elizabeth Moreno, Juan Carlos Segura, Marta Cabrera, Catherine Bloch, Elissa Rashkin, Debra Castillo, Laura López, Tunico Amancio, Gabriela Pulido, Adriana González Mateos, Fernando Muñoz and Héctor Manjarrez.

And we must especially thank those close to us, who have remained unwavering in their support for us even as we have left them alone so often as we visited archives, presented at conferences and met each other at diverse locations far from home: Esteban, Rafael, Marcelo and Daniel.

Finally, this project would have been far lengthier had it not been for the financial support obtained through institutional funding sources, including most especially a Chancellor's Fellowship from the University of California, Davis, along with additional funding from the Tecnológico de Monterrey and the University of California, Davis.

Introduction: 'El Cine Mexicano Se Impone'

Robert McKee Irwin and Maricruz Castro Ricalde

A visit to South America – for example, to Bogotá – from Mexico provokes a feeling of familiarity that goes beyond the recognition of globalising processes of Americanisation, or of Latin American commonalities. There are tequila bars, mariachi clubs, menus featuring guacamole and salsa picante – there is a significant presence of certain common signifiers of Mexican culture. Indeed, Mexican culture is not only well known throughout Latin America, but it is habitually consumed, whether through images of Frida Kahlo's artwork, the iconography of the Virgin of Guadalupe, *charro* hats, tacos and enchiladas, *ranchera* music, or even *narcocorridos*. What many Mexicans think of as national symbols are often part of everyday life elsewhere, especially in Latin America. And what is particularly remarkable is that there is not an equal reciprocation. While the cumbia is well known in Mexico, no classic Colombian cumbia artist has the iconic status in Mexico comparable to that of Mexican superstars Jorge Negrete or Los Tigres del Norte in Colombia. The bandera paesa or ajiaco, Colombia's most emblematic national dishes, are virtually unknown in Mexico; most Mexicans would not have any idea of what traditional folkloric costumes, dances, or archetypes are the most widely accepted symbols of national culture in Colombia. Of course, there are Colombians whose cultural expressions are well known in Mexico, including painter Fernando Botero, novelist Gabriel García Márquez and singer Shakira. And *Yo soy Betty, la fea* (1999–2001), although remade under a different name by Televisa, is only one of many Colombian soap operas well known in Mexico. Still, it is clear that what cultural exchange exists between the two countries is not equal, and the same could be said for many other Latin American countries, including relatively large ones such as Venezuela, Chile and Peru.

Discussions of globalised media and the patterns of cultural flows in the context of globalisation often tend to be constructed in binary terms, with the USA or other major metropolitan media centres positioned against the rest of the world. While many studies are conscious that heightened states of globalisation have not led to the smothering of media flows from poorer areas of the world – with the case of Latin American telenovelas being a major case in point, even these studies often fall into the tendency to posit movements in terms of hegemonic-subaltern contexts, and nearly all of them ignore the complexities of Latin American media flows in the early years of the cultural industries' rise: the 1930s, 40s and 50s. However, as Brazilian film historian and critic Paulo Antonio Paranaguá notes, studies of Latin American film history bring to life 'mythologies capable of transcending borders long before the rise of telenovelas and world music' (*Tradición*, p. 106);[1] or as US film historian Seth Fein puts it, 'the transnational logic of today's cultural economy ... is not an entirely new phenomenon' ('Myths', p. 161).

This book studies the early years of what has been called the 'golden age' of Mexican cinema, a period that runs for about two decades, roughly from 1936 to 1956, during which Mexico's film industry became one of the most productive in the world, exercising a decisive influence on constructions of national culture and identity in Mexico. The golden age of Mexican cinema, at one time dismissed as a commercially oriented and aesthetically uninteresting project whose product was largely derivative of Hollywood models, has been taken much more seriously by the current generation of film critics, who have argued decisively for the centrality of its role in building an imagined national community in Mexico through the use of distinctively Mexican genres, narratives, archetypes, sounds and images. Indeed, critics have for the most part focused their arguments on Mexican cinema's national project: its representations of national culture, symbols, history and geography – and its interpellation of Mexicans, who, in identifying with much of what they saw of Mexican culture on the silver screen, soon began to 'plagiarise' Mexican film in their everyday lives (Monsiváis, 'Mythologies', p. 117; see also Noble, pp. 70–94). While historians and critics have occasionally noted that Mexican golden age film quickly gained the attention of a broadly international Spanish-speaking public (e.g., García Riera, 'The Impact', p. 128; De los Reyes, p. 164; Mora, p. 45; Monsiváis, *Aires*, p. 58), and not a merely national audience, no study to date has looked beyond a couple of individual case studies, or presented any broad hypotheses on exactly how Mexican golden age cinema was received, and what impact it exercised outside of Mexico. As Aurelio de los Reyes declared in 1987: 'The study of Mexican cinema as a conquest that has impeded and obstructed the development of national cinematic expressions, but also as a phenomenon of Latin American identity has yet to be realised' (p. 182), an observation that remains relevant today. This study addresses just these issues.

The consumption and reception of Mexican cinema outside of Mexico during its golden age was a complex phenomenon, involving a wide range of factors of transnational exchange, and taking vastly different forms in different parts of the world. For example, as our study makes evident, in much of the Spanish-speaking Americas, Mexican cinema was the film product with which local audiences most identified. Hollywood, while always the dominant competitor, produced films in English that represented a US perspective that was well known for its lack of precision (or worse) in its representation of Latin America and Latin Americans, and since most Latin American countries produced very little cinema in those years, Mexican film was the closest their audiences had to their 'own' cinema. In the USA, in cities such as Los Angeles, many Mexican emigrants were able to nostalgically enjoy fantasies of their home culture through film, while Mexican movies became part of the cultural landscape of other Latino diaspora cities such as New York, where its visibility helped play out a key element of 'good neighbour policy'. In Argentina and Spain, the case was different, as each had a significant infrastructure of film production. Both these countries saw Mexico's industry as a competitor, one that eventually came to dominate them, and with whom they entered into collaborative agreements of different kinds, when it was to their advantage to do so. The case was completely different in Europe beyond Spain, where Mexican cinema began to gain critical acclaim when a Mexican film, *María Candelaria* (Emilio Fernández, 1944) earned a Palme d'Or in Cannes in 1946, gaining exposure for a Mexican film aesthetic that played on European fantasies of Mexico's revolutionary exoticism, obtaining entry for a particular style of Mexican film in countries such as France, Italy, Czechoslovakia and, especially (as we shall see), Yugoslavia. This study looks at multiple aspects of Mexican cinema's production, distribution, reception and long-term impact in seven different external markets: Cuba, Colombia, Venezuela, Argentina, the USA, Spain and Yugoslavia, reconstructing a series of locally situated stories that together capture the important role that Mexican cinema came to play around the world during its golden age.

MEXICO CITY AS THE HOLLYWOOD OF LATIN AMERICA

We show that, through its golden age film industry, Mexico indeed positioned itself at that time as Latin America's cultural centre. It was the film industry most trusted to bring Latin American stories, characters and culture to the world. As the region's biggest film producer, Mexico City became the 'meeting place for Latin American cinema' (*Cinema Reporter*, 16 September 1944, p. 30), the place to go for many up and coming Spanish-speaking artists and other film industry workers, and Mexico's industry became a sought-after collaborator by local producers in countries with weaker film production infrastructure, including not only smaller countries nearby, like Venezuela and Cuba, but also Spain, one of Mexico's strongest competitors.

We also argue that, as a local cultural powerhouse, Mexico managed to put itself in the unique position of being able to challenge, albeit to a limited degree, Hollywood's dominance in world film markets, most especially in Latin America. There, audiences formed deep but ambivalent relationships with Mexico. On the one hand, they identified more with Mexican film than they did with Hollywood film or European film, and were proud that Latin America was able to produce a high-quality product capable of gaining sufficient market share to make a significant cultural impact throughout the hemisphere. On the other hand, they resented Mexico's success, especially in the face of local failure, whether, in the case of Spain and Argentina, it meant recognising Mexico's superior market position, or, in the case of other Spanish-speaking countries, it reflected a bitter disappointment at the impossibility of establishing a homegrown industry that could compete with Mexico, if only at a local level. While Mexican cinema was welcomed and in many cases loved by Spanish-speaking fans, its dominating role was also resented, much in the way Hollywood was resented as an imperialistic enterprise.

After all, not only did Mexico have the opportunity to deploy its cinema to promote its own image – its customs and culture, its landmarks and touristic attractions, its status as a leader in technology and modernisation for the region – but many in other countries were conscious that such opportunities simply did not exist for them. So, while Ecuadorian peasants, Nicaraguan fisherman and Dominican housewives fell in love with Mexican cinema's dashing *charros*, sexy rumba dancers, romantic *boleros*, noble monuments, picturesque desert landscapes and revolutionary history, none had any idea of the equivalents of these iconic images for other Latin American countries, such as Ecuador, Nicaragua, or the Dominican Republic, and as a result they did not develop the kind of affection for these lands that they had for Mexico. And Ecuadorians, Nicaraguans and Dominicans knew well that their countries did not have the means to aspire to the special status that Mexico had attained throughout the hemisphere through the cinematic diffusion of its culture.

Moreover, Mexico, as Latin America's leading producer of movies for the two decades in which film established itself as the world's most influential genre of cultural production, set the tone for film production style in the region. Mexico's industry not only became the model for Latin American success, but it diffused an entire stylistic and aesthetic repertoire to which Latin American audiences became accustomed, thus defining these audience's tastes and expectations, at least with regard to Spanish-language product. Thus, Mexican genres such as the folkloric musical comedy (e.g., *Allá en el Rancho Grande*, Fernando de Fuentes, 1936), the urban melodrama (*Cuando los hijos se van*, Juan Bustillo Oro, 1941), the piquant cabaret musical melodrama (*Aventurera*, Alberto Gout, 1950), or the stylised nationalist drama (*Flor silvestre*, Emilio Fernández, 1943) became models for autochthonous endeavours of film production elsewhere in Latin America. And as Mexico's industry gradually came to assume a dominant market position *vis-à-vis* its best-funded competitors in Spain and Argentina, Mexican Spanish – including accents, intonations, regionalism – came to supersede peninsular Spanish as the region's standard, particularly in the context of mass media culture, where the Castillian 'z' and the Argentine 'vos' are thought of as regional idiosyncrasies.

It should also be noted that, while Mexican cinema attained critical success through the particular story lines and visual aesthetics of a nationalist genre emblematically represented in the work of director Emilio Fernández in the 1940s and early 50s, its popularity among the masses is attributable largely to its correlation to Hollywood models. The sophistication of its stars, with their elegant dress, the constant press coverage of their appearances at fashionable nightclubs and their often extravagant lifestyles brought Spanish-speaking audiences closer to the distant world of Hollywood luminaries. For different reasons, this kind of glamour faded from the public life of cities such as Buenos Aires, Havana and Madrid in the 30s and 40s, while at the same time the grandiosity of tours of Mexican megastars such as María Félix, Jorge Negrete or Dolores del Río to Spain and throughout the Spanish-speaking Americas, along with the gala ceremonies for their highest awards, the Ariels, served to authenticate Mexico's new role as the Latin American movie mecca.

National pride among external audiences redoubled, directed through a Mexican filter, as their compatriots assumed central roles in the Mexican industry, with homegrown stars often playing Mexican characters. The care taken by Argentine Libertad Lamarque or Colombian Sofía Álvarez in their wardrobe shows that the Mexican industry was not merely imitative of Hollywood excess, but also was constructed in accordance with local values, while the immense popularity of even the more racy live shows of Cuban *rumberas* María Antonieta Pons or Ninón Sevilla shows that Mexico's stars were managed in such a way as to titillate without radically challenging the norms of the region. Mexico's film studios sometimes pushed limits, but always remained conscious of their audience's needs, an ideologically compatible option in tune with the tensions of the era, and in many ways not a mere imitation of, but an answer to the brazen capitalism and frivolity that Hollywood represented.

Mexican studios attracted a parade of foreign talent, including Cuban *rumbera* María Antonieta Pons, who became a Mexican film superstar

Mexico, as Latin America's cinematic mecca, attracted a constant parade of talent from other countries, including major figures such as Argentine tango superstar Lamarque, Cuban dancer-actors Pons and Sevilla, Puerto Rican vedette Mapi Cortés, Cuban mambo king Dámaso Pérez Prado, Spanish heartthrob Jorge Mistral, the great Spanish avant-garde director Luis Buñuel, talented Canadian-born cinematographer Alex Phillips and even Czechoslovakian beauty Miroslava Stern, to name just a few. It also was often in a position to do what other Latin American countries could not do themselves: represent their national cultures for large national and international audiences. Thus, Mexico played an important role in establishing notions of Venezuelan, Cuban, Colombian and even Spanish and Argentine cultures that would be disseminated throughout Spanish-speaking markets during the period, whether through co-productions in which Mexican producers, directors, actors and technicians played dominant roles: *Jalisco canta en Sevilla* (Fernando de Fuentes, 1949) in Spain, *Mulata* (Gilberto Martínez Solares, 1954) in Cuba; other collaborations of various kinds (e.g., Venezuelan production houses hiring Mexican directors or other experts to realise productions in Venezuela: *Amanecer a la vida*, 1950, directed by Mexico-based Fernando Cortés and starring Mexican Susana Guízar); or Mexico's incorporation of foreign themes and characters in its own homegrown productions, as occurred, for example, with the early 1940s superproduction of the life of Simón Bolívar (*Simón Bolívar*, Miguel Contreras Torres, 1942). Even when fledgling national industries were in a position to produce their own films, without Mexican intervention, they still had to deal with the fact that local audiences had expectations about what a national picture should be based upon years of conditioning as fans of Mexican cinema; representing any Latin American national culture in film in a way that did not somehow reference well-known Mexican models either of that culture, or of national cultures in general – that is, as cultures based upon popular music, folklore, story lines involving romance and melodrama, etc. – was difficult, if not impossible.

However, more often than not smaller countries were not in any position to launch a local film industry. Aside from lacking infrastructure, they also lacked expertise, and any startup inevitably was ill prepared to put out a product that could compete in technical and aesthetic terms with what local audiences were used to seeing. Indeed, on any occasions when local productions were released, even those that offered an initial promise of success (e.g., Venezuela's Bolívar Films, which achieved international critical success with *La balandra Isabel llegó esta tarde*, directed by Argentine Carlos Hugo Christensen, 1950), they did not succeed in drawing adequate audiences to keep national production companies afloat. It was not that audiences did not care about seeing their own cultures represented on the big screen; the problem was that Mexican cinema already offered an approximation that they had got used to accepting. It was not Colombian or Uruguayan or Peruvian, but it was Latin American, and as such it was certainly more their own than Hollywood output.

The process of identification here is complex and multilayered. For Mexican fans, according to Carlos Monsiváis, the process was clear. On the one hand, national cinema was a dream factory: 'Amid urban congestion, rural solitude, disorientation from interminable working hours, "the intimate" is not what is lived, but what one wishes to live, the flow of dreams that when collective seem more personal' ('Vino todo el público', p. 62); but on the other, 'Devotees of comedies and melodramas were not seeking to "dream," but to learn skills, to lose inhibitions, ... to understand how they belonged to the nation. In this school-in-the dark the people were educated in suffering and relaxation' ('Mythologies', pp. 117–18). Mexican audiences recognised themselves, or people of their 'category', on the screen, but rather than judge their accuracy, they saw their film idols as ideals to which they might aspire, or about which they might at least fantasise. Their authenticity – especially in comparison to Hollywood's thoroughly unconvincing portrayals of Mexicans – was so obvious as to be taken for granted.

Regardless of whether Monsiváis has overstated the case here – one counts on his wisdom and the astuteness of his powers of observation and analysis, as he cites no empirical evidence to back up his claims – it is difficult to know how to extrapolate these conclusions to the context of Mexican cinema's foreign audiences. While Mexican (and, according to Monsiváis, some Central American) fans' identification with these films might have been excessive [*desbordada*], it is not at all clear how Monsiváis's conclusions about Mexicans might apply to other Latin Americans, even as he argues that 'outside of Mexico, their representations of customs and traditions become amusing exoticism, and their archetypes and stereotypes fascinate without turning into lifestyles' (*Aires*, p. 58). The evidence presented in this study suggests that Latin American fans' identification with Cantinflas's fast-talking and lazy urban rogue, Sara García's saintly and devoted mother, Ninón Sevilla's impulsive and free-wheeling rumba dancer, or Tito Guízar's cheerful and uncomplicated cowboy may not have been as 'excessive' as that of Mexican audiences; however, it is also not clear that they maintained as much emotional distance from these characters as Monsiváis's somewhat casual observation implies.

Mexican cinema is, in many instances, 'our' cinema, just as Latin America is 'our America'. While there may be no *charros* in the Amazon jungle or the Andean highlands, Latin American fans from all over clearly found something 'theirs' in Mexican *ranchera* films, perhaps related to values, attitudes, or personal style. For Mexicans, in the words of Roberto Cantú Robert, editor of the Mexican trade journal *Cinema Reporter*, Central and South Americans are more than just 'our brothers of the South', they are 'a continuation of ourselves' (27 November 1943, p. 8). Some process of interpellation did occur – and not only in films that were directed specifically towards certain audiences. Venezuelan Rómulo Gallegos's adaptations of his novels in Mexican cinema were meant to interpellate Venezuelans, but also came to satisfy many Latin American fans, who ultimately preferred the films of their favourite Mexican actors over national productions with whose plots, landscapes, characters and cultural contexts it might have been easier to identify.

MEXICAN CINEMA'S IMPOSING NATURE

Interestingly, there is a word that comes up repeatedly, not only in the industry's promotional materials, but also in later historical analyses, both in Mexico and abroad: *imponerse*. The word '*imponer*' in Spanish has two relevant meanings. The first one is relatively neutral in tone: 'to become firmly established, in a leadership role'; the other is more like the English usage of 'impose': 'to force oneself into a situation where one is not wanted'. When commentators write that 'el cine mexicano se impone' [Mexican cinema imposes itself] they may be referring only to Mexico's solid incursions into export markets – but the connotation of imposition is always palpable.

As early as 1934, Mexico's industry-leading trade magazine at the time, *Filmográfico*, celebrating the earliest successes of Mexican sound film, which were actually quite modest, declared:

> The national movie industry continues on the rise ... There is no longer any human power that can hold it back, nor any project that will not crystallise in the end. Our cinema has imposed itself not only in Mexico, but in all countries that think and speak to God in Spanish. (June 1934, p. 31)

A market evaluation in 1942 called for the industry to 'conquer [Spanish-speaking] markets, a conquest that besides money, allows us to exert a spiritual influence' (*Cinema Reporter*, April 1942, p. 21), and soon after that (a few months after the international release of *Simón Bolívar*), Paul Kohner, husband of veteran Mexican actress Lupita Tovar, announced to the Mexican press: 'Mexican cinema has imposed itself' (*Cinema Reporter*, January 1943, p. 28). Soon Mexican cinema was reported as having become the product of preference in Guatemala, El Salvador, Nicaragua and Honduras where 'the public seeks new customs', and having 'imposed itself' in Argentina, and in Venezuela (*Cinema Reporter*, 10 June 1944, p. 12; 15 April 1944, p. 27; 11 November 1944, p. 31), with studio executives calling Mexican cinema 'an enormous moral force and a formidable vehicle of propaganda' (*Cinema Reporter*, 30 June 1945, p. 10). By the late 1940s, with Mexican cinema taking hold in New York and in European markets, the industry bragged that 'Mexican cinema, thanks to its quality, has imposed itself all over the world' (*Cinema Reporter*, 8 October 1949, p. 31). By 1952, which for some scholars marks the end of Mexico's golden age of cinema (e.g., Tuñón, *Mujeres*, p. 13), industry insiders continue to brag that 'Mexican cinema has achieved an unquestionable universality due to the international success' of its product, and that 'it is imposing itself' worldwide (*Cinema Reporter*, 30 August 1952, p. 5).

Contemporary critics also have reconstructed film history to reflect the Mexican industry's ambition in the 1930s – one of 'imposing itself in external market', showing how in only a few years 'the longstanding desire of Mexican film-makers: imposing on the world a filmic image of our nationality and our history, contemplated with elements of "legitimate pride" is consummated' (De la Vega Alfaro, *La industria*, pp. 28, 34). They call it a project of 'ideological conquest' (De los Reyes, p. 182) or even 'cultural imperialism' (Jorge Ayala Blanco, quoted in De la Vega Alfaro, *La industria*, p. 35).

Outside of Mexico, too, as early as the late 1930s, observers were reporting an 'invasion of Mexican films' (*Écran*, 15 March 1938, n. p.). However, the tone was not necessarily one of victory and conquest in foreign markets. By 1942, a Colombian critic wrote with some resentment, and not a little bit of awe, about the consequences of Mexican cinema's international triumphs: 'let's also recall Mexico, which with its most recent movies has imposed and popularised its music, its style of dress, its customs, its monuments and natural beauty. In the field of fashion, tastes, aesthetic preferences, everyday life and styles of courtship, cinema exercises an absolute tyranny' (*El Tiempo*, 12 December 1942, p. 5). This same rhetoric of imposition likewise appears in the writings of Latin American film historians and critics, as is the case with Venezuelan Antonio Soto Ávila, who argues in 2005 that 'Mexican cinema imposed itself because it responded to the popular needs' of Latin American audiences of the era (p. 9).

The deployment of the term 'imposition' is noteworthy given that, especially in the 1930s and early 40s, when, at least at some moments, it appeared that any of the competing industries of Mexico, Spain, Argentina – or even Cuba or Chile – might rise up and become a formidable industry, the Spanish-speaking market was quite competitive. In Argentina, the press wrote of the competition in sports or even battle metaphors: 'one wins one round, the other wins the next ... in the competition in which the Argentine and Mexican industries have entered in the Spanish-language market' (*Cine*, 4 December 1942, p. 4) at a moment when Cuba remained 'without a doubt the strongest and most loyal bastion of Argentine cinema in the Americas' (*Cine*, 17 April 1942, p. 4) – a situation that would soon be definitively reversed. In other words, at least into the early 40s, film journalists saw the possibility of either of these players winning out in the end, thus implying that, in going to the movies, audiences form alliances, reveal sympathies and support favourites in national terms. Over time, Mexico's supremacy would become clear – and this rhetoric would become more aggressive in its implications. However, in accordance with the idea of panamerican fraternity (actively promoted in Mexican films such as *Simón Bolívar*), there is a concurrent insinuation that this is a competition in which all participants win, as the advantage obtained by any player also is a victory for the entire region over Hollywood. Even in Argentina, whose industry competed most fiercely with Mexico's, most especially in those early years, commentaries take on an ambivalent tone: 'Mexican cinema is our clearest and most unwavering competitor', but, 'It is not our enemy. It is a stimulus. It obliges us to stay alert' (*Cine*, 30 April 1943, p. 2).

However, this rhetoric of invasion, conquest and imposition, as can be seen in the many examples above, also relates to a propagandistic function of cinema of which most, if not all, of those cited above are quite conscious. It is not just about box office, but about exerting influence. As a Mexico City film journal put it in 1943, our cinema is the 'maintainer of continental mores' (*El Cine Gráfico*, 2 May 1943, p. 2). Mexico's film exports promoted Mexican culture and Mexico's image abroad, determined fashions and tastes, and provided a model for regional customs. The same article, cited above, goes on: 'our films strengthen our national prestige everywhere' as they provide evidence of 'our material and industrial progress' (ibid.).

Mexico, through its film production, imposed itself as the regional leader, the cultural epicentre of the Spanish-speaking world. This study tracks the history of Mexican cinema's conquest of seven foreign markets, paying special attention to the ambivalent reactions to its imposition, which oscillate between celebration, jealousy and offence, as well as to the consequences of its popularity in terms of cultural influence, most especially with regard to national film production in those countries where it was most popular.

HISTORICAL OVERVIEW

In order to better understand Mexican cinema's 'imposition', it would be useful to locate its rise and fall within a broader early history of film in Mexico, Latin America and the world. Most historians mark 1896 as the beginning of Mexican film history, with the arrival of representatives of the Lumière brothers in July of that year to demonstrate and market their new moving-image projection technology (e.g., De los Reyes, p. 8; Mora, p. 6; Dávalos Orozco, pp. 12–13). While production was limited to shorts and newsreels for a number of years as entrepreneurs in Mexico and elsewhere in Latin America gradually began establishing an initial infrastructure for production and exhibition, by the mid-1910s, the first feature-length fiction films were coming out in countries like Argentina and Mexico (King, pp. 11, 19). While many countries began realising some silent film production by the 20s, very little product travelled outside national boundaries, and, even within many countries, distribution networks were not yet solid enough to assure ample exhibition.

With the introduction of sound technology, by the early 30s Latin American studios began producing films of wider appeal. Silent film, which relied on visual language and subtitles, offered Latin American producers no special communication advantage. Sound film, however, which required subtitles or sound dubbing for international audiences, made it harder for audiences to understand or enjoy films not made in their own language. Hollywood initially attempted to produce Spanish-language movies, filming, for example, *Drácula* (George Melford, 1931), a Spanish-language version of *Dracula* (Tod Browning, 1931), starring Spanish actor Carlos Vallarías in Bela Lugosi's role. However, the casts of these movies included actors who were randomly Spanish, Mexican, Cuban, Chilean, Argentine, etc., and the mix of accents was off-putting for Spanish-speaking audiences. As a result, Hollywood's Spanish-language films never really caught on, with production peaking in 1931, and fizzling out entirely by the late 30s (King, p. 32; Dávalos Orozco, p. 61). With the exception of the US-produced films of Carlos Gardel, including, for example, *Melodía del arrabal* (Louis Gasnier, 1933), *Cuesta abajo* (Louis Gasnier, 1934) and *El día que me quieras* (John Reinhardt, 1935), Hollywood's incursions into Spanish-language production produced few real hits. Meanwhile, Argentina's first big hit was Luis Moglia Barth's *¡Tango!* (1933), which featured performances by several figures who, together with Gardel, would come to be counted among Latin America's first international film stars, including Libertad Lamarque and Luis Sandrini. Mexico scored an early international hit with *Santa* (Antonio Moreno, 1932). There is still debate regarding which production should count as Mexico's first sound feature film: *Santa*, *Dios y ley* (Guillermo Calles, 1930), *Más fuerte que el deber* (Raphael Sevilla, 1931), or *Contrabando* (Antonio Méndez Bernal, 1932) (see Mora, pp. 34–5; De los Reyes, p. 121; King, p. 42; Dávalos Orozco, p. 62; Monsiváis, 'Vino todo el público', p. 91; De la Vega Alfaro, '*Contrabando*'), but *Santa* is unquestionably the first important work in the category. Early sound production elsewhere in the Spanish-speaking Americas was insignificant to nonexistent (Pérez Llahi).

While Mexico, Argentina and Spain all saw significant production in the early to mid-1930s, with Spain emerging as an early leader for Spanish-language markets (103 films by 1936), and Mexico (eighty-three films) and Argentina (thirty-one) also contenders, the potential for the international marketing of Spanish-language films became crystal clear only in 1936 with the release of the Mexican musical *Allá en el Rancho Grande* (Fernando de Fuentes), which became the first real box-office sensation of Spanish-language film all over Latin America, as well as in the USA and later in Spain. From 1936 through 1938, Mexico was the leader in production and exportation in Spanish-language markets. Spain's industry, disrupted by civil war, saw production plummet to only four films by 1938 and thirty-three in total for the period; while Argentine production, with a total of eighty-four films during this period, was rising annually; and Mexico led production with 120 films produced during the three-year time frame. Much of Mexico's production followed on the coattails of *Rancho Grande*'s success. Its most beloved actors, comedians and singers, Tito Guízar, Esther Fernández, Lorenzo Barcelata and Carlos 'Chaflán' López, were called on to appear in one *ranchera* comedy after another, until audiences became weary of the formula. This allowed Argentina's industry to step in and become the market leader for four years, from 1939 through 1942 (202 films), with Mexico faltering significantly after reaching a peak production of fifty-seven films in 1938 (151 films for the period 1939–42), and postwar Spain just beginning to recuperate (142 films) (Peredo Castro, *Cine y propaganda*, p. 477).

During this latter period, Mexico began producing some key successes in genres that departed from the *ranchera* musical formula, including the breakthrough comedy of Mario Moreno (better known as Cantinflas), *Ahí está el detalle* (Juan Bustillo Oro, 1940), and the family melodrama *Cuando los hijos se van*, starring the actors who would become the emblematic mother and father in numerous films of the era, Sara García and Fernando Soler – all while renewing the *ranchera* comedy by introducing charismatic new actors such as Jorge Negrete, star of *¡Ay, Jalisco, no te rajes!* (Joselito

Rodríguez, 1941) and *Así se quiere en Jalisco* (Fernando de Fuentes, 1942), both huge hits in domestic and international markets. By 1942, Mexican studios, whose production rose from a low of twenty-nine films in 1940 to thirty-seven in 1941 and forty-seven in 1942, was in a position to aim to assume a leadership position once again (ibid.). Meanwhile, Argentina, refused to break off relations with the axis powers of World War II, leading the USA, which had stepped up its 'good neighbour policy' with Latin America, to intervene and not only begin collaborating with Mexican studios to help them modernise, but also cut Argentina off from celluloid distribution, forcing that nation's studios to buy raw film at exorbitant prices on the black market (ibid., pp. 114–29).

By early 1943, the Mexican industry was reporting (likely with some exaggeration) that '50 per cent of the films showing in the swankiest houses' throughout much of Central and South America were Mexican (*El Cine Gráfico*, 1 January 1943, p. 38). Demand was up all over Hispanoamerica, with new box-office records being set in Havana, Lima, Costa Rica, Panama and Los Angeles during the first months of the year, and earnings up by as much as 500 per cent in key markets, such as Caracas (*El Cine Gráfico*, 17 January 1943, p. 12; 17 March 1943, p. 9; 21 March 1943, p. 2; 18 April 1943, pp. 5, 15; 25 May 1943, p. 15). Earnings records in Chile seemed to confirm Mexico's dominance and 'the definitive collapse of Argentine cinema' appeared to be imminent (*El Cine Gráfico*, 10 January 1943, p. 6). Mexican film magazines bragged that Mexico had become 'the mecca of Spanish-language cinema' and that its cinema 'had succeeded in imposing itself in markets throughout Latin America' (*El Cine Gráfico*, 28 March 1943, p. 12; 21 November 1943, p. 2).

Mexico, during these years, launched what could be called a Latin American offensive by producing a handful of heavily marketed superproductions designed to appeal to broad Latin American audiences, including *Simón Bolívar* and *Doña Bárbara* (Fernando de Fuentes, 1943), the latter film based on the novel by the great Venezuelan writer Rómulo Gallegos (Peredo Castro, *Cine y propaganda*, pp. 235–48, 187–93). Also, with great fanfare, director Emilio Fernández brought Mexican-born Hollywood headliner Dolores del Río back to Mexico to star in *Flor silvestre*, the first of a series of critically acclaimed dramas directed by Fernández and filmed by the great cinematographer Gabriel Figueroa. In the three-year period from 1943 to 1945, Mexico 'imposed itself' dominantly throughout most of the Spanish-speaking world, producing 227 pictures, in comparison with Spain's 120 and Argentina's mere eighty (ibid., p. 477).

In 1946, Fernández would win top prize at the Cannes Film Festival for *María Candelaria* (1943), starring del Río and Pedro Armendáriz. That same year, Mexico would launch its own film awards, the Ariels, which this production team would dominate through 1950, earning three best film awards (*Enamorada* in 1947; *La perla* in 1948; *Río Escondido* in 1949), three best director awards for Fernández (for the same films), four best cinematography awards for Figueroa (for those same three films, as well as for *Pueblerina* in 1950), one best original story award (Fernández and Mauricio Magdaleno for *Río Escondido*), one editing award (Gloria Schoemann for *Enamorada*), seven best actor/actress awards (to del Río for *Las abandonadas* in 1946, María Félix for *Enamorada* and *Rio Escondido*, Armendáriz for *La perla*, Carlos López Moctezuma for *Río Escondido*, Roberto Cañedo for *Pueblerina* and Marga López for *Salón México*), as well as one for best supporting actress (Columba Domínguez for *Maclovia* in 1948). These critically acclaimed films, endorsed at an international level with the Cannes prize, opened up new markets to Mexican producers, especially in postwar Europe, while earning them the respect of many critics who found Mexico's usual musical comedy or melodrama fare to be lacking in artistic or social value. The aesthetic and ideological tendencies of Fernández's films, for which the production team would come to be known as 'the Mexican school of cinema', were embraced abroad by critics anxious to learn about revolutionary Mexico through their nationalist stories, often set during the Mexican revolution, or in rural zones or urban slums. These films promoted a collection of national ideals, idealised visions of Mexican landscapes and indigenous beauty that would satisfy both national audiences in their desire to see their history and culture presented artistically to the world, and foreign audiences who appreciated the unique, exotic and noble vision these films painted of postrevolutionary Mexico (Tuñón, 'Emilio Fernández'; Tierney).

In addition to the actors mentioned above, during these years, the Mexican industry also incorporated Argentine star Libertad Lamarque, who had been blacklisted in her home industry after a dispute with Eve Perón and who, with hits such as *Soledad* (Miguel Zacarías, 1947), would soon become one of Mexico's biggest-grossing stars in international markets. Mexican actor Pedro Infante would also score several megahits, including *Los tres García* (Ismael Rodríguez, 1947), *Nosotros los pobres* (Ismael Rodríguez, 1948) and *Angelitos negros* (Joselito Rodríguez, 1948), that would establish him as one of the hemisphere's most beloved screen heroes. Another new superstar launched during this period was the comedian Germán Valdés (known to fans as Tin Tan), with the triumph of such films as *Calabacitas tiernas* (Gilberto Martínez Solares, 1949). Finally, the success of such films as *La reina del trópico* (Raúl de Anda, 1946), starring María Antonieta Pons, *Humo en los ojos* (Alberto Gout, 1946), featuring Meche Barba, and *Aventurera* (Alberto Gout, 1950), with Ninón Sevilla, gave rise to a genre of musical melodramas known as *cabaretera* films, whose lead actresses were skilled rumba dancers and whose settings were tropical locales or urban nightclubs. During these years, Mexican producers and actors also began collaborating actively with colleagues in Spain, producing such films as the Jorge Negrete vehicle *Jalisco canta en Sevilla*, and also in Cuba, where Figueroa filmed *María la O* (Adolfo Fernández Bustamente, 1948). Mexico's success between 1946 and 1950 was unprecedented, with production surging to 440 films versus Spain's 219 and resurgent Argentina's 224 for the period.

While there were intermittent attempts to establish local film industries elsewhere in Latin America – endeavours which even produced occasional local hits, such as Cuba's *El romance del palmar* (Ramón Peón, 1938), Colombia's *Allá en el trapiche* (Roberto Saa Silva, 1943), Chile's *La dama de las camelias* (José Bohr, 1947), or Venezuela's *La balandra Isabel llegó esta tarde* – production in many countries was largely nonexistent during the golden age years. No Spanish-speaking country besides Argentina, Spain or Mexico had the knowhow, the funds, the talent pool, or the infrastructure to get much going, and these occasional hits were never enough to give local producers sufficient momentum to produce more than a handful of films. While market shares varied, and on the whole Hollywood was always the biggest player, Mexico maintained a significant audience throughout the region, especially from the early 1940s through the late 50s and even into the early 60s in many countries (see Heuer, pp. 71–3). However, the 50s did not reproduce the creative renovation that brought Mexico so much success in the 40s – although there were a few exceptions.

In 1951, Spanish-born, Mexico-based director Luis Buñuel won Mexico's second major Cannes prize with his *Los olvidados* (1950). While Buñuel's urban realism was rewarded with an Ariel, it differed so much from the industry's most popular genres that it discomforted audiences and its influence in Mexico was minimal – the industry preferred to stick to proven formulas for success (Pérez Turrent), and the early 1950s produced few new trends of importance. Mexico's greatest stars (especially Cantinflas, María Félix, Tin Tan, Libertad Lamarque), all well established by this time, continued to achieve substantial commercial and popular success abroad, with Mexico making surprising inroads in places such as France, Italy and even Yugoslavia. By the early 1960s, while a few Mexico-based directors were making films that were increasingly experimental, artistically inspired, or overtly political – a few examples: Luis Buñuel's *Vidiriana* (1961), Roberto Gavaldón's *Macario* (1960), Julio Bracho's *La sombra del caudillo* (1960), the latter of whose exhibition would be blocked by Mexican censors for a generation for political reasons – Mexican film had clearly fallen into decadence, and its golden age was evidently over. Jorge Negrete died of liver disease in 1953; Czech-born Miroslava committed suicide in 1955; Pedro Infante died in a plane crash in 1957; directing pioneer Fernando de Fuentes passed away in 1958. Many of the nation's most admired actors were aging; for example, Dolores del Río, who had had a successful career in Hollywood for nearly two decades before becoming a star of Mexican movies, and turned fifty in 1955, significantly curtailed her screen appearances.

While a few new stars emerged, including Silvia Pinal and wrestler Santo, they failed to generate the excitement that the classic luminaries had. Elite critics, becoming accustomed to much more artistically inspired and socially conscious fare from Europe, and the increasingly high-tech Hollywood model, became ferocious in their condemnation of Mexican *churros* – cheaply made, low-quality, formulaic and frivolous films, and middle-class audiences were gradually lost, not only to higher-quality imports usually in languages other than Spanish, but also to growing competition from television. In late 1955, Mexican producers organised a meeting of their international distributors, with representatives coming to Mexico City from Venezuela, Cuba, Chile, Brazil, Colombia, Puerto Rico, Uruguay, Panama, Peru and the Dominican Republic; their guests agreed that in order to compete internationally, Mexican studios needed to improve the quality of their films, especially with regard to the originality of story lines (*Cinema Reporter*, 7 December 1955, pp. 20–1). However, attempts at innovation, such as the use of costly CinemaScope technology, yielded little success. Studios began to close, and those that remained open resorted to ever cheaper and lower-quality productions to stay afloat. The suspension of the Mexican Academy's Ariel awards beginning in 1959 is symbolic of the era's demise. While activity continued to be substantial – with film production varying from eighty-nine to 136 films per year throughout the 1950s, and only falling off slightly in the 60s, ranging from seventy-one to 110 movies annually during the decade – it could no longer compete with Hollywood as audiences at home and abroad tired of its formulas, and exports and earnings plummeted.

An important new strategy that yielded limited success in the late 50s and 60s attempted to lure the middle classes back to movie houses by focusing on younger audiences in productions filmed on studio sets or locations representing new and wealthier Mexico City suburbs (Las Lomas, el Pedregal, for example), visually and culturally distinct from the inner city *barrios* that had been the settings of earlier hits such as *Los olvidados*, *Salón México* (Emilio Fernández, 1949) or *Nosotros los pobres*. These new locations presented a Mexico situated within an international modernity, with young protagonists living it up in the swimming pools of grand mansions or on the beaches of Acapulco; however, these movies did not necessarily appeal to all audiences as many did not identify with their themes of adultery and romantic promiscuity, implied not only in the representation of casual romantic relationships, but also through the introduction of female nudity, and indeed they largely failed to connect with the industry's most loyal audience, the popular classes. Other genres emerged that were more attractive to these audiences, including wrestling and *fichera* films [movies set in bordellos]. This segmentation effectively weakened the industry's capacity of mass appeal, which had been its strength during its golden years. This is the moment in which the common affective link that had once joined spectators in Maracaibo, Medellín, Los Angeles, Montevideo and San Juan into a transnational community that together learned to cope with the social and cultural changes occurring throughout the hemisphere – as cities and populations grew and rapidly modernised – effectively broke apart. Mexican cinema had ceased to impose itself (De la Vega Alfaro, 'The Decline', pp. 176–91).

MEXICAN FILM CRITICISM: TRANSNATIONAL AUDIENCES

Latin American film criticism as practised by intellectuals and academics was slow in coming to take Mexico's golden age seriously. Emilio García Riera's *Historia documental del cine mexicano*, whose first seven volumes (ten volumes in the 1990s edition), covering the early sound era through 1960, were published between 1969 and 1971, along with Jorge Ayala Blanco's *La aventura del cine mexicano* (1968), established the field's foundation. Some other key early texts of Mexican film history and criticism include Carlos Mora's *Mexican Cinema* (1982), Aurelio de los Reyes's *Medio siglo de cine mexicano* (1987) and Paulo Antonio Paranaguá's compilation *Mexican Cinema* (1995 – published originally in French in 1992). In the 70s and 80s, the Universidad Nacional Autónoma de México, the Universidad de Guadalajara and the Cineteca Nacional sponsored the publication of books and essays dedicated to key figures of Mexican national cinema, including directors Fernando de Fuentes, Julio Bracho, Emilio Fernández, Alberto Gout, Juan Orol and Raúl de Anda. Later texts have treated other major directors, as well as actors such as María Félix, Sara Garcia, Cantinflas and Lupe Vélez, among many others. The focus of these texts was largely historical and biographical, although in some cases studies focused on filmic production (De la Vega Alfaro, *Alberto Gout*; García Riera and González Rubio; Tuñón, *Los rostros*); only occasionally did they consider questions of reception (Peredo Castro, *Alejandro Galindo*).

These texts, along with more recent books of history and criticism that include notable materials on the golden age, such as Chon Noriega and Steven Ricci's edited anthology *The Mexican Cinema Project* (1994); Julia Tuñón's *Mujeres de luz y sombra en el cine mexicano: la construcción de una imagen, 1939–1952* (1998); Joanne Hershfield and David Maciel's compilation *Mexico's Cinema: A Century of Film and Filmmakers* (1999); Susan Dever's *Celluloid Nationalism and Other Melodramas* (2003); and Andrea Noble's *Mexican National Cinema* (2005), all exhibit a strong tendency to view Mexican cinema as a national industry, and to think about its impact in the context of Mexican national culture. A few books, among them: Ignacio Durán, Iván Trujillo and Mónica Verea's compilation *México-Estados Unidos: encuentros y desencuentros en el cine* (1996); Antonio Soto Ávila's *La época de oro del cine mexicano en Maracaibo* (2005); Rogelio Agrasánchez's *Mexican Movies in the United States* (2006); Sara Vega et al.'s *Historia de un gran amor: relaciones cinematográficas entre Cuba y México, 1897–2005* (2007); and Eduardo de la Vega Alfaro and Alberto Elena's special issue of *Cuadernos de la Filmoteca* titled *Abismos de la pasión: relaciones cinematográficas hispanomexicanas* (2009), treat particular cases from a broader, usually binational context. Meanwhile, studies that assume a more broadly Latin American context, including: John King's *Magical Reels* (1990); John King, Ana López and Manuel Alvarado's compilation *Mediating Two Worlds: Cinematic Encounters in the Americas* (1993); Julianne Burton et al.'s multiauthor anthology *Horizontes del segundo siglo: investigación y pedagogía del cine mexicano, latinoamericano y chicano* (1998); and Paulo Antonio Paranaguá's *Tradición y modernidad en el cine de América Latina* (2003), tend to either treat different national contexts from a comparative perspective (e.g., Mexican national cinema versus Argentine national cinema), or cover discrete binational cases (Mexican cinema in the USA). However, there is a dearth of information on Mexican cinema as a multinational enterprise.

Eduardo de la Vega Alfaro's *La industria cinematográfica mexicana* (1991) provides an important foundational enquiry by focusing less on questions of representation, and placing greater emphasis on diffusion. But it is the work of US-based critic Ana López that has most aimed to open up the critical vision of Mexican golden age cinema to a broadly transnational perspective. A series of essays, including 'A Cinema for the Continent' (1994), 'Historia nacional, historia transnacional' (1998) and 'Crossing Nations and Genres: Traveling Filmmakers' (2000), lays out key arguments aiming to transform critical practice in the field. She writes:

> Mexican cinema has been the only Latin American cinema to have successfully and consistently exceeded the limits of its national borders: since the 1930s and especially in the 1940s and 50s, almost all Latin Americans with access to the cinema watched and loved Mexican films ... In the poorer sectors of large urban centers and in rural areas where illiteracy was the norm, the easy-to-understand Mexican cinema was, for decades, almost synonymous with cinema itself. ('A Cinema', p. 7)

She argues: 'Although the process of rescuing the history of national cinemas has been of great importance, the focus on the national has not allowed us to observe the transnationality of all Latin American cinema' ('Historia nacional', p. 75), and: 'This focus on nation has unfortunately obscured important intercontinental forces in the classical period' ('Crossing Nations', p. 34). However, her call for action has not produced significant transformations in the way Latin America's golden era of cinema has been studied.

The most transnationally focused full-length study to date, Francisco Peredo Castro's *Cine y propaganda para Latinoamericana: México y Estados Unidos en la encrucijada de los años cuarenta* (2004), focuses on the Mexican industry's relationship with the USA in the context of World War II, and the shared ideological project that underlay its film production in the early 1940s. This context is not just binational, as it addresses issues related to Mexico's influential incursions into national cinema markets throughout Latin America, as well as to the Mexican industry's competitive relations with those of Argentina and Spain. Interestingly, Peredo Castro does not list any of the López texts mentioned above in his bibliography. While this is a notable oversight, it indicates that the impulse to 'transnationalise' Mexican golden age film criticism comes from multiple sites.

Another characteristic of much of the criticism on Mexican golden age cinema has been its focus on the history of film production and its stylistic tendencies. Much of the material published, then, focuses on major directors (Emilio Fernández, Fernando de Fuentes, Luis Buñuel, Roberto Gavaldón, Matilde Landeta), movie stars (Pedro Infante, Libertad Lamarque, Cantinflas, María Félix, Dolores del Río), genres (*ranchera* comedy, family melodrama, *cabaretera* musical, nationalist drama, literary adaptations) and periodisation (according to Paranaguá: '1931–1936: artisan and experimental sound period; 1937–1946: industrial apogee with fixed codes and genres; 1947–1964: industrial decadence and the regressive repetition of old formulae' ['Ten Reasons', p. 13]). Representation has also been a key category of analysis, with studies treating Mexican cinema's portrayal of national culture, womanhood (mother, prostitute), family, the middle class, machismo, indigenous peoples, etc. (see Castro Ricalde, 'El género', p. 65). Meanwhile, few authors attempt to broach the topic of reception in a serious way.

An important exception is Carlos Monsiváis and Carlos Bonfil's *A través del espejo: el cine mexicano y su público* (1994), which offers influential conjectures on the experience of going to the movies in Mexico during the silent and early sound years. Some of these authors' observations are insightful and provocative:

> In neighbourhood cinemas of poorer areas, audiences acquire basic skills that help them to orient themselves in an expanding city by assuming a sense of intimacy within the crowd, and its complement: a taste for affiliating with communitarian pleasures, for being part of the group, and being among people, undifferentiated and unique ... (p. 60)

> Mexican movies are 'authentic', which I define here by their cultural essence, the inability to separate them from their spectators. Every movie is, in a psychic sense, a full-length mirror of the theatre ... (p. 65)

> With the move from silent to sound cinema a certainty is solidified: what happens on the screen is the most real reality. It does not reject us, it allows us an instantaneous identification, it directs itself straight at us, it makes us share its idea of nation, family and society. (p. 68)

While this text is often cited for its profound understanding of the period and its fresh socially focused approach to cinema from the perspective of its audiences and everyday life in Mexico during the period in question, many of its conclusions are speculative, and have yet to be confirmed by other researchers.

Early incursions among Latin American researchers such as Monsiváis who are not specialists in film studies, but rather stake out a more interdisciplinary perspective that has come to be associated with Latin American cultural studies also begin to take questions of reception seriously. A notable text in this regard, while not concerned specifically with film history, is Jesús Martín Barbero's *De los medios a las mediaciones* (1987), which does focus its attention briefly on golden age cinema in a chapter titled 'Un cine a la imagen de un pueblo' [A Cinema in the Image of a People] (pp. 226–30). Likewise, Néstor García Canclini's edited volume *Los nuevos espectadores* (1994), while again presenting a much broader study that does not concentrate specifically on film or the time period in question here, dedicates a significant amount of space to the period through a study of visitors' engagement with an exhibition titled 'Revisión del cine mexicano' [Review of Mexican Cinema] in order to map out themes, actors, directors, film and situations that stood out in golden age production for late twentieth-century spectators.

However, like most golden age film criticism, Monsiváis and Bonfil, Martín Barbero and García Canclini focus almost exclusively on the Mexican national context, indeed showing a strong bias towards the experience of spectators in Mexico City. While a handful of studies spend at least a bit of time addressing foreign spectators of Mexican films in specific national contexts (the USA in Agrasánchez; Venezuela in Soto Ávila; Colombia in Hernando Salcedo Silva's *Crónicas del cine colombiano 1897–1950* [1981]), none considers the broadly transnational trajectory of Mexican golden age cinema from the angle of consumption and reception. This study aims to follow the lead of De la Vega Alfaro, López, Peredo Castro, and Monsiváis and Bonfil, and the work of recent critics of Hollywood cinema who have begun considering that industry's reception in a broadly transnational context: for example, Richard Maltby and Melvyn Stokes's co-edited anthology *Hollywood Abroad: Audiences and Cultural Exchange* (2004) and Toby Miller et al.'s *Global Hollywood 2* (2005). Thus, it looks both at,

> the way in which a cultural artifact of demonstrable semantic complexity at its point of
> production and initial domestic consumption is liable, when exported, first to be simplified
> and then rendered semantically complex in different ways by the conventions through which
> the artifacts of its originating culture are perceived in the second, host culture. (Maltby,
> 'Introduction', p. 2)

along with the 'mix of indebtedness and *ressentiment* [that] characterises the relation of import to export cultures, where taste and domination versus market choice and cultural control are graceless antinomies' (Miller et al., p. 65). While it has no pretence of comprehensiveness – indeed book-length studies might easily be realised for every national market, or even more local ones, as is the case of Soto Ávila's 217- page *La época de oro del cine mexicano en Maracaibo* – this study aims to present a broad overview of the kinds of issues raised in different parts of Latin America, as well as in the USA and Europe, by the massive distribution of Mexican films in the era of its golden age.

METHODOLOGY: ISSUES AND STRATEGIES

These questions of reception and impact point to a range of possible methodologies, while the project's scope signals a series of potential logistical complications. First, while some tools of media studies such as audience questionnaires, participant observation, or ethnographic interviews might prove useful for a study of contemporary or recent media consumption, the time period in question (1930s through 50s) makes these methodologies difficult or impossible to apply. For example, while a study such as this one might be based on interviews with elderly individuals who habitually went to see Mexican movies fifty to seventy-five years ago, such a methodology would present several significant and troubling biases. For example, many more moviegoers of the 30s would be deceased than those of the 50s, and those who experienced both periods would likely remember the 50s with more clarity than they would the 30s. The demographic in both cases would be skewed young – that is, it would be much easier to find filmgoers who had been teenagers during the period than those who were, say, in their thirties at the time. In addition, memories of old films may have been shaped by television's treatment of Mexican golden age cinema, with local television networks' reconstruction of the era potentially affecting individual memories significantly.

Another alternative is archival research. Movie magazines and other press, for example, might provide insights into the period that would not be tainted by favouring one age cohort over another, nor would problems of fading memories or television's reconstructions of the period figure. Archival sources of this kind would likewise provide important clues in understanding audience tastes in the period, without their having passed through the filter of what has become Mexican cinema's canon. While this latter-day reconstruction has relied a great deal upon the critical eye of specialists – as well as the availability of films, whether in the form of commercial DVDs or archival materials such as original celluloid reels or scripts – the absence of audience reception studies implies that this canon has been built more around critical and aesthetic criteria than popular tastes of the era. Archival materials, especially dedicated film journals, or regularly published newspaper sections or columns specialised in the movies, offer additional insights into the histories of local markets and industries in each country – for example, through evaluations of: subjects treated, the number and duration of such publications, the number and profiles of contributing critics and columnists, etc.

However, archives present their own problems, including four important ones. The first is something of a class bias: although the film press was directed towards all kinds of movie fans, and it was certainly capable of addressing the experience of different audience segments, the majority of spectators in many countries were illiterate and neither read nor, much less, published opinions in these volumes.

Second, it is important to take into account the tendency of film publications to include reports and interviews that had been paid for by studios without revealing that they were really little more than a form of advertising. Like Hollywood studios and distributors, Mexican producers and distribution agencies, along with movie houses in general, invested a great deal in film promotion. It is at times difficult to discern between unbiased criticism or reporting and publicity materials, which might, for example, make heavily promoted but less popular films appear to be bigger successes than some other relatively profitable films that were released with less fanfare in a given market.

The third possible bias is seen in the greater amount of material available in major urban centres. In order to make such a large-scale transnational study that covers several decades feasible, it would be necessary to limit its focus to only some journals. The most efficient way to proceed would be to rely upon those journals with the largest readership, which were either major newspapers of large cities, or movie magazines usually published in national capitals. While there was certainly a greater variety of film product available in cities than in small towns or rural zones, and it is likely that the proportion of film viewing in urban versus non-urban environments was substantially greater than that of the overall population mix, these selection tactics would create a bias in favour of urban spectatorship.

Finally, such a methodology recreates a temporal bias related to the history of the cinematic enterprise and its affiliates: just as there were fewer films made in the 1930s than in the 50s, there were fewer dedicated journals in the earlier years, and the film writing that was published was for the most part less sophisticated in the first years of sound cinema than two decades later; in other words, film criticism developed significantly during the period in question, and the kind of film coverage that appears in the 50s is very different to that of the 30s. While these bias issues are similar in the ethnographic approach mentioned above and the archival approach described here, they are ultimately more pronounced in the former. For example, while ethnography would likely yield virtually no information at all about filmgoers born before around 1910 – that is, spectators aged twenty-six and up in 1936, or forty-six and up in 1956 – film journals, while less abundant and less sophisticated in the 30s than the 50s, were not nonexistent in the earlier period.

Ultimately, the research team for this study elected to avoid, for the most part, the complications implied by the use of ethnographic methods, and to rely principally upon the print media of the period for its primary source material. Supplemental material incorporated into our research includes film history and criticism, along with published interviews and occasional interviews realised by the researchers themselves. In the end, film reviews and other similar coverage published during the period of the study revealed ample information about consumption and reception of Mexican golden age cinema in its markets abroad over the entire period in question.

Certainly as film reviews came to be more and more commonplace in newspapers, they would become an ever better source of information. Daily newspapers such as *El Tiempo* in Bogotá and *La Opinión* in Los Angeles incorporated coverage of cinema during the entire period of sound film. A handful of more specialised sources also documented the bulk of the period in question: Mexico's most important, comprehensive and widely read film magazine, *Cinema Reporter*, began publishing in 1938 and continued throughout the golden age period; in Venezuela *Mi Film* first appeared in 1940 and ran throughout the period. Thus, primary materials, especially those covering the 40s and 50s, were surprisingly abundant, often to the point of being overwhelming. However, movie magazines were not seen as culturally important among academics and cultural administrators until recent decades, and were rarely archived in libraries back in the 30s, 40s and 50s. While major newspapers can easily be consulted nowadays, often on microfilm, and sometimes even through searchable electronic archives, specialised film journals are notoriously difficult to locate today; indeed many have been lost entirely. *Cinema Reporter* is, fortunately, available for consultation at Mexico's Cineteca Nacional and Mexico's *El Cine Gráfico* can be found at the Hemeroteca Nacional, while a nearly complete collection of Spain's *Primer Plano* is housed in Madrid and *Heraldo del Cinematografista* is archived in Buenos Aires. In most cases, however, such journals can be found in only one national archive, often with many issues missing. The case of the important Cuban magazines *Bohemia* and *Carteles* is paradigmatic as, despite their having issued approximately 100,000 copies weekly (with figures occasionally reaching as high as 2 million), they suffer from the problems described above, but with an additional aggravating factor: not even Cuba's José Martí National Library holds complete collections that are in good condition.

While some countries present more challenging cases than others, whether because they lacked specialised movie magazines, or because existing library collections are incomplete, nowhere can they be simply taken at face value. Each journal, and in many cases each writer or article – and it should be noted that much movie writing during the period is by unnamed authors – represents a particular perspective, social position, or set of values. In very general terms, film journalism of the period can be divided into at least seven categories: 1) promotional materials that appear to be based on studio press releases or propaganda provided by distributors and exhibitors (who were often prominent and regular advertisers in those journals); 2) erudite criticism that focused principally on issues of 'quality', routinely denigrating Mexican film as too commercial and frivolous, and calling for a more aesthetically sophisticated and intellectually complex product; 3) conservative criticism that limited its scope mostly to issues of morality and censorship; 4) nationalist criticism that focused on national collaborators in Mexican cinema, Mexican representations of national culture and the state of national cinema production; 5) populist criticism that observed and interpreted audience reception and reactions; 6) criticism that insisted upon representing a local perspective, which many times was presented in explicit contrast with Mexican tastes, and revealed local preferences, rejections and, above all, the emotions awakened by the penetration of Mexican movie production; and 7) materials that combine two or more of the above categories. For example, criticism that defended the national interests may also be tinged with elitism; and promotional articles often insisted upon a film's relevance for local audiences. The publications studied indeed presented within their always changing teams of contributors a variety of examples of all these categories. The Cuban journal *Bohemia*, for instance, would often include in its 'La farándula pasa' section detailed reviews, publicity oriented interviews, general film news and the more frivolous commentaries of correspondent Don Galaor.

The first category of film journalism is of little use to this study, except in providing some insights regarding marketing strategies in different arenas. These insights do not directly offer information regarding questions of reception; however, they may be suggestive of audience expectations. For example, the amount of press and the rhetoric of consequence in promotional articles for *La vorágine* (Miguel Zacarías, 1949), a film based on the great 1924 Colombian national novel by José

Eustasio Rivera, likely had a significant impact on attendance in Colombia, and on how audiences perceived the film.

The second category is, on the one hand, of limited use for its clear elitist bias, especially with regard to its interest in cultivating a minority audience segment of well-educated, upper middle-class filmgoers. For example, Gabriel García Márquez, who became a regularly published film critic in Colombia in the mid-1950s, stated that his mission was to educate his readers, whom he assumed to be mostly passive viewers who sought only distraction and entertainment in the cinema, in film appreciation, a more active and critical style of movie viewing. Critics like García Márquez did not have any pretence of representing the average filmgoer; assuming the role of expert critic, their authority lay in their superior knowledge on film techniques and aesthetics. On the other hand, the growing importance of this style of criticism during the period is noteworthy as it reflects a new sophistication on the part of movie viewers, who increasingly sought higher-quality film production. Indeed, it has been argued that the growth in this elite market segment, which showed less and less appreciation of Mexican cinema by the 1950s, contributed significantly to the Mexican industry's downfall. It should be added that such criticism is occasionally useful for this study's purposes, for example, when after an audience protest over the Bogotá premiere of the art film, *La red* (Emilio Fernández, 1953), a critic commented:

> the clamour during the exhibition of *La red* was not caused by the ignorance of the spectators ... but on the contrary by their sophistication, brought on by years and years of attending fourth-class movies, and by the mental and sentimental habits created by the influence of commercials for cosmetics and chocolates (*Cromos*, 12 December 1953, p. 40)

around the same time that, in the same column, an anonymous critic (perhaps the same one) complained of Tin Tan's 'absolute lack of talent', while conceding his 'enormous influence in Latin America' (*Cromos*, 12 September 1953, p. 24), thereby giving some insight into audience preferences, and the power of Mexico's industrial production with the masses.

Another interesting case is that of Mirta Aguirre, who is better known in Cuba as a poet, but was a highly visible film critic, especially from 1944 until 1953 when she published regularly in *Hoy*, the journal of Cuba's Popular Socialist Party (PSP). Her interventions in that journal ceased when the Fulgencio Batista regime declared the PSP illegal; however, she continued writing for other journals, such as *Fundamentos*, *Cuba Socialista*, *Bohemia* and *La Palabra*, publishing hundreds of reviews, indeed enough to warrant their compilation in a book, *Mirta Aguirre: crónicas de cine* (Miranda and Castillo). Her writings reveal the contrast between a well-educated left-leaning intellectual sector, with its eyes fixed on European vanguards, and the traditionalist, folklore- and customs-oriented cultural policy of the US-backed Batista regime. Aguirre points to an evident separation between the tastes of university-educated filmgoers and those of the vast majority of Cuban spectators, as she ignores many of the most popular films of the day, including even those that were made in Cuba or featured beloved Cuban actors. She leaves aside nationalist impulses to even remark upon Cuba's or Cubans' participation in the films she reviews, not making any attempt to appeal to everyday fans, but instead aiming to cultivate an appreciation of expressions of elite culture.

The social politics of film criticism varies significantly by country. For example, Cuba's *Cine Guía* published film reviews that evaluated films based on their moral content, and 'prohibited' its readers from seeing certain films, while other countries lacked church-influenced journals dedicated to the movies. However, the conservative government of Franco's Spain, which ruled from 1939 until well beyond the period in question, actively censored many Mexican films, especially those of the *rumbera* genre, and implicitly mandated a more sexually conservative approach to film criticism in general than in, say, Yugoslavia. While such conservative criticism aims to be prescriptive (or proscriptive) rather than representative of audience tastes and preferences, the very fact of its prominence implies an interest on the part of a not insignificant segment of readers, and an implicit degree of influence in viewing habits.

The fourth classification in the list above is more important to this study than the previous three since it seeks to represent not a commercial sector (producers/distributors/exhibitors), an elite minority, or a conservative market segment of indeterminate size, but the entire nation. This criticism articulates a range of native views, often negative but many times positive as well, on Mexican film imports. It focuses on the participation of local artists in a foreign industry, its representations of local culture, and co-productions and other forms of international cooperation through film. It also analyses competition between locally produced cinema and foreign imports, and seeks to explain the popularity of foreign-made films among local audiences.

Also of great relevance to this project is what has been categorised above as populist criticism. This genre looks to evaluate the popularity, or lack thereof, of certain films among 'the masses'. This category of criticism can reflect an identification with the masses, or can be critical of them for their 'poor' taste. However, these critics' observations regarding what aspects of Mexican film are attractive to large segments of the population, including especially poorer urban filmgoers who attend *cines de barrio*, offer insights, undoubtedly of varying degrees of reliability, into the reception of Mexican film by those least likely to have the opportunity to articulate their preferences in print.

Likewise, regionalist criticism that looks to understand, for example, why films that depicted what were understood to be Mexican traditions and folklore (*Allá en el Rancho Grande*; *Río Escondido*) were so popular in Spain, while films about more modern urban life (Tin Tan movies, the *Nosotros los pobres* series) were less favoured among Spanish viewers, provides important information on the preferences of local audiences and their relationship to Mexican movies. While these critics often present their own opinions rather than concrete and verifiable data on audience experiences, they offer insights not easily found elsewhere.

The archival research carried out for this project, then, has not been a mere survey of materials, but instead an active evaluation that has aimed: 1) to ensure an adequate treatment of both earlier and later periods, although with particular temporal focuses in each chapter, depending on the questions being addressed; 2) to critically assess all archival materials to determine to what extent they represent relevant information regarding mass audience reception and impact, as opposed to the mere opinion of a small minority or single critic; and 3) to pay attention to issues of audience segmentation, attempting to tease out how markets were divided (by social class, education level, income level, moral values, age, sex, etc.) – although it should be noted that the study does not pretend to identify and evaluate all segments, but rather to identify the largest ones or those most likely to view Mexican films.

Questions of geography also complicate this study. On the one hand, the aim of addressing a range of issues in culturally distinct markets located throughout the Americas as well as in Europe also contributed to making ethnography impractical as a research tool, and archival research expensive to carry out. It would have been extremely difficult to obtain ethnographic data in sufficient quantities for it to be meaningful for each of the seven geographical areas in question. As the research questions in each chapter of this study vary according to the place, in order to incorporate ethnographic evidence meaningfully, it would have been necessary to design and carry out distinct studies in Cuba, Venezuela, Colombia, Argentina, the USA (this chapter's focus on both Los Angeles and New York would likely have necessitated two separate studies), Spain and ex-Yugoslavia. Migration patterns (especially of Cubans to the USA following the revolution of 1959, and the Argentine diaspora brought about by the dictatorship in the 1970s) might have introduced their own biases – or required transnational samples of data that included appropriate proportions of emigrants.

In the end, archives were deemed less biased, and much more logistically practical than ethnography, especially when supplemented with existing film historiography and occasional interviews realised by the investigation team, or previously published in other sources. However, as can be seen clearly from the questions discussed above, there is an inevitable interpretive, sometimes even speculative element to this study that cannot be resolved by tinkering with research methods. While, for a local study focused on one market, there might be some practical and affordable way to incorporate ethnographic research meaningfully, it would be utterly unruly to attempt to apply ethnographic research tools to a large transnational study such as this one.

This geographical complication – also a linguistic issue in the case of Yugoslavia – called for some creative planning on the part of the research team. Indeed, this project did not start off as a team project, but quickly turned into one when it became apparent that it would take years and years for one person to carry out adequate archival research to broach the issues at hand. The project started out in Mexico, and a great deal of research was carried out there at the Cineteca Nacional and in other Mexico City archives. It also built on a certain degree of existing expertise on the part of the two researchers who became the principal investigators for the project, both of whom were specialists in Mexican culture, broadly defined; had a fairly extensive familiarity with Mexican golden age cinema and its cultural impact in Mexico; and had ample experience working in Mexico City archives. However, it quickly became clear that merely acquiring a general familiarity with film history and cultural history, especially with regard to the 1930s through the 50s, in each of the seven countries researched for the project – which could be achieved to a large extent by reading existing publications, such as the work of film historians of those countries – would not be adequate. Indeed, this project's originality lay in the newness of the topic at hand: transnational reception. National film historians' treatment of film imports was sketchy at best, and consultation of primary sources: newspapers, film journals, etc. was essential. However, this meant extensive and often multiple visits to archives in at least eight different countries. For this reason three additional investigators joined the project, with each of them taking responsibility for archival research in one country. The principal investigators then worked with the other three researchers to ensure that materials available only in Mexico or occasional references to one country made from another country were incorporated into their chapters, and that each chapter was presented in such a way as to tie it to the other chapters.

In the end, this project is not a collection of essays on a related theme, but a cohesive monograph co-written by multiple authors, coordinated by the project's two principal investigators and supported by a transnational team of researchers who have applied an interdisciplinary approach to an archive-based project. This is, then, not a summary of relevant film criticism, nor a critical reading of key films, nor a history of industrial production, nor an analysis of discourse on film in historical journals, but a fusion of these – and sometimes other – methods, always in sustained interaction with each other. This interdisciplinary approach sets the tone in each of the chapters, each of which is written by one or two authors, but is also the product of continuous dialogues realised over the past five years or so among the various members of the project team, whether in occasional one on one meetings or sometimes frequent email exchanges, or at conferences where several of us have presented pieces of this project together, specifically at events sponsored by the UC-Mexicanistas collective at the University of California, Irvine; the Stone Center for Latin American Studies at Tulane University in New Orleans; the Sociedad Argentina de Estudios de Cine y Audiovisual at the Universidad Nacional del Centro de la Provincia de Buenos Aires in Tandil; the Latin American Studies Association at the Pontifícia Universidade Católica in Rio de Janeiro; and the Instituto Tecnológico de Estudios Superiores de Monterrey in Toluca. While this type of collective writing is not common in the humanities, this team believes that it is the only way to answer the kinds of broad transnational questions that are increasingly relevant in today's globalised world – and indeed have been important for many decades, as this study shows.

CONSUMPTION, RECEPTION, AUDIENCE, IMPACT

The rhetoric of 'imposition' so prominent in the coverage of the Mexican movie industry's forays into foreign markets implies a certain notion of reception that has been central to many discussions on Mexican golden age cinema's audiences. Carlos Monsiváis's much quoted comment that Mexican audiences of the era 'plagiarized the cinema as much as possible' in their daily lives ('Mythologies', p. 117) might easily be extrapolated to the experience of non-Mexican spectators to yield a conclusion such as that articulated by Jorge Ayala Blanco: that Mexican golden age cinema, as the most powerful film industry in Latin America, came to,

> function in an imperialistic way in the majority of Spanish-speaking nations of the hemisphere that lacked their own film industry. That is to say, it puts forth aesthetic tastes and values to the vast semi-literate masses, constructs or topples individual and social myths, and inaugurates and exploits markets at will. (Quoted in De la Vega Alfaro, *La industria*, p. 35)

On the one hand, Ayala Blanco's reference to the notion of cultural imperialism would seem to be overstated. It reflects a common strain of Latin American communication studies of its time (1960s–70s) based upon a notion of the spectator, put forth by such theorists as Harold Lasswell, that assumed naive passivity on the part of spectators – injected as if by a cultural 'hypodermic needle' – that made their experience of reception susceptible to being moulded and manipulated by the will of communications media producers (DeFleur, p. 169). This vision, representative of a vast sector of journalists as well as academics, portrayed the public as a largely undifferentiated mass, levelled of any possible differences in social context, cultural identity, or processes of consumption. Ayala Blanco nonetheless adroitly identifies the power of Mexico's cinematic machine in a period when the focus of critical attention was on less subtle disequilibriums of communications flows related to questions of Latin American dependency (Hamelink, p. 22; Moragas, p. 85). Both ideas (hypodermic needs, cultural dependency) assume a lack of agency, even a defencelessness, on the part of audiences (Schiller, p. 42).

Discussions of Hollywood's cultural imperialism are foregrounded by the powerful political position of the USA, as well as the ways in which the 'American lifestyle' promoted in Hollywood film benefitted the US economy in a broad way that deepened relations of economic dependency. As critics have observed,

> As early as 1912, Hollywood exporters were also aware that where their films travelled, demand was created for other US goods. ... By the late 1930s, stories of heroic merchandising links between cinema and sales were legion, such as the ones that told of a new Javanese market for US sewing machines ... and a Brazilian taste for bungalows that mimicked Angelino high life ... By the 1950s, the industry confidently claimed that 'business follows the film as well as the flag'. (Miller et al., pp. 65–6; embedded quote from William Irving Greenwald's 1952 text, *The Motion Picture Industry*)

The question, then, of whether Mexico's golden age cinema was 'imperialistic', cannot be answered simply. Mexico's industry was a powerful cultural machine that exercised a remarkable influence over many foreign viewers, playing a key role in contributing 'to the sentimental education of the masses' throughout the hemisphere (García Canclini, *Consumers*, p. 112). However, even if such viewers are assumed to have passively accepted whatever was put in front of them and to have lacked any capacity to discern or interpret film content, it cannot be said that Mexican film's promotion of a Mexican lifestyle did much to sell Mexican goods, aside from other cultural products (music, other films), abroad. The success of Mexican movies abroad did not generate great demand for molcajetes, huipiles, talavera tea cups, or epazote in Chile or Spain. Mexico, while larger and richer than some other Latin American countries, has never exercised the kind of political and economic power that the USA has held over them, nor has it been argued that its cinematic triumphs afforded other Mexican industries important advantages in export markets in the Americas.

In any case, discussions of cultural imperialism have generally been moderated in more recent decades by reconceptualisations of the experience of the film spectator (see, for example, the summaries presented in Sunkel; Wortman). Monsiváis's discussion of Mexican spectatorship, cited above, assumes a certain passivity on the part of film audiences, a naivety perhaps attributable to the relative newness of the medium in the early years of sound cinema. It was, after all, the same period in which Walter Benjamin famously concluded that,

> reception in a state of distraction ... finds in the film its true means of exercise ... The film makes the cult value recede into the background not only by putting the public in the position of the critic, but also by the fact that at the movies this position requires no attention. The public is an examiner, but an absent-minded one. (p. 18)

However, while it may be true that audiences in the 1930s or 40s were more 'distracted' and therefore less critical than contemporary audiences, who have grown up with cinema and are accustomed to a level of astuteness in media criticism uncommon a couple of generations ago, it is difficult to sustain an absolutist position. Even Monsiváis's concept of golden age cinema as a 'school-in-the-dark' ('Mythologies', p. 118) presupposes a learning process, not a mere process of absorption, that would implicitly involve some degree of conscious participation on the part of spectators.

The notion of an active audience becomes especially relevant when thinking about the international market segmentation evident in the distribution of Mexican golden age film. Intuition dictates that a Mexican audience would not have the same experience as a non-Mexican Latin American audience or a European audience. And depending on film content (nationality of actors or characters, setting, cultural context of plotlines, other cultural signs such as musical numbers), audiences from individual countries might experience Mexican films in very obviously different ways. In addition, political relations (e.g., Mexico's severed of diplomatic relations with Franco's Spain) or economic relations (e.g., the Mexican film industry's direct competition with the Argentine industry) might also influence the particular way that spectators of a given country experienced Mexican golden age films.

Stuart Hall's notions of encoding and decoding are clearly relevant for this context. Regardless of how the process of encoding is imagined on the part of producers, directors, screenwriters, editors, or actors, the decoding process, which initiates with local marketing by distributors and exhibitors, local critics and is fully realised by local audiences, and through which meanings are produced for individual spectators, clearly follows distinct trajectories in different international contexts:

> cultural studies argues that the spectator is the result of various discourses put into play by the text, but also the subject of social, economic, and political practices beyond the text, which are brought to bear at the moment of screen/viewer interaction. (Pribham, p. 159)

While discussions of individual subjectivity open up discussion to an infinite range of interpretative experiences, the relevant context in this case will be that of the nation, and the questions asked will be fairly general ones about the reception and impact of Mexican films for Venezuelan or Argentine or Spanish audiences.

The process of encoding and decoding might be thought of in different ways for different films. Producers assign 'preferred meanings' to a film text (Hall, p. 912), which may or may not result in the same experience of final meaning production for different audiences. For example, the highly publicised casting of white Mexican actress Dolores del Río, who had spent most of her career to date as a Hollywood star, in the role of indigenous heroine María Candelaria in the film of the same name likely required a conscious suspension of belief on the part of many Mexican viewers, but at the same time signified a degree of honour and importance for the film that no other Mexican actress could have brought to it. Meanwhile, French critics at the Cannes Film Festival of 1946, for many of whom *María Candelaria* represented a first filmic portrait of Mexican culture, remarked on the authenticity achieved in this role by del Río, who appeared, in their view, 'without artifice, her pure face framed by long braids, and dressed with the simple clothes of a Mexican peasant' (Georges Sadoul, quoted in Tierney, p. 84).

Mexican golden age film likewise evoked different forms of interpellation on different audiences. *Allá en el Rancho Grande*, *Flor silvestre*, or *Nosotros los pobres* undoubtedly called upon Mexican audiences to identify with specific Mexican cultural traits represented in these films, while for many non-Mexican audiences, such films followed more in the tradition of what Ana López has called cinema's 'ethnographic' function ('Are All Latins'): that is, these films might have been interpreted as offering insights into Mexican rural ranch life, the experience of the Mexican revolution, or contemporary urban reality in Mexico City's most impoverished neighbourhoods. French or Yugoslavian audiences, for example, might accept any of the above mentioned films as authentic representations of Mexican otherness, with which they might not identify at all. The particular position of Latin American audiences is more complex. While Uruguayans or Panamanians would unlikely identify with some specific cultural signs or markers, there were enough elements common to Latin American culture in these films, elements (e.g., Spanish language, popular music, certain landscapes or cityscapes, Catholic idols, etc.) that differentiated them from Hollywood films and made them more familiar to Latin American audiences, that they evoked a certain degree of identification, perhaps not as strong as that experienced by Mexican spectators, but an identification robust enough to make it common to refer to elements of Mexican cinema as 'ours'. Thus, in the Colombian press, Cantinflas was 'the greatest comic actor of our America' (*El Tiempo*, 5 March 1943, p. 5), and Venezuelans comprehended the ways in which Mexican cinema 'helped to buttress a spirit of fraternity in Latin American communities' (Soto Ávila, p. 9).

Mexico's relationship with the rest of Latin America, and to a strong degree with Spain, as well, constitutes what film studies scholar Mette Hjort calls 'epiphanic transnationalism', which she defines as 'the cinematic articulation of those elements of deep national belonging that overlap with aspects of other national identities to produce something resembling deep transnational belonging' (p. 16) – in this case a common Latin American unity. However, Mexican cinema's relationship with Spanish-speaking audiences of other nations would seem to be founded even more on what Hjort calls 'affinitive transnationalism', which depends on a notion of cultural similarity, specifically defined 'in terms of ethnicity, partially overlapping or mutually intelligible languages, and a history of interaction giving rise to shared core values, common practices, and comparable institutions' (ibid., p. 17). Spanish America's long shared colonial history and many parallelisms in postcolonial experiences, including at the most basic level a shared nationally dominant language (Spanish) and religion

(Catholicism) encourage both these tendencies. Shared socioeconomic phenomena characteristic of the period in many parts of Latin America – many of which would seem to foreshadow later globalising trends – made this perception of a shared culture more pronounced. Some examples include: trends of emigration from country to city, resulting in unchecked, unplanned urban growth concomitant with a weakening of provincial social structures; and fractures among different segments of the population, especially with regard to questions of ethnicity and social class. These shifting demographics coincided roughly with the golden age of Mexico's cinema, and while other forms of cultural production, including literature and theatre, had long stimulated such transnational connections, the movie industry's wide accessibility and appeal significantly intensified them.

Marvin D'Lugo argues that music, a central component of various Mexican movie genres, including the *ranchera* comedy and the cabaret melodrama, began with the rise of the recording, radio and film industries to cultivate what he calls a transnational 'aural' identity through popular musical genres, songs and artists beloved all over the Spanish-speaking world: 'The distribution of Spanish-language musical films determined by markets that defied political boundaries ... contributed to the formation of a transnational Hispanic audience whose cultural outlook was no longer shaped exclusively by national themes and interests' ('Aural Identity', p. 163). Ana López agrees that Mexican film, more than any other cinema of the golden years, absorbed genres associated with other nations: Argentine tango, Cuban rumba and mambo, 'and even sambas' of Brazil:

> Thus, perhaps on a smaller scale, but no less pervasively than in Hollywood, the Mexican cinema outside the ranchera genre posited Latin American music and dance as general markers of a 'Latin-ness' increasingly dissociated from any national specificity ... Other national differences could be assimilated into a broadened, cosmopolitan vision of a 'Mexico' that could absorb all the Latindad of Latin America. ('Of Rhythms', pp. 324–5)

Thus, even the most nationalist films, including those likely encoded to evoke identification with Mexican national symbols, were often capable of being decoded in such a way as to evoke a broader transnational Latin American identification. However, other films were consciously encoded with transnational symbols as Mexico's industry courted fans in other countries. Some, such as *Simón Bolívar*, called up well-known references evocative of pan-Latin American unity, while others, including *La vorágine* or *Doña Bárbara*, targeted audiences of specific nations. Meanwhile, Mexican cinema's prominent use of actors from throughout the Spanish-speaking world also served to attract fans from their countries of origin. As one Cuban critic commented in 1944,

> It goes without saying that the powerful magnet of cinema has mobilised an endless caravan coming from every corner of the Americas ... This artistic exchange will forever be one of the ways of opening the doors to markets because in every country that exhibits a Mexican film whose cast includes figures of that nationality, they will be welcomed with double sympathy, because everyone likes to see their own well treated. (*Cinema Reporter*, 16 September 1944, pp. 31)

Jorge Negrete experienced overwhelming popularity in Cuba, both as an actor and *ranchera* singer

The question of encoding and decoding bears significantly on the theme of 'imposition'. It is clear at many moments not only that the imperialist argument is diluted by the process of decoding, with the idea of spectator agency that the term implies, but also that the case for Mexican cinema as an imposition falls flat when processes of encoding are considered carefully. While the Mexican golden age industry may have influenced tastes and preferences at home and abroad, it also took into account audience demand in all its markets. Time and again critics noted the connection between Mexican cinema and the Latin American masses. In April of 1942, prior to the release of *Simón Bolívar* or *Doña Bárbara*, Mexican cinema was praised in Venezuela for the attention it paid to external markets: 'The Mexicans make movies for the public, for their distributors and for investors' (*Social Cine*, 4 April 1942, quoted in *Cinema Reporter*, 12 June 1942, p. 8). An international distributor of Spanish-language cinema in Venezuela and the Caribbean was quoted in the Argentine press, explaining the Mexican industry's competitive edge over that of Argentina in Latin American markets as the result of the former's attention to the preferences of audiences throughout the hemisphere, claiming that Argentine movies 'are incomprehensible and of little interest to the majority of Latin Americans to whose taste productions coming from Mexico are better adapted as they are less profound and more accessible to the popular mindset' (quoted in *El Cine Gráfico*, 3 October 1943, p. 12). Years later, Spanish-born film-maker Néstor Almendros, who lived much of his adult life in Cuba, experiencing firsthand the success of Mexican golden age movies there, likewise praised the Mexican industry – in contrast with that of Argentina – for its ability to judge popular tastes, describing Mexican cinema as 'always attentive to the demands and fluctuations of Iberoamerican taste' (quoted in Martínez Pardo, p. 152).

Latin American audiences had choices. For the most part, their first choice was Hollywood cinema, which was abundantly promoted throughout the hemisphere: as Ana López notes, 'even at the peak of its popularity, the Mexican cinema never had more than 25–35% of any one Latin American market' ('A Cinema', p. 7). However, Latin American audiences could choose among various foreign-language products (imports from the USA, France, Italy, etc.), as well as various Spanish-language products (imports from Mexico, Argentina, Spain, or even Hollywood, as well as, at certain times and in certain countries, locally produced national cinema). Mexican cinema dominated the Spanish-language sector of most Latin American markets because of its appeal to popular tastes, an appeal not achieved by luck or by force, but by Mexican producers' consciousness of their customers' preferences. Not only might audiences appropriate sounds and images for their own purposes, as Yugoslav audiences did with Mexican cinema in the 1950s, but viewing publics might influence film production much more indirectly as producers sought to appropriate the popular culture of the masses – songs, jokes, dances, style of dress, language, etc. – for the medium in order to win over audiences. Cinema functioned neither as an imposition from studios, nor as a purely democratising assertion on the part of audiences, but as a process of mediation between the two (Martín Barbero). As García Canclini puts it, 'The consumer is not a pure creator, nor is the transmitter omnipotent' ('El consumo', p. 38).

CASE STUDIES

Each chapter of this project focuses on a particular foreign market, aiming not to present a complete history of Mexican film reception in that country, but to follow through on a handful of arguments pertinent to the local context. Taken together, these arguments offer a broad panorama of issues raised by Mexican golden age cinema's exportation to, consumption in and impact on different parts of the world. Our objective is not to offer a comprehensive history of Mexican film reception in the period for any country, nor do we attempt to include every major Mexican market – we leave out, for example, Peru and Chile. Our selection of Cuba, Colombia, Venezuela, Argentina, the Spanish-language markets of the USA, Spain and Yugoslavia merely allows us to propose critical paradigms relevant to the cinematic relations between Mexico and these national contexts, as well as to the reading of a range of codes, including audiovisual (cinema), auditory (music) and printed codes (newspapers, magazines, posters and other promotional materials). While film industries are ultimately the axis of our analysis, the context brings into play links with literature and its representatives (Rómulo Gallegos), the life histories of popular actors (Libertad Lamarque, María Antonieta Pons), the discourses of panhispanism and their metaphorisation in romances of Jorge Negrete and Carmen Sevilla, or music and its unexpected repercussions in lands as far away as Yugoslavia.

The first chapter, 'Rumba Caliente Beats Foxtrot: Cinematic Cultural Exchanges Between Mexico and Cuba' immediately raises several key issues, many of which will be further developed in later chapters. Most importantly, it addresses the imbalance of power in cultural exchange between the two nations in favour of Mexico with its well-developed cultural industries. It reviews the history of reception of Mexican cinema in Cuba, one of Mexico's biggest export markets, and analyses how Mexico's film industry gradually came to dominate other Spanish-language producers there. It did so through popular genres such as the *ranchera* comedy, but also by incorporating elements of Cuban culture into its repertoire, and by employing Cuban film professionals; it looks especially at the case of one of Cuba's biggest film stars of the era, *rumbera* María Antonieta Pons, and Cubans' ambivalence regarding her phenomenal success, which brought Cuban culture to huge international audiences, but always under the control of a Mexican industry whose representations of Cuba drew freely from racialised stereotypes. While attentive to these questions of national reputation for national audiences, it also takes into account the diversity in strains of film criticism generated in Cuba, reflective of differences in taste and values among different market segments. It also analyses the fact that whatever criticism some Cubans may have had for Mexican cinema, Cubans saw no way to develop film production in their country except through collaboration, and it was the Mexican industry that Cuban producers most sought out to realise such collaborations.

The second chapter focuses attention upon another of Mexico's most important external markets, that of Colombia. '*Así se quiere en Antioquia*: Mexican Golden Age Cinema in Colombia' addresses the rise of Mexican cinema in Colombia and its role in both influencing Colombia's own self-representations in its attempts to launch a national film industry, and the role of Mexican cinema's deeply entrenched popularity in Colombian producers' ultimate failure to establish autochthonous film production. Mexico's panamericanist strategies evident in the production and marketing of *Simón Bolívar* in late 1942, which would be repeated with the highly touted launch of *La vorágine* in 1949, cemented Mexico's dominant position *vis-à-vis* other Spanish-language competitors in Colombia, and even allowed Mexico to pose a serious challenge to Hollywood there. As in Cuba, Colombians' consumption of Mexican film generated ambivalent sentiments that ranged from a celebration of Mexico's success as a victory for Latin America, which implied a Colombian appropriation of Mexican cinema as their own, to a frustration with Mexican cinema's popularity, both for its market strength that effectively shut Colombian producers out of the market and for its catering to the masses by producing a commercially oriented cinema of limited artistic value, and of repetitive themes.

An interesting dynamic of mediation and exchange develops, with Latin American audiences appropriating Mexican cinema for their own purposes, while Mexican producers appropriate and profit from their use of Latin American culture. The next chapter, 'Mexico's Appropriation of the Latin American Visual Imaginary: Rómulo Gallegos in Mexico' turns to another of Mexico's top markets, Venezuela. The Mexican industry's inroads in this market have much to do with the launching of two films: the previously mentioned *Simón Bolívar*, as well as *Doña Bárbara* in 1943, the latter based on the great national novel by Venezuelan author and politician Rómulo Gallegos. Gallegos's abandonment of nascent Venezuelan film production projects and moving to the well-established Mexican studios to realise the production and triumphant release of the Mexican industry's adaptation of his novel *Doña Bárbara*, with rising Mexican superstar María Félix in the lead role, firmly establish Mexican cinema both as an immensely popular cultural supplier for Venezuelan audiences, and as an enormously

Libertad Lamarque's incorporation into Mexican cinema symbolised the Mexican industry's dominance in its rivalry with Argentina

powerful vehicle for representing Venezuelan culture – and for ultimately influencing how its first massively disseminated media representations were constructed. Gallegos's production of five films in Mexico, including *Canaima* (1945), starring Jorge Negrete, would contribute significantly to transforming the Venezuelan market into the biggest Latin American export market for Mexican films (in terms of number of films exported) by the decade's end (*El Cine Gráfico*, 4 May 1952, p. 6), despite its limited capacity (as measured by number of theatres, seating capacity, attendance) in comparison with more populous countries such as Cuba, Colombia, Chile and Peru (Ivers and Aaronson, pp. x–xi).

Chapter 4, 'Latin American Rivalry: Libertad Lamarque in Mexican Golden Age Cinema', reviews the dynamics of Mexico's rise to become the dominant player, over Argentina, in Latin American golden age film production. It traces out the dynamic of the rivalry, reviewing how both US market intervention and domestic policy seriously hampered the Argentine industry's advancement. It focuses in particular on the controversial move of one of Argentine cinema's top stars, Libertad Lamarque, to Mexico upon being blacklisted in Argentina following a dispute with Eva Perón, and how Lamarque's incorporation into Mexican cinema played out, with regard to Mexico's reputation as the cultural centre of Latin America, as well as to Mexico's cinematic representations of its market rival, Argentina, through Lamarque's enormously popular films. The chapter, which plays upon the background of World War II and Peronism (the populist politics of Eva Perón's husband, president Juan Perón), highlights the role of global politics in the Latin American film market.

World War II era 'good neighbour policy' played an important role with the opening of new theatres in New York dedicated to Mexican cinema. In cosmopolitan

New York, Mexico's most acclaimed films played with subtitles, while a broad array of movies played in Spanish Harlem and other key Spanish-speaking neighbourhoods to mostly Puerto Rican audiences. Meanwhile, in Los Angeles and other cities in the southwest, Mexico found its most loyal and profitable foreign market in a public made up mostly of Mexican emigrants. While states such as California had long-established Mexican American populations, with market growth following the advent of the Bracero Program in the 1940s, borderlands cities like Los Angeles came to function practically as part of Mexico's domestic market, even as Mexican cinema produced films that were critical of emigration, as was the case with *Espaldas mojadas* (Alejandro Galindo, 1955), which nonetheless was a box-office hit in Los Angeles. This chapter, 'Mexican National Cinema: Good Neighbours and Transnational Mexican Audiences' traces out the history of Mexican cinema's consumption in the USA, and underscores the US market's key role in the success of Mexico's golden age industry.

Chapter 6, 'Panhispanic Romances in Times of Rupture: Spanish–Mexican Cinema', looks at Mexican cinema's relationship with former colonial power Spain. While Spain initially held the upper hand over Mexico as a rival producer of Spanish-language cinema, Spain's civil war, along with its postwar isolationist politics, damaged both production capabilities and complicated export flows by the late 1930s. The Spanish film industry's recovery would never be sufficient to seriously challenge Mexican domination in Spanish-speaking markets. Eventually Spain's industry adopted the strategy of teaming with Mexico's more powerful studios in a series of co-productions. Spanish audiences were especially enamoured with Jorge Negrete and María Félix, two of Mexico's most iconic superstars, and their preference for folkloric musicals gave rise to a genre of co-produced romantic films featuring Mexican *rancheras* and Spanish flamenco music that drew from Mexican cinematic paradigms. This chapter's analysis of films like Negrete's *Jalisco canta en Sevilla* and Félix's *Mare nostrum* (Rafael Gil, 1948) tease out several ways in which Mexican cinema impacted on Spanish cultural production, a reversal of the colonial legacy that assumed Spain's role as the leading player in Spanish-language cultural production.

The final chapter, '"Vedro Nebo" in Far Off Lands: Mexican Golden Age Cinema's Unexpected Triumph in Tito's Yugoslavia', follows Mexican cinema's postwar trajectory into European markets, exploring its resounding success in Yugoslavia in the early 1950s. Following the triumph in Cannes of *María Candelaria* in 1946, Mexican film, especially the stylish social dramas of director Emilio Fernández, became hits in new markets for Mexico, such as France, Italy and Czechoslovakia, where Mexican cinema was praised for what European audiences saw as its authenticity. Mexican cinema's introduction into Yugoslavia in the early 1950s, filling a void left by the removal of Soviet cinema from the market in a period of conflicts in Eastern Europe, scored an unexpected success with a lesser-known Fernández film, *Un día de vida* (1950). The triumph of this film, and of the *ranchera* music it featured, would have a long-lasting impact in Yugoslavia, where 'Yu-Mex' music would become a long-term trend, an example of the far-flung possibilities of cultural impact for Mexican golden age cinema that went well beyond the expected circuits.

EL CINE MEXICANO SE IMPONE

The 'imposition' of Mexican cinema in foreign markets was a complex process that was both welcomed and resented. Its many internationally popular films – some key titles: *Allá en el Rancho Grande, Ahí está el detalle, Simón Bolívar, Doña Bárbara, María Candelaria, Jalisco canta en Sevilla, Un día de vida, Espaldas mojadas* – were decoded to produce vastly different meanings in different places. Some audiences identified directly with Mexican symbols, appropriating them as their own. Others appreciated the Mexican camera's ethnographic eye from a distance, soaking in what functioned as promotional propaganda for the benefit of Mexican culture. Audiences were deeply impacted by Mexican cinema in a variety of ways, but this did not mean that it was imposed on them against their will; Mexican cinema both shaped and responded to the tastes and preferences of its viewers. The Mexican golden age film industry employed a variety of strategies to grow its markets. It engaged in co-productions with foreign producers; it represented aspects of the cultures of its fans; it employed foreign professionals, often in starring roles. It was so successful that local startup production companies in countries where it had established a strong presence could not compete with it and, when they tried, they felt compelled to adopt Mexican styles and formats, or to invite in Mexican professionals or production companies as collaborators. Mexican cinema thus shaped not only tastes but creative expression, and not only in Latin America, but as far away as Eastern Europe. Mexico became, for a magical period of about twenty years, the Hollywood of Latin America, the centre of Spanish-language cultural production. It positioned Mexican culture in a powerful regional leadership role. Though Mexican cinema would never truly threaten Hollywood's dominance, its remarkable international success during its golden age complicates binary notions of north–south cultural relations, and establishes a precedent for the often complex regional hierarchies in the realm of cultural media in the contemporary globalised world.

NOTE

1.   Note that this and all subsequent translations from Spanish or other languages into English are our own, unless otherwise indicated.

Rumba Caliente Beats Foxtrot: Cinematic Cultural Exchanges Between Mexico and Cuba

Maricruz Castro Ricalde

AFFECTIONS AND REJECTIONS

This chapter explores multiple aspects of the cinematic links established between Mexico and Cuba during Mexican cinema's golden age. These links brought the countries closer together, and even though Mexico's industry was stronger and wielded greater influence in Cuba than vice versa, from the beginning to the end of its golden age, Mexican culture was not immune to the influence of the rhythms, songs, costumes, settings, behaviours and plots of a genre created by Mexican cinema based around the cluster of lovely Cuban women known as *rumberas* (rumba dancers) who began to arrive in Mexico, where they became mainstays of its cinema. Although some Cubans were not happy with the way in which these movies, whether filmed in Mexico or in Cuba, constructed Cuba through stereotypical notions of the island as a Caribbean paradise, others were grateful to see a Cuban presence magnified throughout Latin America that was only possible thanks to Mexican cinema's intense interest in Cuban culture.

Some Cuban critics were vigilant, pointing out fictions, errors, falsifications, rejecting the many representations they saw as excessively primitive, lustful or exotic. But others, perhaps underestimating Mexican cinema's reach, 'remained silent, a common phenomenon throughout the golden age of Mexico's cinema, considered mainly massive, popular, industrial and, therefore, disdained by the haughty Latin American intelligentsia' (Verdugo Fuentes). While Cuban journals celebrated the international success its stars achieved through the Mexican industry, they lamented the way it portrayed Cuba, or simply wished its defects away by ignoring its existence.

The *ranchera* comedy is what initially established Mexican cinema's foothold in the Cuban market with the astounding triumph of *Allá en el Rancho Grande*, although this genre fell quickly into disfavour, opening up opportunities for Argentine cinema to become the leading exporter of Spanish-language product to Cuba in the late 1930s. But the *ranchera* and other genres rooted in Mexican popular culture would again become the favourites of Cuban audiences even as most Cuban critics remained lukewarm. The success of the *ranchera* comedy and *rumbera* musical, a genre that became a huge hit in the late 40s, allowed Mexico to assume an unchallengeable leadership position among Spanish-language producers through the 50s, with Mexican product circulating in quantities three times greater than those of all other Spanish-language producers combined (Douglas, pp. 318–19). While the *ranchera* genre was understood to be essentially Mexican in content, the *rumbera* films were more ambivalent in their focus, with Mexican Gulf coast contexts blurring into Cuban ones, with Cuba's Afro-Latin American roots ultimately coming to define its culture in opposition to that of mestizo Mexico. Cuban audiences identified with superficial elements essential to stereotypes of the Caribbean: music, landscapes, exuberance, colour that could be imagined (in the mostly black-and-white films) in the paradox of costumes that were baroque in their scantiness. Likewise, the phenomena of migration and industrialisation, experienced in these years through all of Latin America, allegorised in stories about innocent girls from the provinces trying to make it in rough, modern cities by dancing in cabarets, allowed recent arrivals to the city (whether Mexico City, Havana, Los Angeles or Bogotá) to find a cultural anchoring in the titillating cinematic representations of the *rumbera* genre.

Meanwhile, as Mexico became Latin American cinema's mecca, its studios received a great number of Cuban artists and professionals, many of whom established permanent residency in Mexico City, including pioneers in the Mexican industry such as director Ramón Peón and actor Juan José Martínez Casado, and some of its biggest all-time stars, including *rumberas* María Antonieta Pons and Ninón Sevilla. However, there was also a moment in the latter half of the 1940s of a certain fluctuation in flows as the possibility arose that Cuba's own film industry would gain momentum. During that period, Cuban expatriots and Mexicans alike travelled more often to Havana in hopes of participating in different media projects, very few of which came into fruition. Only those in the music business were able to return to Mexico with signed contracts, and by the mid-1950s Cubans were resigned to seeing their culture represented mostly through Mexican–Cuban co-productions whose content was usually determined by the Mexican industry's need to export them widely – to audiences that wanted to see Cuba represented as a sensuous and exotic island paradise and that had little interest in other themes, including representations of major Latin American heroes and writers, such as José Martí, whose biopic, *La rosa blanca* (Emilio Fernández, 1954), was a box-office flop.

Reactions to Mexican cinema would turn ambivalent in these years as Cubans' dreams of founding their own sustainable industry faded, and Mexican cinema began to lose its lustre as well, although it remained very popular in Cuba right up to the revolution of 1959. Throughout the 1950s, Cubans continued to travel to Mexico to learn the ropes of the business and perhaps meet eager investors or sign on to fruitful collaborations. Others complained: 'it is time that Mexican cinema realised the enormous responsibility it has as an industry that exercises a huge influence on the multitudes' (*Bohemia*, 21 March 1948, p. 86). Mexican cinema had indeed imposed its cinema not only as a product for Cuban moviegoers, but also as the best Spanish-language medium for Cuban performers including actors, dancers and musicians to work in, and the most frequent portrayer of Cuban culture on the silver screen.

This chapter lays out the complexity of the cinematic relations between Mexico and Cuba, marked as they nearly always were by contradictory attitudes oscillating between affection and rejection. As in the case of other countries, although audiences continued to express their own tastes, a segment of the press attempted to implant a vision of cinema as artistic expression. This vision would be realised following the revolution of 1959, after which the only Mexican films remaining in circulation were those exhibiting a social realism that privileged dramatic narrative structures differing significantly from the bulk of golden age cinema, which had built on traditions of musical revue or vaudeville-style theatre, especially in the cases of Cuban audiences' favourite genres: the *ranchera* comedy and the *rumbera* musical.

MUSIC: A LANGUAGE WITHOUT BORDERS

While the rise of the tango was key for the appropriation of certain aspects of Argentine culture in Mexico and the rest of Latin America, from the first decade of the twentieth century, Cuban popular music made its own mark. The incorporation of rhythms dear to Cubans such as the son, the rumba and the habanero (antecedent of the popular danzón) into everyday life in Mexico City and Mexico's cities most connected to Caribbean culture, such as Veracruz and Mérida, was reinforced thanks to the appreciation shown for Caribbean sounds by Mexican composers such as Juventino Rosas or Manuel María Ponce. Postrevolutionary Mexico saw its dancehalls come alive with danzóns and other Caribbean-influenced music, along with Argentine tangos, which began to take hold alongside more traditionally Mexican rhythms.

Of course, the seduction exercised by melodies from places like Argentina and Cuba was possible only when they were disseminated through international cultural industries (the recording industry, radio, film); when these cultural interactions did occur (as they did with Cuban, Mexican and Argentine music, but did not with, for example, Chilean, Venezuelan or Bolivian music), they promoted the national cultures they represented to the world while their reterritorialisations abroad, where foreign artists incorporated them into their repertoires, simultaneously made it ever more difficult to discern origins. Just as the cultural industries strengthened notions of national culture by nationalising once regionally identified musical genres, their transnational reach and the cultural exchanges they promoted diluted these marks of identity, favouring the incorporation of formerly 'national' genres throughout Latin America, and the promotion of what has been called a 'transnational aural identity' (D'Lugo, 'Aural Identity'). Thus, 'Cachita' – put to music by the New York-based Puerto Rican Rafael Hernández and whose lyrics were written by Mexico-based Spaniard from Bilbao, Bernardo San Cristóbal – set a whole generation dancing following its 1936 broadcast on Mexico City's XEB radio, sung by Yucatecan crooner Wello Rivas in a duet with Mexican Margarita Romero (Granados, p. 24).

Convergences of this sort, of artists from different locations, both in music and in film, began to transform Mexico's capital into the Hollywood of Latin America that it would definitively be by the mid-1940s. Moreover, the unprecedented triumph of 'Cachita' is emblematic of the changes in taste occurring in the epoch in which, in effect, the foxtrot, a genre associated with metropolitan style (US big bands), was being cast aside for its 'coldness' and replaced by rhythms that had previously been rejected for their association with marginalised groups, spaces and symbolic realms. The *arrabal* (a term used for poor neighbourhoods in Argentina and Uruguay) and *carpa* (informal mobile theatre set up inside tents, once common in Latin America), with their *caliente* (hot) rhythms such as the rumba or the cha-cha-cha, were conquering audiences all over the world, a trend allegorised in song lyrics about their popularity among the French and other non-Latin Americans – 'The Frenchman has fun like this/as does the German/and the Irishman has a ball/as does even the Muslim' ('Cachita') – even as they filtered in the presence of a blackness – 'and if you want to dance/look for your Cachita/and tell her "Come on negrita"/let's dance' – denied in the official discourse of those Spanish-speaking countries wielding the greatest economic power in the region: namely, Argentina and Mexico, the latter of which would eventually incorporate Afro-Latin American culture into its cinema – although being careful to mark it as Cuban and not Mexican.

The recording industry and the power exercised through its greatest channel of transmission, the radio, in the 1930s would be accompanied by cinema, which, with its incorporation of sound technology, would absorb for the Latin American market the most popular Cuban artists of the era, including Rita Montaner and the ensemble Caribe, as seen already in the early sound film *La noche del pecado* (Miguel Contreras Torres, 1933), or Juan Orol's *opera prima*, *Madre querida* (1935), which featured the music of Cuban artist Bola de Nieve. Over the course of the years associated with Mexican cinema's golden age, Cuba's musical community would grow significantly in both number and influence, producing internationally acclaimed artists such as Kiko Mendive, Dámaso Pérez Prado, Benny Moré, Trío Matamoros, Celio González, Celia Cruz and Sonora Matancera, among many others. This music was incorporated into movies, and was further promoted in the popular artistic caravans that toured for months at a time through the small towns and big cities of Mexico and the rest of Latin America and the Caribbean. It is not easy to imagine a movie starring a Cuban *rumbera* such as María Antonieta Pons, Ninón Sevilla, Amalia Aguilar or Rosa Carmina without the intervention of one of the Cuban musicians mentioned above.

The exchanges between Cuba and Mexico not only involved Cuban musicians and singers coming to Mexico, whether on tour or to stay temporarily or permanently, but also led to the incorporation of Mexican popular songs and styles into the repertoires of Cuban artists. At the same time, Mexican recording composers and artists such as Agustín Lara, María Grever, Toña la Negra and Trío los Panchos made Caribbean genres such as the *bolero* Mexican.

While actors who happened to be talented singers, as was the case of tango chanteuse Libertad Lamarque in early Argentine sound cinema or *ranchera* composer and singer Lorenzo Barcelata in 1930s Mexican film, had played an important role in Latin American talkies from the beginning, with the rise of the international recording industry and the diffusion of the recordings of Latin American artists across the hemisphere, film-makers began to give significant screen time to musicians who were not experienced as actors, as was the case of 'mambo king' Dámaso Pérez Prado in *Al son del mambo* (Chano Urueta, 1950), a film in which the beloved Cuban singer and actress Rita Montaner also starred. Without playing a speaking role, but instead forming part of the musical groups that added so significantly to the atmosphere of many films, Kiko Mendive became a universally known face through his visual (and musical) presence in Juan Orol productions such as *Balajú* (Rolando Aguilar, 1944), *La reina del trópico* or *Embrujo antillano* (Geza Polaty, 1947), among many others, or in plots protagonised by other *rumberas* such as Rosa Carmina in *Tania, la bella salvaje* (Juan Orol, 1948) or Ninón Sevilla in *Señora Tentación* (José Díaz Morales, 1948).

Mexican films, such as *Al son del mambo* (1950), featured Cuban musicians and dancers

Although music was one of the main channels through which Cuban culture was able to reach other regions, it is important not to leave out the sizable contingent of Cuban actors that began appearing in Mexican cinema from the first years of sound production. For example, Juan José Martínez Casado played the memorable role of the Spanish bullfighter 'El Jarameño' in Mexico's first major sound film, *Santa*, while René Cardona was one of the lead actors in the milestone 1936 film *Allá en el Rancho Grande*, and Enrique Herrera played Emperor Maximilian in the historical drama *Juárez y Maximiliano* (Miguel Contreras Torres, 1934). And over the years, the list grows much longer, with nearby Cuba being one of the foreign nations most present in the casts of Mexican golden age films. Marta Elba Fombellida, who had acted in the Cuban movie *La que se murió de amor* (Jean Angelo, 1942), upon moving to Mexico, began writing for the era's most important film magazine, *Cinema Reporter*. She mentions numerous Cubans (born and/or raised on the island) who were working in Mexican film: Pituka de Foronda and her half brothers Rubén and Gustavo Rojo (born to Spanish parents), Carmen Montejo, María Antonieta Pons, Chela Castro, Blanquita Amaro, Lina Montes, among a half dozen others (16 September 1944, pp. 29–31). Other names that might be added to this list include: Issa Morante and the next generation of Cuban *rumberas* (Ninón Sevilla, Amalia Aguilar, Rosa Carmina, Mary Esquivel), along with Otto Sirgo and Dalia Íñiguez, to name only a few of the most successful. This list includes actors who established long-term, solid careers in Mexican film, and others whose presence was less memorable; this exodus illustrates where Cuban artists went to pursue a film career once that, in the words of Fombellida, 'Mexico had become the place of Latin American cinematic assemblage' (ibid., p. 30).

Cuban cinema prior to the revolution is little studied, as Cuba's own golden age of cinema was born of the 1959 revolution and the foundation of the Cuban Institute of Cinematographic Art and Industry (widely known as ICAIC). Earlier Cuban film production, to the extent that it has been studied at all, has been largely disdained by critics for its adherence to popular styles of the era and its lack of originality, as well as its lack of adequate production financing and the resulting aesthetically and technically inferior quality of its product. Co-productions have likewise generally been ignored as not authentically national, despite the fact that such films as *Más fuerte que el amor* (Tulio Demicheli, 1955) and *Mulata* were launched with fanfare and became big box-office earners as vehicles for some of the biggest stars of the epoch: Jorge Mistral and Miroslava, and Ninón Sevilla and Pedro Armendáriz, respectively. And even though Mexican studios produced megahits using scripts based on Cuban radio soap operas, the emblematic case being *El derecho de nacer* (Zacarías Gómez Urquiza, 1952), these too have been little studied. There are numerous possible reasons for the oversight on the part of Cuban critics: for example, the feeling that Mexican investors only used the island's resources and talent without leaving behind anything worthwhile; or the conviction that these films' representations of Cuba's history and culture were distorted; or the idea that the Mexican industry's appropriation or Mexicanisation of the Hollywood melodrama genre did not take into account Cuban tastes, in that way exhibiting its own 'neo-colonialist' tendencies. Criticism on Cuban cinema prior to 1959 is relatively recent and has largely been built upon the premises mentioned above, which represent the principle lines of investigation of the era to date (Guevara; Valdes Rodríguez; Piñera; Paranaguá, *Le Cinéma*; Chanan; Podalsky).

It is impossible to refute the conclusions of critics such as Paulo Antonio Paranaguá or Michael Chanan when they refer to Cuba's 'submission' to the Mexican film industry, which took advantage of both the scenic locations and cheap labour of the island (Paranaguá, *Le Cinéma*, p. 7; Chanan, p. 86). The frank declarations of Mexico-based director Juan Orol support this view in his looking to Cuba to escape pressure from the unions to hire unnecessary personnel: 'In Cuba ... films turned out to be much cheaper and got a lot of attention from authorities because cinema was new there' (Meyer, vol. 2, p. 32). The idea that Mexico was more interested in saving money than in engaging in meaningful collaborations with the Cubans is further supported in a report by Marta Elba in *Cinema Reporter* asserting that Cubans are limited to second- or third-tier roles when hired by Mexican production companies, even in Mexican–Cuban co-productions (16 September 1944, pp. 29–31); furthermore, critics are justified in their complaints of the lack of authenticity in Mexican cinematic representations of Cuba. However, these interpretations suggest a singular direction of influence that greatly impacted Cuban culture and left Mexican culture intact. They also turn a blind eye to the various exchanges generated between the two nations' cultural industries (including both film and music production), even though they may not always be evident in the number of cinematic products realised or in the intensity of the echoes they produced throughout Latin America. The earliest sound cinema productions indeed reveal cultural changes, accommodations, ratifications, negations and syncretisms in which interventions from both countries are apparent.

MEXICAN GOLDEN AGE CINEMA IN CUBA

The persistence of Mexican cinema's penetration into the Cuban film market can be illustrated through various anecdotes. A particularly memorable one takes place in the context of the Cuban revolution:

> In Cuba, the groups of peasants who came down from the hills to combat the Batista government's army singing the chorus of Jorge Negrete's '¡Ay, Jalisco, no te rajes!' are distinctly memorable, as are the first Cuban films produced after the revolution, which included allusions to Mexican cinema: a song interpreted by Jorge Negrete or Pedro Infante supposedly being played on the radio, a mention of a popular actor's name or of specific films. (De los Reyes, p. 180)

Another story that demonstrates the significance of Mexican golden age cinema in Cuba is the popular certainty that the reason Cuban authorities decided in the 1970s to cancel the television show *Cine de ayer* [Cinema of Yesterday], which featured old Mexican and Argentine films, was that the devotion of its audiences provoked tardiness on the part of evening school students, as well as surges in electricity usage (Vega et al., p. 7). The programme brought together three different generations, fans of both sexes, variables indicative of the relevance these movies continued to have for Cubans over the years. The meanings propagated through the power of the mass culture industries prior to the arrival of Fidel Castro maintained their vigour due to the fact that their products had become entwined with what was considered to be the cultural heritage of the island. Even today, the online vendor Cuba Collectibles, which caters principally to Cuban Americans in the USA, has a *Cine de ayer* product line. This collection features, among its 'fine Cuban memorable treasures', DVDs of various Mexican productions or co-productions, evoking Mexican golden age cinema as a central element of nostalgia for prerevolutionary Cuba (http://www.cubacollectibles.com/).

From the early 1930s – and even earlier as there is evidence that Cuba was one of only a handful of foreign countries that exhibited Mexico's first major silent feature film, *Santa* (Luis Peredo, 1918) (*Cinema Reporter*, 26 April 1952, p. 28) – the rise of Mexican cinema was remarkable, as was the Cuban–Mexican connection in everyday Cuban life. By 1934, early Mexican sound films directed by Cuban expatriot Ramón Peón, including *Sagrario* (1933) and *La llorona* (1933), were already breaking box-office records on the island (*El Cine Gráfico*, 25 Febuary 1934). The inauguration of Radio Cine, a movie house that would become a major reference point for movie fans of the following decade, took place on 7 November 1937, with the Mexican film *Mujeres de hoy* (1936), directed by Peón and featuring a multinational cast including another Cuban, Juan José Martínez Casado, who had become an early star of Mexican sound cinema.

Even at that time, when no clear Spanish-language market leader had yet emerged among film-producing nations and a certain optimism regarding the consolidation of a national film apparatus in Cuba still prevailed, no Cuban film would make a significant impact in Mexico, much less provoke the euphoria of *Allá en el Rancho Grande*. An early Cuban sound film *El romance del palmar* (Ramón Peón, 1938) raised the hopes of Havana's critics that Cuban movies would begin to conquer audiences beyond the island when it premiered in Mexico City just a few months after it was first released in Havana in the centrally located Alameda theatre as part of the official activities organised in honour of then military chief Fulgencio Batista. Directed by Peón, who was known for his work in Mexico, including hits such as *La llorona* and *Sagrario*, both of 1933, and starring Rita Montaner, admired in Mexico for her performances a few years earlier at the Politeama nightclub, it was expected to be a big hit. However, it played for only a week. The reception was different in Cuba, where the film earned applause from audiences, praise from critics and even symbolic national awards (Douglas, p. 81); however, the astounding triumph of *Allá en el Rancho Grande* in Cuba was bigger and long lasting, enhanced and extended further after a promotional visit from leading man Tito Guízar. The tumult provoked by his arrival resulted in the injury of three fans in Santiago and huge crowds of enthusiasts in Havana (ibid., p. 82).

The repercussions of this moment in film history, which launched the *ranchera* comedy throughout the Spanish-speaking world, were immediate in Cuba, and are reflected in Cuba's first locally produced sound films. Peón, who had established himself early in Mexico's sound cinema industry and worked regularly in Mexico throughout the golden era, would repeatedly attempt to jump start film production back in Cuba. Peón, who had no doubts regarding the cultural proximity of the two neighbouring nations, and whose perspectives were undoubtedly influenced by his professional experience in and his affections for Mexico, hesitated before deciding upon a title for the film that would be known as *El romance del palmar*, with other possibilities including 'La guajirita', 'La verguerita' (both titles evoke the idea of a Cuban country peasant), then 'La rancherita' (the farm girl – this time recalling *Rancho Grande*), then 'El rincón del palmar' [the place of the palm trees] before assuming its definitive name (*Cinema Reporter*, 23 September 1938, p. 7; 7 October 1938, p. 3). This oscillation points to a translatability of national identities (which would be seen later in Colombia, with the release of *Allá en el trapiche* in 1943) at a moment when such concepts were still somewhat unstable, as well as a desire to make the picture personally relevant to as many viewers as possible, including those outside Cuba. In 1938, *Rancho Grande* was a common point of reference throughout the Spanish-speaking Americas.

Soon after the release of *El romance*, and with the backing of the (short-lived) production company that Peón founded in Cuba, PECUSA, *Estampas Habaneras* (Jaime Salvador, 1939) was promoted as *Chaflán en La Habana* in order to cash in on the popularity of the Mexican comic Carlos López, who became Mexico's first international comic star for his role as supporting actor in *Allá en el Rancho Grande*. These examples point to the confidence that Ramón Peón had in the direction taken by the Mexican film industry – and he was not mistaken. While intellectuals writing about cinema never fully accepted these pictures as 'works of art', the box-office response in Cuba was enthusiastic.

CONCERNS OF CRITICS

Typical was the review of *El romance del palmar* by Francisco Ichaso, who would become a veteran film reviewer and president of the Association of Theatre and Film Editors; he is happy to recognise 'our landscape, our music, our women, our local colour, all the picturesque characteristics of typical creole life in the country and in the city', which he praises as 'tailored and ... integrated, with the detailed precision in settings and indispensible autonomy of an artistic work' (*Diario de la Marina*, 6 December 1938, n. p.). The conservative character of the *Diario de la Marina* attracted many readers, including Cubans with more liberal ideas who trusted its seriousness. Ichaso's commentary on Peón's film is significant as it denotes the existence of a perception of 'Cubanness': landscapes, music, women, local colour, expressed through a mixing understood in racial terms, but also as a reference to the fusion of the urban and the rural. This description does not deviate much from what were often identified as the key elements exploited by Mexican cinema of the era, which have been touted as axes constitutive of national identity (paradigmatic landscapes that only touch on a handful of key locations; *ranchera* music and *boleros*, the latter being the emblematic genre of modern urban life; feminine stereotypes that legitimise the mores of the moment; identity traits that are born of a vocabulary, an accent, certain topics, modes of entertainment; see, for example, Monsiváis and Bonfil; D'Lugo, 'Aural Identity' and 'Gardel'). This coincidence might explain the gradual adhesion on the part of Cuban filmgoers to Mexican cinema's style of representation: spectators of both countries began to see in these films a series of cultural repertoires in which they could recognise themselves and, at the same time, understand things they did not know of.

The movie press of course came to play a key role in the integration of cultural stereotypes in the mindset of readers. Ichaso underlines what 'belongs' to Cuban culture, producing generalisations through the use of possessive pronouns. At the same time, his interest in 'artistic' elements reveals the tension between the position of superiority of the writer as member of an intellectual elite and that of the masses, the filmgoing public that, according to these critics, without valid criteria, keep filling theatres playing films of appalling quality week after week. Meanwhile, this artistic quality was apparently of little interest to the average Cuban movie fan; furthermore, aesthetic criticism was not given importance by the nation's more conservative journals. Therefore, while liberal intellectual critics such as Ichaso completely ignored the *ranchera* genre, conservative publications such as *Guía Cinematográfica*, published by an organisation affiliated with the Catholic church, placed a great deal of attention on popular films, including *ranchera* comedies, although its critical assessments were principally moral in nature, focusing on the treatment of certain topics, such as family unity, intergenerational respect, virginity, bodies as taboo and matrimony as a fundamental institution. The critical vocabulary of these writers is simple and repetitive: 'agreeable', 'nice', 'discreet', 'good', 'tasteful', 'well made' – indicative of the public to which it was directed, its unobjectionable clarity aimed at facilitating the reader's discernment. The schematisation of each entry in this annual 'guide' to filmgoers reinforced its aim of moral influence, in contrast with the liberal intellectual tendency, much more lavish and varied, and eager to make comparisons with other cinema styles and films, as well as to relate the films under review to elements of the socioeconomic context they portray. The response of film viewers tended to go against both these extremes, failing to leave aside the repetitive plots of *ranchera* comedies detested by intellectuals, or to stay away from racy *rumbera* films censured by conservative critics, although undoubtedly published commentaries in widely read journals bore an influence on filmgoers' interpretations of what they saw.

It is worth noting that the influential journal *Bohemia*, which boasted a peak circulation of 200,000, and which covered political, social and cultural news from a liberal perspective, dedicated space in its main pages to Mexican cinema: when an item was deemed too important for treatment only in its performing arts section, the story would get much more prominent coverage. From 1945 to 1957, despite the journal's marked preference in its entertainment news for Hollywood luminaries such as Mickey Rooney, Charlie Chaplin, Shirley Temple, Orson Welles or Elizabeth Taylor, Mexican cinema was never left out of the mix. Likewise, the magazine *Carteles*, whose profile is comparable to that of *Bohemia*, had a regular section undoubtedly inspired by that of *Bohemia*, entitled 'On the Performing Arts', featuring news on Cuban artists in Mexico, and the ups and downs in the personal and professional lives of Mexican screen idols, along with those of other figures related to the business, including producers, composers and directors. Through periodicals such as *Bohemia* and *Carteles*, as well as *Cinema* and *Chic*, among others, Cuban readers could follow the rise of new Cuban stars and their establishment in the international entertainment scene through their work in Mexican cinema. These journals served, albeit obliquely, to promote for Cubans the Mexican film industry's central role in determining who would represent Cuba and how Cuba would be portrayed to international audiences.

AUDIENCE SEGMENTS

In some ways, however, it would seem that critics played less of a role in shaping public opinion than more structural elements of the film business, including distribution networks, which defined different niche markets that helped consolidate distinctions among different audiences. For example, there were theatres dedicated exclusively to Hollywood films, and others, fewer in number, that also featured some European films, while others, also a minority, specialising in Spanish-language cinema, were often so-called '*barrio* cinemas' (Douglas, p. 67). As Mexican cinema gained market share in the 1940s, more Cuban theatres, including some more elegant urban venues, began to exhibit Mexican films, especially the more stylised productions of certain directors such as Emilio Fernández and Roberto Gavaldón, while the more popular genres, including *ranchera* comedies, *rumbera* musicals, romantic melodramas and the urban comedies of Cantinflas and Tin Tan dominated the screens of the working-class *barrios* and poorer rural areas. Even as the handful of Cuban films, a few of which are mentioned above, were released in the late 1930s, signalling the potential for the consolidation of a national cinema industry, the biggest Spanish-language hit of the late 30s remained *Rancho Grande*, and it was Mexican cinema that most reliably filled working-class movie houses.

HIGHS AND LOWS

However, by the end of the 1930s, the excitement ignited by *Rancho Grande* had died down and Mexican films saw viewership fall in Cuba, as occurred elsewhere in Latin America. The tendency could be sensed as early as 1938 and, by 1940, the Cuban public was expressing a clear preference for Argentine over Mexican productions. Mexican films, along with live revues and plays, were booed (*Cinema Reporter*, 29 June 1938, p. 1; 23 September 1938, p. 7; 14 October 1938, p. 5), and among the few that remained popular were musical acts such as Trío Calaveras and tenor Juan Arvizu, who were willing to internationalise their repertoire with tangos and *boleros* (*Cinema Reporter*, 9 December 1938, p. 2). Another exception was the young Jorge Negrete, who experienced tremendous success on all three of his trips to Cuba, including his debut visit of 1939, which coincided with the inauguration of Havana's Tropicana nightclub, a few years before his breakout cinema success with *¡Ay, Jalisco no te rajes!*, a second trip in 1944 for a benefit function for hurricane victims and a third trip in 1950 (*Bohemia*, 16 January 1944; Lam).

Part of Cuban audiences' problem with Mexican films may have lain not only in what seemed to be an increasing repetitiveness of plots, but in its general orientation towards a particularly Mexican configuration of popular cultural production rooted in the *carpa* or tent theatre. In Mexico, the poverty of live shows and the precarious conditions of the theatre business were not an obstacle to these works drawing large crowds. Due to the increasing hard-line position of public officials with regard to public criticism, these spaces became essential safe sites for the public to voice an opinion. Their relevance in the public sphere is even greater when considering the broad variety of audiences they attracted, which diluted differences in social class, cultural levels, places of origin, or professions (Normland, p. 189).

The existence in Mexico of sections dedicated to popular theatre in widely distributed entertainment publications – often featuring photos of young aspiring actresses, wearing very revealing clothing – in a context increasingly restrictive with regard to public criticism of the government, allowed for something of a public catharsis through mockery of official decisions and ironic challenges to incessant campaigns of 'moral cleansing', revealing some of the contradictions of Mexican society, which would become more marked during the presidencies following that of Lázaro Cárdenas (1934–40). However, these nuances would unlikely have been perceived by Cuban audiences. Interestingly Ramón Peón's first attempt at a Cuban film, *Sucedió en La Habana* (1938) flopped, and its lack of success (*Cinema Reporter*, 22 August 1938, p. 2; *El Crisol*, December 1938, n. p.) in Cuba may have had to do with the fact that it was following the Mexican formula of revue cinema typified by Cantinflas's first feature film *Aguila o sol* (1938); indeed, Cantinflas built his screen success upon an earlier career as a popular comedian of the *carpas* – although his international success, solidified with *Ahí está el detalle* (1940), which includes no musical numbers, assumes a less skit-like and more conventional narrative style typical of full-length feature films. *Aguila o sol* was not a hit in Cuba, where audiences both wearied of too many *ranchera* comedies, which soon fell 'out of fashion' (*Cinema Reporter*, 23 September 1938, p. 7), and were disappointed at the flimsy formal structure of some Mexican films. Meanwhile, Argentine films such as *La rubia del camino* (Manuel Romero, 1938) were popular with Cuban audiences and critics alike (*Cinema Reporter*, 4 November 1938, p. 2), and Argentine cinema, which privileged plot development over endless musical numbers, even in the hit films of wildly popular tango crooner Libertad Lamarque, such as *Madreselva* (Luis César Amadori, 1938), was fast becoming the top preference in Spanish product among Cubans.

However, the success of other Mexican titles in the late 1930s shows that audiences were not so fed up with Mexico's insistence on its stylistic paradigms, and that some critics misunderstood the functioning of a still new culture market that privileges popular tastes. Indeed, maybe the Cuban public just needed to get used to Mexican cinema's idiosyncrasies. Other genres would develop with family conflicts and love stories set far from the context of traditional rural life, and certain actors of Mexican cinema would begin to consolidate their status as audience favourites, including Martínez Casado, Joaquín Pardavé and Manuel Dondé, while fresh young faces such as that of Gloria Marín also earned praise and raised hopes: 'All exhibitors are anxiously awaiting the arrival of *La tía de las muchachas* to see if they can improve the profitability of Mexican material, which has been awful' (*Cinema Reporter*, 14 October 1938, p. 5).

However, this general atmosphere allowed the Argentine press to brag that Argentine cinema had become the favourite of Spanish-speaking audiences on the island – even a few years later when the trend had begun to reverse:

> Cuba is without a doubt the strongest and most loyal bastion for Argentine cinema in the Americas. The public of 'the Pearl of the Antilles' keeps up with the latest on Argentine cinema with an attraction similar to that generated by Hollywood. Libertad Lamarque, Niní Marshall – especially in the role of Cándida – and Delia Garcés head up the list of favourite artists. (*Cine*, 17 April 1942, p. 4)

In 1942, the promotional reviews prepared by Cuban distributors for Mexican readers continued to list Mexico, as a business, behind Argentina and Spain. Even in 1944, the competition between the two industries remained significant, notwithstanding Argentina's difficulties in producing movies during the war years due to its lack of access to celluloid:

> Movies in Spanish, with a preference for Mexican and Argentine films, are indispensible in our theatres, as can be seen in the case of 'exclusive' venues such as América, Fausto and Auditorium, which, although reluctant and hesitant to exhibit Spanish-language films, have hosted the very successful Cuban premieres of such films as *Doña Bárbara*, *Flor silvestre*, *Casa de muñecas* and other titles of true artistic significance. (*Cinema Reporter*, 5 May 1944, p. 18)

The examples given are Mexican, in the first two cases, Argentine in the third. Cuban eyes, then, remained turned towards the film production of these regions, and even that of Brazil, although this interest would develop mainly in the years to come as Cuban *rumbera* stars of Mexican cinema began acting in Brazilian movies – and hope would remain alive for the development of Cuba's own national film industry. A 1947 article extrapolated on the success of María Antonieta Pons in an article optimistically titled 'Cuban Cinema, National Reality', stating that Havana 'could become one of the great cinematic centres of the continent, along with Mexico City, Buenos Aires and Rio de Janeiro' (*Chic*, January 1947, p. 26).

While it is evident that the obligatory reference for the industry, the name synonymous with success, was Hollywood, from the late 1930s into at least the mid-40s, a major struggle played out for market leadership in Latin American film production, with the epithet of 'the mecca of Spanish-language cinema' among the most disputed. The Cuban market's case reflects Mexico's momentary weakness: despite physical proximity and a history of cultural collaboration, Cuban fans tired of Mexican production, ceding their favouritism to the Argentine industry, and clung to Argentine affections until Argentina lost its capacity to incite them, after which Cuba would become, from the mid-40s through the late 50s, one of Mexico's largest and most loyal audiences. In this context, the Cuban film market, Latin America's fourth largest market (after Argentina, Mexico and Brazil) – despite the island's relatively small population compared to that of Colombia, Peru or Chile – throughout the 40s, was of crucial importance to Mexico (and Argentina).

Mexico's crisis from roughly 1938 into the early 40s can be seen both in the indifference of spectators towards its films and in the harshness of the commentaries and reviews of Mexican movies. Nevertheless, public sympathies during the 40s would follow a different trajectory, and Mexican cinema would be given ever greater attention in the Cuban press, where it would be treated with an increasingly admiring tone. Mexico would turn from a possible competitor, or a second-rate producer (compared to Argentina), into a sister nation, and references to the longstanding solidarity between the two countries would be recurrent. In 'Mexico and Cuba: Fraternity, a Sacred Word', Leandro García sustained happily in 1944 that Argentine production had fallen significantly, and Mexican cinema had begun to impose itself definitively in the Cuban market (*Cinema Reporter*, 16 September 1944, p. 8; Peredo Castro, *Cine y propaganda*, p. 477).

THE TREND REVERSES

The indifference to or frank rejection of Mexican cinema in Cuba did not last. *La noche de los mayas* (Chano Urueta, 1939), released in Cuba in December of 1940, awakened curiosity at its subject matter, which diverged significantly from previous formulas. The good fortune of this film, an indigenist drama, would foreshadow the future success of Emilio 'el Indio' Fernández's acclaimed works, which would be among the few Mexican films to compete seriously with Hollywood in world markets beyond Latin America. By early 1941, there came another sign of reversal as *Cinema Reporter* announced to its Mexican readers that two Mexican films had been given awards in Cuba, a pair of comedies (with no *ranchera* tendencies): *En tiempos de don Porfirio* (Juan Bustillo Oro, 1940) and *Pobre diablo* (José Benavides hijo, 1940) (*Cinema Reporter*, 3 January 1941, p. 1).

The fact that several of 'the most significant films released in Cuba', according to Cuban film historians, are Emilio Fernández signature works: *Flor silvestre* (1943), *María Candelaria* (1944), *Bugambilia* (1945) and *Pueblerina* (1949) (Douglas, pp. 300–1) – all of which can be said to build on the critical success of *La noche de los mayas* in that they were dramas featuring characters of indigenous origin or from the lowest social strata as protagonists – signals a tendency of Cuban critics to favour topics corresponding to social justice, national identity and human integrity in stories that might end tragically over the idyllic and vacuous visions of reconciliation that characterised *ranchera* comedies. Interestingly, the preference for precisely these traits would crystallise in the style of cinema produced in Cuba immediately following its 1959 revolution: on the one hand, it draws attention to impoverished sectors abandoned by the official discourse of the previous regime while seeking to portray the 'truth' of the everyday life of the people rather than the artificial likeness constructed by earlier cinema (Podalsky, 60); on the other, it employs strategies similar to those of documentary film-making, and to those of some Mexican golden age directors, including the early Chano Urueta, Emilio Fernández and, later, Benito Alazraki (e.g., *Raíces*, 1954): highly stylised cinematography with a focus on landscapes, filming on location, emphasis on formal elements.

Janitzio (Carlos Navarro, 1935) and *La noche de los mayas* would be mentioned frequently as paradigms of 'pure art'. The positive reception of the first two of Emilio Fernández's films listed above permitted the consolidation of a cluster of ideas that linked the concept of art with the essence of national culture, promoted on multiple fronts. His distribution company, Films Mundiales, referred to these films as 'authentically Mexican' because 'they are not merely a mix of songs, guitars, pistols and wide-brimmed sombreros, but have been brought to life by a true feeling of the expression of our nationality' (*Cinema Reporter*, 30 June 1945, p. 10). One Cuban critic distinguishes carefully between 'Mexican movies' and 'movies produced by Mexicans', the former represented by 'such jewels of inestimable value as *Janitzio* and *María Candelaria*', gifts to the world, while the latter (and here the author refers especially to those produced by Juan Orol, who was establishing a reputation as a specialist in sexy *rumbera* musicals) were artistically irresponsible: 'ridiculous', 'sickeningly sweet, corny' (*Bohemia*, 21 March 1948, p. 87).

This strain of patriotic exaltation inherent in Mexican film-making in the mid- to late 1940s placed less emphasis on folkloric and popular themes as studios were not targeting the less favoured social classes, but rather emerging urban middle-class audiences, although the profit motive kept producers filming stories set in the country or small provincial towns, adorned with musical numbers, as, even in the 50s, many such films continued to be hits. The *ranchera* comedy genre in fact continued to be relentlessly popular in Cuba among rural peasants and recent arrivals to the city (Vega et al., p. 31). New immigrants to Havana or other cities identified not with the specifics of Jalisco ranch life, but with the nostalgia they generated for idealised notions of traditional rural life. This was one of the fundamental reasons for their successful penetration: 'Mexican movies have been able to portray the national spirit, institutions, character, and social organism of Mexico, which to a large degree are similar to those in Cuba' (Chanan, p. 78).

In 1942, the distributor Tropical Films de Cuba released *Así se quiere en Jalisco*, 'the Mexican film with the greatest box-office earnings to date' (*Cinema Reporter*, 29 May 1944, 1938). With the already locally popular singer Jorge Negrete in the lead role, the movie repeated and magnified the phenomenon incited by Tito Guízar and the first version of *Allá en el Rancho Grande*. The second, released in 1949 and directed (as with the former) by Fernando de Fuentes, with Negrete in the lead role, earned him more fans and provoked these reactions upon his promotional visit to Cuba:

> In Havana, the crowds formed a human wall upon his arrival that led from the airport to the centre of the city, where businesses closed up and everyone ran out into the street to see their most beloved artist up close. The homage that the Cuban people paid him was greater than the tribute offered to the late president Roosevelt upon his first visit to this country. Our compatriot was honoured with the loftiest decoration that can be given to distinguished foreigners and he received the Cuban flag for his safekeeping. (Rangel and Portas, p. 10)

The actor was practically a brand, and his face served as its logo (Vincenot, p. 224).

A 1947 US report on the Cuban market noted: 'Film distributors and theatre owners say that Mexican movies are more popular in Cuba outside the two large cities of Havana and Santiago than the productions of any other country' (quoted in Chanan, p. 78), confirming a report by Marta Elba in late 1946 that more Mexican than Hollywood films were showing in Cuba (*Cinema Reporter*, 7 September 1946, p. 23) – although it should be noted that this data is contradicted by other sources that insist that Mexico's market share was never more than 40 per cent that of Hollywood (Douglas, pp. 318–20). But critics were in unanimous agreement that 'Mexican movies hold a unique, high place in the affections of the representative Cuban theatregoer' (Chanan, p. 78). By the mid-1950s, reports in Mexico referred to Cuba as 'one of the countries in which Mexican films are most widely received' (*Excélsior*, 14 July 1954, p. 4b). Indeed, this period might have been the apex of Mexico's success, and one of its most successful films in Cuba was the *ranchera* comedy *Dos tipos de cuidado* (Ismael Rodríguez, 1953) starring two of Mexico's most beloved stars, Negrete and Pedro Infante (although the genre soon would soon enter into its definitive decline). This was the same moment as the launching of the insurrection against the Batista regime which would culminate in the triumph of the revolutionary forces in 1959. It is not surprising, then, that the guerrilla groups, composed of university-educated youth, peasants and members of the urban working class, would sing the chorus of the Negrete song that had been so fashionable just a few years earlier ('¡Ay, Jalisco, no te rajes!') as what appeared superficially to be mere Mexican nationalism morphed into a pan-Latin American spirit of popular camaraderie.

FRUITLESS EFFORTS

Cuba's early attempt at establishing some kind of trajectory in sound film production in the late 1930s was hardly successful. Cuba produced three films in 1938 and remarkably managed to make nine in 1939. This figure would not be surpassed until 1950, while in the intervening years production was shaky at best, with only one film made in 1941, 1942 and 1944, and two in 1943. Beginning in 1945, foreign producers (mainly from Mexico, and to a lesser extent from Argentina) helped augment, if only slightly, the quantity of pictures filmed on the island – with the aid of foreign capital, technicians and actors, and an inevitable loss of domestic production control.

The possibility that this sector might actually develop into something warranted that closer attention be paid to the island. *Cinema Reporter*, from its founding in 1938, featured a column titled 'What They're Saying in Cuba' that appeared by its second issue, and by September a long-lived section was established under the name 'Cuba habla' [Cuba Speaks] (23 September 1938, p. 7). The Mexican weekly *El Cine Gráfico* also included a section titled 'Notes from Cuba', whose content documents the rise of the Mexican industry, with a focus until the early 1940s on what is being produced in Cuba, followed by a shift towards discussion of the impact of Mexico and its artists in Cuba thereafter.

Ramón Peón's efforts to stimulate film production in Cuba date back to 1916, when he had participated in the creation of a film production company (Golden Sun Pictures) with the goal of jump-starting the sector in Cuba by constructing studios that would both facilitate filming on the island and increase its attraction for foreign producers. His ideas never really caught on in Hollywood, whose studios filmed only fourteen movies in Cuba from 1929 to 1959, nearly all of them favouring (beginning with the titles of the pictures) imaginaries of exoticness, sensuality, attractive women and danger: *The Girl from Havana* (Benjamin Stoloff, 1929), *Rumba* (Marion Gering, 1935), *Sarumba* (Marion Gering, 1937), *Affair in Havana* (Laslo Benedek, 1957), among others. Some featured first-rate casts and prestige directors such as Walter Lang (*Weekend in Havana*, 1941) – although this film's construction of Latin exoticism included Brazilian actress Carmen Miranda singing in Portuguese and speaking with her heavy Brazilian accent in the role of a supposedly Cuban nightclub singer – along with John Huston (*We Were Strangers*, 1949) and John Sturges (*The Old Man and the Sea*, 1958). However, the majority of them were not of great transcendence and were only partially filmed on the island. As Emmanuel Vincenot observes, the relatively sparse production prior to the 1950s, inversely proportional to the boom in feature films being imported from the USA, may have been related to the difficulties in filming outside the big studios at the time (p. 231), combined with the factor of Cuba's inferior crews in terms of their level of technical skill, which increased costs of relocation and set design. For this reason, Hollywood would only send small teams of secondary units to film landscapes and picturesque locations.

The momentum that Cuban production seemed briefly to be generating in the late 30s was, seen from a distance, illusory. In those years, due to the untiring efforts of Peón, 'the symbol of that ardent desire to make cinema in Cuba between 1920 and 1960' (Piñera, p. 69), to set up a local cinema infrastructure, it is quite evident that the press saw in this endeavour an opportunity for investors, as the very first issue of *Cinema Reporter* frets that not only Argentine but also Cuban producers 'will not waste time with internal squabbling [and] are lying in wait in hopes of displacing Mexican cinema, which will occur if we are not careful' (22 June 1938, p. 5). But by 1945, when the situation was quite clear regarding the real infeasibility of a profitable cinema power emerging in the Caribbean, Peón was still referring to Cuba 'as a country that aspires to figure among Latin American production markets' (*Cinema Reporter*, 5 May 1945, p. 8); however, the prevailing sentiment was one of a 'failed' industry, in spite of the numerous 'so often discussed plans' (*Cinema Reporter*, 28 September 1946, p. 16).

By the next decade, no one could refute the following pronouncement: 'our cinematography already has its history, albeit not as brilliant as that of other industries' (*Cine Guía*, July 1954, p. 8), although critic Manuel Fernández still held some hope for its growth in Cuba, building on the filming of *La rosa blanca* (Emilio Fernández, 1954). This picture was subsidised by the Batista government as part of the festivities planned for the centenary of José Martí's birth. The project unleashed a major polemic on both shores of the Caribbean, given the audacity – according to many – of letting a Mexican production team film the life of the Cuban national hero, casting Mexican actor Robert Cañedo in the role of Martí and ignoring the cinematic talent available on the island (Castro Ricalde, '*La Rosa Blanca*'). Manuel Fernández saw the process differently, pondering the advantages in collaborating with 'a country near to ours both geographically and spiritually, and one that already moves confidently across cinematic terrain'. Some of the principal deficiencies in Cuba's film- making included: 'the small domestic market, the scarcity of resources and of technical personnel, and above all the lack of experienced directors and screenwriters'. However, he added: 'Alongside Mexico's artists and technicians, Cubans can learn a great deal in order to later launch an industry of their own' (*Cine Guía*, July 1954, p. 19).

CUBA LOOKS TO MEXICO

The logic of taking advantage of Mexico's knowhow had been a topic of discussion since much earlier. This was one of the reasons why journalists were sympathetic to the exodus of artists to Latin America's mecca of cinema production, as seen in positive evaluations of the professional advancement of Cuban stars such as María Antonieta Pons and Ninón Sevilla in Mexico (*Chic,* January 1947, p. 26; *Carteles*, 24 February 1952, n. p.). Cubans' interest in Mexican cinema can be measured by taking into account both the number of show business-oriented journals produced in Cuba and the amount of space these and other journals dedicated to the Mexican movie business. Between 1944 and 1948, Mirta Aguirre maintained a column in the socialist party journal *Hoy*, in which she reviewed newly released films and frequently focused on Mexican film production, taking special care with 'el Indio' Fernández's work, showing interest in the films of Cantinflas and dedicating attention to screen adaptations of literary works as well as to the melodramas of Alejandro Galindo and Ismael Rodríguez (Miranda and Castillo). Meanwhile, two weekly publications with wide circulation, *Bohemia* and *Carteles*, devoted special sections to Mexican film, as did newspapers such as *Diario de la Marina*, *Crisol* and *El País*. Other relevant journals include *El Cine Gráfico*, *Chic*, *Cinema* and various 'women's magazines' such as *Vanidades* and *Ellas*. Taken together, the amount of press space dedicated to Mexican cinema dwarfs that seen in other major markets such as Colombia, which did not have a major movie magazine until well into the 1950s, and Venezuela, where *Mi Film* was the only specialised journal of importance of the era. This wide coverage helped to naturalise Mexican culture, filtered through its cinema, and over time constructed an idea of its being representative of Latin American culture in general.

Despite the size and enthusiasm of the Cuban market, this proximity and exchange, and particularly the growing success of Cuban actors and musicians in Mexican cinema, along with the growing Mexican interest in co-productions may have, in the end, been the downfall of efforts to boost fledgling Cuban homegrown production. Once the Mexican industry had firmly imposed itself in the Cuban market, Cubans became addicted to it – and identified enough with it that a low-budget nationally produced product could not compete, especially as Mexican films increasingly featured Cuban settings and stars.

MEXICAN–CUBAN CO-PRODUCTIONS

A commenatary by Alfredo Guevara, the founding director of the ICAIC, passes harsh judgment on film production in Cuba prior to the revolution of 1959:

> The films made in our country during the past twenty years are nothing more than tear-jerkers whose plots are constructed out of songs and cabaret or television shows, and co-productions of horrendous quality in which Cuba offers some 'tropical flavour' with a handful of landscapes, a luxury hotel, a pair of rumba dancers and a villain in a Panama hat with a twisted moustache. (*Cine Cubano*, June 1960, p. 5).

While 1960s-era critics were most vehement in their critiques of Hollywood's interventions on the island, this critic's allusions to projects that had been undertaken in the previous decade in partnerships between Mexico and Cuba is also evident. Although it is important to note that the observations generated after the revolution completely erased other aspects worthy of consideration, regarding the relationship established between the two countries, it would also be fair to lay out the ways in which these films contributed, on the one hand, to promoting certain aspects of Cuban culture, while keeping in mind that they helped little in altering stereotypes that had been forged long before regarding the island, its inhabitants and its cultural idiosyncrasies. In a seminal article, Laura Podalsky demonstrates how the co-productions realised prior to the revolution are no less 'authentic' than the films produced exclusively from Cuban capital, but that they merely delineated 'different representations of the nation' (p. 67).

Any of the titles of the Mexican co-productions fit at least partially if not totally within the scheme presented by Guevara for their set designs, characters or plots. Juan Orol's productions correspond point by point, as do those directed by Juan José Ortega, including *Frente al pecado de ayer* (1955), *No me olvides nunca* (1956) and *Tropicana* (1957), along with those of Miguel Morayta: *Morir para vivir* (1954) and *La fuerza de los humildes* (1955), or emblematic films such as *Mulata, Una gallega en La Habana* (René Cardona 1955) or *Yambaó* (Alfredo Crevenna 1957). Even story lines that presaged the fashion of playing out struggles between good and evil, whether in urban or rural contexts, such as those of the Santo films that Joselito Rodríguez filmed in Cuba in the late 1950s: *Santo contra hombres infernales* (1961), *Santo contra cerebro del mal* (1961), or the Villalobos series: *Los tres Villalobos* (Fernando Méndez 1955), *La justicia de los Villalobos* (Enrique Zambrano, 1961), *Aquí están los Villalobos* (Enrique Zambrano, 1962) tended to take for granted stereotypical aspects of Cuban culture.

According to María Eulalia Douglas, Mexico began pursuing partnerships for feature-length co-productions in the mid-1940s, with *Embrujo antillano*, a model *rumbera* film, and concluded these activities with the Villalobos films, the last of which was filmed in

María Antonieta Pons in *Embrujo antillano* (1947), the first of many Mexican–Cuban co-productions

1959 (pp. 260–70). She does not take into account projects in which creative, technical or acting personnel from Mexico work in Cuba-produced films, nor cases in which a shared investment is made in a Cuban company as is the case of Peón's films or those that Jaime Salvador directed for PECUSA, or even *Siboney* (Juan Orol, 1940). Nonetheless, the nearly thirty movies she lists as collaborative works between the two countries dwarf the mere handful co-produced with other countries, including only one Argentine film, *A la Habana me voy* (Luis Bayón Herrera, 1949) or the few Orol productions financed under the auspices of the nominally Spanish España Sono Films, which in reality were essentially Mexican–Cuban co-productions: for example, *El amor de mi bohío* (1946), *Sandra: la mujer de fuego* (1954), *El sindicato del crimen* (1954), *La mesera del café del puerto* (1957), *El farol en la ventana* (1958), *Thaimí, la hija del pescador* (1960). And of the forty-five pictures Douglas lists as having been made in Cuba from 1953 to 1959, twenty-five are collaborations with Mexican producers (pp. 265–70). Indeed, Mexico, due to questions of geographic proximity, reduced production costs and concrete opportunities, would collaborate more with Cubans, film more in Cuba and incorporate Cuba into its movie plots more than occurred with any other Latin American nation.

Rumba Caliente Beats Foxtrot

53

Seen from a Cuban perspective, a significant portion of prerevolutionary Cuban cinema is inextricably linked to the Mexican industry, whether due to economic interests or because of the participation of Mexican technical labour or actors, or Cubans who had relocated to Mexico years before and were essentially representatives of the Mexican industry. This was the case of actresses Blanquita Amaro and Dalia Íñiguez, as well as Ramón Peón – in the latter case, of the nearly sixty sound films he directed, only six were made in Cuba. The 'Mexican seal' was imprinted on these films: the majority of cast and crew were Mexicans or Mexican residents, and their themes and perspectives were often more Mexican than Cuban. For example, *María la O*, a historical drama set in colonial Cuba, incorporated music by Cuban composer Ernesto Lecuona and starred Cubans Rita Montaner and Issa Morante, but employed more leading actors from Mexico and even from Spain than from the island. While much of the movie was filmed on location in Cuba, it was through Mexican eyes, including not only those of its Mexican director and screenwriter Adolfo Fernández Bustamente but also those of its award-winning cinematographer, Gabriel Figueroa, who, beginning with *Allá en el Rancho Grande*, forged an international reputation for visually defining Mexico for the world.

The words of Alfredo Guevara cited earlier resonate deeply regarding the Mexican industry's penetration into Cuban film production. Regarding the representations of Cuba in films made on the island, postrevolutionary criticism expressed two principal grievances. The first points to the stereotype forged of Cuba in which tropical landscapes, chaotic clamour and exotic women were fundamental components – even as these were images that through their massive dissemination endeared Cuba to many spectators. The second signals the vision of the island as a refuge for all sorts of criminals and delinquents lodged in grand hotels or living in the sugar plantations they greedily exploited, a perception that permeates Mexican co-productions much less than it does the image of Cuba transmitted by Hollywood, whose favoured images draw from a vision of Havana as a vacation paradise full of nightclubs, diversion and permissiveness.

These configurations of Cuban culture ironically diverge only slightly from those projected in the late 1930s when *El romance del palmar* – with its focus on representing local customs, humour and styles, but also featuring rural tropical landscapes centred on idyllic plantation life, contrasted with a corrupt urban modernity represented in the cabaret, a site of drinking, gambling and even an assassination plot – was considered Cuba's own expression of its culture. José Manuel Valdés Rodríguez would aver, shortly after the revolution's triumph, that by 1940 'there is no film that merits attention as part of our own expression' (p. 13). However, that does not mean that Cubans did not flock to see films such as the beautifully photographed *María la O*, the star-studded *Más fuerte que el amor*, or the award-winning (two Ariels) *Yambaó*, starring Cuba's own Ninón Sevilla, learning in this way about their own national culture from the powerful Mexican film industry.

'CUBANOS EN MÉXICO'

The proliferation of references to Mexican movies and their protagonists and the gradual disappearance of news about Argentine film in the Cuban press are indications of the trend that would solidify by the mid-1940s – although even in 1940, a year in which Argentina produced forty-nine films to Mexico's twenty-nine, the total number of Mexican imports to Cuba exceeded that of Argentina forty vs thirty-six (Douglas, p. 318; Peredo Castro, *Cine y propaganda*, p. 477). With the title 'Cubanos en México' [Cubans in Mexico], a regular column of *Bohemia* reported the latest gossip. But the column's biggest feature was the interviews carried out by 'the king of the entertainment world' Don Galaor (pseudonym of Germinal Barral) with such artists as Ninón Sevilla, 'the girl who has triumphed so resoundingly in Aztec cinema'. The anonymous editor of the column did not hesitate to proclaim that 'Mexico is now, artistically speaking, an extension of Cuba' (29 September 1948, pp. 34–5).

The inseparable link between cinema and music is evident in *Bohemia* with its frequent focus on the promotional tours to Cuba of Mexican musical artists, or of Cuban artists residing in Mexico. The journal assiduously covered these activities and promoted frictions with the goal of increasing interest in their commentaries. For example, they played up a supposed rivalry between Rita Montaner and the internationally popular Mexican singer Toña la Negra (María Antonia del Carmen Peregrino Álvarez). Both famous for their voices as well as their cinematic performances, they also shared the common physical trait of dark skin. Their continuous trips between Cuba and Mexico, added to the previous factors, contributed to confusions regarding their origins. In Mexico and other Latin American countries, Toña was often referred to as being from Cuba as the presence of black and mulatto communities in Mexico was routinely denied or overlooked (*Bohemia*, 23 May 1948, p. 36).

Mexico's construction as a mestizo (mixed-race country), product of the fusing of Spanish and indigenous cultures, made – and continues to make – invisible any other racial component. Mexican cinema's adopted custom (at a time when it was no longer socially acceptable in the USA) of employing blackface makeup for actors playing the role of black or mulatto characters – including even the mulatta actress Rita Montaner, for example, in *Angelitos negros* – reinforces the idea of their absence from Mexican society. Toña and her unobjectionable public persona made her into a somewhat provocative screen character: an Afromexican actress. Her image, in conflict as it was with national stereotypes, was dismantled to some degree by confusing her birthplace, even through the emphasis placed on her being from the gulf coast state of Veracruz, a region linked symbolically to the Caribbean and therefore less 'authentically' Mexican than, say, Jalisco.

NATION, RACE, OTHERNESS

Mexican cultural historian Ricardo Pérez Montfort argues that,

> as a synthesis of a series of representations and values, the stereotype tended to become hegemonic: that is, it sought to gather together something that would be valid for the totality of a social conglomerate, and aimed to impose itself as a central element of definition. ('Un nacional ismo', p. 178)

National stereotypes, then, went beyond musical rhythms, visual landscapes or traditional dress. In this vein, the following anecdote is significant: in Buenos Aires Toña la Negra's Cuban but indigenous-looking piano accompanist, Juan Bruno Tarraza, was assumed to be Mexican, while she was identified as Cuban, and specifically from the province of Camagüey (*Bohemia*, 23 May 1948, p. 36). In other words, physical traits were generalised to the point that Indians, so prominent as characters in Mexican cinema, belonged to a single human conglomerate associated invariably with Mexico, while another set of traits based on skin colour, vocal style and preference for certain Afro-Latin American rhythms could belong to only one place: the Caribbean. What is especially curious is that these same standardisations appear regularly in Cuban, Mexican and Argentine publications.

This view was often promulgated in Mexican cinema. In *Salón México*, there is a stark contrast between those presumably Mexican contestants competing in a danzón contest and the subtle sensuality in their movements, and the assuredly Afrocuban drummers and wildly frenetically sexual rumba dancers whose performance provides a segue between several scenes of the movie, a contrast that plays out in skin colour (some of the Mexicans are dark skinned, but not black like the Cubans) and in the style of movement. Mexican cinema habitually juxtaposed lighter-skinned and more 'civilised' Mexican characters against more 'primitive' Cubans. For example, in *Víctimas del pecado* (Emilio Fernández, 1951), in Cabaret Changó, Rita Montaner's character plays piano and sings '¡Ay, José!' surrounded by musicians marked as Cuban by their frilly outfits and dark skin, after having seen the blonde Violeta (played by Ninón Sevilla) dance a stylised mambo, directed by Dámaso Pérez Prado, dressed in formal attire; all these artists are Cuban, but the fashionable Mexico City cabaret seems to hold them in check. But when Violeta falls into disgrace, she is forced to dance in a low-class dive and her degradation is symbolised by a change in register in her dance performances: now they are unabashedly Afrocuban, marked by the unrestrained beat of the drums and the 'savage' movements of the actress. As in the previous case, no one dares to intervene; everyone stares, transfixed, at Violeta's corporal convulsions.

Thus, the manufacturing of confrontations between Rita Montaner and Toña la Negra, two of the biggest singing stars of the moment, is not surprising. One putative clash is especially provocative due to its somewhat nonsensical plot. During the preparations for one of the early Mexican–Cuban co-productions, *María la O*, it was rumoured that since no role had been offered to Toña, Rita Montaner could not be given the starring role. In reality, any dispute would have been over a supporting role, not that of the character who would interpret film's title role, taken from the popular song composed by Cuban Ernesto Lecuona. Montaner's age, approaching fifty at the time, was enough to make clear the absurdity of the rumour. Nonetheless, Toña, albeit involuntarily, allowed the rumour to grow and even to take other turns. Don Galaor titles his interview based on her comment, 'It wasn't me, it was Jorge Negrete!', with the intention of blaming the leader of Mexico's actors' union for keeping Montaner from getting the part (*Bohemia*, 9 May 1948, pp. 48–9, 77); earlier rumours had claimed that Montaner would not be cast because she had bad-mouthed some Mexican actors (*Cinema Reporter*, 13 December 1947, p. 29). In the end, another Cuban actress, Issa Morante, a light-skinned Cuban mulatta with large light-coloured eyes, played María la O, with Montaner cast in a supporting role that in the end was a good one, as it allowed her talents to shine. Toña la Negra, who acted in several dozen films of the era, did not get a part.

Another high-profile Montaner role that same year was that of Mercé in *Angelitos negros*, in which the already dark-skinned actress appeared in blackface to emphasise her Cubanness. What becomes clear is that Cuba, the foreign country perhaps most often represented in Mexican golden age cinema, is repeatedly portrayed without great care taken to accurately depict Cuba's national culture, which was undoubtedly of little interest to Mexican producers. Instead, Cuba is constructed in contrast with Mexico, its culture exaggerated as an exotic other to the more familiar Mexican context. Its always exotic otherness is often visually represented in clearly racialised terms, in which a Mexico's own civilised, modern and mestizo nature is reaffirmed in contrast to Cuba's wild, hypersexual and Afro-Latin American character. When, in *Al son del mambo*, an Afrocuban musician played by Dámaso Pérez Prado intuits, in a primitive way, exciting new rhythms from listening to nature, it is only through the savvy interventions of a visiting light-skinned Mexican music producer that mambo is invented. Likewise, an exotic *bembé* ritual in *Mulata*, in which light-skinned Cuban actress Ninón Sevilla acts in blackface, portrays Afrocuban culture through a visually wild and sensual display of erotic excess and utter lack of inhibition that must be explained in a voiceover by a light-skinned Mexican character, played by Pedro Armendáriz, with whom the audience is meant to identify, the melodrama briefly assuming the form of an ethnographic documentary (Irwin, 'Memín'). Mexican cinema effectively erases Afromexican culture by so frequently associating blackness with Cuban difference.

ASPIRATIONS: TO MAKE IT IN MEXICO

Whether or not its audiences, critics or performers were conscious of the Mexican industry's lack of concern regarding the accuracy of its represenations of Cuban culture and their power in disseminating them across the world, Mexican film remained the best show in town: more authentic than Hollywood, more powerful than Argentinian production and certainly better funded than Cuba's handful of short-lived and struggling film companies. In an interview with Carmen Montejo carried out by Don Galaor in 1944, it is evident that the best opportunity for a Cuban to perform in a cinema with international reach lay in Mexico, even more than in Hollywood. In only two years, she had acted in five films; she added that she turned down offers to work in Hollywood at the invitation of the great actress Lillian Gish and Joseph Schenck, the powerful chairman of 20th Century-Fox studios. This was because 'she wanted to make a name for herself in Mexico' (*Bohemia*, 6 February 1944, pp. 38–9). This formula would be constant in the Cuban press. Feature coverage of María Antonieta Pons in *Bohemia*, which identified her as a 'Cuban and rumba dancer', was accompanied by a photograph of the artist dressed up in a wide-brimmed Mexican sombrero and a sensualised Caribbean-tinged (pleated and fringed wide-necked collar, large earrings and bracelets) but otherwise archetypically Mexican *china poblana* outfit (21 December 1947, p. 64). Ninón Sevilla is admired as both 'our compatriot' and 'Cuban star of Mexican cinema' (*Carteles*, 24 February 1952, p. 55).

It is evident that this type of coverage served to exalt the success of Cubans, promoting a national pride that was dependent upon Mexican collaboration and, furthermore, creating a perception of shared fame. It was of little importance that many Cuban artists no longer filmed on the island, whether due to their own lack of interest or the dearth of projects, and that many only returned to their homeland sporadically to visit family, even going so far as to initiate processes of naturalisation in Mexico (Pons, for example, would become a Mexican citizen): the entertainment press followed their every move and reported it all to eager readers. While the dynamic activity in Mexico had begun to 'immunise' viewers regarding the national origin of its stars, who often played Mexicans roles, even if they were born in Cuba (or Spain or Argentina or even Czechoslovakia, in the case of Miroslava), Cuban reception was reportedly a case apart. 'There is no nation more enthusiastic about artistic figures from other countries than Cubans, but when it comes to their own, their love is boundless,' sustains Cantú Robert (*Cinema Reporter*, 20 May 1944, p. 8).

Seen from another angle, some reviews seem to go out of their way not to mention the country of origin of Cuban actors, as can be seen in Mirta Aguirre's review of *Nosotros los pobres* (*Hoy*, 30 April 1948, p. 5), or in *Cine Guía*'s coverage of *Estafa de amor* (Miguel Delgado, 1955) (November 1955, p. 12), both films featuring Cuban actress Carmen Montejo. Curiosity about these popular personalities grew, along with their achievements, and readers made them their own through a process of metonymy that either ignored or assimilated the fact that they so often represented Mexican characters. The personal proximity was based on their ability to stay up on the latest news, especially when it related to readers' affinities for music and dance. Parallel to Monsiváis's arguments regarding how Mexican melodramas imposed themselves on Mexican audiences of the era, the ideological effect of the *rumberas* on their Cuban fans,

> can be attributed to the virtues of continguousness, to their proximity to the public that sees and hears them, to the familiar scenes, to the popular sound – not less credible for being fabricated – of the city, to the instantaneous comprehension of the dialogues. (Monsiváis and Bonfil, p. 137)

However, the difference is, in this case, that Mexican cinema is not fomenting a cohesive Mexican, but rather, a Cuban identity.

MARÍA ANTONIETA PONS, 'MEXICAN MOVIE STAR'

The genre of movies that most visibly brought Cuban culture to the world was that of the *rumberas*, a genre built around rumba dancers, and always featuring multiple solo dance numbers in which the *rumberas* performed in frilly and revealing outfits. These dances were circumscribed within a repetitive range of story lines, narrative strategies and cinematic atmospheres that gave it few possibilities for originality; their typical casts included young wide-eyed girls trying to make it in the big city, abusive agents with criminal proclivities and ardent admirers from good families who do not suspect the unsavoury aspects of these women's lives. The *rumbera* genre's box-office success in

Latin America offered relief to the Mexican industry at a time – beginning in the early to mid-1940s – when the genres that had proved most durably popular – the *ranchera* comedy and the urban melodrama – had been overexploited, signalling the need for something new. Audiences' eager acceptance of the *rumbera* films, whose principal attraction lay in the suggestive dance numbers and rhythmic songs with racy lyrics that often functioned as a commentary on or illustration of the movies' plots – some films were even based on popular songs: for example, *Humo en los ojos*, *Aventurera* – or as a distraction from a dull story line, flung open the doors for the entrance of a handful of incipient Cuban actresses into starring roles in the Mexican film industry, including, notably, María Antonieta Pons, who began acting in Mexico in supporting roles in 1942, caused her first stir with *Konga roja* (Alejandro Galindo, 1943) a year later and became a headliner soon thereafter.

Notwithstanding the diversity in nationality among Mexican cinema's rumba stars – for example, Meche Barba's father was Spanish and she was born in New York, but raised in Mexico; Mapy Cortés was Puerto Rican – their tendency to speak with a Cuban accent, to favour rumbas and other song-and-dance genres associated with the Caribbean, and to collaborate with Cuban musicians such as Mendive, Montaner or Pérez Prado associated them intrinsically with the island, even though Cuba is not the usual setting for *rumbera* films (Castro Ricalde, 'Cuba exotizada'). These variables stand out when taking into account that many of the biggest stars of the genre: Pons, Sevilla, Carmina and Aguilar were indeed Cuban.

None were professionally trained actresses, and their experience as dancers was limited, learned as a pastime and practised casually since childhood. They were essentially trained in Mexico and, as their careers quickly advanced, each took on a particular personalised style that together came to structure the stereotype of the *rumbera*. These artists offer another interesting link between the two countries and how Mexican–Cuban relations developed over time, which can be analysed through their reception back in Cuba and the constructions of Cuban culture that circulated throughout the Spanish-speaking world in their popular films.

Essential elements of the existing stereotypes of the Caribbean can be seen at the beginning of the nineteenth century, as can be inferred from the descriptions of Cuba by the traveller, statesman and botanist Joel Roberts Poinsett: 'The land is gently undulating, the hill sides covered with fresh verdure, and the valleys present the dark foliage and luxuriant vegetation of the tropics' (p. 210). His descriptions of land and nature suddenly turn into metaphors for the local women, whose curves are standardised in the description of their sinuosity, their exuberance and the lust they awaken. The types of women represented by these Cuban artists, whose forms and movements, along with their way of speaking, could easily be identified by Cuban fans, aroused diverse reactions. While many became their most devoted fans, others disputed their authenticity, denying that they were an 'expression of their musical tradition and that their dancing incorporated the cultural heritage of their homeland' (Vega et al., p. 41).

Following success in films such as *La reina del trópico* and the Cuban–Mexican co-production *Embrujo antillano*, Pons soon reached the height of her popularity, becoming one of the best-known stars of Mexican cinema. However, her position was threatened by fierce competition. Between 1947 and 1950, the genre proliferated: *La sin ventura* (Tito Davison, 1948) was one of a dozen Pons films made in that period; but Amalia Aguilar was featured prominently in another ten, including *Al son del mambo* and *Ritmos del Caribe* (Juan José Ortega, 1950); Meche Barba stepped out in another dozen, including *Tania, la bella salvaje* and *Cabaret Shangai* (Juan Orol, 1950), and another half-dozen films starred director and Pons's ex-husband Juan Orol's new wife Rosa Carmina, while Ninón Sevilla made her screen debut in 1947 and quickly became a screen sensation through her high-octane performances in films such as *Pecadora* (Juan Díaz Morales, 1947), quickly earning top billing in such pictures as *Coqueta* (Fernando Rivero, 1949) and *Perdida* (Fernando Rivero, 1950). Sevilla gave a tour de force performance in *Aventurera*, a controversial feature that earned critical acclaim and was one of the most popular movies of the year in Mexico, sealing once and for all the now indissoluble link between cabaret and prostitution in a genre that had often titillated through innuendo. Sevilla would be the only *rumbera* to star in a prestigious 'el Indio' Fernández picture, the critically acclaimed *Víctimas del pecado*, a film that, along with *Salón México* (which starred the Argentine actress Marga López, who was not a *rumbera*), raised the *rumbera* or *cabaretera* genre to a new level of prestige.

This huge wave of cabaret films placed the tragic destiny of female nightclub performers ('bad girls') at the core of a sexualised contemporary urban life. This mix of ingredients (music, gritty but clearly modern urban nightlife, sexual fantasy) brought about a change in Pons's roles, which had often told a story of a young girl from the provinces seeking her fortune in the big city, and now simply presented her as the *reina* [queen] of the cabaret in films such as *La reina del mambo* (1951).

La bien pagada (Alberto Gout, 1948) was discussed at length in *Bohemia*, which insisted on a fundamental lack of acting talent on the part of Pons, but admitted that she had one singular ability: 'María Antonieta Pons is a formidable rumba dancer. She has managed, without knowing anything of our popular dance, to impose herself through her beauty and, above all, through the electrifying movements that her daunting figure knows how to produce.' The anonymous critic noted that it is possible to dance rumba 'without knowing anything' about the dance and, in addition, signalled the 'fabrication' of steps and the transformation of the genre's standard moves, marking a distance in speaking of 'our popular dance', expelling Pons from this 'we' (*Bohemia*, 21 March 1948, p. 86).

Two months later, Rosa Carmina's *Tania, la bella salvaje* was reviewed, in a similar but even more virulent tone, especially regarding its Mexico-based, Spanish-born director, Juan Orol, who was responsible in many ways for both his first wife Pons's rise to fame and that of his soon to be second wife, Carmina. The reviewer deplores the ineptitude of Orol's new muse for this style of dance, along with Orol's ignorance of the authorship of the songs to which she dances:

> Ah, and let us tell you before concluding that neither Rosa Carmina nor Juanita Riverón knows how to dance rumba! Furthermore, the movie's opening credits claim that the music of the songs and rumbas are original compositions by Armando Valdespí. Don't believe it! (*Bohemia*, 23 May 1948, p. 88)

Having been born on the island does not give Carmina a natural ability to dance to Cuba's rhythms, nor does it imply that she knows about its cultural traditions. The critic does not recognise the cabaret sets, the landscapes, or the female protagonists of the movie as Cuban, characterising it all as part of its 'savage' setting. Another critic affectionately mocks the casting of Carmina as 'the beautiful savage … a monicker that she, with this pose, deserves, because, truly, the girl is simply that way. Savage!' (*Chic*, June 1948, p. 61). The author of this latter publicity-oriented note had not seen the movie and assigned a Mexican nationality to its Cuban-born star.

However, during the mid- to late 1940s, the *rumbera* genre was eminently popular in Cuba as it was everywhere else Mexican movies played. Ninón Sevilla, in fact, came to be quite popular beyond the Spanish-speaking world, with her films playing regularly in France (*Cinema Reporter*, 9 February 1952, p. 23; 3 November 1954, p. 18) and Brazil, where she and Pons were both invited to make movies in Portuguese (*El Cine Gráfico*, 11 May 1952, p. 6; 27 July 1952, p. 9; *Cinema Reporter*, 23 August 1952, p. 6; 24 January 1953, p. 10; 24 October 1956, p. 33). Apart from the films' success, the press reported again and again on the huge crowds these performers would draw to their live shows. An avalanche of spectators paid three times or more the usual price of admission, lined up for hours to get tickets and obliged them to repeat their favourite numbers again and again, with stories avidly reported of the *rumberas'* triumphs on tours all over the Americas, as exemplified in Pons's concerts in Los Angeles in 1947 where 'a long queue, five people wide, that wound around the block … waited for tickets. I have never seen anything like it!' (*Bohemia*, 21 December 1947, p. 88).

Audience response reveals the position that this genre of cinema had obtained: by the late 1940s its stars had quickly risen to the level of Mexico's greatest *astros*, as can be seen in the following commentary on the popular reception of *Embrujo antillano* (1947), an Orol-directed Mexican–Cuban co-production featuring both Pons and Blanquita Amaro, who would soon afterwards carve out her niche as the leading *rumbera* of Argentina cinema (which unfortunately would severely limit her potential to compete with Pons and Sevilla):

> The truth must be told, and it is the following: *Embrujo antillano* has triumphed in Cuba and in all countries where it has been exhibited, among them the USA and Puerto Rico … In the USA, its earnings have surpassed those of María Félix and Jorge Negrete. (*El Cine Gráfico*, 26 January 1947, p. 9)

The success of the genre, of course, likely had more to do with its sexual titillation than with its music and other signifiers of Cuban culture, and its critical reception in Cuba, as elsewhere, was mixed. While, in an issue of 1956, *Cinema* promotes two Pons films, one on its cover: *La culpa de los hombres* (Roberto Rodríguez, 1955) and another in a captioned photograph: *Casa de perdición* (Ramón Pereda, 1956), praising 'such exciting and well-produced rumbas and songs' (22 June 1956, p. 41), the *Guía Cinematográfica 1956–1957* judges both of these films harshly. *Casa de perdición* is 'forbidden' to readers due to its 'provocative costumes' along with 'the obscenity of its dances and the bad intentions of the camera's point of focus' (p. 75), condemnations that carried little practical weight and may have ultimately done more to promote the films than to keep spectators away. Sevilla's *Mulata*, which included the depiction of a *bembé* ritual identified with Cuban *santería* that censors found to be 'denigrating' and 'immoral', most probably because in the middle of the ritual some of the young and

Ninón Sevilla starred in the provocative *Mulata* (1954)

attractive Afrocuban women begin deliriously (and gratuitously) ripping off their blouses. The *Los Angeles Times*, reviewing its extended exhibition in Spanish-language cinema houses in California, lauded its 'voodoo ceremonies' and 'wild dancing ... shown with barbaric restraint' (3 August 1955, p. 87). While the tone of the scene suggests that these are merely 'primitives' whose nudity is no different from that portrayed in illustrations of anthropology texts – 'native scenes', according to the *Los Angeles Times* (ibid.) – Cuban authorities apparently saw it as pornographic, or in their words, 'dirty, cheap and indecent', and banned its distribution, even after its premiere in seven different cinemas had been announced (*Cinema Reporter*, 17 July 1954; Douglas, p. 136) – although they eventually did allow it to open, some months later (Paranaguá, *Le cinéma*, p. 167; Douglas, p. 137).

In fact, Pons's films were the target of repeated censorship. In Colombia, an anonymous critic declares: 'We find it incomprehensible that the Censorship Board tolerates the films of Señora María Antonieta Pons who acts only in movies with frankly pornographic content, such as *La bien pagada*' (*Cromos*, 19 February 1949, p. 12). When Pons, along with mambo king Pérez Prado, faced censorship in Venezuela for being 'the true incarnation of the devil', a young Gabriel García Márquez rose up to their defence in a Barranquilla newspaper, suggesting that distributors quote the Venezuelans, using that very phrase in their publicity campaigns (*El Heraldo*, 19 June 1951, quoted in Gilard, vol. 1, p. 674). However, generally speaking, censors did little to restrain *rumbera* cinema in Latin America. In Spain, however, it was a different story. The contrast between her generalised triumph in Latin America and her utter lack of penetration in the Spanish market reveals the characteristics of the market of Spain, whose cinema was severely limited by the Franco regime's strict censorship (Castro Ricalde, 'We Are Rumberas').

ABRUPT ENDING

The Cuban press's predilection for the Mexican movie industry continued on even into the late 1950s, when Mexican cinema was losing its lustre. However, the Cuban press noted that Mexico remained the second-biggest film importer to Cuba as late as 1960, with a market share (calculated in terms of number of films imported) that went from 8 per cent in 1940 (forty Mexican films vs 360 from Hollywood), to 16 per cent in 1946 (sixty-four vs 257), to 22 per cent in 1950 (105 vs 274), down to 15 per cent (sixty-seven vs 256) in 1958, and remaining surprisingly steady at 14 per cent even in 1960 (fifty-three vs 210), although from that point, it would fall precipitously (Douglas, pp. 318–21; Ramsaye, *1947–48*, pp. 958). For example, Mexican cinema stars Elsa Aguirre, María Antonieta Pons and Martha Roth would be featured on covers of the journal *Cinema* (20 January 1955; 20 July 1956; 21 December 1956), which would maintain its section 'Activity in Mexican Cinema', along with related notes and reviews, throughout the 1950s. A typical issue of *Cinema* from these years includes an article by Walfredo Piñera on the season's latest Mexican films scheduled to premiere in the Teatro Negrete, a review of Cantinflas's *Caballero a la medida* (Miguel Delgado, 1954) and another article entitled 'Mexican Cinema' (29 May 1955).

While the *rumbera* pictures lost their lustre as the world changed, their suggestiveness was gradually replaced with a franker sexuality. A generation of younger Mexican actresses, who were not known as talented dancers, including Ana Luisa Peluffo, Kitty de Hoyos and Columba Domínguez, gained fame in the mid-1950s for baring their breasts before the camera, making the *rumberas*' hip shaking, bared midrifts and veiled references to prostitution seem tame (García and Aviña, pp. 68–9). While Pons continued filming until 1966, Carmina shifted to more dramatic roles and Sevilla's last major film was *Yambaó* in 1957, although she continued filming in Mexico, Brazil and Spain for another two years. Cubans, meanwhile, remained loyal fans of Mexican cinema throughout the 1950s, just as Cuban producers continued to seek collaborative arrangements with Mexican studios throughout the decade. While in some other markets imports gradually fell off as audiences tired of the deteriorating quality and lack of innovation in Mexico's film product, in Cuba Mexico's golden age ended more abruptly, for entirely different reasons associated with the revolution of 1959. Just as the new culture of revolutionary Cuba rejected the cultural imperialism of the USA, it could not tolerate the cheap commerciality of Mexican cinema in its decadence, with its emblematic manifestation being the *rumbera* genre that portrayed Cuba as a sexual playground, not an image congruent with a communist revolution, nor one that the new revolutionary government wished to project to the world. The founding of the ICAIC in 1959 effectively signalled the end to Mexican–Cuban co-productions and would quickly lead to the shutting down of Mexican film import channels.

What was the golden age of cinema in Mexico, in Cuba saw only the stumblings of a movie industry unable to reach maturity, thus preventing its inhabitants from questioning themselves about their own images produced in their own films, and essentially leaving spectators to accept those images produced in foreign, mainly Mexican works, which incorporated, with a certain efficacy that Hollywood could not achieve, physiologies, landscapes and behaviours that Cubans assumed as their own, at least until their own golden age of film production taught them differently. Audiences of other nations would experience the era differently. Smaller nations located farther away from Mexico would not engage in many co-productions, nor would many of their compatriots become headlining stars in Mexico, nor would the Mexican industry be motivated to produce many movies about their culture. Countries such as Colombia lost the opportunity to use the medium of film to consolidate national identity during the period, instead being offered only the option to identify with the Mexican cinema that came to dominate their market through a regional affiliation, as Latin Americans.

2

Así se quiere en Antioquia: Mexican Golden Age Cinema in Colombia

Robert McKee Irwin

THE IMPOSING PRESENCE OF MEXICAN FILM IN COLOMBIA

With the rise of Mexico's golden age film industry, Colombia would quickly become one of its most consistently profitable markets. The case of Colombia represents in many ways what was a typical situation for Latin American film audiences. Colombia, like other smaller Latin American countries during the 1940s and 50s, never developed its own national film industry – nor did it see much in the way of tentative advances such as those of Venezuela, Cuba or Chile. Mexican film filled a void, coming to represent a viable substitute for Colombian audiences for an authentically autochthonous product that never came to be. While Colombians celebrated Mexico's ability to compete with Hollywood as a Latin American feat, their sometimes problematic identification with the Mexican cinema project in effect made it impossible to launch a local industry in Colombia. Mexican film's reception in Colombia, as in most other Latin American countries, was always ambivalent: on the one hand, it was welcomed as 'our' own Latin American cinema; on the other, it always was something of an imposition that established from the earliest years of the culture industries a somewhat hegemonic – or even imperialistic – position for Mexico within the region.

RANCHO GRANDE

While Colombia was, in 1936, the fifth-largest Latin American market for movies, with 210 theatres in operation, it had many fewer theatres than fourth-ranking Cuba, with 350 cinemas in 1936, despite Colombia's having close to double Cuba's population (see Ramsaye, *1937–38*, pp. 1120–1). Moreover, the presence of Mexican imports was negligible, with Hollywood holding an 80 per cent market share in 1936 – that is until the premiere of *Allá en el Rancho Grande* in late September of 1937. The sensation it caused in Bogotá that year was unprecedented. At a time when films from anywhere rarely played in more than one movie house at a time, *Rancho Grande* premiered simultaneously in four cinemas. Accompanied by a clamorous advertising campaign, it reportedly began breaking box-office records within only a few days (*El Tiempo*, 3 October 1937, p. 16), and generated rare newspaper coverage at a time when film criticism was virtually nonexistent in Colombia, with an anonymous reporter observing that 'Mexico is the Spanish American nation with the most character or talent for film making' (*El Tiempo*, 4 October 1937, p. 4). It would remain in theatres for the rest of the year, even while competing for the last seven weeks with the follow-up hit *Jalisco nunca pierde* (Chano Urueta, 1937), and would be rereleased on multiple occasions in years to come (*El Tiempo*, 3 July 1941, p. 13; *Cinema Reporter*, 10 January 1953, p. 18).

Various *comedia ranchera* pictures continued to attract audiences in Colombia over the next couple of years, with films like *Las cuatro milpas* (Ramón Pereda, 1937), *Amapola del camino* (Juan Bustillo Oro, 1937), *¡Ora Ponciano!* (Gabriel Soria, 1937) and *Bajo el cielo de México* (Fernando de Fuentes, 1937) keeping up the momentum, although the Tito Guízar vehicle *Amapola del camino* generated Mexican cinema's first mini-controversy in Colombia when it was claimed that the film's theme song had been composed by Colombian Guillermo Quevedo, who remained officially uncredited (*El Tiempo*, 8 March 1938, p. 4). *Ranchera* troubadour Guízar, comic actor Chaflán and musicians Trío Calaveras, all stars in *Rancho Grande* along with several films with similar themes and settings of the next few years, visited Bogotá on promotional tours, and were received with great enthusiasm (*El Tiempo*, 24 May 1939, p. 12; 3 March 1939, p. 15; 18 May 1940, p. 16) in what can be seen as a clear instance of an affinitive transnational identification (Hjort, p. 17); however, not all Mexican films were big hits in those years, including those most likely to interpellate Colombian spectators. Mexico's attempt at producing a cinematic representation of Colombia's great foundational novel, Jorge Isaacs's *María* (Chano Urueta, 1938), was a clunker, generating very little press at all in Colombia, where it was remembered later by Gabriel García Márquez in his early years as film critic as 'technically rudimentary' (*El Espectador*, 10 December 1954, p. 4, quoted in Gilard, vol. 3, p. 942), and indeed had provoked discomfort even prior to its release for being a foreign production of a Colombian literary classic (*El Tiempo*, 19 February 1939, p. 11), signalling from the start that Mexico's incursion into international markets would not always be welcomed.

And despite the fact that Mexican cinema had improved its technical quality to the point that it deserved to be exhibited in cinemas previously dedicated only to more polished Hollywood imports (*El Tiempo*, 6 January 1939, p. 13), by the end of the 1930s, it had lost substantial momentum and risked permanently ceding market share to its Argentine competition (see Ramsaye, *1939–40*, p. 932), which was fast becoming the leading producer of Spanish-language cinema.

NEW ENERGY IN THE 1940s

However, Mexico's luck would begin to change by the early 1940s, a period when it took particularly deep root in the Colombian market. Announcements for the return of the now classic *Allá en el Rancho Grande* listed it as holding the all-time box-office record in Colombia (*El Tiempo*, 3 July 1941, p. 13). A few months later, *¡Ay Jalisco no te rajes!* (Joselito Rodríguez, 1941), starring rising star Jorge Negrete and Carlos 'Chaflán' López, caused a sensation by drawing 10,000 spectators in five days (Martínez Pardo, p. 130), a record topped the following year by the film *Casa de mujeres* (Gabriel Soria, 1942) when it sold 20,000 tickets at a single theatre, the Lux (ibid., p. 131). Yet another record was reportedly set in 1944 with the opening of Cantinflas's *Romeo y Julieta* (Miguel Delgado, 1943) in Bogotá (*Mi Film*, 14 December 1944, p. 18).

The film world was still a relatively small one in Colombia at this time, with Bogotá boasting only twenty-one theatres as of 1942, but it is significant that Mexican films captured more screens than did those of Hollywood that year, with Argentine product in a distant third place (Martínez Pardo, p. 130). In January of 1943, for example, of seventeen films running at capital city theatres, eight were from Mexico, seven from the USA and one each from Argentina and France (ibid., p. 131). The weekly culture magazine, *Sábado*, remarked in 1944 on the 'avalanche' of Mexican films inundating Colombian theatres (26 February 1944, p. 15), while in Mexico it was reported that Mexican films were commonly attracting up to four times the number of spectators as Hollywood films, and as a result playing more than twice as long in Colombian movie houses (*El Cine Gráfico*, 20 February 1944, p. 12). Meanwhile, statistics show that the movies had become the favourite pastime in paid entertainment of Colombians. A study carried out in the first half of 1944 found that over 3.1 million spectators had attended movies in Bogotá, while only 192,000 had gone to see live theatre, and just 45,000 had been to bullfights during those six months. Considering that Bogotá had only about 500,000 inhabitants, it would seem that Bogotanos were going to the movies an average of more than once per month per person (Martínez Pardo, p. 132).

Colombians' passion for film continued to grow during the period. By 1944, twelve new movie houses had opened in Bogotá, raising the total to thirty-three (ibid., p. 163), with another fifteen opening by 1949. At a national level, in 1945 Colombia boasted 280 cinemas, a total bettered in Latin America only by Argentina, Brazil and Mexico – Latin America's three largest countries and most important centres for film production – and Cuba, a country well known for the zeal of its movie fans, which had 357 (*Cinema Reporter*, 10 November 1945, p. 27), and by 1951, Colombia, with 641 theatres with a total seating capacity of 410,000, had surpassed even Cuba's 600 theatres and capacity of 360,000 (Kann, p. x). A 1952 report indicates that, in the first two years of the decade, Colombia was the Mexican industry's third-largest market, after the USA and Venezuela, as measured in the number of features imported (*El Cine Gráfico*, 4 May 1952, p. 6). It can be assumed that Mexican imports were the most important factor in keeping Hollywood's percentage of total Colombian screen time down to 50 per cent in 1948 and 60 per cent in 1951 (Ramsaye, *1949–50*, p. xvi; Kann, p. x).

While Mexico's wartime alliance with the USA was important for its industry's growth, its rapidly increasing viewership in Colombia can be attributed to a number of factors, including Mexico's savvy introduction of new subject matter, its openness to foreign participation and questions of startup costs and economies of scale that made it difficult if not impossible for smaller countries such as Colombia to establish film studios of their own that were capable of producing product of sufficient technical quality to compete with those of Mexico.

GOLDEN AGE CINEMA GOES INTERNATIONAL: BOLIVARIAN PANAMERICANISM MEXICAN STYLE

The Mexican industry, whose success in the late 1930s and early 40s had been achieved mostly through the popularity of films of universal themes – for example, class conflict: the poor devil who confounds both the bourgeois snobs who abhor his social class and the institutions that routinely abuse the lower classes (*Ahí está el detalle*); family conflict: the new generation who aspire to a better life in the city and separate themselves from their loving but old-fashioned parents (*Cuando los hijos se van*); romantic conflict: the ranch owner who unwittingly tries to seduce the fiancée of a beloved employee (*Allá en el Rancho Grande*) – that are nonetheless always set in recognisably Mexican spaces, began to think strategically about promoting further expansion of its product into international markets by better representing, on the screen, its target markets. While Central and South Americans identified with Mexican films more than they did with Hollywood or French or Italian films, some Mexican film-makers realised the potential for increasing their success abroad by producing features capable of evoking a more direct identification among non-Mexican Latin American audiences.

The first director to sense and act on this potential in an important way was Miguel Contreras Torres. Although official 'good neighbour policy' would not yield a formal pact between Mexico and the USA until June of 1942, as early as January of 1941, Contreras Torres had begun laying the groundwork for production of the film that would be Mexico's first big-budget blockbuster. This film was designed to be a vehicle for establishing Mexico's not just as a strong national industry, but as the leading movie production enterprise of Latin America, one that represented not only Mexican national culture, but a unifying panamericanist vision. Indeed, the panamericanist propaganda emanating from the USA to promote political and economic cooperation across the Americas during the war coincided with the Mexican film industry's own goals of continental expansionism. Its first significant tactical move in promoting a panamericanist agenda would logically be through the heroic historical figure most associated with the term in Latin America: Simón Bolívar. In early January of 1941, Contreras Torres travelled to Venezuela to carry out on-site research and garner support for the film he intended to make depicting the life of South America's great *Libertador* (Peredo Castro, *Cine y propaganda,* pp. 236–40). From there he travelled to Colombia, where he continued to do research, and to seek 'cooperation' and 'goodwill' in support of his project (*El Tiempo*, 31 January 1941, p. 3).

Contreras Torres, after debuting as an actor in *El Zarco* (José Manuel Ramos) in 1920, soon began making his own films, and indeed became Mexico's most prolific film-maker of the 20s (De los Reyes, pp. 89–91). He directed no less than twenty films during that decade, sixteen of which he produced and five for which he authored screenplays. He also acted in eleven of them, edited thirteen of them and was cinematographer for ten. None of these films achieved much distribution or critical recognition as Mexican film remained primitive and underfunded until the 30s. He achieved his first significant success with an early sound film, *Juárez y Maximiliano* (1934), and soon became known as Mexico's most accomplished director of patriotic historical dramas (Peredo Castro, *Cine y propaganda*, pp. 235–6). His Simón Bolívar project was designed to solidify his position as one of Mexico's greatest directors, a feat he hoped to achieve by obtaining significant government subsidies, which he could seek due to the fact that a film about Bolívar would promote the panamericanist cooperation favoured by the Mexican, Venezuelan and Colombian governments. While

Julián Soler in the 1942 Mexican blockbuster, *Simón Bolívar*

there is no evidence that he obtained anything more than 'moral support' that opened
doors to facilitate filming on location in the latter two nations, his heavy lobbying of
Mexico's government yielded him financial backing that guaranteed *Simón Bolívar*'s
release in 1942 as the Mexican industry's first international blockbuster (ibid.,
pp. 236–42).

   The film was advertised as costing a million pesos to produce (*Cinema Reporter*,
4 July 1941, p. 7), an unprecedented budget at the time – indeed, the average film
production cost in Mexico in the early 1940s was only about 15 per cent of that
(Peredo Castro, *Cine y propaganda*, p. 165) – and was promoted as the 'first Mexican
production of continental interest' (*Cinema Reporter*, 13 June 1941, p. 5), 'the golden
dream of the Latin American people' (*Cinema Reporter*, 18 July 1941, p. 7) and
nothing less than 'the most significant and ambitious movie that has ever been filmed
in the Spanish language' (*El Tiempo*, 29 July 1941, p. 7), generating publicity – and
controversy – in Colombia and Venezuela long before its release in July of 1942, when
it premiered in Venezuela (9 July), Mexico (15 July) and Colombia (21 July). A regular
stream of prerelease publicity generated much buzz, but also some concern.

Venezuelans debated whether Mexican actors could accurately portray the protagonists of South American history (*Cinema Reporter*, 5 December 1941, p. 4), while Colombians predicted that the Mexicans' accent and dialect would undermine the project's historical precision (*El Tiempo*, 24 September 1941, p. 5) and questioned whether some of the film's supporting characters even existed (*Cinema Reporter*, February 1942, p. 9).

In Venezuela, the *Simón Bolívar* premiere generated great fervour. The fact that it was a big-budget production representing Venezuelan history and that it was produced in Latin America and not in Hollywood impressed and even surprised critics: 'let's be frank – we didn't believe that Mexican cinema could achieve so much ... we never dreamed of having a film as well documented and as complete as this one' (*Mi Film*, 23 July 1942, quoted in Tirado, p. 95). The Venezuelan press raved that *Simón Bolívar* had been 'marvellously realised', that it had 'greatly exceeded our hopes' (*La Esfera*, 11 July 1942, quoted in *El Tiempo*, 21 July 1942, p. 20), that its most elaborate battle scenes were 'stunning' (*Últimas Noticias*, quoted in *El Tiempo*, 20 July 1942, p. 16) and that the production, 'magnificently monumental', evoked 'intense emotion' (*El Heraldo*, 10 July 1942, quoted in *El Tiempo*, 17 July 1942, p. 12). A publicity blitz reprinted in Mexico, Colombia and other markets quotes many of these reviews, along with endorsements of the Venezuelan president and other dignitaries, all of whom 'enthusiastically applaud the extraordinary film' (*Cinema Reporter*, 10 July 1942, p. 11), and claimed, moreover, that the movie earned 'unanimous praise' from 'all social sectors' (*Cinema Reporter*, 17 July 1942, p. 7). A few months later, reports came in that *Simón Bolívar* was breaking all records in South America, having earned more than US$100,000 in Venezuela alone (*Cinema Reporter*, 19 March 1943, p. 31); indeed, despite its exorbitant production budget, the film reportedly earned all of it back on its first three months of Venezuelan box-office receipts (Peredo Castro, *Cine y propaganda*, p. 241n113). In 1943, the Venezuelan embassy staged a homage to Julián Soler, who played Bolívar in the film (*Cinema Reporter*, 10 July 1943, p. 24), and both he and Contreras Torres were given honorary titles in Venezuela (Peredo Castro, *Cine y propaganda*, p. 241). In an era when most films came and went in a week, *Simón Bolívar* became a mainstay on Venezuelan screens, and was still playing in Caracas nearly two years later (*Cinema Reporter*, 15 April 1944, p. 30). Likewise, in Colombia, the movie's release became a major cultural event as it was, according to the local press, 'the first time that the great figures of history, embodied and interpreted with intelligence and mastery, have come to the Spanish-speaking screen' (*El Tiempo*, 2 August 1942, section 2, p. 2). It later was also a hit in such places as Argentina (*Cinema Reporter*, 26 June 1943, p. 28), Ecuador (*Cinema Reporter*, 3 June 1944, p. 30) and Chile – and reportedly as far away as Spain and England (Tirado, p. 95), meeting and even exceeding the designs of Mexican film promoters, who claimed that *Simón Bolívar*, 'without a doubt will elevate our industry to the place it deserves to hold in Spanish-speaking film markets' (*Cinema Reporter*, June 1942, p. 14).

Latin American press on the film was not all positive, with one Venezuelan critic claiming that the film is nothing more than 'a mere educative film for elementary school students' (Alberto Posse Rivas of *La Esfera*, quoted in Tirado, p. 96). This sentiment was echoed a decade later by Gabriel García Márquez, who remarked that the film 'seemed as if it had been taken from a public school textbook' (*El Espectador*,

10 December 1954, p. 4, quoted in Gilard, vol. 3, p. 942) – an assertion not at odds with Mexican actor and screenwriter Enrique Uthoff's defence of the film, in which he sustained that it 'fulfils a pedagogical function' (*Cinema Reporter*, August 1942, p. 5). The film, unlike some other early box-office hits, including *Allá en el Rancho Grande*, *Cuando los hijos se van*, *Ahí está el detalle* and *¡Ay, Jalisco, no te rajes!*, has not held up over time, as one critic puts it, eventually falling 'into a bottomless well where memory inexorably devours itself' (Izaguirre, *Acechos*, p. 75). *Simón Bolívar* has never been released commercially on video or DVD – although a handful of scenes can be found on YouTube.

But, at the moment of its release, *Simón Bolívar* represented a major cultural event in Colombia and Venezuela, an event that located national history in a broader hemispheric context that confirmed the importance of Colombia and Venezuela's place within a common Latin American culture, but also confirmed their subordinate position to Mexico, whose cultural industry was the only one powerful enough to represent their history to the entire hemisphere in the grandiose style it deserved. The public clearly enjoyed the invitation to identify with Mexican cinema in a way that undoubtedly felt more authentic and complete than what they felt with Chaflán, Cantinflas, Sara García or Jorge Negrete, but it also generated distrust regarding historical accuracy and linguistic credibility, and its appropriation of Simón Bolívar and Venezuelan and Colombian history seemed, to some, ultimately like something of an imposition.

COLOMBIA'S MEXICANISED STARS

A major attraction of Mexican cinema, aside from its newly internationalised themes, and in contrast with that of Hollywood (or of Argentina or Spain), for Colombian audiences, was the participation of Colombian artists. While they would never achieve the visibility of Argentine (Libertad Lamarque, Niní Marshall, Marga López), Spanish (Armando Calvo, Emilia Guiú) or Cuban (María Antonieta Pons, Juan José Martínez Casado, Carmen Montejo) film stars, Colombians participated actively in Mexican film throughout its golden age, and the Colombian press was careful to keep these stars' fans abreast of their activities.

Colombia's most celebrated star of the period was Sofía Álvarez, a performer well known as a vocalist during her lifetime, but best remembered nowadays as Joaquín Pardavé's wife in the classic Cantinflas film *Ahí está el detalle*. Álvarez launched her film acting career with the inauguration of sound cinema in Mexico, appearing as an unnamed prostitute in *Santa* (1932), and eventually becoming one of the era's most respected actresses, co-starring with such luminaries as Fernando Soler and Pedro Infante in twenty-nine Mexican films, including *México de mis recuerdos* (Juan Bustillo Oro, 1944), *Si me han de matar mañana* (Miguel Zacarías, 1947) and *Soy charro de Rancho Grande* (Joaquín Pardavé, 1947).

Álvarez was interviewed frequently by the Colombian press, and when she launched a tour of the country in 1946, after living fifteen years in Mexico, her visit, timed to coincide with the local premiere of *La reina de la opereta* (José Benavides hijo, 1946), in which she starred with Joaquín Pardavé and Fernando Soler, she remained in

Columbia's greatest star of Mexican cinema, Sofía Álvarez

the local headlines for weeks. Álvarez was received with 'fervent applause' at her live vocal performances in Bogotá (*El Tiempo*, 23 April 1946, p. 3) and admired for 'bringing prestige to the name of our country' (*El Tiempo*, 30 March 1946, p. 16a). However, her success as an actress and singer in Mexico, which brought her a level of international celebrity unknown to Colombians working in Colombia, also inspired a certain ambivalence among Colombians.

Álvarez, a foreigner in an industry thought of as a Mexican national resource, herself had to tread a fine line. In an interview with *Cinema Reporter* (1 May 1943, pp. 8–10), her interviewer commented that she possessed 'the quality of being tremendously Mexican'. Álvarez protested that she was Colombian by birth, however concluded 'with pride' that 'I don't believe that there is any artist more Mexican than I, in terms of sentiments' (p. 10). Such flirtation with a Mexican identity – especially for an actress who had acted in many Mexican roles, including that of the popular icon la Valentina (*Revolución*, Manuel Contreras Torres and Antonio Moreno, 1933) – did not sit well with her Colombian fans. In 1947, a rumour that Álvarez planned to become a Mexican citizen (*El Tiempo*, 1 August 1947, p. 8) caused a minor uproar in her homeland. Her response:

> I was born in Colombia. I feel Colombian. If life has brought me to Mexico, where the traditional generosity of its peoples has allowed me to triumph in art, and has bonded me to the nation with a love born of gratitude and recognition for their distinguished qualities, that does not mean that I don't think of my homeland with the devotion that its heroic history and the nostalgia that its landscapes inspire, desirous that back home they consider me, until death do us part, as Colombian as bambuco music. (*El Tiempo*, 31 October 1947, p. 8)

Just as it was imperative that she maintain her love for her adopted homeland, the devotion of her fans in Colombia required that she bind herself, at least rhetorically, to Colombia. Indeed, Álvarez was occasionally victim of xenophobic attacks in the Mexican press for taking jobs away from Mexican actresses, as the Colombian press revealed in an article provocatively entitled 'Sofía Álvarez is Attacked in Mexico for Being Colombian' (*El Tiempo*, 25 September 1949, p. 10). Despite continued proclamations of being 'more Mexican than pulque' (*Cinema Reporter*, 9 October 1948, p. 29), campaigns against foreign artists would eventually lead Álvarez to temporarily retire from acting and devote herself to her career as a vocalist for much of the 50s, although she would act again in a handful of minor Mexican films beginning in the late 50s until her definitive retirement from the screen in 1968.

In addition to Álvarez, Alicia Caro, Alicia Neira and José Gálvez rose to be minor stars in Mexico – although the latter initiated his career when Mexico's golden age was already waning. However, other hopefuls failed. For example, the well-publicised debut of Carlota Linsell (*El Tiempo*, 25 May 1946, p. 8) – in a minor role in Ramón Peón's forgettable *Se acabaron las mujeres* (1946) under the name Carlota Cook – quickly fizzled as she never acted in another film; and rising star Gloria Cancino, billed as a María Félix look-alike (*El Tiempo*, 13 November 1949, p. 14), managed to secure minor roles in only a handful of films. Likewise, a contest to send a Colombian to Mexico to become a film star, despite a great deal of hoopla, fell flat when the winner, Lilia Hurtado, failed to make a splash in Mexico. *El Tiempo* celebrated her arrival in Mexico City, where she was given a bit part in the film *Novia a la medida* (Gilberto Martínez Solares, 1949); quickly met María Félix, Diego Rivera, Blanca Estela Pavón and Fernando Soler; and even experienced the thrill of dancing with Gabriel Figueroa and 'el Indio' Fernández at a gala event, entering, as the contest promised, directly into the dream factory. However, despite an announcement that she had signed on with producer Alfredo Ripstein for her next role, perhaps starring like Álvarez before her alongside Cantinflas (*El Tiempo*, 29 April 1949, p. 18), there is no evidence of her being cast in any other Mexican movie. Apparently, having married soon after arriving in Mexico, she left acting. Then, upon marrying for a second time in 1954, she began negotiating to get back into the movie business; but before anything concrete happened, she got into a 'minor argument' with her new husband that ended with her murdering him with a pistol, sealing the end of her screen career (*Cinema Reporter*, 26 October 1955, p. 13).

ARGUMENTS IN FAVOUR OF COLOMBIA'S OWN CINEMA

While Colombians were happy to see a handful of their own making it big in Mexico City, many wished that Colombia could simply establish its own homegrown film industry in which local talent could act. But those who advocated repeatedly for the establishment of Colombia's own film production apparatus were more conscious than anyone of the power of Mexican cinema's appeal. By 1944, it was clear that,

> the enthusiastic reception that Mexican films with typical and folkloric motifs have received from us is the most obvious proof that if these same criteria were applied to our own initial

Allá en el trapiche (1943),
an early attempt to produce
sound cinema in Columbia

cinematic production, it would yield greater results in every way. We possess vast autochthonous artistic material that is just waiting to be exploited intelligently. (*El Tiempo*, 19 April 1944, p. 5)

The natural solution would be to reproduce the success of Mexican cinema, with the milestone of *Allá en el Rancho Grande* raised repeatedly as an example of how to succeed: a simple and entertaining plot, well-known elements of national folklore, catchy music and at least a rudimentary level of technical competency (*El Tiempo*, 25 October 1947, p. 8; 17 September 1950, p. 11). However, the idea of basing a possible Colombian cinema on a Mexican formula was not a solution with which other critics felt comfortable. Mexico's success inspired what to some was little more than an imposition of a foreign style that went to the extreme of 'plagiarisation of titles' (a clear reference to Colombian director Roberto Saa Silva's substitution of sites emblematic of national folklore in his 1943 *Allá en el trapiche*, recalling the Mexican blockbuster *Allá en el Rancho Grande*), leading one critic to insist: 'The orientation of our national cinema must be authentically Colombian, with a clear definition of what our culture is' (*El Espectador*, 26 December 1948, p. 16).

Colombian critics such as Álvarez Lleras realised that Mexico's benefits went beyond the direct income generated by the film industry, which could also be thought of as a 'formidable system of propaganda' that provided an enormous boost for Mexico's growing tourism industry: 'cinema has given Mexico more prestige and has made Mexico better known everywhere than have its statistics, its diplomats or, though it hurts to say it, its writers'. He further laments that 'a country without film production is an unknown country' (*El Tiempo*, 11 December 1948, p. 22). Mexican production designer Luis Moya, in an interview in *El Tiempo*, asserted that Colombia's lack of a film industry had cost the nation millions in lost opportunities (17 September 1950, p. 11).

However, mere imitation of Mexico was not the solution. Unfortunately, the few films that were produced in Colombia during these years were often criticised for being more than merely influenced by – for actually copying – Mexican cinema (Salcedo Silva, p. 193). Film critic Camilo Correa, upon viewing the Colombian picture *La canción de mi tierra* (Federico Katz, 1945), a major box-office failure, proposed: 'If we are to persevere in film-making to the point of making it a new Antioquian industry, it would be quite desirable for our actors to get rid of a detrimental Mexican influence' (*El Colombiano*, 22 February 1945, p. 5, quoted in Martínez Pardo, p. 144) so as not to build a national art 'on an antinational foundation'; 'it would be horrible if *Allá en el Rancho Grande* and *Ay Jalisco no te rajes* were to serve as the norm for what we film here' (ibid., p. 144), implying that Colombian film-making entrepreneurs insisted on mimicking the folkloric atmosphere of the ranches of Jalisco: character types, dress, situations of everyday life, musical styles – adjusting them just enough so that they could be recognised as Antioquian, a regional culture that was imagined to be Colombia's equivalent to that of Jalisco, rather than simply making films about Colombian people, history, traditions and cultural paradigms. However, the public's apparent identification with Mexican film signalled the value in using it as a model – and, for an industry that never was able to get off the ground, a better model did not exist. As a result, 'legislation, commentators and producers stagnated the development of Colombian cinema with their obsession for the autochthonous that they identified with songs, landscapes and customs, taking Mexican cinema as an example' (ibid., p. 149). Colombian culture existed only in comparison to Mexican culture – or to the notions of Mexican culture promulgated through its popular cinema. As film historian Hernando Martínez Pardo puts it, 'It's one thing for the public to like Mexican movies and another very distinct thing for them to like a pseudo-Colombianized copy of Mexicanness' (ibid., p. 151).

The problem is that Colombians had been devouring Mexican films since the late 1930s and were deeply accustomed to their style. Meanwhile, Colombia had to start from scratch if it wanted to compete with Mexico. It had no infrastructure: no experienced directors, producers or technicians, no star-quality actors aside from the handful of second- and third-tier talent working already in Mexico; worse, it lacked the state-of-the-art technology that Mexico possessed, especially once the Mexican studios began collaborating with Hollywood during World War II. The same Colombians who eagerly consumed Mexican movies were 'implacable' when confronted with Colombia's technologically inferior product: they 'would not tolerate the systematic technical flaws of Colombia's sound films, much less their lack of attractive story lines, for which no nationalist consideration could compensate' (Salcedo Silva, pp. 192–3). As a result, while Colombian films often played only for brief runs in neighbourhood movie theatres of the inner city – that is, not the first-run theatres of the elite, but in popular *barrio* theatres – the best films of big Mexican stars ran for weeks on end all over town (Martínez Pardo, p. 149). In other words, it seems that for many Colombians, Mexico's cinema was close enough to being *nuestro* – that is, to being their own – that they did not really need a Colombian national cinema, particularly one that was inferior to the Mexican product that they consumed in abundance and to which they had become eminently accustomed.

Unfortunately, technical quality did not guarantee acceptable content, especially for those critics most passionate about Colombia's making its own movies; for these critics, the majority of films imported to Colombia, including the bulk of Mexican product received, 'constitute[d] a true affront to culture, morality and aesthetics' (Camilo Correa, in *El Colombiano*, 11 January 1949, p. 5, quoted in ibid., p. 206). In the end, Mexican cinema's powerful presence in Latin America was something of 'an ideological conquest' that 'impeded and hindered the development of national cinematic expressions' (De los Reyes, p. 182).

The imposition of a Hollywood model for Colombian films no doubt would have been assessed by Colombian critics as a form of cultural dependency, and ultimately a product of cultural imperialism, a concept normally associated exclusively with the cultural industries of metropolitan nations (see Fernández L'Hoeste). Mexico's status as a less-developed, semi-modern nation with little economic clout would make a parallel critique difficult to sustain. However, it is impossible not to recognise key aspects of what has been called 'cultural imperialism' in the dominant role Mexican cinema came to play in Colombia during its golden age. Certainly the constant flow of Mexican films into the Colombian market assured the promotion of Mexican values, traditions and lifestyles in a context in which Colombia lacked avenues of response; there is no doubt that Colombians became 'dependent' on Mexico for film entertainment; however, it is more difficult to argue that Mexico benefitted economically or politically in other ways as the USA did, for example, by gaining in political influence or in demand for the importation of products and technologies as a result of the successful promotion of 'the American way of life' in Hollywood films. Mexico was neither a political nor economic powerhouse; however, it was – and remains – a major centre of cultural production in the Spanish language, and Colombian critics were no doubt justified in resisting its 'imposition' on them. Other solutions, whether to invite Mexico to make more films in Colombia or about Colombia, or to aim to enter into co-productions with the Mexican studios, 'which have been so successful in Cuba and other countries' (*El Espectador*, 28 February 1954, p. 38), humbly located Colombia in a position of dependency.

REALITIES OF COLOMBIAN NATIONAL CINEMA

The precedent of the 1920s might have suggested an optimistic picture for the possibilities of establishing a national film industry in Colombia later on. Colombia's first full-length feature film, an adaptation of the great nineteenth-century novel, *María* (Máximo Calvo Olmedo, 1922), is remembered as 'the most famous and most viewed movie in the entire history of Colombian cinema' (Salcedo Silva, p. 79) – although it should be noted that concrete supporting evidence to sustain these lofty claims has not been located. What is surprising is that the film was such a hit in Colombia that its producers sent the negatives to the USA to print up more copies to satisfy demand both in Colombia and throughout the Spanish-speaking Americas (Máximo Calvo, quoted in ibid., pp. 69–70). Another literary adaptation, *Aura o las violetas* (Vincenzo di Doménico, 1924), based on the popular novel by José María Vargas Vila, was also reportedly 'a commercial triumph' in Colombia (and Panama) (ibid., p. 40). A third film from the 20s, *Bajo el cielo antioqueño* (Arturo Acevedo Vallarino 1925), was also successful in Colombia – and abroad (ibid., p. 95), and is remembered as the 'Colombian *Gone with the Wind*', earning it a rare rerelease in Medellín in 1942 (ibid., p. 97). Yet another Colombian silent, *Garras de oro* (P. P. Jambrina, 1927) is a polished-looking (for the era) film critical of US intervention in Panama's separation from Colombia and, implicitly, US president Theodore Roosevelt's expansionist projects in Latin America, of sufficient profile to warrant calls for its censorship from the USA. Less successful than the other films mentioned, it did open to applause to a sold-out audience in Cali in March of 1927, but apparently did not play in other major Colombian cities (Suárez et al.). While there is no evidence to show that these films were megahits – indeed, if they were, production would probably not have fizzled out as it did by 1926 – all, even those for which only the smallest fragments remain in Colombia's film archives (complete or almost complete copies exist of *Bajo el cielo antioqueño* and *Garras de oro*, and indeed are commercially available thanks to the Fundación Patrimonio Fílmico Colombiano, while only twenty-five seconds of *María* remain), evoke an era of optimism regarding Colombia's possibilities for establishing a strong national film industry.

However, the period from 1926 to 1941 is one of marked inactivity in Colombian film production, save for newreels and a handful of documentaries (Salcedo Silva, p. 147), a pattern broken with the release of *Flores del valle* (Máximo Calvo Olmedo, 1941) in Cali in late February of 1941. Once again Colombia would enter into a short period (four years) of attempts, all failed, to found and keep in operation national production companies. Other films from this era include the local hit *Allá en el trapiche*, *Anarkos* (Roberto Saa Silva, 1944), *Golpe de gracia* (Hans Brückner, 1944), *Antonia Santos* (Miguel Joseph y Mayol, 1944), *La canción de mi tierra*, *Bambucos y corazones* (Gabriel Martínez, 1945), *Sendero de luz* (Emilio Álvarez Correa, 1945) and *El sereno de Bogotá* (Gabriel Martínez, 1945). During this period, which coincided with that of Mexico's rise to domination in the Spanish-speaking film market worldwide, despite occasional enthusiastic reception of Colombian audiences, moral support from the government including presidential attendance at premieres and sometimes (perhaps not often enough) even positive critical reviews, few of these films were profitable and there is no evidence of any of them being distributed outside Colombia.

The spectre of Mexico's industry weighed heavily and relentlessly on Colombian production. Director Máximo Calvo, in a 1960 interview, describes the difficulties he encountered as early as 1943 in obtaining exhibition space in Bogotá for *Flores del valle*, a film that had been well received in Cali, where it was filmed. After playing the film with a test audience that responded with applause, the manager of the Bogotá theatre where Calvo had hoped to launch the film declared: 'We can't exhibit the film any more because we just had a meeting of exhibitors and distributors, and … the distributor of Mexican movies … threatened that whatever theatre that shows this movie will no longer be supplied with Mexican film' (quoted in Salcedo Silva, p. 75) – although it should be noted that Colombian films' threat to Mexico's market share was probably minimal, a fact undoubtedly realised by distributors who appear to no longer interfere thereafter with the exhibiting of Colombian films in Bogotá.

While films such as *Allá en el trapiche* did indeed bring in respectable box office (Martínez Prado, pp. 94–5), this did not mean that audiences did not perceive their inadequacies. And when audiences forgave shortcomings, critics were not hesitant to point them out. Technical and logistical problems indeed abounded. *Allá en el trapiche*, for example, apparently lacked a working script (Arango, p. 58). *Golpe de gracia* and *Sendero de luz* were filmed with the camera operator sealed in a glass cage so that the excessive noise made by the camera would not interfere with the sound recording, making it impossible for the cameraman to move his apparatus, or to even understand directions from the director (Martínez Pardo, p. 98). Sound recording and editing presented particularly pronounced problems that became characteristic of films of the era. Radio reviews had reported that *Sendero de luz* included a 'kiss that sounded like cannonfire', which had moviegoers laughing out loud (ibid.). *Antonia Santos*, for its part, was recorded without sound, then synched with recorded dialogues that were spliced together with great difficulty as the 'recording had to be suspended every time a streetcar passed' (ibid., p.105). *El Espectador* complained of *Anarkos* that 'the sound technicians are a disaster: nothing can be understood. The effort of the public to get part of the dialogue is heroic, and the result nil' (21 April 1944, p. 4, quoted in ibid., p. 117). *Sendero de luz* experienced another technical problem associated with filming on location in the countryside where the crew's 50 metre-long extension cord connected to the only available power source, severely limiting their ability to vary backdrops and landscapes (ibid., p. 98). Film fans reportedly, upon hearing the film panned, made a point of going to theatres where *Sendero de luz* was showing only to boycott it (ibid.).

A critic in *El Espectador* reports being unable to decide how to evaluate the 'isolated applause' for *Sendero de luz* 'since at some moments it had an unmistakable accent of irony' (23 November 1945, p. 4, quoted in ibid., p. 99). Critics of *El sereno de Bogotá* railed, demanding that censors be put in place to 'defend the rights of the public, attending not only to moral but also artistic questions' (*El Espectador*, 5 November 1945, p. 6, quoted in ibid., p. 114), while the panning of *La canción de mi tierra* involved proposing that 'the crematorium would prevent such a crime from being put within the reach of spectators of all kinds, including those of miserable villages where they have never heard of the invention of Lumière' (*El Colombiano*, 9 February 1945, p. 5, quoted in ibid., p. 120). Even more appreciated films such as *Allá en el trapiche* could not escape the wrath of Colombia's most acerbic critics, one of whom was utterly unforgiving: 'in its photographic and sound technology, directing, acting, script, background music, and even in its title the unfortunate *Trapiche* gathers as many errors as can possibly committed in making a film' (*El Colombiano*, 18 April 1943, p. 12, quoted in ibid., p. 96). If *Allá en el trapiche* was meant to found a national cinema and define a national culture, 'then it's sort of an idiot-land' (ibid.).

The national press, then, was not about to cut fledgling national production companies any slack for their technological or artistic inadequacies. Moreover, there was often some underlying resentment as national productions were never fully Colombian, an issue dating back to *María*, a project produced to a significant degree by Spaniards – including Máximo Calvo, its director (as well as that of *Flores del valle*).

Practically all directors of Colombian films in the era were foreign: Austrian Hans Brückner, cinematographer for *Allá en el trapiche* and *Sendero de luz*, and director of *Golpe de gracia*; Swiss Federico Katz, director of *La canción de mi tierra*; Chileans Roberto Saa Silva, who directed both *Allá en el trapiche* and *Anarkos*, and Gabriel Martínez, who directed *Bambucos y corazones* and *El sereno de Bogotá* – as well as *Antonia Santos*, although official credit was given to the director who originated the project, Spaniard Miguel Joseph y Mayol (ibid., p. 105). Of the nine domestically produced feature films released during the 1940s, only *Sendero de luz* was directed by a Colombian (Emilio Álvarez Correa). Some of the most prominent performers in these enterprises were also Chilean, including Lily Álvarez (wife of Gabriel Martínez) and Humberto Onetto (stepfather of Lily Álvarez), both of whom acted in *Allá en el trapiche*, *Bambucos y corazones* and *Antonia Santos*, often in leading roles. While the contributions of Brückner, along with those of Frenchman Charles Rioux, a technical advisor on several films of the era, were appreciated (Salcedo Silva, p. 181; Martínez Pardo, p. 94), many of these foreign interventions have been looked upon with disdain – Camilo Correa charges that Federico Katz 'knew nothing about cinema' and was only in Colombia waiting to obtain a Colombian passport so that he could move to the USA (quoted in Martínez Pardo, p. 102) – with one critic concluding that 'foreign participation was definitive, which implies its colonisation of Colombia's film-making enterprise' (Salcedo Silva, p. 180).

Interestingly, there were no Mexicans who figured prominently in any of these homegrown productions of the early to mid-1940s. Nonetheless, it was the Mexican influence on Colombian cinema that most troubled critics. If the title of *Allá en el trapiche* suggested that producers and screenwriters looked to Mexico for inspiration, it was also inevitable to imagine that the films themselves were mere variations of Mexican models – indeed, one contemporary critic, who has probably not seen the recently reconstituted fragments of the film that the Fundación Patrimonio Fílmico Colombiano holds in its public archive in Bogotá, assumes that *Allá en el trapiche* 'exhibits a marked Mexican influence' (Ardila, 'Cine del sur').

The plot of *Trapiche* actually had little to do with that of *Rancho Grande* except that both took place in rural environments. *Allá en el trapiche*'s plot included the threat of an arranged marriage, a trip to New York, kidnappings, devastating debts, a romantic rivalry, a comic case of mistaken identity and an excess of music, whose function, according to one contemporary critic, was probably partly to 'dissimulate the problems implied by the poor synchronisation of dialogues' (Arango, p. 58). Headstrong Dorita (Lily Álvarez) is not comparable to the pathetically helpless orphan Cruz (Esther Fernández) of *Rancho Grande*, nor is the urbane Leonardo (Tocayo Ceballos) at all similar to the macho and somewhat ingenuous José Francisco (Tito Guízar). Although one might make a connection between Crucita's arranged interlude with Rancho Grande's owner Felipe (René Cardona) and the marriage Dorita's parents attempt to set up for her with a disagreeable but wealthy neighbour (who, it turns out, is already married, with fifteen kids), the tone of the two films is quite distinct. *Rancho Grande*, whose romantic rivalry is essentially about male honour, has been criticised for its 'openly reactionary sentiments' in its construction of an idyllic ranch life unaffected by class conflict, let alone postrevolutionary agrarian reform (García Riera, 'The Impact', p. 130), while *Trapiche*, like other Colombian films of the era, is 'not nostalgic nor a celebration of Arcadian countryside'; though set in the countryside, its romantic leads meet in New York and have clearly assumed big-city tastes and attitudes: 'Their modern customs clash with tradition, and the filmmakers take sides with the modern' (Vélez-Serna).

Nonetheless, *Trapiche*'s success must be attributed both to the previous success of various participants in the film's production, especially that of its lead actors, many of whom are associated with the mostly Chilean Álvarez-Sierra performance troupe, both in theatre engagements and on the radio, as well as to the producers' knowledge of what works for Colombia's movie audiences: that is, a range of Mexican, and to a lesser extent Argentine, conventions. Thus, the plot's main tension involves how the romance, introduced from the beginning, between its two protagonists, will be, despite numerous obstacles, inevitably resolved; its pace is uneven as the camera must pause over gorgeous national landscapes, and rural folk music makes numerous and sometimes lengthy interventions; modernity, symbolised in national terms, in the form of an Avianca aeroplane, looms over the quaint, but old-fashioned customs of the family ranch, a nice place for Dorita's parents, but not for her and the boyfriend (ultimately husband) she met in New York.

Similarly, although the convoluted plot of *Sendero de luz* – about the hunt for a criminal fugitive in a remote rural village that turns into a romantic rivalry between the two friends who are pursuing the assassin – recalls no specific Mexican film of the era, yet does draw from certain formulaic elements of Mexican golden age movies, including 'rural settings, simple romantic plots and a tone that oscillates between comedy and melodrama' (Vélez-Serna). In this case, according to Martínez Pardo, the film-makers take a Colombian novel and turn it into a Mexican melodrama by making the novel's central theme of 'the possession and working of the land' tangential to the movie, which introduces 'the presence of the girl, which is what unleashes the conflict', which then follows,

> the schemes of Mexican melodrama: the rivalry that emerges between the buddies over the same woman … the bet in which the stronger will get her, the presence of a drunk that introduces comic relief, the indispensible scene of the serenade, the jokes based on word play. (Martínez Pardo, p. 100)

Golpe de gracia also fails to recall any specific Mexican movie, actors or plot elements, while nonetheless recalling numerous Mexican film conventions. It is the story of a radio announcer who falls in love with a secretary and, while attempting to win a radio contest, ends up involved in a confusing situation of a holdup and criminal accusations that turn out to be the plot of his best friend, who runs off in the end with the woman. While the plot is convoluted and mostly incredible, the film is fast-moving and full of music. However, what is most notable is that it lacks the depth of pathos of Mexican melodramas such as *Cuando los hijos se van, Historia de un gran amor* (Julio Bracho, 1942), *Flor silvestre*, or other early international hits (including *Rancho Grande* and other *ranchera* comedies, such as *¡Ora Ponciano!* and *Así se quiere en Jalisco*, in which tear-jerker elements were an essential part of the formula). Despite an ironic marketing campaign – the film debuted in Bogotá just two days after a failed *golpe de estado* [coup d'état] and was advertised as: 'the true "golpe" … *Golpe de gracia*'

(Martínez Pardo, p. 97) – this movie did not make much of an impact. Its star, Tocayo Ceballos, again does not recall any Mexican star of the era with his cheerful bourgeois urban singing persona, and his co-star Sofía Hernández is not especially charismatic in her role as an apparently irresistibly charming young working woman, and again does not compare in any way to Mexico's dancing vamps, suffering mothers, devoted *soldaderas*, or innocent *hijas de familia* [good daughters]. The film is built around the radio business in which its performers were more comfortable, although once again many common themes of Mexican cinema are incorporated: the dream of making it big in show business, the rivalry among two male friends over the same woman, the glamorous aspects (and dangers) of modern urban life, the capricious and ultimately deceitful woman, etc.

In the end, critics claims that Colombian cinema of the 1940s is a mere imitation of Mexican film are unconvincing. However, their speculation that Colombian films would never generate enough revenue to allow national studios to establish themselves in the long term due to audience's preferences for – and even identification with – Mexican movies rings true. For many Colombian movie fans, as for Mexican audiences, the cinema had become a 'school of customs' (Monsiváis, 'Vino todo el público', p. 56), and Colombians, taught to expect a certain (Mexican) approach to Spanish-language film production, sought in Colombian productions a (Mexican) style and quality that they did not deliver. By the mid-40s, Colombia would enter into another extended period of inactivity lasting until 1955 with the release of *Colombia linda* (Camilo Correa) and *La gran obsesión* (Guillermo Ribón Alba) (Arango, pp. 64–5), leaving its market for Spanish-language cinema open for Mexico to dominate.

COLOMBIA IN MEXICAN FILM

The critical and popular success of *Simón Bolívar*, whose historical subject matter gave it special meaning in Venezuela and Colombia, Ecuador, Peru, Bolivia and Panama, seemed to lead immediately to Rómulo Gallegos's project of bringing his great Venezuelan novels such as *Doña Bárbara* and *Canaima* to the screen. However, this did not lead Mexican producers to quickly seek out projects in Colombia. Perhaps the failure of *María* in 1938 remained fresh in their memories; and there was certainly no Colombian Gallegos beating down their doors with ideas.

However, by April of 1947, Jesús Grovas, producer of both *Simón Bolívar* and *Doña Bárbara*, was announcing the filming of the great Colombian novel, *La vorágine* by José Eustacio Rivera, with a teaser that the film would debut the talents of 'a pretty Colombian girl' (*El Tiempo*, 25 April 1947, p. 16), who would turn out to be Alicia Caro in her first starring role. Like *Bolívar*, this film was the product of 'a squandering of money' (García Saucedo, p. 125). Colombian writer and critic Eduardo Mendoza Varela was among the first to view footage of the film, leading him predict its 'sure success' (*El Espectador*, 19 December 1948, p. 18), while playwright and novelist Antonio Álvarez Lleras, one of the first to see the film in previews, described it as 'exceptional ... most original and audacious' (*El Tiempo*, 26 April 1949, p. 3). An anonymous critic added: 'Every Colombian heart will be filled with emotion' upon the long-awaited arrival of 'the great work of Hispanic cinematography, which was inspired from that colossal work of our literature' (ibid.). In addition, Luis Eduardo Nieto Caballero, Colombia's ambassador to Mexico, and Javier Arango Ferrer, cultural attaché to the Colombian embassy in Mexico, also profusely praised the film to the Colombian press prior to its national release (*El Tiempo*, 20 May 1949, p. 3). However, other early reports warn that director Miguel Zacarías has been 'mutilating scenes and adding situations that radically alter the atmosphere of the novel' (*El Colombiano*, 23 January 1949, p. 5, quoted in Martínez Pardo, p. 203).

Upon its opening in Mexico, Bogotá's *El Tiempo* reprinted a detailed review from the Mexican journal *El Universal* that, despite several misgivings, rated it 'a great film', noting that, notwithstanding its international cast (including Spanish actor Armando Calvo and Colombian Alicia Caro in starring roles, along with several Cubans) and its Colombian story line, 'if any praise is due this film, it should be tallied in the column of national cinema' (*El Tiempo*, 8 May 1949, p. 2). Despite any bad taste that Mexico's insistence on the film being classified as Mexican and not Colombian may have provoked, its premiere in Colombia on 24 May, a gala event timed to coincide with the celebration of the twenty-second anniversary of the opening of the theatre Cine Colombia in Bogotá, ended with the film being 'rewarded with a long and impassioned applause' (*El Tiempo*, 27 May 1949, p. 18). *El Tiempo*'s anonymous reviewer blew off *El Universal*'s critique of Calvo's out of place Spanish accent, arguing that both he and Alicia Caro sounded like 'any cultured citizen of central Colombia', while complaining that the supposedly Colombian plainsmen spoke with a characteristic Venezuelan tone (ibid.). Ultimately the review was strongly positive, with the reviewer concluding that its success ought to 'open the eyes of Mexican producers to the endless mine of material that our nation has to offer film' (ibid.), an opinion not shared by all critics, one of whom, in the newspaper *El Colombiano* of Medellín, objected that 'Colombian literature and music now run the risk of Mexico's recording and thereby coopting and inevitably distorting them' (23 January 1949, p. 5, quoted in García Saucedo, p. 128).

La vorágine was a box-office smash in Colombia, where it drew over 42,000 spectators in its first week (*Cinema Reporter*, 25 June 1949, p. 31), and was soon showing simultaneously in an incredible twenty-one of Bogotá's sixty-three movie houses (*Cinema Reporter*, 13 August 1949, p. 24). As was the case with *Simón Bolívar*, reviews were mixed. The fact that it was a megaproduction with artistic pretensions based on a great national novel brought out the public in droves; but its box-office success does not imply that everyone was happy with it. One reviewer in Medellín tried to see the big picture, noting that different audiences left having formed distinct impressions of the film. *La vorágine*, the review argued, was largely well made in technical terms and was mostly satisfying for a passive audience that goes to the movies to be entertained – but for those seeking to 'appreciate what has been done with one of our great works' and to experience 'cinema as a form of artistic expression', *La vorágine* was a failure, particularly due to the inappropriate casting of the lead actors, among whom Alicia Caro is mediocre and the rest utterly 'out of place' (*El Colombiano*, 30 August 1949, p. 13, quoted in García Saucedo, p. 127). Other critics complained that the film 'was mutilated by its own producers, for inexplicable reasons, but it would seem that they were forced to do so due to its extremely high production costs' (*Dominical*, 4 June 1950, p. 28). Martínez Pardo summarises Colombian critics' views of what he calls the 'Mexicanised' *La vorágine* as 'not at all laudatory' (p. 203).

Ironically, García Márquez, who later came to embody a style of criticism that heavily favoured art films and auteur cinema, in his very first film commentary, published five years before he became a regular film critic, was sympathetic, remarking that:

> the worst that could befall a movie is what has happened with the Mexican version of *La vorágine*: we have all gone to see it with the secret aim of pointing out its defects or signalling its quality – not that of the film itself, but rather from a comparative perspective *vis-à-vis* Rivera's novel. (*El Universal*, 23 October 1949, p. 4, quoted in Arango, p. 159)

In the end, he judged the product not disappointing, a faithful representation of Rivera's novel, produced 'with a mastery not at all common in the cinematic merchandise of Mexico' (ibid., quoted in Arango, p. 160).

Soon after the release of *La vorágine*, rumours surfaced that Emilio Fernández would be making a new colour version of Isaacs's *María* (*El Tiempo*, 15 January 1950, p. 10), or that Fernando Soler would make this film in Colombia, with Alicia Caro or Alicia Neira in the starring role (*El Tiempo*, 29 October 1950, p. 11). But, despite the growing importance of the Colombian market for Mexican sales, Mexico cinema would not bother to remake *María*, and *La vorágine* would remain the only major Mexican production of the era set in Colombia. Perhaps due to Colombia's inability to produce its own films, the Mexican industry became complacent about keeping Colombian audiences interested in its films. But almost immediately critics demanded: 'Mexican producers must take into account our tastes' (*El Tiempo*, 5 February 1950, p. 16), trying to make an urgent case even as the Mexican industry's box-office earnings continued to rise at a rapid pace in Colombia (*El Tiempo*, 10 January 1954, p. 13).

THE LAST YEARS OF THE GOLDEN AGE

Mexican cinema's popularity began to wane in Colombia only in the late 1950s, although not necessarily in absolute terms. A new generation of critics, including most notably the young Gabriel García Márquez, who believed that cinema should not be mere entertainment for the masses, but that it could be elevated to a sophisticated form of art, complained incessantly in journals such as *El Espectador*, *El Tiempo* and *Cromos* of Mexican cinema's repetitiveness and low artistic quality. For example, an article in *El Tiempo* (27 January 1955, p. 18) is titled 'Mexican Cinema: Notorious Deficiency in Quality'; while film criticism in *Cromos* regularly complains that 'there is no solution for Mexican cinema' (24 May 1954, p. 49). A review of the popular Libertad Lamarque–Pedro Infante vehicle *Ansiedad* (Miguel Zacarías, 1953) proposes: 'The Mexican movies that have been arriving lately to the country are so noxious that it would be worth studying limiting their importation or banning those that are lacking in aesthetic value' (12 July 1954, p. 21). García Márquez claims that the artsy Franco-Mexican collaboration *Les orgueilleux* (Yves Allégret and Rafael Portas, 1953), which portrays 'a Mexico that is livelier, more visceral, more human and authentic than in all Mexican films, including the best of Emilio Fernández', could teach 'an exemplary lesson' to Mexican film-makers (*El Espectador*, 13 November 1954, quoted in Gilard, vol. 2, p. 58) in an era when Mexican production can be summed up, as he put it, in the phrase 'progressive decadence' (*El Espectador*, 31 December 1954, quoted in Gilard, vol. 2, p. 434). But even as Mexican cinema ceased to keep up with changing tastes of elite audiences, advances in production technology, intensified competition from Hollywood and Europe, and the rise of the new medium of television, it continued to draw audiences in Colombia, especially among less-educated publics, with Cantinflas's *Abajo el telón* (Miguel Delgado, 1955) making headlines by playing simultaneously in thirty-five Colombian theatres upon its Colombian release in 1956 (*Cinema Reporter*, 29 August 1956, p. 22), and the Mexican industry's earnings from the Colombian market went on growing well into the 1960s, peaking only in 1963, with Colombia remaining Mexico's second-biggest foreign market, after Venezuela (Heuer, pp. 72, 93).

However, as the Mexican cinema project gradually lost prestige, Colombians' last major collaborations with it were increasingly impoverished. Alfonso López Michelsen, a highly respected Colombian intellectual and politician – son of former president Alfonso López Pumarejo, and a future president himself (1974–78) – exiled with his family in Mexico from 1952 to 1960, published *Los elegidos* there in 1953, a novel that according to García Márquez would provide the argument for a Mexican movie script (*El Espectador*, 10 December 1954, p. 4, quoted in Gilard, vol. 3, p. 942). This planned collaboration brought Mexican producer Alfonso Rosas Priego, along with German-born director Alfredo Crevenna (a veteran of Mexico's industry), to Colombia to seek exteriors to film typical landscapes, cityscapes and touristic locations; *El Tiempo* reported enthusiastically that 'it will be a propaganda film for our homeland, worthy of our country's prestige and importance', realised with the enviable budget of $100,000 and the collaboration of some of Mexico's greatest – still to be named – stars (13 February 1955, p. 18). The project, however, did not turn out as planned, with Crevenna's landscapes being used instead for *Pueblo, canto y esperanza* (1956), a film that included a 'Colombian episode' (not based on López Michelsen's work) as one of the film's three (the others being Mexican and Cuban). The movie, whose Colombian episode was directed by Crevenna, was produced not by Rosas Priego but by Alfonso Patiño Gómez. The film did feature several major stars, including Pedro Infante and Joaquín Pardavé, with the Colombian piece acted by Roberto Cañedo, Columba Domínguez and Víctor Manuel Mendoza, all acclaimed actors, and cinematography by Gabriel Figueroa. While *Pueblo, canto y esperanza* was reasonably well made, it did not generate buzz anything like that of *Simón Bolívar* or *La vorágine*, and the fact that the Colombian episode was reduced to a third of the screen time was undoubtedly a disappointment to those who had been expecting a Mexican film dedicated to promoting Colombian culture.

Around the same time, López Michelsen signed on as co-producer with Rosas Priego of *Llamas contra el viento* (Emilio Gómez Muriel, 1956), a film about the adventures of three Mexican stewardesses in Venezuela, Cuba and Panama inspired by a poem by Colombian Porfirio Barba Jacob. While advertised initially in the Colombian press as being based on – once again – *Los elegidos* (*Cine-Noticias*, 27 August 1955, p. 18), there is no obvious connection to the novel in the final product, which is based on a script co-written by Crevenna and Edmundo Báez, with no mention of López Michelsen in the film's credits except as producer. Early reports on the making of the film signal difficulties in original plans to film in Bogotá, Medellín and Cali that resulted in a move to locations in Caracas, Panama and Los Angeles, as well as

Cartagena and Baranquilla (ibid.), although, according to the Mexican press, filming was actually realised only in Venezuela, Panama and Cuba (*Cinema Reporter*, 11 July 1956, p. 30). In the end, while actress Annabelle Gutiérrez quotes the Barba Jacob poem with exaggerated frequency throughout the film, and Colombian musicians Alejandro Durán and Delia Zapata Olivella perform, Colombian culture in the film is overshadowed by that of Venezuela – and that of Panama (which had been a part of Colombia until 1903). In a film co-produced by a Colombian that 'functioned to allow Mexican cinema to throw a complacent gaze, in full colour, over its "natural markets"' (Emilio García Riera, quoted in Tirado, p. 305), it is striking that Colombia again played a supporting role. Meanwhile, in Venezuela, a country that was featured centrally in the film's plot, *Llamas* provoked 'an angry protest, indicating as unjust and totally erroneous the idea of collaborating in a cinematic "pool", putting in 33 per cent for a foreign production without any merit or value' (Tirado, p. 305). Despite its apparent positive, if muted, reception in Colombia (*El Cine Gráfico*, 21 October 1956, p. 3), this film marked the end of López Michelsen's brief period of activity in the Mexican film industry, and more or less the conclusion, as the industry fell ever deeper into economic crisis, of its interest in promoting Colombian culture.

THE IMPOSITION OF MEXICAN CINEMA

An anonymous critic in Colombia observed in 1942: 'In the fields of fashion, tastes, aesthetic preferences, everyday and sentimental life, cinema exercises an absolute tyranny' in its ability to impose its worldview on audiences (*El Tiempo*, 12 December 1942, p. 5). He was conscious of how Mexico had recently 'imposed and popularised its music, its dress, its customs, its monuments and natural wonders' on Colombian audiences (ibid.). Colombians were aware that Mexicans were quite conscious of the power of influence of their film industry. An excerpt from an article published in the Mexican journal *Revista de América* confirmed this:

> Without any doubt Mexican cinema has become one of the most efficient instruments of propaganda for our country throughout the world. It takes to America, Africa, Asia, Europe cinematographic productions that present the problems, life and men of Mexico, and those works obtain praises for Mexican producers and artists. But, in addition, it exercises over the men and women of Hispanoamerica an irresistible attraction. (Quoted in *El Tiempo*, 11 December 1949, p. 15)

There was some resentment in Colombia for Mexico's powerful self-promotion through its cinema across all of Latin America. Mexico's music, its customs, its folklore, its dress all became well known everywhere. Mexican *ranchera* music, Colombians complained, had become more popular than the Argentine tango. Jorge Valdivieso Guerrero, in an article in which he interviews Argentine singer and actress Libertad Lamarque, opines:

> Tangos and milongas and Libertad Lamarque are from other times, from another epoch that will be unforgettable, like the memory of Gardel. The films then were only a pretext for the

songs, sentimental tangos and milongas whose notes have been silenced by the loud brashness of Jorge Negrete and his followers. Even in old Buenos Aires, you hear only *sones jaliscenses* and *huapangos*. (*El Tiempo*, 31 May 1946, p. 18)

As Colombian poet Gregorio Castañeda Aragón noted in an article published in 1943, a biting criticism of Mexican cinema for its lack of thematic or stylistic innovation, just as Mexican film 'has been gradually dislodging US film, Mexican songs have been taking over the continent. Other Latin American countries do not count at all. Regarding Colombia, *pasillos* or *bambucos* are never heard in the north' (*El Tiempo*, 19 January 1943, p. 4). Amid the clamour of a Pedro Infante tour appearance that brought an estimated 15,000 spectators to Plaza Santamaría in Bogotá, a reporter observed meekly that Colombians 'become excited and joyful to the point of delirium with the music that comes from Mexico' and that Latin Americans adore Mexican artists 'more than their own singers' (*El Espectador*, 30 May 1954, p. 9).

Recent studies have shown how musical genres such as the *bolero* functioned to promote a Latin American cosmopolitanism (e.g., D'Lugo, 'Aural Identity' and 'Gardel'). In the context of Colombia, Carolina Santamaría Delgado has studied the particular issue of the consumption of the *bolero* in the context of 1930s–50s Medellín, concluding that this cosmopolitanism 'constructed as sound and image by the Mexican cultural industries was assimilated and adjusted by local Medellín society to articulate its own values and prejudices', thus emphasising not only the importance of the cultural power exercised by Mexico's music and film industries, but also the agency maintained by consumers in decoding and interpreting the products they received. In Medellín, consumption of Mexican *boleros* by middle-class consumers 'served to clearly demarcate differences of class, race and sex' in ways that differed from those in which these categories were understood in Mexico (Santamaría Delgado). In other words, while the industries maintained control of what products were amply circulated, they could not fully control the process of audience reception.

On the other hand, just as Hollywood imposed its worldview on its international audiences, promoting an idealised 'American way of life,' Mexico achieved something similar – and in countries like Colombia that shared Spanish as their native language, Mexican film also served to 'normalise' Mexican-style Spanish in terms of pronunciation, vocabulary, inflection, etc. Reporter Jorge Cabarico Briceño was aware of this issue, as is evident in a pointed question he asks Colombian actress Alicia Neira regarding her experience working in Mexican film: 'Why do foreign artists adopt a Mexican accent and idiomatic expressions soon after going to live in the country? Do they oblige you or imply that you must do so?' (*El Tiempo*, 9 December 1950, p. 19), to which Neira replied in the negative, claiming that she just picked up a Mexican accent naturally by living there. Although it should be noted that the Colombian press shared Mexicans' indignation when Spanish authorities decided to dub with Spanish voices a pair of Mexican films 'because "the language of the Mexicans" is not understood in Spain' (quoted in *Magazin Dominical*, 17 January 1954, p. 24), and never discussed substituting Colombian soundtracks for those already recorded in 'Mexican'.

By the end of the golden age, the average Latin American film fan knew a great deal about life in Mexico: history, landmarks, customs, music, food, geography, popular legends, city life, details of national culture of which few Mexicans had corresponding knowledge regarding any other Latin American country, and which in some cases did not even experience wide diffusion at a national level due to the lack of strong domestic cultural industries.

CONCLUSIONS

What some critics have seen as 'the powerful influences ... of Mexican cinema, probably more assimilated than is usually assumed' (Salcedo Silva, p. 195) undoubtedly had far-reaching effects on Colombian culture. While this chapter's objective has not been to trace out specific influences, it has attempted to get a pulse of Colombian audience reception of Mexico's films during its golden age. This enthusiastic reception of many films, including some that featured Colombian actors, history or story lines, was based on an identification with a product that not only represented recognisable Latin American characters, landscapes and cityscapes, sensibilities and values, traditions and lifestyles, but also signalled the potential for Latin American success and visibility in a high-tech industry at an international level. Whether Mexican cinema determined the content of Colombia's incipient attempts to create its own industry is debatable, but Mexican cinema's ability to beat Colombian cinema out of existence during the period is evident. In the end, one conclusion is clear: Mexican golden age cinema indeed imposed itself in Colombia, a situation that would repeat itself in another of Mexico's largest markets of the era, that of Venezuela.

3

Mexico's Appropriation of the Latin American Visual Imaginary: Rómulo Gallegos in Mexico

Robert McKee Irwin

VENEZUELA: MEXICAN FILM'S BIGGEST AUDIENCE

The film exhibition business took root gradually in Venezuela, but once it became clear that a film product was available that had long-term appeal to the Venezuelan masses, the country quickly became one of the most important markets on the continent. At the end of the 1930s, capital city Caracas had only eighteen formal theatres – as opposed to travelling exhibitors that improvised shop in traditional theatres, temporary structures such as tents, or in other non-dedicated spaces – but a decade later there were over sixty (Roffé, p. 245). At the national level, one source counts 111 theatres (including mobile ones) in 1936, a number that spikes to 147 within two years, reflecting the growing financial success of film entrepreneurs (distributors, exhibitors) in the country (ibid., p. 246). This particular moment of rapid growth coincides with the excitement generated over the film *Allá en el Rancho Grande*, which opened in Mexico in late 1936 and became a major hit in Venezuela in 1938 (Hernández, p. 17), outdoing 'even the biggest Hollywood-made product' (anonymous critic quoted in/translated by Alvaray, p. 34). In 1936, US-produced films held a 91 per cent market share in the country, but within two years the rapidly increasing popularity of Mexican as well as Argentine films had cut that percentage in half (Roffé, p. 250). Indeed, distributor and sometime producer Salvador Cárcel, one of the leading forces in bringing Mexican cinema to Venezuela during its golden age, got his business off the ground with the profits earned from Mexico's first box-office blockbuster (ibid.). Another important event promoting the movies as a major national pastime was the launching in 1940 of *Mi Film*, one of the most important movie magazines in Latin America during the period. In 1940, Venezuela ranked seventh in Latin America in number of functioning movie theatres, following, in order, Brazil, Argentina, Mexico, Cuba, Colombia and Peru (Tirado, p. 81). However, growth accelerated once more in the 1940s, with the total number of movie theatres in the country doubling again by 1945 (ibid., p. 310), and Venezuela's market overtaking that of Peru (Ramsaye, *1947–48*, p. xv), and film spectatorship peaking only around 1960 both in terms of absolute number of spectators and in attendance per capita (Roffé, p. 248). Venezuelan audiences' partiality for Mexican film remained notable, and by the late 50s, Venezuela represented by far Mexico's largest foreign market, bringing in significantly more than number two market Colombia, and three to four times the box-office earnings of third-place earner Peru by the end of the decade (Heuer, pp. 71–3).

Film came to occupy a very important place in Venezuelan culture, perhaps because it was endorsed by a popularly elected president and leading intellectual of the era. Rómulo Gallegos, author of several of Venezuela's great national novels, including *Doña Bárbara*, *Cantaclaro* and *Canaima*, among others, maintained a strong interest in the medium, first attempting to help try to establish a national film industry in Venezuela, and later seeing greater potential in producing film versions of some of his greatest works in Mexico. Initial forays included adapting his early novel *La trepadora* into a screenplay in 1925 for a silent film of the same title that he co-directed with Edgar Anzola, and significant participation in the production enterprise Ávila Films, producer of *Juan de la calle* (Rafael Rivero, 1941), for which Gallegos authored the screenplay. However, by the early 1940s, it was clear to Gallegos that Venezuela lacked the resources to produce a film of the quality that his works deserved. During a period of less than three years, Gallegos participated as screenwriter in the production of five films, four of which were based on his novels: *Doña Bárbara*, a remake of *La trepadora* (Gilberto Martínez Solares, 1944), *Canaima* and *Cantaclaro* (Julio Bracho, 1946), the fifth being an adaptation of a short story, *La señora de enfrente* (Gilberto Martínez Solares, 1945). The year following the Venezuelan premiere of the last in the series, *Cantaclaro*, Gallegos ran for president. He won and took office in early 1948 – although, before the year was out, his liberal government was overthrown by a military coup, which would keep him in exile until 1958. In the meantime, a sixth Mexican film was made, *La doncella de piedra* (Miguel Delgado, 1956), based on Gallegos's novel *Sobre la misma tierra*. Whether or not Gallegos's participation in the Mexican film industry contributed significantly to its economic success in Venezuela, what is clear is that no other Latin American country saw so many of its greatest literary works and icons represented by Mexico's golden age film industry. This chapter will examine the circumstances behind Gallegos's collaborations with Mexican film studios, the reception of his films in Venezuela and the cultural implications of these endeavours.

THE EARLY YEARS OF THE MOVIE INDUSTRY IN VENEZUELA

Venezuela's first feature-length dramatic film was *La trepadora*, a major hit, achieving distribution for the first time for a Venezuelan film in Colombia, Peru, Chile and Argentina (Tirado, p. 32). Gallegos, who not only wrote the screenplay, but also collaborated in the film's direction with Edgar Anzola, was meticulous in his attention to how his novel was adapted to the new genre of film, and went so far as to pull the film from screens at the height of its popularity for a re-edit, with the ostensible goal of making the film more comprehensible. The consequence, according to critics, was that it ended up too 'literary', which explained its disappointing box-office results following its rerelease (ibid.), a criticism that would remain with Gallegos throughout his career as a screenwriter.

However, in the early years, almost all films screened in Venezuela were imports, principally from Hollywood, as well as from Italy and France. While a few films began to arrive from Spain and Argentina, very few silent or early sound-era films from Spanish-speaking countries made it to Venezuela. Although as late as 1934 no Mexican films at all had been screened in Venezuela (Soto Ávila, p. 53), by 1935 early sound films such as *Chucho el Roto* (Gabriel Soria, 1934) began to show in Caracas (Sidorkovs, p. 71). With the huge success of *Allá en el Rancho Grande* a few years later, Spanish-language film began to take over the Venezuelan market. Indeed, *Rancho Grande* set box-office records in Venezuela (Alvaray, p. 34), giving Mexican cinema an early edge on its Argentine competition, especially among the masses, due to the 'prestige' it held for its 'authenticy'. As Venezuelan film historian Antonio Soto Ávila puts it, 'the cult of machismo that that folklore brought with it incited feelings of complicity and satisfaction among peoples living in submission and humiliation, as do the majority of Latin Americans' (p. 71). As in Colombia, one immediate reaction was a desire to recreate the Mexican film industry's paradigm for success in Venezuela: 'Venezuelan producers copied not only Mexico's mode of film production but also its narrative and formal patterns' in hopes of reproducing Mexico's formula for box-office success (Alvaray, p. 37). This endeavour would prove impossible (Sidorkovs, p. 92); while a few entrepreneurs attempted to establish some film-producing infrastructure in Venezuela, Mexico's industry began to fabricate and inspire dreams, including 'the longing to know Mexico and the new idols that its cinema introduced' (Soto Ávila, p. 94), establishing, as it were, Mexican culture as an important part of Venezuelan everyday life.

MEXICAN CINEMA 'SE ESTÁ IMPONIENDO'

Something of an addiction began to form among Venezuelans. As we have seen, the Mexican industry, which had begun to lose market share to Argentina in the early 1940s, by 1942 was establishing itself as the undisputed market leader, earning its 'definitive consolidation' among Spanish-language producers in the Venezuelan market (from *Social Cine*, a short-lived journal published in Caracas, reprinted in *Cinema Reporter*, 12 June 1942, p. 8). Indeed, during the first three months of 1942, among forty-nine movie premieres in Venezuela, including thirty-four Hollywood pictures, nine from Argentina and only six from Mexico, four of the eight biggest box-office triumphs were Mexican, with *Flor de fango* (Juan Ortega, 1941), *La liga de las canciones* (Chano Urueta, 1941), the Cantinflas film *El gendarme desconocido* (Miguel Delgado, 1941) and Jorge Negrete's smash *¡Ay, Jalisco, no te rajes!* (Joselito Rodríguez, 1941) playing at least two weeks in first-run cinemas (*Cinema Reporter*, 12 June 1942, p. 8). By early 1943, it was being reported that earnings for Mexican films in Venezuela had increased fivefold (*El Cine Gráfico*, 21 March 1943, p. 2). As was occurring through much of Latin America, 'Mexican films, due to their quality, are imposing themselves decisively in the hearts of our audiences' (*Cinema Reporter*, 12 June 1942, p. 8).

DOÑA BÁRBARA: MEXICAN CINEMA 'SE HA IMPUESTO'

Rómulo Gallegos got caught up in the excitement of the rapidly expanding international film industry and, some sixteen years after his initial venture into silent cinema, he joined forces in 1941 with a group of local entrepreneurs to found Estudios Ávila, with the goal of establishing a high-quality national industry in Caracas.

María Félix stars in the Mexican film version of the great Venezuelan novel *Doña Bárbara* (1943)

Gallegos's ultimate goal from the beginning was to film his most acclaimed novel, *Doña Bárbara*, a project he had already been discussing with executives in Hollywood, where Joan Crawford would act in the starring role – although Gallegos himself would have preferred popular Hollywood-based Mexican actress, Dolores del Río (Tirado, p. 81). However, *Doña Bárbara* would be filmed by neither a Hollywood studio nor Ávila, whose first and only feature film would be *Juan de la calle*, scripted and produced by Gallegos, and deemed in one early review 'the first movie filmed in Venezuela worthy of being shown, as much for its technical merit as for its story, in any cinema abroad' (*El Universal*, 10 December 1941, quoted in Tirado, p. 89). The film, about a street kid who gets into trouble and ends up being saved by admitting himself into a reform school for juvenile delinquents, was widely praised in the Venezuelan press (Tirado, pp. 89–91), but in the end did not earn a profit, which would lead to the liquidation of the Ávila venture (Izaguirre, *Acechos*, p. 58).

    Much more profitable was the release of the Mexico-produced *Simón Bolívar* (see discussion in previous chapter), which was 'the most important event in Venezuelan life, at least as far as cinema goes', in the early 1940s (Izaguirre, 'Del infortunio',

p. 118), and its success, along with that of other films of lesser critical acclaim, began to lead to an ever warmer reception of Mexican films in Venezuela. In early 1943, for example, Cantinflas's *Los tres mosqueteros* (Miguel Delgado, 1942) was breaking box-office records in Caracas (*Cinema Reporter*, 26 February 1943, p. 32), a city in which no less than eleven Mexican films were playing at once (*Cinema Reporter*, 19 February 1943, p. 31), a figure that would grow to fourteen just a few months later (*Cinema Reporter*, 26 June 1943, p. 28).

The technological capabilities and increasingly vast international reach of Mexico's film industry were not lost on Gallegos, who, as Estudios Ávila fell apart, departed for Mexico to continue to pursue his dream of making feature films of his best novels, especially *Doña Bárbara*. This time, his luck would be better. His presence in Mexico generated a buzz from the beginning (*Cinema Reporter*, 13 November 1942, p. 1; 20 November 1942, p. 3), while in Venezuela speculation on the casting of the film began almost immediately, with the names of Dolores del Río, who had recently returned from a successful career in the USA to begin acting in her native Mexico (her first Mexican film, *Flor silvestre*, under the direction of Emilio Fernández, would debut in April) and the lesser known Isabel Corona (*Mi Film*, 28 January 1943, p. 5) immediately suggested. Ultimately, *Doña Bárbara* would be the career-defining film for another lesser-known but promising actress, María Félix, who from this film on would be forever known as 'La Doña' and 'La devoradora de hombres' [the man-eater]. The definitive casting was soon announced, also featuring Julián Soler (now Mexico's quintessential Venezuelan leading man: first as Simón Bolívar, now as Santos Luzardo), Adrián Soler and María Elena Márquez (*Mi Film*, 25 February 1943, p. 5), whose photos would appear a few weeks later in *Mi Film* (11 March 1943, p. 10).

This film would be a major commercial success, would play a key role in the Mexican film industry's strategy of US-backed internationalisation and would ultimately become an all-time classic of Mexico's golden age (Tirado, p. 111), all while firmly establishing Gallegos's importance as a major player in Mexican film – certainly making him the literary author of greatest international importance to enter into direct, hands-on collaboration with film-makers. Promoted internationally to be a major blockbuster – for example, earning a full-page spread in the weekly *Sábado*, where it was billed as 'the loftiest and best-realised of Mexican film production' when it debuted in Colombia in 1944 (27 May 1944, p. 7) – it opened to rave reviews in September of 1943 in Mexico (*Mi Film*, 1 October 1943, p. 5) – where its premiere would be marked by gestures of goodwill, including a benefit screening for flood victims in Venezuela (*Cinema Reporter*, 18 September 1943, p.13), with news arriving in Venezuela just in time for its premiere in Caracas (*Cinema Reporter*, 30 October 1943). It opened on 21 October in Caracas, where it was promoted with María Félix featured on the cover of *Mi Film* (21 October 1943) and a special edition of the daily newspaper *Mi País* (Tirado, p. 112). Its Venezuelan premiere was attended by President Isaías Medina and by Gallegos himself (*Mi Film*, 4 November 1943, p. 5), the author immediately proclaiming that he was pleasantly surprised and entirely satisfied with the result of his collaboration in Mexico (*Mi Film*, 21 October 1943, p. 15).

The film quickly turned him into 'the author of the moment' (*Mi Film*, 4 November 1943, p. 5), and earned him a formal homage event in Mexico (*Mi Film*, 6 December 1943, p. 15), as rumours of additional projects began to circulate, including one that would feature another rising Mexican star, Jorge Negrete (ibid., p. 14). Venezuelan distributor, Salvador Cárcel, meanwhile, gushed that he expected *Doña Bárbara* to be the biggest hit of the year (*Cinema Reporter*, 25 September 1943, p. 27). Indeed, the film, whose premiere showing in Mexico lasted an impressive six weeks (Paranaguá, *Tradición*, p. 113), would bring in the largest worldwide returns of any Mexican film for the third trimester of the year (Tirado, p. 112), and would break 'all cinematic records' in Venezuela (*El Cine Gráfico*, 31 October 1943, p. 8).

In Venezuela, while the release and international box-office triumph of the film generated excitement and a certain patriotic glee, the film itself drew mixed reviews. An inevitable problem had to do with authenticity. While audiences outside of Venezuela, whether in Mexico, Chile or Spain, would not likely notice or care, in Venezuela details – such as scenes in which the plainsmen used pillows on their hammocks or donned Mexican-style serapes, or in which a rural political boss wore gloves – weighed heavily on some audience members, who were not trusting of Mexico's ability to represent a work of such symbolic weight for Venezuelan national culture as *Doña Bárbara*, critiques with which Gallegos himself was forced to concur (*Cinema Reporter*, 27 November 1943, p. 4). Some reviews focused on issues less specific to the translation of Venezuelan culture to the Mexican film industry than to the translation of a literary work to film – indeed, the film has been roundly criticised for being too literary, especially for its reliance on dialogue rather than visual language. Venezuelan film historian Rodolfo Izaguirre sums up this critique:

> Mexico threw itself eagerly at the novels of Gallegos only to take from them the merely anecdotal, distorting the author's positivist preoccupations with the civilization–barbarism binary ... and exaggerating even more the literariness of the dialogues ... dehumanising the characters and turning them into strictly literary figures, portrayed, moreover, by a cinematography that preferred to locate them closer to the book than to the camera or the actors, and without making the least effort to situate them within the real geographic space of Venezuela since they were content to insert stock shots sent from the plains by Venezuelan cinematographer Antonio Bacé. (Izaguirre, 'Del infortunio', p. 119)

Ultimately the issue of the film being shot in Mexico would somewhat dampen the enthusiasm of its reception, and not all criticism in Venezuela has been positive, with one critic more or less gratuitously calling *Doña Bárbara* 'one of Fernando de Fuentes's worst movies' (Marrosu, 'Los modelos', p. 36). However, in 1943 Venezuela, the film was a must see, and 'an object of admiration without any precedent' (Soto Ávila, p. 130).

The film is about a young man (Santos Luzardo, played by Julián Soler) returning to his family's ranch after having studied at the university in Caracas, and being confronted with a backwards ('barbarous') provincial culture – represented in the figure of Doña Bárbara (played by María Félix) – that resists his attempts to modernise ('civilise') local land management, politics, etc. The ultimate victory of civilisation over barbarism is symbolised in Luzardo's education of and ultimate union with Doña Bárbara's daughter, Marisela Barquero (María Elena Marquéz), who was abandoned by her mother and raised wild, like an animal. While the plot is clearly set in the *llanos* [plains] of Venezuela, the script includes various regionalisms copied from the novel, and several supporting characters make a reasonable attempt at a Venezuelan accent, many of its actors, including María Félix, who presents a memorably iconic performance as a woman capable of paradoxically fusing feminine beauty and masculine power, did not come across as distinctively Venezuelan; indeed, there is much about the movie's main themes (civilisation versus barbarism, obstacles to modernisation, conflicts in traditional gender roles) that is universally Latin American.

The Mexican spin was that Gallegos's own objective was to 'bring Venezuela closer to the other countries of the Americas' and that '*Doña Bárbara* inaugurates ... the Era of Latin American Film', explicitly locating the grand designs of both Gallegos and the Mexican film industry within the context of 'our America' (*Cinema Reporter*, 27 November 1943, p. 4). It is, of course, no coincidence that *Doña Bárbara* was produced just at the moment that the Mexican industry, through circumstances stemming from the accidents of world war and the national politics of the various players in the Spanish film-making market, was able to position itself as the dominant industry in Latin America. And, ultimately, *Doña Bárbara* helped Mexico to realise its potential, particularly in Venezuela where Mexican production executive José Calderón reported just a month after the premiere of *Doña Bárbara* in Venezuela that 'our movies have taken over the market' (ibid., p. 9).

The use of the first-person plural is interesting in the two articles cited above, each taken from the same issue of *Cinema Reporter*. On the one hand, Gallegos is an artist of 'our America' (ibid., p. 5), a term, coined by José Martí, that weighs heavily in a history of rhetoric of Latin American fraternity and unity; on the other, the journal's editor Roberto Cantú Robert defines 'those fraternal peoples' as 'a continuation of ourselves' (ibid., p. 8). Cantú Robert perceives a cultural unity, but it is a unity centred around a *nosotros* [we] that is clearly Mexican: 'Our movies' (ibid., p. 9) are not Spanish or Argentine. A transformation is occurring in Venezuela, the result in part of the fraternal relations implied in the collaborative project of *Doña Bárbara*, but also of the 'magnificent acceptance' of Mexican films in general in Venezuela (ibid.). Calderón raves to Cantú Robert: 'they prefer our movies. You have no idea what everything that is Mexican means to these people. Mexican music is heard all over and their battle cry might easily be "Ay Jalisco ... no te rajes!"' (ibid.). It would seem that Mexican film's pan-Latin Americanist market strategy aims to replace nationalist sentiments with feelings of Latin American fraternity based upon symbols that are specifically Mexican. Indeed, recent critics have read the film, most especially the intervention of María Félix as an 'appropriation' of Venezuelan cultural production (Ocasio).

BOOM IN VENEZUELAN MARKET

This same period coincides with what seems to be a boom in growth in the film exhibition business in Venezuela in general, with annual spectatorship more than doubling between 1943 and 1944 (Roffé, p. 248), and with the growth in popularity of Mexican films a major factor in the fuelling of the boom. Already in late 1943 the number of Mexican films screening in Venezuela – thirteen (*Cinema Reporter*, 4 December 1943, p. 4) – was greater than the total in Cuba, where only ten Mexican films were in circulation (*Cinema Reporter*, 30 October 1943, p. 17) despite the fact that Cuba boasted double the number of theatres (*Cinema Reporter*, 10 November 1945, p. 27). By year end, Venezuela had become Latin America's biggest importer of Mexican movies (*El Cine Gráfico*, 19 March 1944) and, by April of 1944, the Venezuelan market seemed insatiable, with an amazing thirty-three Mexican films showing in a single week (*Cinema Reporter*, 15 April 1944, p. 30), approximately the same number – now thirty-one – simultaneously appearing on Venezuelan screens a few months later (*Cinema Reporter*, 30 September 1944, p. 29), and box-office records being set nationally and regionally – for example, with a single-day business of over 10,000 customers for three Mexican films in Maracaibo (*Panorama*, 5 July 1944, p. 9, quoted in Soto Ávila, pp. 149–50). By year end, Mexicans were declaring, using the familiar phrase, that 'our material has imposed itself definitively in Venezuela, the country that represents Latin America's best market' (*Cinema Reporter*, 11 November 1944, p. 31).

MORE GALLEGOS FILMS

Premiering in September of 1944 in Mexico and in November in Venezuela, *La trepadora*, an adaptation by Gallegos of the same Gallegos novel that had been produced in the silent age in Venezuela, was 'very well received', but ultimately did not mimic the box-office success or impact of *Doña Bárbara* (Tirado, p. 119). The Caracas-based magazine *Élite* raved,

> It is important that without reaching the level of *Doña Bárbara* it left us open-mouthed at its magnificence, and we must give thanks to director Gilberto Martínez Solares for a film that is full of light and romanticism and respects the colour and flavour of Gallegos's novel. (11 December 1944, quoted in Tirado, p. 119)

This film, not marketed like *Doña Bárbara* to become an international blockbuster, did nonetheless maintain some degree of the excitement generated in Venezuela by Gallegos's presence, now clearly established, in Latin America's leading film industry.

The elation was not to wane as another superproduction was known to be in the works, starring Jorge Negrete, who had already established himself as a megastar with the success of films such as *¡Ay, Jalisco, no te rajes!* and *Así se quiere en Jalisco* (this time he would be the protagonist of Gallegos's *Canaima*), with publicity circulation beginning soon after the premiere of *Doña Bárbara* in Venezuela (*Mi Film*, 6 December 1943, p. 14), and heating up with a visit by Negrete to Caracas a year later (*Mi Film*, 28 December 1944, p. 11). What one critic calls 'the furore for Mexican cinema' among Venezuelan spectators thus continued (Soto Ávila, p. 154), with twenty-nine films in exhibition in a single week in September of 1945 (*Cinema Reporter*, 22 September 1945, p. 27).

Canaima, another film with a civilisation versus barbarism theme (with a setting this time in the jungle during the rubber boom), which premiered in Mexico in early October of 1945, and in Venezuela on 16 December, once again was a major national event, winning fervent praise from reviewers in the Caracas-based journals *Últimas*

Noticias and *La Esfera* (21 December 1945 and 23 December 1945, respectively, both quoted in Tirado, pp. 131–2) – along with two Ariel awards in Mexico. The film played in Caracas for over a month, with three sell-out screenings three times a day during the week and five at weekends. However, amid all the applause, there began to emerge an increasing uneasiness that it was the Mexican industry that was making these great Venezuelan movies 'in the face of the inability to do so on the part of Venezuelan national cinema' (Tirado, p. 132).

Gallegos soon had to start defending his decision to work in Mexico. In an interview published in early 1946 in *Élite* and titled 'Venezuelan Cinema and Its Problems as Seen by Rómulo Gallegos', the great writer had to explain the lack of Venezuelan participation in his Mexican films: 'we're talking about an industry whose product, in this case movies, must, and it is important to understand this, feature names established through cinematic experience and popularity' (quoted in ibid., p. 151). Not only was Mexican Jorge Negrete chosen to star, but a high billing was also given to Argentine actress Charito Granados, with Venezuelans overlooked entirely. However, his interviewer expresses concern that Mexico 'has figured out how to capitalise, robbing subject matter and market share from us' (ibid.). Meanwhile, efforts would heat up to establish a national film industry in Venezuela, with the invitation of a team of Mexican consultants – although apparently similar endeavours in the past had failed when the Mexican 'experts' turned out 'not to know anything' (*Mi Film*, 13 December 1945, p. 26).

Elsewhere in Latin America, *Canaima* itself would be criticised for its lack of authenticity. Colombian writer Manuel Zapata Olivella had been in Mexico at the time of its filming, and decided to do some tongue-in-cheek investigative reporting, infiltrating the film's sets disguised as an extra. Zapata Olivella in fact posed as an authentic Venezuelan *cauchero* [rubber harvester] and was disappointed that many of the other extras – 'saloon singers, pretty boys planning to become stars without making any effort, sexual hybrids and delinquents' (*Cromos*, 11 June 1949, p. 43) – were not impressed. However, he was able to exude a certain authority, especially regarding costuming, due to his speech, which differed, of course, from everyone else's Mexican accent. His authority (along with his cover) was briefly challenged when they brought in Venezuelan actor Luis Jiménez, known as 'Pajarote', for the role he had previously played in *Doña Bárbara*, but he was relieved to learn that the Venezuelan was from Caracas and not the jungle provinces of the *caucheros*. Zapata Olivella played up his supposed expertise, criticising the outfits provided to the extras: 'This is all grotesque. I have never seen *caucheros* like us beardless and with well-ironed trousers in the middle of the jungle' (ibid., p. 42). When word got to director Juan Bustillo Oro that there was an authentic *cauchero* on site, he had everyone rough up their costumes according to his recommendations (ibid., 43).

While for many critics Negrete's star power as 'the most popular Mexican artist throughout the Americas' was an asset (Tirado, p. 132), helping to make *Canaima* 'one of the most clamorous hits' of the moment (*Últimas Noticias*, 21 December 1945, quoted in Tirado, p. 131), others found the film to be too literary (Izaguirre, *Acechos*, p. 63) and rough around the edges, with jungle backdrops represented via 'painted fabric' (Tirado, pp. 129–30). But Negrete in particular stood out in his role as Marcos Vargos for his acting limitations:

Negrete was unwilling to transform his own personality ... In the middle of the jungle, if Jorge Negrete had to sing, he would do it 'his way', in accordance with his personality, even when this was at odds with the character he was playing. (*Magazin Dominical*, 13 December 1953, p. 5)

The same critic concludes that 'he was a bad actor, an awful actor. And he really was because Jorge Negrete was born a *charro* and could not be anything else' (ibid., p. 43); thus there is 'a startling contrast between the two Marcos Vargases', the literary and the cinematic ones (Marrosu, 'Notas', p. 19).

The problem with Negrete is not seen in merely personal terms, but in national ones, and in the critiques there can be sensed a resentment of the infiltration of distinctly Mexican cultural traits into a monumental work of Venezuelan culture: 'Jorge Negrete ... brings to the character Marcos Vargas his "immortal *charro*" halo ... which makes possible that sex appeal of the badder the better, in its sickening sweet and typically Mexican incarnation' (ibid., p. 24). Jorge Negrete as Marcos Vargas – and the same could be said for María Félix as Doña Bárbara or Julián Soler as Simón Bolívar (or Santos Luzardo) or, the following year, Antonio Badú as Cantaclaro – 'by being very Mexican was very [Latin] American' (*Magazin Dominical*, 13 December 1953, p. 5); in other words, Mexico had become a synechdoche for all Latin America in a way that no other nation – not even Argentina, much less Venezuela, Cuba or Colombia – could. And when Negrete sings 'Maigualida' in the film – a song created for *Canaima* by the greatest music composer of Mexican golden age film, Manuel Esperón, who would go on to win his first Ariel for best musical score for *Cantaclaro* – the Venezuelan joropo, a genre with minimal diffusion outside of Venezuela (in comparison with the popularity of the Mexican *ranchera* or *bolero* throughout the hemisphere), becomes well known all over Latin America as part of the great Mexican *charro cantor*'s repertoire. The joropo is validated as a legitimate and worthwhile Latin American musical genre because Negrete (not Marcos Vargas) sings it, and Maigualida is better known as a female lead character, played by Gloria Malín, from a popular Mexican film (remembered by many through another Mexican reference, Negrete's hit song) than as a protagonist of a Venezuelan novel.

The process of identification with Negrete, then, implied for non-Mexicans a particular manoeuvre of interpellation that required subordinating national to Latin American identity, a Latin American identity defined always with a Mexican accent:

The Colombian from Caramanta sees Jorge Negrete with his guitar, his big sombrero, his pistols, and reacts to the hero in the same way as the little Indian from Tlaxcala, the *cholo* from Cuzco, the Juan Bimba from Mérida. He too longs to have a girlfriend with bottomless eyes and black braids, a spirited horse, a noble guitar full of songs, and a wonderful manly voice to sing them. Jorge Negrete was, in the movies as in life, what millions of American men, poor and sad, alone, without a woman, a horse or songs wished to be. (*Magazin Dominical*, 13 December 1953, p. 5)

With *Canaima*, the stream of Gallegos films appeared to have become steady, with *La señora de enfrente*, starring Sara García and Carmen Montejo, making its debut in Caracas in January of 1946, but this time with minimal impact. While the excitement of *Canaima* was revived when *Mi Film* named it picture of the year (30 January 1946, quoted in Tirado, p. 153), *La señora de enfrente*, apparently not much appreciated by audiences or the press, 'passed almost unnoticed from the first' (Tirado, p. 152). In March, *Cantaclaro* followed, generating, for the last time, significant buzz in Venezuela about a Venezuela-inspired Mexican film. Praised for its authenticity in *Últimas Noticias*, *Mi Film* added, 'Both from an artistic and a technical point of view, it deserves our most sincere praises' (quoted in Tirado, p. 154; see also *Mi Film*, 4 April 1946, p. 14). By this time, Gallegos was immersed in local politics as a player in a 1945 coup d'état that would elevate him to a brief stint as president for ten months in 1948, until he would, in turn, be deposed in a military coup. While some contemporary critics have generally labelled *Cantaclaro*, along with most or all of the Gallegos films, 'mediocre' (e.g., Izaguirre, *Acechos*, pp. 115, 119), it has for others gone down in Venezuelan film history as 'a hit right on target' (Soto Ávila, p. 131). Again, there is a sense of pride in the criticism of the film at the representation of a great Venezuelan novel and of Venezuelan music on the silver screen in a context (that of Mexican golden age cinema) that guarantees a broad diffusion that Venezuela's own cultural industries were incapable of affording; however, despite the fact that the film is described as 'real' (*Últimas Noticias*, quoted in Tirado, p. 154 – no date given), more recent Venezuelan critics express an ever greater impatience with these films' lack of authenticity 'despite the effort of Mexican actors to speak with a startling singsong quality attributed to inhabitants of our plains' (Tirado, p. 154). With *Cantaclaro*, Gallegos once again came away with a film of the year award from *Mi Film*, along with the pleasure of seeing the film awarded three Ariels in Mexico, including one for Manuel Esperón for best musical score.

Cantaclaro's *Mi Film* award would essentially end the Gallegos era of Mexican film, a period short in time but long on impact. This high-profile collaboration would ensure that Venezuelans saw the Mexican film enterprise not as absolutely foreign, as was the case with Hollywood, but as one of 'our America' that was open to investing significantly in partnerships with Venezuelan collaborators – and that Mexicans, having established a substantial and loyal market in Venezuela, saw the value in continuing to include Venezuela or Venezuelans somehow in Mexican films. Gallegos himself would not make any return to the film-making business, although rumours of Mexican film adaptations would continue for years. These rumours seemed to intensify during his presidency, when some Venezuelans hoped he would support the firm establishment of a national film industry (Tirado, p. 167). He was undoubtedly the only sitting president who was also a screenwriter, a fact not lost on Venezuela's diplomatic corps, which ran a high-profile screening of *Doña Bárbara* in the Venezuelan embassy in New York in early 1948 (*Cinema Reporter*, 13 March 1948, p. 32). In that year, it was reported that Mexico would adapt his novels *Pobre negro* and *Sobre la misma tierra* (*Cinema Reporter*, 31 July 1948, p. 27; 21 August 1948, p. 32). This latter novel would actually get filmed, but only years later, under the name *La doncella de piedra*. Its premiere in Caracas in January of 1956 did not make headlines. In fact, despite playing for several weeks in Caracas and Maracaibo, the press virtually ignored the film, perhaps because Gallegos remained in exile as an enemy of the military regime that had deposed him in 1948 and was still in power at the time (Tirado, p. 302). Luis Álvarez Marcano, in the Caracas daily *El Nacional*, was perhaps the only critic to

The final Gallegos film produced in Mexico, *La doncella de piedra* (1956)

address the film seriously, giving it a negative review, blaming the director and screenwriters for its flaws (ibid.). Rodolfo Wellisch, director of *Mi Film*, notes its use of new technologies (CinemaScope), but otherwise denies the film any mention in the journal (23 February 1956, p. 14).

FILM IN VENEZUELA BEYOND GALLEGOS

By the mid-1940s, film had become perhaps the preferred form of entertainment for Venezuelans, and many clearly favoured the Mexican product over that of any other production centre. Film historian Antonio Soto Ávila finds that, in the period 1946–52, 'the majority of Venezuelans continued enjoying Mexican film, which we assumed as our own' (p. 160), and that demand for Mexican movies continued to increase throughout the period in Maracaibo (ibid., p. 184), where they remained favourites for the majority until the end of the 1950s (ibid., p. 206). The journal *Cine-Venezuela* confirmed in 1949 the failure of the Argentine industry to compete with Mexico due to the former's 'distancing itself from popular themes' that Venezuelan audiences preferred (quoted in Tirado, p. 176).

Meanwhile, Venezuelan entrepreneurs continued to make mostly unsuccessful attempts to start up a national film industry in the country. Bolívar Films was the most promising project, winning a cinematography award at the Cannes Film Festival in 1951 for *La balandra Isabel llegó esta tarde* (1950), which imported top talent including Argentine director Carlos Hugo Christensen and Mexican box-office favourite Arturo de Córdova, earning praises from the Venezuelan press. *Mi Film* downplayed Spanish-born cinematographer José María Beltrán's award-winning work and made short shrift of the contributions of Christensen and leading man Córdova, instead praising the acting of Venezuelans Tomás Henríquez and Néstor Zavarce, Eduardo Serran's soundtrack and the screenplay based on a short story by Venezuelan writer Guillermo Meneses. While noting that the work is a collaboration with Argentines (including both technical crew and actors), reviewer José Hernán Briceño insists that 'thanks to Meneses and to those incomparable landscapes of ours ... *La balandra Isabel* is a 100 per cent Venezuelan film' (20 September 1951, quoted in Tirado, p. 230), in this way emphasising the importance of its having been not only based on a Venezuelan literary work – as was, of course, the case with the Gallegos blockbusters (and flops) – but also, in contrast with *Doña Bárbara* and *Canaima*, actually filmed in Venezuela and interpreted by Venezuelan actors. For others, Bolívar Films failed to contribute meaningfully to constructing an autochthonous Venezuelan cinema due to its 'reliance on foreign talent and narrative techniques' (Alvaray, p. 40). Unfortunately, despite the high-profile international award and general excitement it generated upon its release in Venezuela, *La balandra* has long been forgotten, while *Doña Bárbara* and *Canaima* are readily available today on DVD. Indeed, *Doña Bárbara* in particular is remembered as an all-time classic of the era for its importance in establishing once and for all the star power of María Félix. Regarding Bolívar Films, after a few years the enterprise fizzled after producing only a handful more mediocre films (Izaguirre, 'Del infortunio', pp. 124–5).

The more viable way for Venezuela to be involved in film producing was to enter into co-productions, a strategy which seemed to be paying off by the 1950s for Cuba. However, co-productions probably did not do a lot for national morale, especially when films came accompanied by advertising copy such as the following, which promoted the film *Los años han pasado* (Agustín Delgado, 1945): 'A Venezuelan movie, with music, story and songs that is very much ours, MADE IN MEXICO, with all the Aztec perfections' (quoted in Tirado, p. 155), with the strident reference to its Mexican production appearing as a certification of its quality – and an implication of the opposite had it been a purely Venezuelan project. Venezuela distributor Salvador Cárcel, in the Venezuelan journal *Cine-Canción*, felt the need to defend his collaboration as co-producer in a range of Mexican Films, including *Simón Bolívar*, *La trepadora*, *El secreto de la solterona* (Miguel Delgado, 1944), *Cantaclaro* and *Los años han pasado*, a pattern of international cooperation that would continue throughout the golden age of Mexican cinema. He explained that it only makes sense to invest in films that are likely to earn a profit: 'I am neither a benefactor nor a patron of the arts ... This is a business' (August 1946, quoted in Tirado, p. 156).

However, by the 1950s, when Bolívar Films – in which some still held hopes regarding its potential to lay the foundation for a national film industry capable of competing, as *La balandra Isabel* did, on an international level – chose to team with Mexican producers Gustavo de León and Modesto Pascó in making the film *El cuarto cerrado* (Chano Urueta, 1952), despite public enthusiasm, probably due to the presence of popular Venezuelan actor Luis Salazar in a featured role, and an extended premiere run, the press expressed outrage that Bolívar had chosen the route of a Mexican co-production, as opposed to a national project. In part reacting to this polemic, the Venezuelan Association of Film Exhibitors released a treatise that was published in six

Venezuelan producers could not capitalise on the critical success of *La balandra Isabel llegó esta tarde* (1950)

Caracas dailies (*El Universal*, *La Esfera*, *El Nacional*, *Últimas Noticias*, *El Heraldo* and *La Religión*). An important point was to defend the concept of the co-production, not as a drain of national funds to foreign companies, but as a project of 'mutual benefit' (Tirado, pp. 260–1).

While Argentine studios likewise engaged in numerous collaborative projects, Argentines saw Mexico's eagerness to enter into co-production agreements, in Cuba and Venezuela in particular, as a strategy to dominate those markets: 'it has allowed them to impose their films' (*Set*, 10 August 1949, quoted in Tirado, p. 176). Indeed, when foreign distributors – such as Cárcel – signed on as co-producers, a certain visibility for these films was guaranteed in their countries. Meanwhile, the power dynamic between the wealthy Mexican industry and Venezuelan entrepreneurs, of course, was not equal, although the latter would not have entered into agreements if there had not been reasonable chances of profitability. From a historical point of view, it is unfortunate to note that many co-productions are not remembered as such, with Mexican partners – in the case of *El cuarto cerrado* – routinely going down in history as sole producers (e.g., in Viñas, p. 130, or in the Internet Movie Database). While Venezuelan sources on film history list Salvador Cárcel as co-producer of dozens of Mexican golden age films, Mexican sources do not credit him at all. Even films that are key to Venezuelan film history, such as *La doncella de piedra*, which Venezuelan film historians report has having been co-produced by Venezuela Sono Films and Salvador Cárcel, are listed by Mexican sources with mentions of Mexican producers only

(Filmadora Chapultepec: e.g., Viñas, p. 162) – and it is this latter data that makes it into international references.

In any case, as early as the late 1940s, notwithstanding the dominant position Mexico's film industry had achieved among Venezuelans seeking cinema in Spanish, middle-class viewers in particular,

> had other aspirations that were not necessarily related to a preference for native culture, recalling that Mexican cinema was assumed to be our own. That middle class of professionals, oil executives, bureaucrats, businessmen, small industrialists, etc. began to reject Mexican film 'for not having the glamour of US cinema'. (Soto Ávila, p. 160)

As the 1950s advanced, 'colour, special effects, the American dream, television and other factors began little by little to win terrain from Mexican film' (ibid., p. 206).

MEXICAN FILM IN VENEZUELA

Many Venezuelans think of Mexican golden age film as part of their own national history, not because they think it was produced there, but because they know it was amply enjoyed among Venezuelans in the 1930s, 40s, 50s and beyond, as old favourites were shown again and again on television. Spectatorship is, after all, a form of cultural production. One critic avows, 'it's the cinema that we like' (Soto Ávila, p. 9), adding, using a phrase familiar to us, that 'Mexican cinema imposed itself because it responded to the popular needs of a public that saw in movies entertainment and spectacle to make them laugh, cry or simply have a different experience' (ibid.). But it could be said that, more than responding to Venezuelan tastes, Mexican cinema cultivated 'a structure of feeling' among its audiences, including those of Venezuela, through its major genres, especially melodrama, and its charismatic stars (Alvaray, p. 35).

The 'imposition' of Mexican cinema had to do with a process of identification in which a gap was filled for a nation that longed to see itself represented on the big screen. The absence of a cohesive and enduring native film industry in Venezuela was not a serious problem for Venezuelan filmgoers since audiences learned to identify with Mexican films: 'our peoples … saw themselves somehow reflected in Mexico's popular cinema, which, incidentally, helped establish a spirit of fraternity among Latin American communities' (ibid.). This process of identification was fostered and enhanced by collaborative projects with Venezuelans. As long as Salvador Cárcel continued to earn money from his investments in Mexican film as both distributor and co-producer, he would vigorously promote Mexican films not as foreign imports, but as Latin American products that naturally belonged on the Venezuelan market. Thus, it was not unusual to employ a rhetoric of shared culture in film advertising, with the quintessentially Mexican *Así se quiere en Jalisco* promoted as showing 'the bravura of our men, the passion and beauty of our women' (Sidorkovs, p. 189), allowing for an ambiguity in the reading, in which 'we' might be Mexicans (or even Jaliscans), but might also be 'Latin Americans'.

It is not insignificant that iconic figures such as Doña Bárbara or Marcos Vargas of *Canaima* are best known, in visual terms, through interpretations by quintessential

Mexican actors of its golden age of cinema (Félix, Negrete), or that the star of Venezuela's most lauded film of the era was Mexican (de Córdova). And while Venezuelans (Luis Jiménez Morán, Rafael Lanzetta, Rosa Castro) obtained minor roles in these films, their presence did little more than produce somewhat confusing 'soundtracks with mixed regional accents' (Alvaray, p. 36). Even the beloved Venezuelan poem 'Píntame angelitos negros' (Andrés Eloy Blanco) was popularised through its being put to music by Mexican composer Manuel Álvarez Maciste and later recorded by Mexican actor-singer Pedro Infante, who starred as well in the Mexican film by the same name (Joselito Rodríguez, 1948), whose non-Mexican references and characters were not Venezuelan, but Cuban.

As one critic laments:

> the influence of Mexican cinema on that of Venezuela in those years, the 1940s, was notorious. Not only with regard to formal aspects ... but also in the selection of themes, management of actors and opportunistic co-production agreements without any goals beyond that of making some money, which contributed to prolonging and reaffirming even more the Mexican cinematic presence among mindless Venezuelans incapable of finding another model to follow except that proposed by Mexican cinema. (Izaguirre, 'Del infortunio', p. 116)

Contemporary film scholar Luisela Alvaray confirms the power of Mexico's popular industry in shaping audience expectations and producers' conceptions for a national film product, concluding that 'Venezuelan producers copied not only Mexico's mode of film production but also its narrative and formal patterns, which guaranteed some commercial success at the local box office' (p. 37). Despite occasional bright spots such as *El balandro Isabel llegó esta tarde*, the moviegoing experience with which Venezuelans most identified during the 1940s and 50s was profoundly Mexican.

Even as Mexico's golden age fizzled in the late 50s, Venezuelans' still tentative attempts to produce their own cinematic vision have repeatedly been assessed as being deeply embedded in a Mexican aesthetic. For example, Venezuela saw a cinematic milestone produced in *Caín adolescente* (Ramón Chalbaud, 1959), a film emblematic of the transition from the golden age era of popular musical melodramas and comedies to the social cinema most associated with Latin American production in the 60s and 70s. Its director, Ramón Chalbaud, had trained with Mexican director Víctor Urruchúa while he was in Venezuela working with Bolívar Films, and was a great 'enthusiast of the Mexican golden age' (Alvaray, p. 43); according to Paulo Antonio Paranaguá, *Caín* 'includes many elements of the golden age of Mexican films: melodramatic climaxes, bar and the cabaret locations, typical characters, gestures and forms, and, above all, the young girl, who is seduced, abandoned, and continually rejected because of her loose morals' (quoted in ibid.). Even Margot Benacerraf's astounding documentary *Araya* (1959) has often been said to share a cinematic aesthetic with Sergei Eisenstein's *Thunder Over Mexico* (1933, remade as *Que viva México* [1979]), a film seen as fundamental to the aesthetic of the most emblematic golden age works of director Emilio Fernández and cinematographer Gabriel Figueroa, including also the latter's award-winning collaboration with Luis Buñuel, *Los olvidados* (1950) (Burton Carvajal, pp. 55, 61, 69). Even if *Araya* is 'the first authentically Venezuelan film' (Marcel Martin quoted in ibid., p. 67), or if *Caín adolescente* 'is a very clear vision of what our cinema ought to be' (Amy Courvoisier, quoted in Tirado, p. 338), beneath the surface of both lies the mark of the Mexican golden age film industry, which had entertained and perhaps overwhelmed Venezuelan audiences for so many years that it became difficult to imagine a national cinema that did not coincide somehow with the pan-Latin American aspirations of Mexico's golden age industry.

But it must also be remembered that Venezuelan culture was key to Mexico's transnationalist strategies of the 1940s and 50s. When Mexican cinema embraced Rómulo Gallegos and went on to produce a series of highly publicised and high-quality films based on his novels, it seemed that Mexican film was no longer just about *charros* and *mariachis*, but that it could also accommodate *caucheros* and *llaneros*. This inclusion, also noted in co-productions that featured Venezuelan actors such as Rosa Castro and Luis Salazar, helped facilitate this process of identification for Venezuelans, who were apt to overlook minor differences of accent with Mexican actors more than with Spaniards or even Argentines. Of course, the dominant force in film was always Hollywood, and while audiences were entertained by Hollywood films, deep identification with them was not so likely. But the idea of cultural similarity that was fomented by conditioning audiences to suspend disbelief at seeing Mexicans María Félix as Doña Bárbara, Julián Soler as Simón Bolívar and the quintessential *charro* Jorge Negrete as Marcos Vargas of *Canaima* enabled Mexican film to 'impose itself' comfortably into the Venezuelan market. As Soto Ávila puts it: 'This cinema is appreciated for a series of values common to our societies that serve as a reinforcement of tradition and as a resource to resist the tendency of western culture to dominate' (pp. 10–11). Indeed, the consumption of Mexican cinema was something of a political act of 'protest for the abuse of which we cinephiles in this part of the world have been victims, which concerns the exclusivity that Hollywood has imposed in cinematic product' (ibid., p. 11). Mexican cinema, then, was less imposition than redemption? Maybe so, but the question becomes more complicated when we take into account the consumption of golden age Mexican film in Argentina, the market belonging to its greatest rival.

4

Latin American Rivalry: Libertad Lamarque in Mexican Golden Age Cinema

Mónica Szurmuk and Maricruz Castro Ricalde

The departure of Libertad Lamarque for Mexico has become one of the great myths of Latin American cinema. Steeped in melodrama, a story that has circulated for decades asserts that, during the filming of *La cabalgata del circo* (Mario Soffici, 1944), Lamarque, one of Argentine cinema's biggest stars, squabbled with the young actress Eva Duarte and, in a moment of fury, gave her a *bofetada* [slap across the face], the culmination of a situation of deep tensions between the two of them. Soon afterwards, the younger actress, now married to President Juan Domingo Perón (and known as Eva Perón), endeavoured to make sure that Lamarque would never work again in Argentina. Lamarque has denied the accuracy of this story, as have historians (e.g., see Fraser and Navarro, p. 42); however, it is clear that the newly installed first lady was offended by certain attitudes of the radiant star, which led to the latter's decision to leave the country. Nuria Madrid de Susmel, daughter of film's screenwriter Francisco Madrid, who as a young girl assiduously attended the filming of *La cabalgata*, also refuted the story of the mythic *bofetada*, concurring that there were ongoing disagreements between Duarte and Lamarque during the shooting of the film, but insisting that there was never any physical aggression.

Of course, as frequently is the case with media anecdotes, this one has served the purpose of framing within the argument of a melodrama a much more complex story, indeed one whose broader context is that of the competition between the two most successful Spanish-language film industries, the role of the USA in the consolidation of Latin America's cultural industries and a series of prevailing tensions in international movie markets in the final years of World War II. This chapter will explore the industry battle between Mexican and Argentine cinema, which had been particularly intense since the latter half of the 1930s, but which would resolve itself in Mexico's favour by the mid-40s, a time when, as we have seen, Mexico's industry succeeded in imposing itself throughout the Americas, and thereby establishing its cinema as the most successful cultural export product of all Latin America. The particularities of the Peronist project, more concerned with internal development than expansion, contributed to the international decline of Argentine cinema, punished during the war by boycotts in other countries and by Argentina's exclusion from access to celluloid markets. The successful move of Libertad Lamarque to Mexico, where she worked steadily for thirty years, points to the Mexican industry's strategic flexibility in incorporating talent from other areas of the hemisphere.

Eva Duarte and Libertad
Lamarque in *La cabalgata
del circo* (1944)

Although, as this chapter will show, Lamarque was excluded from working in Argentina during the Perón presidency (1945–55), there were clearly other reasons for her exile. Mexico's was the most powerful industry in the Spanish-speaking world and therefore Lamarque's decision to develop her career there is not illogical. In addition, at the moment of her departure, the actress was having a series of professional and personal problems in Argentina, which she largely resolved by moving to Mexico. The endless number of starring roles that she was offered is testament to the durability of her continental popularity, the continued relevance of the tango (the musical genre for which she is best known as a vocalist) in Latin American popular culture, her definitive and long-term establishment as a screen superstar throughout Latin America, and the versatility of melodrama as the most appropriate genre for her starring roles as a mature actress.

This chapter's analysis of the Mexican–Argentine rivalry in Spanish-language cinema markets provides the backdrop for an analysis of Lamarque's decision to settle in Mexico, the role she would assume in Mexican golden age cinema beginning with her Mexican debut in Luis Buñuel's *Gran Casino* (1947) and the belated reception of her Mexican films in Argentina.

THE STRUGGLE OVER THE SPANISH-LANGUAGE MARKET

On 4 December 1942, the Buenos Aires-based movie magazine *Cine*, which since its launch only six months earlier had quickly established itself nationally as the industry's most respected journal, with regular participation of key industry insiders (including producers Francisco Madrid and Mauricio Rosenthal, director Luis Saslasky, one of the era's most prominent critics Domingo di Núbila and set designer Pablo Ducrós Hicken), printed a note titled 'Real and Potential Territories for Argentine Cinema', analysing the possible markets open to the industry, illustrated by a series of maps (of Europe, the Americas, the Philippines) (p. 4). Each country is indexed with a number that references a discussion on its potential as an export market. In addition to the obvious markets (Uruguay, Chile, Paraguay, Central America, etc.), the listed opportunities include countries of southeastern Europe and the USA. The rivalry between Mexico and Argentina is presented in terms of a sports competition: 'one wins one "round", the other wins the next ... in the tournament of the Spanish-speaking market in which Argentine and Mexican cinema have entered' (ibid.). In most markets, Mexico comes out the winner, with the exceptions of the River Plate nations and Cuba. In Cuba – as in Brazil – Argentina comes out ahead thanks to its female headliners Libertad Lamarque, Niní Marshall and Paulina Singerman. The analysis of this same theme in other similar journals of the early 1940s, including *Cine Argentino*, *Sintonía* and *El Heraldo del Cinematografista*, makes evident the preoccupation of Argentine film entrepreneurs and artists with the competition with Mexico, heightened by Mexico's privileged access to raw film stock.

Cine notes a year later, now with some preoccupation, that 'Mexican cinema is our clearest and most decided competitor', although it attempts to soften its position by turning to the rhetoric of panamericanist 'brotherhood' promoted at the time: 'They are not our enemy. They are a stimulus. They oblige us to stay awake' (30 April 1943, p. 2). Argentine film-making had taken off during the 1930s thanks to the international success of the tango and its emblematic figure, Carlos Gardel. According to the chronology laid out by Domingo di Núbila, the years 1939 to 1942 were Argentina's 'golden years' (García Reira, *Historia*, vol. 1). This brief bonanza was seen in Argentina's leadership role both in number of titles produced and in their circulation in Spanish-speaking countries, as well as in their quality and popular appeal. 'Neither Mexico nor Spain can compete with the booming evolution of Argentine cinema', declared Mexico's *Cinema Reporter* in a front-page headline of 1938 (29 July 1938, p. 1). Mexico's penetration into the Argentine market was also sparse at the time. Argentina's *Anuario Cinematográfico* of 1940 registers the exhibition of six Mexican titles, very few compared to the forty-seven locally produced films in circulation, although the figures are reversed with regard to Argentine pictures in exhibition in Mexico during the same period, with one Argentine film showing for every seven Mexican titles (*Cinema Reporter*, 30 April 1941, p. 1G; 20 June 1941, p. 1).

The Argentine industry's collapse is evident in comparing the fifty-six films produced in 1942, a year in which it came out ahead of both Mexico and Spain, to what followed in 1943. Optimism ruled most sectors of Argentina's industry in the years immediately prior to Perón's 1946 election. Lamarque herself, caught up in the enthusiasm, declared in 1943:

> Argentine cinema is in its great moment, the genesis of a formidable age to come, poised to attain the importance it deserves in the grand and fantastic world of celluloid. Our national cinema has now proven itself, taking its first solid steps and establishing the basis for greater accomplishments to come. (Quoted in *Cine*, 2 April 1943, p. 3)

although only a couple of weeks later, up and coming critic Domingo di Núbila, sensing a change in the air, would begin to publish more pessimistic forecasts (*Cine*, 16 April 1943, p. 2). While Mexico's alliance with the USA in the war gave the industry ample access to this indispensible raw material, Argentina's refusal to declare war on the axis powers earned it international sanctions, not only through the limitation of access to celluloid, but also through trade embargos, which besmirched the democratic image of the country, impacting on the reception of its movies elsewhere in Latin America. The Argentine press began to admit defeat, reporting ruefully that the Mexican industry 'has practically absorbed the movie market of Latin America. Argentine pictures have been utterly dislodged ... by Mexican ones'; while demand continued in a few countries, namely Cuba and Venezuela, 'in the rest of the continent, the Mexicans have imposed their films' (*El Cine Gráfico*, 3 October 1943, pp. 12, 19).

By the end of 1943, Mexico had produced practically double the number of films (seventy) that Argentina could muster (thirty-six) and, by 1944, the lack of national product opened up the market for imports; soon there were ten Mexican films showing in Argentina simultaneously, with an average of four new films premiering each month. Observers were in agreement: 'Mexican cinema's conquest of foreign markets has been definitive' (*El Cine Gráfico*, 9 April 1944, p. 2). Demoralising for the Argentine industry was the public response as the release of the Mexican comedy *Los tres mosqueteros* surprised everyone by breaking box-office records and running for three months in the same movie house in Buenos Aires, especially since its star, Mario Moreno, better known as Cantinflas, had been unknown in Argentina prior to that time (*El Cine Gráfico*, 16 April 1944, p. 6); Argentine film critics responded by naming *Los tres mosqueteros* the best Spanish-language movie of the year (*El Cine Gráfico*, 26 March 1944, p. 22).

Meanwhile, in postrevolutionary Mexico, the government fomented a nationalist discourse that translated into a profusion of cultural products that put forth a stereotyped image of Mexican culture. This de facto cultural policy led to an open dialogue among the largest production houses and representatives of the state, who were interested in offering support to ensure the continued prosperity of the Mexican industry. For example, in the face of union disputes in 1944–45, the intervention of Mexican president Manuel Ávila Camacho via union leader Fidel Velázquez of the powerful Confederation of Mexican Workers was evident. Later, various leaders of the National Association of Actors would take advantage of close ties to powerful politicians, including, in the case of Jorge Negrete, Miguel Alemán Valdés, whose presidential term ran from 1946 to 1952. In Argentina, in contrast, the strong reactionary right, following a 1930 coup d'état, would assume an ever greater power, which it would frequently exercise against the national film industry through decrees, restrictive legislation, censorship and even assaults on actors. By the time populist Juan Domingo Perón assumed office in 1945, the battle had been utterly lost: in that year Mexico produced eighty-two feature films versus Argentina's mere twenty-three (García Riera, *Historia*, vol. 4, p. 10). In the last few months of 1945, the Argentine industry was paralysed, launching no new films at all nationally (*El Heraldo del Cinematografista*, 19 December 1945, pp. 193–6).

WORLD WAR II

Despite the notable presence among Argentina's film industry executives, directors and technicians of Spanish republican exiles and European Jews (some exiles of

Nazism), there emerged an ever greater suspicion in an international context that the Argentine industry was collaborating with the Nazis. Tamara Falicov cites an accusation made by Vincent de Pascal in the *Hollywood Reporter* of 20 December 1941 about the putative links between the Argentine studio Sono Films and Nazi Germany, noting that no corroborating evidence of such a collaboration has been found (pp. 253–4). However, this was not an isolated declaration. In Mexico, *Cinema Reporter* published a story with the headline 'Nazi Film Contraband Discovered in Buenos Aires' (26 July 1942, p. 1) and, early in 1943, Argentina's *Cine* reported that 'in Cuba Argentine films are being called agents of Nazism' (26 February 1943, p. 3). That same year, in Mexico, alarmist headlines warned: 'Our Material in Buenos Aires in the Hands of Fascists: Danger' (*Cinema Reporter*, 3 April 1943, p. 31). Meanwhile, in evaluating the poor diffusion of Argentine films in Mexico, an argument pointed to 'a popular resentment for Argentina's delay in joining the United Nations ... and the fact that Argentine films never mention the world war, while Mexican movies are becoming more and more antitotalitarian' (*Cine*, 16 April 1943, p. 2). And if the identification with totalitarianism was not enough to elicit rejection, the Mexican media insinuated that Argentina was not exhibiting goodwill towards other regions of Latin America. There are multiple cases of this, including the launch of *Simón Bolívar* in Buenos Aires: 'Despite the silence of the local press regarding this film, it can be said, looking at public attendance, that it has triumphed' (*Cinema Reporter*, 26 July 1943, p. 31), and Mexican headlines such as 'Argentina Prefers US Movies' (*Cinema Reporter*, 28 September 1946, p. 17) suggest a disdain for Spanish-language production.

The accumulation of these ideas, regardless of whether they were based on facts, functioned marvellously for the Mexican film industry: while Argentine cinema was projected as fascist, Mexican studios invested heavily in configuring their industry as the great promoter of pan-Latin Americanism (see Castro Ricalde, 'Del panamericanismo'; Peredo Castro, *Cine y propaganda*, pp. 177–84). In Mexico, by the mid-1940s Argentina's reputation took deep root; upon Lamarque's death in 2000, amid solemn and nostalgic reminiscences, the Mexican press identified Perón as the 'military dictator who took in thousands of Nazis, which pushed Lamarque into exile in Mexico' (Moral, p. 10).

MEXICAN CINEMA IMPOSES ITSELF IN ARGENTINA

All these factors resulted, over the course of just a few years, in a reduced level of activity that generated an exodus – in some cases temporary, in others permanent – on the part of some of the Argentine industry's best-loved actors, along with directors, screenwriters and technical personnel. In 1946, despite problems in Mexico, including major labour issues, a number of Argentina's biggest stars, among them Luis Sandrini, Hugo del Carril and Tita Merello, spent much of the year working in Mexico. This was also the year that Libertad Lamarque took up long-term residency there. Other Argentines working in Mexico in 1946 included actors Juan José Cibrián, Néstor Deval, Nelly Edison (using the name Nelly Montiel), Inés Edmonson, Charito Granadas, Agustín Irusta, Amanda Ledesma, Ana María Lynch, Vicente Pádula, Héctor Palacios and Julio Villaroel; producer Juan José Guthman; directors Luis Amadori, Leo Fleider and Roberto Ratti; and screenwriter Enrique Santos Discépolo. During the same period, several Mexican film executives visited Argentina in search of actors, as well as to facilitate the dissemination of their films in Argentina – and, purportedly, that of Argentine films in Mexico (*Heraldo del Cinematografista*, 19 December 1945, p. 196).

Cinema Reporter's Roberto Cantú Robert visited Buenos Aires with regularity and, beginning in mid-1946, had a column in the Argentine journal *Heraldo del Cinematografista*, giving this Mexican industry insider a platform for reaching Argentine fans, whom he informed of Mexican studio activity, including the growing presence of Argentine stars there.

The Argentine industry's business model was also working against them, with problems of staff turnover among their foreign distributors (*Heraldo del Cinematografista*, 28 November 1945, p. 16), and generally poor organisation abroad (*Heraldo del Cinematografista*, 19 December 1945, p. 196). While Mexican companies had opted to sell their films directly, sending representatives to the most significant regional markets of Latin America to negotiate, face to face, with local distributors, Argentine firms, in contrast, preferred to sell their titles for a fixed sum. While this practice implied immediate cash payment, it annulled the possibility of negotiating box-office percentages. Mexico's sales system inspired greater confidence in the industry, which appeared to bet not only on its knowledge of audience tastes, but also on the conviction that the very volume of its production permitted the rapid substitution of one movie for another in the case that a given film did not attract the expected level of attendance. Mexicans followed a distribution model developed in the UK and the USA several decades earlier (Briggs and Burke, p. 196), subjecting distribution to movie 'chains' – in other words, subordinating the distribution of certain desired titles to 'package deals' containing other less interesting or lower-budget films. The productions of Cantinflas or other megastars could only be obtained for distribution if purchased along with a collection of other films. All of this assured that movie theatres dedicated to Spanish-language cinema would nearly always be occupied with Mexican product.

MOVIE MAGAZINES SET THE MOOD

The tone of journalistic texts did not help to raise spirits in Argentina. If there were serious and real problems in obtaining celluloid in Lamarque's homeland, in that of Dolores del Río this was not a concern at all, and the Argentine press regularly called attention not only to the crisis at home, but also to the bonanza abroad, as can be seen, for example in a feature story titled 'From a Mexican Daily: There Will Be No Shortage of Film for Our Movie Business' (*Cine*, 16 July 1943, p. 4), or another Argentine item that quotes Francis Alstock, Director of the US's Motion Picture Division of the Office of the Coordinator of Inter-American Affairs, from a story published in the Mexican press: 'the US film industry will collaborate in the Mexican production of Spanish-language movies "until Mexico succeeds in becoming the mecca of cinematic production in Castillian"' (*Cine*, 16 April 1943, p. 2).

A relentless rhetoric emerges in the Argentine press in its endless comparisons of the two film industries, emphasising the many cultural similarities between Mexico and the rest of Latin America, along with (albeit sometimes in the form of negation) the stylistic and thematic differences between Mexican and Argentine cinemas, with one typical article signalling, in hyperbolic terms, a cultural split in a discussion of 'the parallelism in tastes – often questioned to the point of speaking of divorce – of our audiences from those of other Spanish-speaking nations' in an article titled 'The Battle of Cantinflas' (*Cine*, 2 July 1943, p. 1), assertations supported by film criticism in other parts of the hemisphere. In Caracas, for example, critics in 1943 applauded Mexican cinema's ability to produce cinema of appeal 'for all audiences,' while criticising Argentine films, which tended to have 'generally poor arguments that are conceived out of a very narrow view of what the public really wants' (*Mi Film*, 5 August 1943, p. 22); Venezuelan film historian Antonio Soto Ávila concurs, noting that the Mexican industry came out on top because their films were 'more to the taste of the region's masses', to whom they came across as authentic, evoking a sense of 'complicity' (p. 71). In Colombia, critics believed that unwise tactics 'led Argentine cinema away from popular tastes' (Martínez Pardo, p. 152), while the Mexican industry was consistently 'attentive to Iberoamerican demand and fluctuating preferences' (Cuban film-maker Néstor Almendros, quoted in ibid., p. 152). Gabriel García Márquez, in his early career role as film critic, was of the same opinion: while initially Argentines had begun producing 'an authentically national cinema' (*El Espectador*, 27 November 1954, p. 4, quoted in Gilard, vol. 2, p. 390), eventually the Argentine industry settled into a style of 'production without a particular method, without a direction that would make it identifiable and create for it a sure public like that of Mexican cinema' (ibid., p. 391).

CULTURAL POLICY

In addition to international relations, domestic cultural policy also played a significant role in the dynamics of the rivalry. According to the Argentine film press, with the financial support it received, Mexico's industry was elevated to the level of those of France or the USA (*Heraldo del Cinematografista*, 26 September 1945, p. 139), while on the home front there was a proliferation of reports on closed studios, cancelled projects, frustrated film proposals and an utter lack of backing from the state: 'the film industry remains complicated because there is no official support' (*Heraldo del Cinematografista*, 28 November 1945, p. 179). Meanwhile, Mexican producers 'obtained from the government not only the suspension of taxes, but also the creation of the Banco Cinematográfico, created to grant them loans' (Sánchez, *Hojas de cine*, p. 140).

Although earlier administrations, notwithstanding their significant investments in national culture, virtually ignored the movie business, the presidency of Manuel Ávila Camacho (1940–46) was especially interested in stimulating production of films based on versions of Mexican history that supported the ruling party's vision and postrevolutionary discourse. Without openly manifesting its patronage, it offered monetary support necessary to bring such projects to fruition. *Cine*, however, presented a different interpretation of the 600,000 peso state subvention offered to director Julio Bracho in the making of the film *El cura Morelos*, based on the life of the independence-era hero (the final project ended up being a different one, whose focus was not Morelos, but independence heroes Miguel Hidalgo and Ignacio Allende:

La virgen que forjó una patria, 1942); the production subsidy was seen instead as a prize awarded to a promising young director for 'the noble artistic and spiritual lineage exhibited in his work, especially *Historia de un gran amor* (1942)' (15 January 1943, p. 2).

The atmosphere of a Mexican bonanza – high return on investment, availability of credit and a general optimism in the studios – was featured in the Argentine print media from as early as late 1942 (*Cine*, 9 October 1942, p. 2; 15 January 1943, p. 2). Commentaries like the following are a symptom of the sensation of being at a marked disadvantage that became more and more apparent as the decade wore on: 'The grim situation that Argentine cinema is going through is especially evident in the lack of news regarding production projects for 1946. We're at the end of October and no studio has come out with a filming plan' (*Heraldo del Cinematografista*, 24 October 1945, p. 157). Meanwhile, in Mexico, reports from the same period acknowledge the expectation of around 120 new films for the coming year. The announcement of the suspension ('for an undetermined period of time') of the activities of Argentina's Academy of Cinematic Arts and Sciences and the postponement in announcing its annual movie awards for 1944 contrasts sharply with the nominations for and awarding of international prizes for various Mexican films in this period, in places such as Locarno, Cannes, Venice, Moscow and at various festivals in the USA, and the growing lavishness in the awarding of Mexico's Ariel awards, in the style of Hollywood's Oscars, in Mexico City.

The Perón regime would adopt policies in 1946 that mirrored those in place or about to be enacted in Mexico. However, they came into play too late and in some ways produced effects opposite to those intended. Ana López mentions the establishment of obligatory quotas for distribution and exhibition of Argentine films, state funding for film production loans, laws requiring that given percentages of box-office income go towards financing new films and restrictions on foreign companies withdrawing earnings from Argentina (cited in King, p. 41). The consequences turned out to be adverse, given the prevailing atmosphere of state control and censorship: it was no secret that the Subsecretariat of Information and the Press decided which projects prospered and which were held back, and which films were exhibited, whether Argentine or foreign. Most screenwriters, directors and actors opted to remain silent, tacitly accepting the type of content that placated leaders – privileged themes of confrontations between the rich and the poor, social justice, alternated or combined with romantic or other ingenuous plots (Argente, 'Un maya', pp. 70–3) – or simply leaving the country in search of more creative opportunities – and while many went to Mexico, others found work elsewhere: for example, director Carlos Hugo Christensen ended up in Venezuela, where he earned a nomination in Cannes for the film *La balandra Isabel llegó esta tarde* (1950), an opportunity he never achieved in Argentina. This situation did not go unnoticed by local audiences, who quickly became bored with films that repeated the same themes and preferred to see their idols acting in the powerful Mexican industry.

Argentina's defeat went, therefore, far beyond questions of production volume, industry earnings, or the exodus of stars. It impacted on the social and cultural mood of the epoch. This situation perhaps contributed to the popularity of Eva Duarte de Perón, who with the theatricality of her public appearances and her carefully cultivated image as mother of the dispossessed embodied for the better part of a decade the image of a true star, the dazzling protagonist not of a movie, but of Argentine public life. She was just the kind of star figure that was lacking in the dim environment of national cinema.

MEXICAN STARS IN ARGENTINA

If Argentine cinema's actors, from minor players to the biggest stars, fled to Mexico in search of contracts, Mexico's greatest actors, in contrast, had the luxury of turning down advantageous offers such as the one Argentina Sono Films made to Jorge Negrete. He was to film in 1944 in Buenos Aires and maintain the rights for the film's box office in Mexico, but he didn't like the script and the project fell apart, despite having advanced substantially. Meanwhile, 'the most sought-after Argentine actresses filmed with him in Mexico and in that way the Mexican industry took advantage of his popularity in the southern cone' (Serna, p. 20). Thus he took top billing alongside Amanda Ledesma in a film distributed in Mexico as *Cuando quiere un mexicano* (Juan Bustillo Oro, 1944), a film released in Argentina under its original title, *La gauchita y el charro*. The change in name reveals where the international star power lay, sustained in Negrete's image as a stereotype of arrogant virility. Immediately afterwards, Negrete would film *Camino de Sacramento* (Chano Urueta, 1945) with Argentine actress Charito Granados, and would follow up two years later with *Gran Casino* with Libertad Lamarque.

Another case was that of Yucatec actor Arturo de Córdova, born Arturo García, whose stage name came from his time as a student in the Argentine city of Córdoba. Linked affectively and professionally to the region, he rejected, nonetheless, the offer from Sono Films executive Atilio Mentasti, who travelled first to Mexico and later to Hollywood in pursuit of the actor who had triumphed in such films as *Crepúsculo* (Julio Bracho, 1944), *La selva de fuego* (Fernando de Fuentes, 1945) and *La diosa arrodillada* (Roberto Gavaldón, 1947), accompanied by Gloria Marín, Dolores del Río and María Félix, respectively. 'To close the issue, Arturo asked for a very large amount of money.' But there were other reasons that finally determined his trip to Buenos Aires and, eventually, the grand triumph of *Dios se lo pague* (Luis César Amadoni, 1947), in which he co-starred with 'the great star of the Peronist cosmos', Zully Moreno (Argente, pp. 70–3). The contract that tied Córdova to Mexican producer Gregorio Walerstein obliged him to accept this project as the result of an arrangement arrived at between the Mexican mogul and an Argentine counterpart; in other words, if it were not for a legal obligation and a possible rupture with the powerful Walerstein, who was involved romantically with megastar Dolores del Río, he would never have agreed to film in Buenos Aires. In sum, the Mexican industry knew how to exploit the talent, beauty and prestige of its Argentine actors, while the cinematic enterprises of Argentina were losing their attractiveness for Mexican artists, who were becoming less and less interested in travelling to Argentina to work. What they preferred was to tour Latin America to capitalise on the popularity of their films and music, as they became idols throughout the region.

The fame of Mexican stars began to magnify in the early 1940s thanks to presentations organised in central plazas of major South American and Caribbean cities, including Havana, San Juan, Caracas, Bogotá, Buenos Aires and Santiago. The fanfare evoked upon their arrivals and for the shows they put on in those cities utterly dwarfed the receptions of those coming from abroad to visit the Mexican capital. Regarding Jorge Negrete's trip to Buenos Aires in 1946:

> Thousands of people escorted him from the airport to his hotel, forming a human wall several kilometres long. There his admirers were not content in seeking autographs: they left his cowboy outfits in tatters every time he entered or left Radio Belgrano studios or Teatro Broadway, where he put on a series of shows in which the public would make him return to the stage at least six times for curtain calls. (Serna, p. 42)

Similar descriptions can be found from the same period regarding the tours of Mario Moreno (Cantinflas) and María Félix. The Mexican public expressed itself differently, perhaps because it was accustomed to having its idols at home. Thus, there were no huge crowds awaiting Libertad Lamarque when she flew into Mexico City in 1946 upon her first and definitive visit to Mexico, despite the news of her arrival that preceded her, which briefly summarised her trajectory as musical interpreter and actress, calling her 'The Grand Dame of Tango' and 'La Novia de América' [America's girlfriend], the definitive nickname she had acquired in Cuba earlier that same year (Gallegos, 'Libertad Lamarque: mi nombre', p. 1E).

However, it should be noted that Lamarque's visit was not part of a studio-sponsored tour: she travelled to Mexico without any contract to film, nor any appointment with major studio executives (Valdés, pp. 22–4). Her arrival was actually promoted with a focus on her work as a singer and recording artist. Thus, it can be understood that, although actor Arturo de Córdova, who had known her for several years, met her at the airport, she was also met by the great composer Tata Nacho's orchestra, and they took her straight to XEO radio studios to announce her upcoming shows at El Patio, the fashionable nightclub (Zúñiga, p. 18). The Mexican public responded positively to her prestige and the quality of her performances, enabling her to extend her initial contract of three weeks to a duration of three months (*Excélsior*, 23 November 2008, p. 4) – although it should be noted that Jorge Negrete's extended stay at Teatro Alvear in Buenos Aires ended up lasting nine months. Lamarque had entered into a friendly relationship with Mexican Pedro Vargas, a connection that would become closer as they worked together in several movies. Vargas was a highly appreciated singer in Mexico and, thanks to his recommendation, entrepreneur Vicente Miranda, manager of El Patio, had offered Lamarque the gig (Gallegos, 'Libertad Lamarque participó', p. 2E).

END OF THE WAR

In Mexico, the end of World War II implied a challenge in keeping up audience levels. During Miguel Alemán's presidency (1946–52), Mexico continued its efforts to industrialise and advance technologically, but in ever more competitive international markets. In 1946 Mexico's impressive film studio infrastructure saw a series of labour disputes and strikes, which had been attenuated or little discussed in the press during wartime. Neither the weight of Films Mundiales nor Emilio Fernández's star production team (Mauricio Magdaleno, Gabriel Figueroa, Gloria Schoemann) backed by acclaimed actors Dolores del Río and Pedro Armendáriz could accelerate delays in exhibiting *Las abandonadas* (1945), which dragged on for six months due to government censorship as various high-ranked military veterans anonymously exercised pressure to prohibit its release (García, p. 12). To avoid similar confrontations, in 1947, the production of *The Fugitive*, directed by John Ford, with the same team of actors (in collaboration with Henry Fonda), was released without any indication of the setting for its plot, which was based on the Graham Greene novel *The Power and the Glory*, a text that brought to light the corruption of both Mexico's authoritarian political boss Plutarco Elías Calles, who, after serving as president from 1924 to 1928, continued controlling the presidency from 1928 to 1935, and the Catholic church (ibid., pp. 33–4).

Despite these difficulties, the lack of competition from Mexico's greatest Latin American rival and the still effective machinery of Mexico's industry continued to encourage an influx of Argentines. Among those departing for Mexico during roughly the first half of the year: Ángel Magaña, Francisco Petrone, Luis Sandrini, José Le Pera, Juan José Guthman, Carlos Olivari, Sixto Pondal Ríos, Blackie (Paloma Efrom), Alicia Barrié, Leo Fleider, Vilches, Paul Ellis, Atilio Mentasti, Pepita Serrador, Paulina Singerman and Juan Carlos Thorry (*Heraldo del Cinematografista*, 9 January 1946, p. 4; 30 January 1946, p. 12; 6 February 1946, pp. 17–18; 13 February 1946, p. 22; 13 March 1946, p. 37; 3 April 1946, p. 49; 24 April 1946, p. 61; 22 May 1946, p. 74; 12 June 1946, p. 87; 31 July 1946, p. 123). The Argentine press not only registered these movements, but also published a steady stream of reports about Argentines working in Mexico, including Sandrini, Pondal Ríos, Olivari, José Cibrián, Amanda Ledesma, Néstor Deval, José Ramón Luna and José Nájera (*Heraldo del Cinematografista*, 3 April 1946, p. 53; 24 April 1946, p. 62; 26 June 1946, p. 94; 7 August 1946, p. 129; 14 August 1946, p. 153; 4 December 1946, p. 216), along with nearly weekly updates on Hugo del Carril, Charito Granados and Agustín Irusta, among others, as well as on offers made to Mecha Ortiz, Amelia Bence, Zully Moreno and Silvana Roth (*Heraldo del Cinematografista*, 24 April 1946, p. 61). In addition, news releases document the sale of Argentine scripts to Mexican studios (*Heraldo del Cinematografista*, 21 August 1946, p. 137; 4 September 1946, p. 146). All this information worked two ways for the Argentine film fan: it confirmed the acceptance of Argentine professionals abroad while simultaneously raising expectations for an interest in Mexican films. In reality, few Argentines made a significant impact through their Mexican collaborations. Preceded by their fame, the triumphs of Luis Sandrini and Hugo del Carril were ephemeral, and many lesser actors never achieved anything close to star status in Mexico.

Of those stars who were able to integrate themselves fully into the Mexican industry and establish themselves as stars of Mexican golden age film, Libertad Lamarque, Marga López and Rosita Quintana, only Lamarque maintained a marked Argentine identity, and was recognised unhesitatingly as such by national and international audiences. Indeed, in many of her films, Lamarque plays an Argentine, makes no attempt to hide her accent and inevitably sings tangos (along with Mexican or other Latin American genres), although in her autobiography, she describes the efforts she supposedly made to moderate her accent, and approximate a Mexican style of speech. This was not the case with López and Quintana, who quickly neutralised their speech style and played roles of prostitutes and servants, as well as of ladies of Mexican high society. An article introducing the young Marga López to the Mexican public in 1946 in *Cinema Reporter* does not even mention her nationality (11 May 1946, pp. 14–15). For this reason it is not unusual to find odd affirmations such as the following: 'the Argentine-born Mexican actress, Marga López' (Ramón, p. 17).

OURS AND THEIRS

As mentioned previously, by the time Perón came into power in 1945, Mexico had already established itself firmly as the winner in this contest, in terms not only of production, but also of exhibition – even in the Argentine market. In that year, sixty-nine Mexican films premiered in Argentine theatres versus only forty Argentine pictures (*Heraldo del Cinematografista*, 1945, pp. 740–7). In less than three years of Mexico's gaining ground, the results were now all too clear, an early sign perhaps having been the gala premiere of *Historia de un gran amor*, starring Jorge Negrete, the first time a Mexican film had been launched in the Monumental theatre of Buenos Aires, the 'cathedral' of national cinema – and with a very positive reception on the part of the public (*Cinema Reporter*, 10 July 1943, p. 24). Another milestone was the box-office success of the María Félix vehicle *Amok* (Antonio Momplet) in 1944 in what had been an impregnable space, the Normandie theatre, a venue that did not even project Argentine films, dedicating itself until then to Hollywood premieres. An Argentine correspondent of *Cinema Reporter* writes as early as late 1943: 'It can now be said that Mexican cinema has conquered our market' (6 November 1943, p. 5), and within a few months the victory was sealed with a familiar phrase: 'Mexican cinema has imposed itself in Buenos Aires' (*Cinema Reporter*, 15 April 1944, p. 27).

The modus operandi of the US industry, the reference par excellence, had been reproduced in Latin America in both countries, according to a comment by Orson Welles on a visit to Mexico in 1942: 'In Argentina there is a well-equipped mini-Hollywood. There are big studios, movie magazines, the artists give autographs and cruise the streets of Buenos Aires in large automobiles. The imitation is perfect' (*Cine*, 23 October 1942, p. 3). This type of comparison had abounded in the Argentine press as well, where Argentine product was thought to compare favourably with Mexican film in terms of its technical quality, as is seen in an article that quotes the US Department of Commerce's opinion judging the Argentine industry's 'degree of technical perfection, superior to that of Mexico' (*Cine*, 6 November 1942, p. 2). In Mexico, *Cinema Reporter* reproduced an article from Argentina's *Heraldo del Cinegrafista* that, in 1946, continued to assert: 'We know very well – as do audiences throughout the hemisphere – that with regards to technical quality, Argentine cinema is better' (*Cinema Reporter*, 28 September 1946, p. 17). However, the industry's deterioration in the final years of the war produces a different perception on the eve of Perón's assumption of the presidency regarding where the true Latin American

Hollywood is located: 'Mexico, the new mecca of Spanish-language cinema, continues to attract our greatest artists while their films achieve greater success every day among our audiences' (*Sintonía*, 9 September 1945, p. 86).

During the course of 1946, the sense of cinematic crisis in the southern cone had heightened significantly. The Mexico-based Argentine journalist Carmelo Santiago declared that Argentine cinema in Mexico had reached a new low point: 'movies are released without publicity and are poorly exploited' (*El Heraldo*, 4 September 1946, p. 146). In the same vein, in Mexico, an article in *Cinema Reporter* quotes an executive of Argentina Sono Films, who complains of the lack of distribution of Argentine films in Mexico, lamenting that 'there is a manifest lack of sympathy for or disinterest in Argentine movies on the part of the Mexican filmgoing public' (12 January 1946, p. 32). And, despite Argentina's previous run of success in Cuba, a market that had previously preferred Argentine over Mexican cinema, Chas de Cruz, founder and director of *Heraldo del Cinematografista*, a few weeks later cites the opinion of a Cuban comic: 'Argentine cinema is not bad. It is good cinema for them, but not for Spanish-speaking Americans. There are Argentine pictures whose themes are so locally oriented that no one in other Spanish-speaking countries can understand them' (16 October 1946, p. 173). This commentary gets at the heart of the deep-rooted success of Mexican films in other Latin American countries, and even in some non-Spanish-speaking countries. Despite the care taken in giving plots local settings, whether through music, costumes, landscapes, or historical context, producers were fully conscious of the need to allude to much vaster geographies and ways of thinking. This can be seen in a commentary disseminated in *Cine*:

> Mexican cinema has not forgotten what it owes to its homeland, but it has not aimed to ignore the general tastes of the public and it has done well. It has united its national sentiments – which it captures very well – and universal commitments. (30 April 1943, p. 2)

And if, in 1944, in the opinion of *Heraldo del Cinematografista*, 'Argentine cinema is becoming disargentinised', that of its competitor has been more convincing in its achievements because it is 'more authentic, more Mexican' (quoted *Cinema Reporter*, 18 March 1944, p. 4). It might be said, then, that Mexican cinema, far from 'imposing' itself, succeeded by paying attention and responding to audience demands, serving, following Martín Barbero, as an efficient vehicle of mediation, inviting the cultural participation of the Mexican and other Spanish-speaking masses.

The movie press was also an index of how the divisions and the competition in the film business, amplified as they were by the crisis, were fed by the political atmosphere, which in Argentina often acted as a determining variable in deciding which scripts would prosper, who could be hired, which producers would be best accommodated and who ought to be looking for opportunities elsewhere. The social polarisation in Argentina during these years contrasts in many ways with that of Mexico, whose president from 1940 to 1946 promoted a rhetoric of 'national unity'. Mexico's postrevolutionary governments tended to gloss over events of great political gravity (the Cristero war, the outlawing of the Communist party, the repression of dissident union movements), instead, putting forth a unifying discourse that rubbed out ideological differences, even within the ruling party itself.

Mexican cinema and related communication industries echoed this spirit of pacification and social harmony. In the words of Chilean-born screenwriter and director Tito Davison:

> In many countries they wonder why Mexican cinema has been so successful. I would not hesitate in stating that it is due to the spirit of collaboration that animates, without distinction of social class, the 20 million men that make up the population of this beautiful country. From the lady of the stuffiest aristocratic lineage, like those from the times of don Porfirio [Díaz], to the humblest, darkest-skinned peasant, they all do their part to support the film industry. (*Sintonía*, November 1945, p. 92)

Davison's vision perhaps accommodates itself to an unconscious strategy on his part of insertion into the Mexican movie business. A journalist in his native Chile, he took up screenwriting in Argentina and scripted several Mexican films, beginning in 1945, but his career as a director would take off upon getting a break in Mexico in 1948, with the film *La sin ventura* starring the Cuban *rumbera* María Antonieta Pons; upon establishing himself in Mexico, he would become a major collaborator of Libertad Lamarque, directing nine of her films, starting with *Te sigo esperando* (1952), and would come to be known as one of the most successful screenwriters and directors of his generation, winning two Ariels – one as screenwriter for *Bel Ami* (Antonio Momplet, 1947), and another as director of *La dulce enemiga* (1957) – along with a nomination in Cannes for his directing of the María Félix vehicle *Doña Diabla* (1950).

The inclusive 'Mexicanness' promoted by Mexican cinema, as seen in the success of Davison, was transnational in nature. Just as it could be manifested in Pedro Vargas's *ranchera* numbers of Jalisco or Toña la Negra's sones of Veracruz, it could just as easily present itself in the colourful braids of a Libertad Lamarque singing a tango with her characteristic Argentine accent, in the Afrocaribbean dances of Cuban Ninón Sevilla in a Mexico City cabaret, and even in the 'appropriation' of nationalities, in enlisting actors such as Costa Rican Crox Alvarado, Colombian Sofía Álvarez or Cuban Dalia Íñiguez as Mexicans (Serna, p. 39). The following statement about Jorge Negrete is interchangeable with the phenomenon that would later be embodied by Lamarque herself, through the intermediation of the Mexican movie studios:

> Jorge roused in the Latin American peoples a feeling of emotional brotherhood ... In his clear and powerful voice, the music of Jalisco became the music of Cuba, Venezuela, Argentina, and at the same time erased artificial borders, offering to the rest of the world a new way of celebrating life. (Ibid., p. 23)

Indeed, the music and image evoked by Negrete and Lamarque, following the examples of Carlos Gardel and Agustín Lara discussed by Marvin D'Lugo in his article 'Aural Identity, Genealogies of Sound Technologies, and Hispanic Transnationality on Screen', promote 'a Hispanic "transnation"' through a shared 'aural identity', whose importance as a business strategy the Mexican industry well understood.

There was not, then, a single explanation for Mexico's growing market share: some arguments related to 'national' values, while others focused on opening up to more universal themes and contexts, or a mix based on localised themes and making use of talents from other places. In summary, during this period, one of the most controversial topics that had shaken up the intellectual world a decade earlier in Mexico intensified in Argentina: the debate between nationalism and cosmopolitanism, translated into the exaltation of local values versus the impulse of a universalist spirit. This confrontation of ideas crossed paths with the notion of what the social function of cinema should be.

NATIONAL CINEMAS

This tension plays out in the dispute initiated by Domingo di Núbila in *Cine* in 1943: 'The seventh art becomes … a mirror of the spirit of the mother country by bringing together those physical and spiritual manifestations that define the national temper' (16 April 1943, p. 5). The essentialism of this proposal is clear, a notion further ratified in assertions revealing an evolutionary perspective (the existence of stages of national formation that eventually reach maturity) and allude to the 'true forms' of national culture. Di Núbila argued that neither Argentina's melodramatic tear-jerkers, nor its *arrabal* [slum] films provided the answer to how to penetrate international markets – an odd conclusion considering the decisiveness of these two genres in consolidating Mexico's popularity in the rest of Latin America (e.g., *Cuando los hijos se van*, *La mujer del puerto* [Arcady Boytler and Rafael Sevilla, 1936]), instead seeking the solution in those that, apart from being appealing, are based on historical themes (paradigms might include epic dramas, biopics, national legends: *La guerra gaucha* [Lucas Demare, 1942], *Juvenilia* [Augusto César Vatteone, 1943], *Almafuerte* [Luis César Amadori, 1949]), or in political satires and witty comedies. In his reasoning, he underlines the importance of intellect, of elevating the public's critical capacities, elements that are not easily detected in Mexican films of the 1940s (ibid.).

The article provoked immediate reactions, the very next issue of *Cine* accusing the author of promoting 'spiritual fascism' and of not understanding the reality of the Mexican industry: 'which has throughout these American lands an extraordinarily positive reception' (30 April 1943, p. 2). Di Núbila's position seems to reveal aspirations to approach an idealised European cinema, particularly as it would take form after the war, in which the spectators are expected to 'rise' to the level of the art, rather than cinema being required to 'lower itself' to the crude horizons of the masses – presaging debates that would become central to Latin American cinema in the decades following the golden age.

The inclusion of actors from other countries cast no doubt on the mark of origin of a film. 'In this sense, the Mexicans have been accepting and wisely so. They have not closed the doors on anyone,' declared Modesto Pascó, who explained how Spanish, as well as French and US actors had been invited to work in Mexico. The consequences, he sustained, were quite positive:

> In this way they have given their production a 'general appeal' that meets the needs of any public. They have not closed themselves off in a homogeneous production of local appeal, but have endeavoured to move in a more cosmopolitan or universal direction … All of this

encourages an international-style production that, I repeat, captures all Spanish-speaking publics. (*Cine*, 15 January 1943, p. 2)

While all of this would change in a few years when new union rules forbade the hiring of more than one foreigner into a starring role, and completely excluded actors from outside Mexico from supporting roles, in this period of consolidation, Mexico's openness to foreign talent was a key factor in its international success.

The debate about how to deal with the Mexican competition appeared regularly in the press between 1942 and 1946, just as it did from a reverse perspective in the Mexican press. Argentine critics looked back on how the industry successfully responded to the pivotal success of *Allá en el Rancho Grande*, especially by the early 40s, in an articles such as 'The Lesson Has Been Learned' (*Cine*, 9 October 1942, p. 2; see also 15 January 1943, p. 2). The thematic repetition and rehashing of plots (*Cine*, 16 April 1943, p. 5), the concentration in the sector of too few actors and the resorting to formulaic production were severely criticised and identified as the cause of the Argentine industry's decline.

Libertad Lamarque was undoubtedly aware of all these problems, and the great film diva, at the height of her career in Argentina, was conscious of the kinds of roles she was being offered and their implications, as were producers, directors and other protagonists in the industry. As early as 1943, she admitted her desire to renew herself as an actress and begin acting in different kinds of roles in films with more diverse plotlines. She didn't know whether to attribute this infrastructure of artistic stagnation to actors themselves for not moving successfully in new directions, to the public for not wanting to be surprised, or to writers who propose particular kinds of plots with actors in mind (*Cine*, 2 April 1943, p. 3). Once settled in Mexico a few years later, she would work closely with a leading screenwriter, Edmundo Báez, who came up with some of her most smashing triumphs, including *La loca* (Miguel Zacarías, 1952), whose story he conceived not only knowing who would be its protagonist and who was predetermined to be its producer and director (Miguel Zacarías), but also having in mind the particulars of its cinematic genre:

> I came up with a character for a melodrama as it was impossible to do anything else with her; not because she was a bad actress, but because the public was used to this … In *La loca*, she fought to not sing: 'Look, don Miguel, I love the story, it's an actress's part and I …' 'What do you want?' 'To demonstrate that I can be an actress and not just a singer.' However, of course, it was all a commercial mechanism and the producer added: 'It is impossible, Libertad, for me to produce and risk my money for you not to sing, you would probably be defrauding the public.' And he made her sing. (García Riera, *Historia*, vol. 6, p. 48)

This case shows that the logic of the film market was the same, whether filming in Argentina or Mexico, in the early 1940s or the 50s. Lamarque's position, laid out in Buenos Aires in 1943, coincides completely with Báez's anecdote from 1951. It is obvious that these reasons put forth for Argentine cinema's decline were not the right ones, as the Mexican industry that was beating it down operated under the very same premises. As World War II came to an end, European films began to circulate again in Argentina and sweep up market share, pushing out both Mexican and Argentine product, although both industries hung on for another decade before audiences tired of their formerly successful formulas, and the golden age of cinema fell rapidly into decadence.

LIBERTAD LAMARQUE: EVENTS LEADING TO HER EXILE

An early 1942 note in the journal *Cine Argentino* describes Libertad Lamarque:

> She is Central America's favourite actress. And she knows it. But she stays in Buenos Aires. At Argentine Sono Films. Or San Miguel. Which means that she stays and ... that she has yet to show an eagerness to take to the road. (29 January 1942, p. 7)

Libertad Lamarque was, at that moment, an undisputed superstar of Argentine cinema. No issue of a movie magazine in those days lacked some reference to her, and she more often appeared in multiple articles, in full-page photos, in quotes of her statements on any topic from love and cinema to the radio business or raising children. The pre-eminence of Libertad Lamarque in the Argentine cinema of the early 1940s is undeniable. She was the favoured actress of San Miguel studios, earning a salary that rose from a mere 100 pesos in her screen debut in *Adiós Argentina* (Mario Parpagnoli, 1930) to 200 pesos a day for *¡Tango!* (Luis Mogila Barth, 1933), to a sum sufficient to buy a house for *Ayúdame a vivir* (José Ferreyra, 1936), the film that firmly established her as a major star, to the equivalent of six Ford automobiles by 1942 (Argente, 'El génesis', p. 35; *Cine*, 2 April 1943, p. 3; Valdés, p. 17). Her salary, along with that of Niní Marshall (87,000 pesos per movie) (*Cine Argentino*, 23 April 1942, p. 33), triggered a discussion on the upper limits of stars' earnings on the part of the association of producers, although motions to establish fixed limits never went forward.

The diva bragged that from her very first performances she had a say in the kinds of roles and scripts she would accept (Valdés, p. 17); and producers would seek her opinion on which headlining actors she would prefer as co-stars (Lamarque, p. 209). No star exercised more power in the industry than she. Nonetheless, the public story that began to circulate in the years of the celluloid shortage was that Lamarque was beginning to consider multiple offers from abroad, notably from production companies in Cuba, Chile, Mexico and Brazil – and even Hollywood (*Cine Argentino*, 22 January 1942, p. 5). Inevitable rumours of her move to Mexico, in the air for years (*El Cine Gráfico*, 9 May 1943, p. 9; *Cinema Reporter*, 15 May 1943, p. 31), were initially put to rest with the star's definitive response: 'that in her homeland she is much loved; that she has many movies to make; that she is an investor in her movies' (*Cinema Reporter*, 29 July 1944, p. 15).

In the early and mid-1940s, it was hard for her to take these foreign invitations very seriously considering the diva treatment she was receiving in her homeland. By this time, the only viable option was Mexico as it had become all but impossible to launch an industry in smaller countries such as Cuba or Chile, whose film entrepreneurs had never got much production off the ground. As Paulo Antonio Paranaguá argues, only Mexico had what could truly be considered a film industry at that time (*Tradición*, p. 101); Cuba, for example, only managed to produce a total of eight films from 1941 to 1945 (Douglas, pp. 261–2), a level of production that Chile only barely surpassed (Ossa Coó, pp. 40–53), and neither nation had a track record for exporting – hardly a platform from which to make an attractive offer for a career move for Lamarque.

With regard to the more realistic choice and obvious appeal of the offer of a seven-year contract with Paramount in Hollywood, Lamarque thought that the Latin American market was a much safer bet, considering how little success Hollywood's Spanish-language film efforts had seen (Camarena, p. 28). There were other more pragmatic reasons for her to turn down Hollywood, which she would only reveal years later in an interview in which she confessed: 'I wasn't willing to sign, I wouldn't accept; in the first place I would have to study the language and I didn't have time, or maybe I was just lazy' (Valdés, p. 29). To these reasons might be added another related to the actress's personal life at the time, which she undoubtedly did not wish to complicate further by moving somewhere where she had few friends and did not speak the language.

Her family issues included her separation from Manuel Romero, whom she had married at age twenty in 1928. Her marital conflicts were such that her hit records and cinematic triumphs were not enough to discourage rumours of 'a suicide attempt while touring in Chile; due to the difficult situation she was undergoing with her husband, she threw herself off the balcony of a hotel room, but her fall was broken by a canopy' (*Excélsior*, 23 November 2008, p. 4E). This incredible story complements those circulating on the subject of the dispute over the only child of the marriage, their daughter Mirtha. Argentine law at that time invariably awarded custody to the father. It was reported that Lamarque travelled to Montevideo with her daughter without Romero's authorisation, resulting in charges of kidnapping. Another report claimed the opposite, that, angered by the actress's decision to separate definitively from him, Romero kidnapped Mirtha (ibid.). These scandals obscured another that Lamarque preferred not to have leak out as it would have weakened her precarious legal position, given that divorce did not exist at the time in Argentina: her romantic relationship with composer Alfredo Malerba, which had purportedly been going on since 1936 during the filming of *Ayúdame a vivir*. The affair could no longer be hidden during the filming of the movie *Besos brujos* (José Ferreyra, 1937), whose title was that of a well-known tango composed by Malerba that would become an international hit for Lamarque – this professional link presaging the role that Malerba would assume as composer for many of her recordings and musical director for many of her shows and albums. Despite the couple's visibility, the press preferred to keep things quiet, promoting her clean image as 'America's girlfriend'. In this vein, when *Cine Argentino* jokingly asks Lamarque what she has asked for for Christmas, she responds *un galán* [a handsome man] (3 January 1942, p. 19), and frequently refers to Lamarque not as a wife who is unfaithful to her husband, but as a mother who is unwaveringly devoted to her daughter.

Thus, at the moment of the weakening of the Argentine cinema industry, the frank disagreements with Mirtha's father, and Lamarque's desire to marry Malerba, the controversial episode with Eva Duarte was more than a smokescreen to prepare her exit from the country. Without denying the significance of this latter conflict regarding

Lamarque's possibilities for continuing her career in Argentina, the discretion with which she managed her private life upon her arrival in Mexico contrasts deeply with the continuous chatter in the press about her motivations for not returning to her homeland. To the famous slap or the cold shoulder given to Evita, another anecdote was added, a story that was less disseminated but more symbolically dangerous: the rumour that linked her romantically to Juan Domingo Perón. The appearance of a pair of photographs of the then military leader alongside the movie and recording star incited murmurings of the possibility of a secret affair. Lamarque energetically denied this years later and explained that she was not even sure when those photos were taken. Nonetheless, at the time, her sudden departure fitted the logic of any of these stories about her private life. At the same time, the start of the Perón administration and the end of World War II was an excellent time for a tour, for economic reasons; her departure then was personally convenient as well as professionally necessary and politically inescapable – and easy to arrange, given her enormous fan base abroad.

As Argentine cinema was losing international market share, it brought in a new generation of young female leading ladies who would not compete with Lamarque's star power – or her salary. Mirtha and Silvia Legrand, Sivana Roth and Paulina Singerman, among others, represented a different physical type – blonde, blue or green eyes – and acted in headlining roles in a new film genre geared towards a female audience that 'was characterised by syrupy story lines, small-scale domestic dramas and juvenile love stories' (España, p. 78). These new trends represented for Lamarque another reason to leave what seemed to be a sinking ship.

THE MOVE TO MEXICO

In January of 1946, in the company of Malerba, Lamarque launched a Latin American tour that the press referred to as her honeymoon, as she had remarried a week prior (*Sintonía*, February 1946, pp. 42–3). In Cuba she was received by President Ramón Grau, and greeted her fans from the presidential balcony. Behind her public fame and satisfaction in her private life, a range of conflicts still lurked, invisible to her fans as Lamarque preferred not to even articulate them to studio executives. Indeed, even the much talked about *bofetada* story circulated very little in Latin America; a rare exception: Bogotá's *El Espectador* published a few years later a Spanish translation of a gossipy *New Yorker* story clearly aiming to discredit the Perón regime as dictatorial, which does not mention the slap, but does outline Eva Perón's role in Lamarque's departure from the Argentine film industry, the banning of her Mexican movies in her homeland and the shutting down of a magazine (*Qué*) that dared to print an issue highlighting Lamarque's achievements in Mexico (5 September 1948, p. 22).

Regarding her work with San Miguel studios, relations had turned sour (Lamarque accused them of not fulfilling contractual obligations to her) and her frictions with the government were quickly becoming more palpable as her documents had 'disappeared from police files', leading her to consider fleeing 'across any border' (Lamarque, p. 220). She landed in Mexico, for the first time, during holy week in 1946 and settled there by year end, a stay that would last until 1976, during which time she would film forty-five movies.

Libertad Lamarque and Jorge Negrete in Luis Buñuel's *Gran Casino* (1947)

GRAN CASINO: BLURRING THE BOUNDARY BETWEEN ART AND LIFE

In 1946 Lamarque, at age thirty-seven, filmed *Gran Casino* under the direction of Spanish exile Luis Buñuel, in his first Mexican feature. The actress was already well known in Mexico, both as a popular singer of tangos and as an actress, most especially for the 1936 film *Ayúdame a vivir*. It is worth noting the effectiveness of the strategies she employed that year in her concerts in which a range of established Mexican film stars (Cantinflas, Jorge Negrete, María Félix, Dolores del Río, Pedro Armendáriz) made appearances.

Tango was a beloved genre in Mexico, having been popular and influential there for decades (Martínez), as can be seen very clearly in Cantinflas's early hit *Águila o sol* (Arcady Boytler, 1938) in a scene in which three orphans sing a song that goes 'a night of partying, my shadow tired from drinking and dancing', lyrics resounding in Buenos Aires *lunfardo* [slang], evoking an enthusiastic response calling for *¡otro tanguito!* [another tango!]. Tango had established roots among Mexican music fans, rich and poor, at least since the time of Carlos Gardel's musical recordings and movies. The genre's success continued with the triumphs of Luis Sandrini, Pepe Arias and Lamarque herself (King, pp. 37–8).

Gran Casino features the popular Argentine genre, assigning it nearly the same status as the Mexican *ranchera*. In the 'grand casino' – which is represented as more of a show palace than a gambling hall, undoubtedly because of recent legislation in Mexico outlawing gambling – a mature woman sings a Spanish *zarzuela* and is booed off stage by a crowd that is soon pacified by the arrival of Jorge Negrete, singing a *ranchera*. Negrete's character comments on the crowd's reaction: 'Everybody likes what moves them.' As the movie progresses, it becomes clear that the film's Latin American audience is meant to identify with the casino's audience, which consistently rejects European music in favour of Mexican, first and foremost, or other Latin American genres. The latter comes into play with the arrival of Lamarque's character, who does not appear until a third of the way into the film. This is clearly not a Lamarque vehicle, but it was undoubtedly a film role she chose for strategic reasons. Lamarque worked without pay in a film with a mediocre script, in which she gets second billing, and whose director was (at the time) an unknown quantity within the Mexican machine. But her intervention in the film, in alignment with the plot that ultimately joins her romantically with Negrete, symbolises a pact of friendship between Mexico and Argentina.

Lamarque had attempted to negotiate with Mexican producers, trying to get bit parts for some compatriots, a request that was denied due to union rules, but ultimately felt obliged to take the offer. As producer Óscar Dancigers told her, 'This is all I can offer you ... Besides, who knows if we'll have another chance to get Jorge Negrete.' She explained her reponse in her autobiography: 'What can I say! Putting on airs upon my very arrival? ... Impossible! I accepted what they gave me ... and was very grateful' (Lamarque, p. 327). This anecdote shows who was the true leading actor in the film – despite Lamarque's name being listed alongside that of Negrete, and on the left – and the Argentine diva's consciousness of her fragility in an unknown workplace.

This was not the interpretation of the circumstances projected in her home country, whose press celebrated her triumphant arrival onto Mexico's silver screen, alongside the great idol Negrete, following her hit show at El Patio. The accusations lodged against her in the midst of the nationalist Perón regime for being 'anti-Argentine' are understandable, especially from the perspective of readers who may have been surprised to learn that Lamarque did not ultimately support her compatriots in helping them get roles in her film, or that she now refused to act in Buenos Aires – even though it had previously been reported that she was already under contract to make at least two more films in Argentina. Lamarque responded to what appeared to be a publicity campaign against her by publishing a paid ad in *La Nación* and *La Prensa* (ibid., p. 270).

The release of *Gran Casino* in Argentina might have cleared up some of this controversy. While the film was steeped in Mexican nationalism (its plot treated foreign expropriation of Mexico's oil interests, playing off Mexican president Lázaro Cárdenas's interventions to nationalise the oil industry, expelling British, US and Dutch firms – and the film's main villain is Dutch), it establishes a symbolic pact of friendship between Mexico and Argentina, represented both through an oil alliance and through the romantic ties that emerge between Lamarque and Negrete, an affection that is sealed with the interpretation of a musical medley that alternates between Mexican and Argentine songs. And Lamarque plays up her Argentine identity in the film, arriving at the train station decked out in a stylised version of gaucho dress, teaching rumba dancer Meche Barba slang expressions from Buenos Aires and giving her tips on how to sing tangos.

Gran Casino unfortunately made little impression in Mexico, whether at the box office or among critics, despite the significance of the arrival of Buñuel, well known in intellectual circles for his avant-garde films, in the Mexican cinema apparatus. Despite a three-week initial run at a first-run theatre in Mexico City (el Palacio), it did not fare well after that on second-tier and provincial circuits, an indicator of the lack of appeal of the Negrete–Lamarque formula – Lamarque would do better with other leading men, such as Pedro Infante in films such as *Ansiedad* and *Escuela de música* (Miguel Zacarías,

1955) or Arturo de Córdova in *Bodas de oro* (Tito Davison, 1956) and *Mis padres se divorcian* (Julián Soler, 1959). Lamarque's luck would change considerably with time, as her second Mexican film, *Soledad*, was a huge box-office hit (García Riera, *Historia*, vol. 4, p. 142), and she soon became one of Mexico's studios' most reliable box-office draws. In *Soledad*, Lamarque, playing the tragic role of a servant who becomes a singing star only after having to give up her daughter, connected with astounding force with Mexican audiences, and established an important niche for herself in the Mexican industry as a downtrodden, abject mother figure (and cabaret singer) (see Velázquez).

In Argentina, *Gran Casino*'s fate was more dramatic: the Perón administration prohibited its exhibition (Serna, p. 48). Negrete tried to intervene by taking advantage of the sympathy Perón had expressed towards him, having attended one of his Buenos Aires shows as guest of honour. The two had remained in touch, sporadically exchanging small gifts. Negrete wrote to Perón in 1948, thanking him for the gift of a framed portrait, daring to add:

> I would not be absolutely sincere with Your Excellency if in corresponding to the honour and sympathy that you have demonstrated to me I did not express my feelings of disappointment that the news that the exhibition of my latest film, *Gran Casino*, which I dedicated with such affection to the Argentine people, has been prohibited by the General Office of Public Performance has caused me. (Quoted in ibid.)

The ban was not lifted, an indicator of the true weight of the censorship levied against Lamarque.

In her autobiography, she dedicates several pages – 'with the flames of bitterness that undoubtedly pained me at the time now doused' – to a handful of episodes, which she designates *bagatelles*. She returns to Argentina to visit her daughter a year and a half after her initial departure, attracted by a proposal to appear in the theatre. Once there, the entrepreneur, Pascual Carvallo, owner of the theatre Presidente Alvear, informed her that her coffin was sealed; as she put it: 'to not work again in Argentina was to be on a black list of undersirable citizens, banned, my name taboo, no theatre, no movies, no radio, no records, neither my name nor my face in newspapers and magazines' (Lamarque, p. 261). This ban, never announced publicly, involved not only omission, but also attacks: caricaturisations of the diva, public insults (they invite her to a dinner, seat her at the head table, then make a show of asking her to move, reseating her in an insignificant spot), shutting down journals that refuse to censor out her name (ibid., pp. 260–73). It should be added that this censorship in Argentina likely affected distribution of her films in countries allied with the Perón government such as Paraguay and Uruguay.

None of this was especially important for the Mexican film industry and, within a few years, Lamarque was filming an average of three films a year in Mexican studios. The lack of distribution of her films in Argentina was more than counterbalanced by her enormous popularity in Mexico and just about everywhere else. In Argentina, the case of *Gran Casino* was not exceptional: none of Lamarque's films were shown in Argentina as long as Perón remained in power (i.e., until his government was overthrown by a military coup in 1955), but this ban had no effect at all on the distribution of other Mexican films in Argentina.

The films that did arrive from Mexico included many of those that starred visiting artists from Argentina, such as Charito Granados: *Camino de Sacramento*, *Adulterio* (José Díaz Morales, 1945), *Canaima*, *La diosa arrodillada*; and Luis Sandrini: *Yo soy tu padre* (Emilio Gómez Muriel, 1948), *El embajador* (Tito Davison, 1949) – *El baño Afrodita* (Tito Davison, 1949) featured both of these actors. Most Mexican films starring big-name actors made it to Argentina between 1946 and the early 50s. Cantinflas was a big favourite, with many of his Miguel Delgado-directed films becoming big hits, along with comedies starring Tin Tan (Germán Valdés). Other favourite stars include Jorge Negrete, Pedro Armendáriz, Pedro Infante and the *rumberas* María Antonieta Pons and Ninón Sevilla. Works by Mexico's most prestigious directors were also promoted, including those of 'el Indio' Ferández and Roberto Gavaldón.

LAMARQUE AFTER THE FALL OF PERÓN

With the coup d'état that led to Perón's exile in 1955, Mexican studios took advantage of the change in government to begin importing the Lamarque films that had been banned. Perhaps her absence, both physical and symbolic, for so many years produced deeply embedded feelings among audiences and critics that – piqued by the rumours that had circulated about her contentious relationship with Eva Duarte, so beloved and missed since her death in 1952 – adversely affected the reception of these films. It is also possible that the melodramatic tone of the Mexican productions now seemed excessive, especially for audiences that had lived through their own national tragedies. In general, reception was lukewarm, and critics were often brutal.

Some (anti-Peronist) critics that embraced her return, such as Domingo di Núbila, celebrated her as a symbol of freedom (note that her first name, 'Libertad', means 'liberty'). He writes with aplomb: 'When the shadow of tyranny extended over Argentina and all liberties were persecuted, so too was Libertad Lamarque' (*Cinema Reporter*, 11 April 1956, p. 10). He reports that she was received enthusiastically by her fans, not only because they fondly remembered her movies and musical recordings, but because 'she is one of the few very live symbols of resistance' (although it should be noted that she had never assumed any public political stance regarding the Perón government), and declares that the 80,000 pesos she was paid by Radio Belgrano to sing only four songs was well spent (ibid., p. 11).

COMING HOME?

The Peronist government was overthrown by a military coup in September 1955. In February 1956 *El Heraldo* reported on Lamarque's desire to film in Argentina, adding that she had left the country 'for well-known reasons' (22 February 1956, p. 36). In May 1956, Lamarque's 1956 film *Dímelo al oído*, which had been released as *Historia de un amor* (Roberto Gavaldón) in Mexico, became the first of her movies to premiere in Argentina since 1946. A half-page ad ran in *El Heraldo* promising 'a film that will be unforgettable for the viewing public' (9 May 1956, p. 93). The picture was widely

Libertad Lamarque's character, a homeless alcoholic, poses as a wealthy lady of society in *La marquesa del barrio* (1951)

publicised and celebrated, but critics were cold and unenthusiastic. Reviews stressed that the most valuable aspect of the film was Lamarque's singing. The plot was considered 'trivial', 'merely melodramatic in tone' (*El Heraldo*, 9 May 1956, p. 93). That same year, *La loca* received a similar review in *El Heraldo*: 'a melodramatic and naive plot derails this film through clichés, whose only purpose is to employ all available resources to touch the feminine public' (21 June 1956). *Dímelo al oído* and *La loca* were the only golden age Lamarque films that showed in theatres in Argentina. Only a handful of Lamarque's later Mexican films played in Argentina in the following years, usually opening a couple of years after their Mexican premiere. All of them received the same lukewarm reviews: critics commended Lamarque's abilities as a singer, listed the songs she sang and sometimes praised the wardrobe and the set design. While comedies such as *La cigüeña dijo sí* (Rafael Baledón, 1960) – a remake of a 1955 Argentine film of the same title – were thought to have some redeeming qualities such as their tempo, melodramas were always torn to pieces.

It must be mentioned that Lamarque's roles in Mexican cinema were not always flattering to Argentine national identity. In *Soledad* her character is introduced as an abused Argentine servant in a wealthy Mexican household; in *La loca* she is a mentally ill Argentine living in impoverished conditions in a Mexico slum. While she always comes through on top in the end, she must rise up from horrifying conditions unimaginable for her in Argentine film, where she was 'America's girlfriend'. When she is cast as a homeless alcoholic living on the streets of Mexico City in *La marquesa del barrio* (Miguel Zacarías,1951), it might seem as if a condition to her entry into the Mexican industry is that she must accept being cast in utterly humiliating roles. She becomes an iconic mother figure in Mexican cinema, but not merely the saintly self-sacrificing archetype played by Sara García; instead she is a mother who is forcibly separated from her children, whom she struggles against all odds to win back, often through her singing talents (Velázquez). Despite their positive outcomes, her tribulations play out situations, implausible as they might be, in which the Argentine protagonist finds herself in Mexico, miserable and downtrodden, in contrast with the prosperous Mexicans who surround her – situations that in a sense allegorise (and exaggerate) the hierarchies between the two nations' film industries.

Nonetheless, due to Lamarque's substantial Argentine fan base, her films continued to screen in Argentina. If by the late 1950s critics and intellectuals preferred the less commercial, more artistically and intellectually inspired style of film embodied in the internationally acclaimed works of Argentine director Leopoldo Torre Nilsson such as *La casa del ángel* (1957) and *La caída* (1959) to the Mexican style tear-jerkers for which Lamarque was most famous, she had not been forgotten by her fans of the 30s and 40s, who welcomed her return to Argentine recording studios in 1956 (Flores y Escalante and Dueñas, p. 63), although it was not really until her triumphant return to the Argentine stage in 1967 in the 'colossal smash hit' *Hello Dolly* (Bernal Ramírez, p. 68) that she began to recuperate her former status as superstar in Argentina. Although she would never return permanently to Argentina, Argentina never forgot her; she later made a handful of blockbuster films in the country, and was even offered the role of Mother of Plaza de Mayo in the Oscar-winning feature film *La historia official* (Luis Puenzo, 1985), although she turned that role down (*Nuevo Sur*, 21 September 1989, n. p.). A couple of years before her death in 2002, she was designated Ad Honorem Cultural Advisor and declared Public Personality Emerita by the Argentine government (*La Nación*, 13 December 2000, n. p.), and her films continue to be broadcast on public and cable television.

Argentina was, to sum up, as Mexico's great rival in golden age film production, the market that most stubbornly resisted the imposition of Mexican cinema, giving in only at moments of its own industry's weakness and to Mexico's most irresistible products, as were the many films of Cantinflas. While exchanges between the two industries during these golden age years were many, Mexican cinema's ultimate incorporation of Libertad Lamarque is the one that best captures what became an unequal power dynamic. At the other extreme was the case of another of Mexico's great rivals: the USA, whose great film industry of Hollywood happened to be located in the very same region as the Mexican film industry's most avidly devoted foreign audience of all: the Mexican Americans of the US southwest.

5

Mexican National Cinema in the USA: Good Neighbours and Transnational Mexican Audiences

Robert McKee Irwin

Mexican film-makers began exporting their films abroad long before they built national film production into what could legitimately be called an 'industry'. As the first foreign country to begin receiving Mexican film exports, the USA would soon become its most profitable foreign market. Yet the audiences most responsible for that international success were Mexican. In many ways, the distribution of Mexican films to the US southwest might be thought of as much in national as in transnational terms; naturally Mexican films would generate significant demand among Mexicans, even for those living in the USA. Of course, the identities of Mexican Americans living in the USA were by no means uniform, nor were audiences of Mexican golden age films in the USA uniformly Mexican American. Indeed, Mexican golden age cinema's incursions into the US market reflect their attractiveness for a diversity of audiences, including temporary migrant workers, recent immigrants, well-established immigrants, second- and third-generation (and beyond) Mexican Americans, as well as Latin Americans coming to the USA from the Caribbean and elsewhere, along with sophisticated gringos interested in Mexico and Latin America, especially during the 'good neighbour' years, when such Americanist cosmopolitanism was encouraged. While audience composition differed significantly among major cities such as Los Angeles and New York, or between urban and rural settings, together these audiences allowed Mexican golden age cinema to 'impose itself', even in the country whose own film production was thought of as a constant threat, with its imperialistic tendencies, to authochthonous film production throughout Latin America.

The USA essentially was comprised of three markets for Mexican films. The largest and first to be exploited, located in cities such as Los Angeles, El Paso and San Antonio, as well as small towns throughout the US southwest, was composed of Mexican emigrants and Mexican Americans – a heterogeneous group with regard to individuals' strength of identification as Mexicans or 'Americans', but all of whom shared a recognition of their Mexican cultural heritage – for whom Mexican films represented the best mass media technology could offer: an immediate nostalgic connection to their own cultural roots. The export of Mexican film product to these markets was, in cultural terms, not an export at all, but rather the mere dissemination of Mexican culture to deterritorialised Mexican audiences living in the peripheries of 'Greater Mexico'. A second market consisting of non-Mexican Spanish speakers, including especially Puerto Ricans living in New York City, was in many ways like those of other Latin American countries: Puerto Ricans and other deterritorialised Latin Americans in New York identified with Mexican cinema not for its Mexican particularities, but for the ways it represented a common Latin American or Hispanic culture – through its use of Spanish language, popular 'Latin' musical genres, stylistic conventions such as melodrama, and familiar archetypes; Nuyoricans and other Latin Americans living in cities such as New York identified with Mexican film as a Latin American product. New York was, of course, also one of the most cosmopolitan cities in the world, and one with a long history of links to Latin America, and on some occasions Mexican films crossed over in New York, attracting a third market segment: English-speaking audiences. Indeed, by the latter years of World War II, Mexico would become not only the market leader in Spanish America, but was at its apex the third-largest film producer in the world, after Hollywood and Mumbai, and in cosmopolitan New York the best of Spanish-language film, with subtitles added, was of interest to an audience large enough to justify a theatre of its own, the Belmont on Broadway.

TWO KEY CITIES: LOS ANGELES, NEW YORK

Spanish-language film fans in the USA, even those from poor backgrounds, earned dollars, making it easier for them to go to the movies, and allowing theatres to charge them significantly more for the experience than in other countries to which Mexico exported films, making the USA Mexico's most profitable foreign market (Fein, 'From Collaboration', p. 133). Moreover, throughout Mexican cinema's golden age, Mexican imports held a near monopoly on the US market, with over 90 per cent of Spanish-language imports coming from Mexico (Beer, p. 3). While Mexican films were shown all over the country, a look at the history of their reception in two cities will offer a good idea of the range of its cultural impact, which was most profoundly felt by Mexican American audiences, but which was much broader in scope.

The two cities that, over the course of this golden age, arguably represented the USA's two most significant markets for Mexican film are Los Angeles and New York. Los Angeles stands out as being the city with the largest population of Mexicans outside of Mexico City, with over 100,000 residents of Mexican descent by the 1930s. Los Angeles was at the same time coming into its own as the international capital of film production, with the rise of Hollywood's studios. It is ironic that one of Mexican cinema's biggest markets was located right in Hollywood's backyard; indeed, it has been argued that this 'Mexican presence in and around Hollywood' played an important role in shaping 'film production, distribution, and exhibition practices' (Marez, p. 57). Los Angeles was a film town par excellence, a fact reflected not only in production, but in consumption, and by the early years of the golden age, for Mexican Americans living in the Los Angeles area, 'the largest proportion of the recreation expenditures ... was for the movies' (Agrasánchez, p. 8), although often not for the locally produced English-language product. Mexican stars routinely visited Los Angeles for concerts or promotional tours, and virtually all major Mexican-made films were exhibited there; it could be said that Los Angeles was more a part of Mexican film culture than perhaps anywhere outside Mexico City.

New York, on the other hand, was home to very few Mexican Americans, but many Spanish speakers: over 100,000 in 1930, of whom only a little over 3,400 were

Mexican (ibid., p. 80). There Mexican film gained a foothold first among New York's larger Spanish-speaking populations, the most notable being that of Puerto Ricans, and to a lesser extent among cosmopolitan mostly anglophone film buffs for whom Mexico's industry represented a major foreign film production centre, especially during the war years when options for foreign film were slim, and when the 'good neighbour policy' promoted cultural ties with Latin America (Beer, pp. 48–50). Meanwhile, the Cuban and other Latin American music that began to thrive in New York by the 20s and 30s, with the presence (concerts, shows, recordings, films) of such influential figures as Carlos Gardel, Antonio Machín, Xavier Cugat and Carmen Miranda, transformed the city into a major centre of 'Latin' culture, with, by the 30s, 'a plethora of Spanish, Cuban and Argentinean restaurants and cabarets' offering New Yorkers and tourists a taste of the exotic (ibid., p. 36). Many of the most popular films in this market were not emblematically Mexican, but exhibited more of a universal Latin American appeal; for example, *caberetera* films, musical melodramas set in urban nightclubs and featuring rumba dancers, whose best-known protagonists were often Cuban actresses such as New York-born Meche Barba and Cuban Ninón Sevilla, were especially popular in New York (ibid., p. 123).

It could be said that many of the stars of Mexican cinema were especially well known to Spanish-speaking audiences of these two cities, not only for the promotional tours they routinely realised, but because figures such as Jorge Negrete, María Antonieta Pons, los Panchos and Ramón Armengod were established stars for their musical and/or dramatic work in live shows, often having appeared in the same theatres that premiered their movies, years prior to entering Mexico's film industry.

THE SILENT ERA

Mexico began exporting feature-length films to the USA practically as soon as it began making full-length narrative fiction films, although these early exports made little impact. Mexican movie production in these early years was artisanal, at best, and was hardly the kind of organised industrial production that could produce an infrastructure of international exportation. Nor could it be said that a Mexican American or Spanish-language market existed as such: the USA's Spanish-speaking residents had yet to be cultivated, interpellated. But early incursions of Mexican film into markets such as Los Angeles, New York, San Antonio and El Paso clearly helped lay the groundwork for important triumphs later on.

Only a few early silent films managed to reach audiences outside of Mexico. The earliest concrete evidence of international screenings of Mexican films was unearthed by Rogelio Agrasánchez, who notes the 'commercial success' in El Paso in 1919 of *Santa* (1918), a film that would be screened as far away as Boston (*Cinema Reporter*, 26 April 1952, p. 28). A year later, three films, all produced by the team of Enrique Rosas and Mimí Derba, *En defensa propia* (Joaquín Coss, 1917), *La soñadora* (Eduardo Arozamena and Enrique Rosas, 1917) and *La tigresa* (Mimí Derba and Enrique Rosas, 1917), arrived with some fanfare in San Antonio, followed soon after by *Cuauhtémoc* (Manuel de la Bandera, 1919) and the landmark twelve-part serial, *El automóvil gris* (Enrique Rosas, Joaquín Cross and Juan Canals de Homs, 1919), which was such a hit that it was brought back to the same theatre a year later (Agrasánchez, pp. 110–11). Agrasánchez's research reveals no evidence of such early distribution to California – where the first Mexican feature screening apparently was the highly publicised US premiere of *El que a hierro mata* (María Cantoni, 1921) in late 1926 in Los Angeles (p. 48) – much less New York.

These early films included some subject matter that would have been particularly provocative for Mexican audiences in the USA, most especially Miguel Contreras Torres's *El hombre sin patria* (1922), which was filmed on location in San Diego and Los Angeles (Maciel, 'Los desarraigados', p. 179), and whose alternative title was *Los braceros mexicanos*; unfortunately, they left very little trace regarding their reception in US markets. Film criticism in the Spanish-language press was virtually nonexistent, and with production and exhibition sporadic, there is little evidence to suggest that these early films reached many spectators or made a significant impression. However, film became a more and more popular form of entertainment, as it became clear from small triumphs here and there of Mexican films among Mexican Americans living in the southwest that a market existed for Spanish-language films in the USA. When sound technology was introduced in the late 1920s, Hollywood began producing Spanish- language versions of many of its films – the most celebrated example being *Dracula* in 1931 (Tod Browning, English version; George Melford, Spanish version), in this way seeking to gain market share not only in Latin America, but also among Spanish- speaking audiences in the USA. While Hollywood's Spanish-language talkies never caught on (King, pp. 31–2), they ensured the consolidation of a Spanish-language public in Los Angeles, New York and in many other US markets.

FIRST (?) SUCCESS: THE SECOND *SANTA*

The earliest exportation of Mexican sound films appears to also have been not to other parts of Latin America, but to areas of the USA with large Mexican-heritage populations. *Santa* was launched with a grand publicity blitz, first in San Antonio and soon after in Los Angeles, in May of 1932 (Agrasánchez, pp. 50, 113) – arriving in New York only four months later. Based on the same best-selling turn-of-the-century novel by Federico Gamboa that provided the plot for Mexico's first widely seen feature-length silent film (*Santa* of 1918, mentioned above), *Santa* treats the seduction and fall into prostitution of an innocent young girl from a small town near Mexico City, introducing a number of what would become commonplaces in Mexican golden age film: fallen women, bordellos, melodramatic plots and popular music (the movie's theme song, 'Santa', was an early hit by Agustín Lara, who would become one of Mexico's all-time great popular composers). Its gala premiere in Los Angeles (more than that of Mexico City two months earlier) generated buzz across the hemisphere, making headlines as far away as Chile, where film journal *Écran* raved that the film's reception served to demonstrate 'the enthusiasm of the peoples of our race for the efforts of their own people' (2 August 1932, p. 10). But it was not the mere making of a film in Mexico, but its exhibition in Los Angeles, at shouting distance from the great Hollywood studios, that confirmed Mexico's new role as a contender in cinema production. Several of the film's cast and crew were well known in Hollywood, having

Laurel and Hardy pose for a photo reading Mexican trade journal *Cinema Reporter*

worked in numerous films: director Antonio Moreno, a Spaniard, had been acting in Hollywood for two decades; Mexican leading lady Lupita Tovar had recently starred in the Spanish-language *Drácula*; Canadian-born cinematographer Alex Phillips had made numerous films in Hollywood; Donald Reed (born Ernesto Ávila Guillén in Mexico) was also an established actor. Joselito Rodríguez, who had also spent time in Hollywood learning whatever he could about how to make movies in the 1920s, albeit without obtaining any significant film credits, was charged with managing the introduction of sound technology. The film's gala midnight premiere marked the reopening of the newly renovated Teatro California, an event attended by numerous local luminaries, including Hollywood stars such as the comics Stan Laurel and Oliver Hardy, a duo well known to Spanish-language audiences for the numerous Spanish- language versions that they had filmed of their popular comic shorts (*La Opinión*, 19 May 1932, p. 4). The *Santa* premiere would often be remembered in Mexico as a symbol of Mexican cinema's potential for international triumph (*Cinema Reporter*, April 1942, p. 5; 20 October 1945, p. 7).

While the film was about an innocent girl's downfall into prostitution, it was also the tale of a young Mexican, who was uprooted from the small town in which she grew up and forced to move into the modern chaos of the big city, a detail undoubtedly not lost on Mexican immigrants living in the USA. Similarly, many Mexicans, including those involved in producing *Santa*, as mentioned above, had come to Los Angeles to pursue a career in cinema. Dozens of Mexicans and other Latin Americans – Emilio Fernández, Alejandro Galindo, Andrea Palma, José Bohr, Ismael Rodríguez, Roberto Rodríguez, among others – had come to California, but left for Mexico in the 1930s as opportunities in the USA became few following the stock market crash of 1929. Ironically, many of these figures became the founders of Mexico's own industry. Hollywood, unwilling to accommodate these Spanish-speaking immigrants, set the stage for the rise of an industry that would compete with it, bringing down Hollywood's own Spanish-language film production, and capturing Spanish-speaking audiences all over the world, including in Los Angeles itself.

While *Santa* gained notoriety for being Mexico's first sound film exhibited, it appears that another Mexican film, *Contrabando* (1933), was actually produced a few months before filming of *Santa* began. Filmed in and around Tijuana (two versions, one in Spanish, another in English, the latter of which was probably never exhibited commercially), this lost movie's plot dealt with drug smuggling 'or something like that' (De la Vega Alfaro, '*Contrabando*', p. 148). It was released with major fanfare in Los Angeles in October of 1932, five months after *Santa*'s debut, and was subsequently exhibited in numerous US borderlands markets, with limited success (ibid., pp. 154–5). In Mexico City, where it premiered in February of 1933, on the other hand, it flopped (ibid., p. 153), and indeed has for the most part been written out of Mexican cinema history – and producer Alberto Méndez Bernal's dream of building Mexican production studios in Tijuana never went any farther than this film. However, the anecdote of the production of this lost film remains interesting in presenting an alternate history to the foundation of Mexican sound film, establishing its point of origin not in a Mexico City brothel (main scenario for *Santa*), but in Hollywood's shadow, on the California border.

The importance of Hollywood and the US market for Mexico's early forays into film-making is further evidenced in the fact that some early sound films, including the now classic *¡Vámonos con Pancho Villa!* (Fernando de Fuentes, 1936), were purportedly released in the USA prior to their Mexico premieres (Agrasánchez, p. 114), and the early box-office success of films such as *Sagrario* (1933) and *Madre querida* (1935) in California and Texas – as well as in New York City – presaged the boom that Mexican film production would see in exports by 1937 (ibid., pp. 5, 81, 99, 114; *El Cine Gráfico*, 25 February 1934, p. 7; 18 March 1934, p. 6). *El compadre Mendoza* (Fernando de Fuentes, 1934) earned a positive review in the *New York Times* (*El Cine Gráfico*, 2 December 1934, p. 2), an early suggestion of the potential for market exploitation well beyond the context of Spanish-speaking Mexican emigrant audiences. The appeal of films set in Mexico, portraying Mexican national archetypes, or treating events from Mexican history, most especially to emigrant audiences, soon became obvious to distributors.

EARLY FILM 'CRITICISM'

Any success experienced by the Mexican film industry in the USA, especially the southwest, can be attributed in part to the attitude of the Spanish-language press, which was almost exclusively supportive and uncritical. While the fact that theatre owners advertised daily in journals such as Los Angeles's *La Opinión* might be seen as a conflict of interest, it also reflected a collaborative attitude among businesses catering to the same Mexican American population – that is, for journalists, support of Spanish-language theatres was a question of fostering community. Newspapers such as *La Opinión* tirelessly promoted Mexican films, artists as well as movie houses. For example, during Mexican actress Dolores del Río's years working in Hollywood (1925–43), first in silent film and later in sound film as well, *La Opinión*

Dolores del Río's silent films of Hollywood made her a megastar throughout Latin America, as seen in this Argentine playbill of *Evangelina* (1929)

covers her work assiduously, tirelessly celebrating her every success. *Ramona* (Edwin Carewe, 1928), for example, is a 'masterpiece' (30 March 1928, p. 4) – indeed, Del Río's Hollywood films, both silents such as *Evangelina* (Edwin Carewe, 1929) and talkies including *In Caliente* (Lloyd Bacon, 1935), were popular throughout Latin America. When Mexican films begin to circulate in the USA, they are inevitably promoted uncritically, as was the case with *Vámonos con Pancho Villa* (22 November 1936: section 2, p. 3), or lauded day after day, as occurred with Mexico's biggest hits such as *Santa* and *Allá en el Rancho Grande*. When *La Opinión* did assume a critical attitude, it would not address aesthetic or formal flaws, but would focus only on thematic issues. For example, *La Opinión* launched an attack on an anglophone theatre that was exhibiting a film that the journal, in agreement with the Mexican consulate, found to be 'denigrating to Mexico' for 'presenting us as savages' (31 March 1928, p. 4). Ironically, the film in question on this occasion was a Mexican-produced documentary about a charismatic popular healer and his followers, *Vida y milagros de el niño Fidencio* (Jorge Stahl, 1928). More typical was the critique of *Juárez*, the 1939 film starring Paul Muni and Bette Davis, as a 'movie that leaves a lot to be desired' in its treatment of Mexican culture (11 June 1939: section 2, p. 6).

In general, it was not only the Spanish-language press that received Mexican golden age films with uncritical enthusiasm. Audiences made up of Mexicans 'who are far away from their own country are even more patriotic and eager to see anything connected with the land of their ancestors' than Mexicans living in Mexico (*Cinema Reporter*, 23 October 1943, quoted in Agrasánchez, p. 8). Rogelio Agrasánchez sums up the reception of golden age Mexican film in the US southwest: 'People were ... drawn to Mexican movie houses because these places provided ethnic minorities with a sense of identity and cultural pride, amidst an often hostile environment dominated by the Anglo-American way of life' (p. 162). While the English-language press's occasional reviews of Mexican films (e.g., *New York Times*, *Los Angeles Times*) present a more critical perspective, the treatment of Mexican film by the Spanish-language press complicates understanding audience reception *vis-à-vis* the same exercise in other parts of the world where such a strong pro-Mexican bias (in the face of the discrimination and marginalisation of the large population of Mexican heritage living in the USA) did not exist.

THE PHENOMENON OF *ALLÁ EN EL RANCHO GRANDE*

While Mexican producers tried in vain to replicate the success of *Madre querida*, Fernando de Fuentes, a director who had already garnered international critical acclaim for his historical drama of the Mexican revolution, *El compadre Mendoza*, upon its New York premiere (*New York Times*, 19 November 1934, p. 13), scored a surprise hit in Mexico in the autumn of 1936 with a musical melodrama set on a rural Mexican hacienda, *Allá en el Rancho Grande* (1936), immediately generating buzz as far away as Los Angeles (*La Opinión*, 11 October 1936: section 2, p. 6). *Rancho Grande* premiered only a month later at the Teatro Cervantes in Harlem, earning a positive review in the *New York Times* (23 November 1936, p. 17), and soon began playing to packed houses in Los Angeles (*La Opinión*, 21 February 1937: section 2, p. 3; *Los Angeles Times*, 18 February 1937, p. 10), where it became the first Mexican film released with English subtitles (García Riera, 'The Impact', p. 128). It would eventually have a mainstream premiere on Broadway before being released nationally (*Cinema Reporter*, 18 November 1938, p. 1), where it would earn praise in such journals as *Newsweek* (in a 5 December 1938 article titled 'Mexico's Movie Threat', cited in *Cinema Reporter*, 16 December 1938, p. 1).

Soon Mexican production companies were opening distribution offices in major US markets including Los Angeles, San Antonio, El Paso and New York, leading one exuberant Los Angeles executive to proclaim, 'Mexican movies are imposing themselves in foreign markets' (*Filmográfico*, April–May 1937, pp. 8–9). Soon Mexican film production would put Hollywood's Spanish-language talkies out of business; as Los Angeles distributor Frank Fouce averred in 1938, Mexican films were bringing in twice the box office of Hollywood's Spanish films (Agrasánchez, p. 5).

It could be said that it was *Santa* that first generated major excitement about Mexican cinema in the USA, but it was clearly the phenomenal success of *Rancho Grande* that allowed entrepreneurs to establish networks of distribution and exhibition of Mexican films in key markets across the country. And business boomed for a while, although by 1940, audiences seemed to be tiring of the *ranchera* musical formula, and would not tolerate hurriedly produced, low-quality product. While many southern markets had simply shifted to importing more Argentine material, in much of the USA that was not an option, especially in the southwest (*Cinema Reporter*, 7 June 1940, p. 1; 28 June 1940, p. 3).

THE 1940s BOOM

The 1940s in the USA was an important decade for relations with Mexico. The Bracero Program was launched in 1942, legalising the presence of tens of thousands (eventually hundreds of thousands) of Mexican contract labourers annually. Meanwhile, in Los Angeles, a new public assertiveness of Mexican American youth led to the famed Zoot Suit Riots of 1943. At the same time, the wartime 'good neighbour policy' promoted, most notably through Hollywood film, cultural relations between the USA and Latin America. This policy also included new collaborations with and aid to the Mexican film industry that helped the Mexican industry prosper. The early 40s saw the release of a series of high-quality motion pictures of great popular appeal, including comedian Cantinflas's now classic *Ahí está el detalle* and his bullfighting spoof *Ni sangre, ni arena* (Alejandro Galindo, 1941), Jorge Negrete's *¡Ay Jalisco no te rajes!* and its follow-up, *Así se quiere en Jalisco*, the urban melodrama *Cuando los hijos se van* (Juan Bustillo Oro, 1941) and the high-budget biopic *Simón Bolívar*. Between 1941 and 1945 the number of movie houses exhibiting Mexican films in the USA doubled – from nearly 150 to close to 300 (Agrasánchez, p. 8).

'Good neighbour policy' gave Mexican films new visibility among both hispanophone and anglophone audiences. Vice-president Henry Wallace attended the premiere of *Ni sangre, ni arena* (marketed with English subtitles as *Neither Blood Nor Sand*) in Washington, DC (*Cinema Reporter*, 23 January 1942, p. 1), while in California Disney's propaganda pic *The Three Caballeros* (Norman Ferguson, 1944) was released in Spanish-language movie houses on a double bill with *La virgen morena* (Gabriel Soria, 1942), a film about the Virgin of Guadalupe, a national icon for Mexicans, touted by its director as 'the continental movie par excellence, through which the miracle of [the Virgin of Guadalupe's appearance at] Tepeyac, which united Mexicans, will unite all peoples of the Americas' (quoted in Peredo Castro, *Cine y propaganda*, p. 220). The Virgin of Guadalupe was, of course, more than a Mexican national icon, but a major symbol of a shared Latin American Catholicism that represented the mixed-race heritage of the entire region.

GOLDEN AGE CINEMA GOES INTERNATIONAL: BOLIVARIAN PANAMERICANISM MEXICAN STYLE

The political context of US support of Mexican cinema during the good neighbour years required a collaborative attitude on the part of Mexican studios, most particularly with regard to the good neighbour project itself. Thus, a number of films from the era, like *La virgen morena*, actively promoted panamerican unity through references to a shared history, religion and culture, with Simón Bolívar, the Latin American independence hero, often evoked for his own historical advocacy for hemispheric unity. Miguel Contreras Torres's 1942 film, *Simón Bolívar*, was the Mexican studios' boldest panamericanist project. While the film achieved its greatest impact in South America, most especially in Colombia and Venezuela, where Bolívar is revered as a national hero, the symbolic value of the film ensured it a certain amount of attention in the USA, especially among anglophones.

Simón Bolívar indeed was one of the first films to be distributed with English subtitles and marketed to anglophone audiences in the USA (Agrasánchez, p. 23). Upon its premiere in Los Angeles in early 1943, *Simón Bolívar* inspired mixed reviews in the anglophone press, with one reviewer seeing 'innate glamour and glory' in Julián Soler's portrayal of *El Libertador*, but describing the film as 'tedious' and quipping that the protagonist's eventual death 'is a blessed release for the spectator' (*Los Angeles Times*, 3 February 1943, p. 11). The film opened four months later in New York to a similarly lukewarm critical response. *New York Times* critic Bosley Crowther gave a respectful summary of the film, but concluded that *Bolívar*, though cut down from four to two and a half hours, was 'an interminably long and repetitious film, uneven ... and lacking in dramatic drive' (18 June 1943, p. 16), adding a few days later that after viewing 'battle following battle, intrigue following intrigue and speech following grandiose speech ... one begins to wonder whether the film will run as long as Bolívar's life' (20 June 1943, p. X3).

What is especially noteworthy about the film's debut in both cities, but most especially in New York, is that it comes at a time when Simón Bolívar's name appears with an intense frequency in the news. Bolívar was evoked incessantly in the early 1940s as a symbol of panamericanism; the fact that his affectionate designation in Latin America is 'the liberator', but in the USA is known as 'the Latin American George Washington', and had promoted his own version of panamericanism – of course no mention is made of his not inviting the USA to his Panamerican Congress of 1826 – made him something of a go-to name to justify Franklin Roosevelt's 'good neighbour policy' as a gesture of friendship – and not imperialism. The fact that countries such as Colombia and Venezuela (along with Mexico) allied themselves readily with the USA politically further confirmed the authority of the Bolívar trope.

In New York, especially, Bolívar's cultural presence was immense. Biography after biography was reviewed in the *New York Times* book review pages in the early 1940s, including famed Polish-born Swiss citizen Emil Ludwig's *Bolívar: The Life of an Idealist* (8 February 1942, p. BR5), which was soon to be promoted in South America through a Coordinator of Inter-American Affairs-sponsored lecture tour (*Los Angeles Times*, 8 April 1943, p. A2); children's author Elizabeth Waugh's *Simón Bolívar: A Story of Courage* (22 February 1942, p. BR10); R. Ybarra's *The Passionate Warrior* (16 August 1942, p. BR 18); and Marguerite Allis's *The Splendor Stays*, a historical novel that included a romantic episode in which one female character 'encountered the great Simón Bolívar, and thereafter was lost to any other man' (8 November 1942, p. BR12). Meanwhile, Nina Brown Baker was awarded the 'gold Intro-American Award' by the Society for the Americas for her *He Wouldn't Be King: The Story of Simón Bolívar* (15 February 1942, p. BR20).

Also in New York, in early 1942, in celebration of George Washington's birthday, several 'spokesmen for Latin-American organizations' prepared a message on 'inter-American solidarity' for President Roosevelt through 'the International League for Bolivian Action, dedicated to the principles of Simón Bolívar, the Latin-American "George Washington"' (23 February 1942, p. 34); later that year a ceremony was held in Central Park, where a statue is dedicated to *El Libertador*, honouring the 112th anniversary of his death (18 December 1942, p. 24); in March of 1943, Vice-president Henry Wallace travelled to Panama on a panamerican goodwill mission in which he repeatedly evoked and quoted Bolívar, and was appropriately awarded a medal by the Bolívar Society of Panama (24 March 1943, p. 6); four months later, just after the premiere of *Simón Bolívar* on Broadway – notably at the classy Belmont Theater, a mid-town venue that began specialising in Mexican cinema in 1943 (*New York Times*, 4 April 1943, p. X4) – the Pan American and the Bolivarian Societies teamed up to decorate the beloved Central Park Bolívar statue on the occasion of his 160th birthday, an event attended by diplomats from Colombia, Venezuela, Ecuador and Peru (25 July 1943, p. 24); meanwhile, in Los Angeles, a lobbying effort was launched to name a street after Bolívar: 'To make it count we must all learn not to pronounce it Bollyvar but Boleevar, as all Spanish-speaking persons do' (*Los Angeles Times*, 5 November 1943, p. A4).

Regardless of how boring audiences may have thought the film, in the USA, it was clear, most especially in New York, that its release amid the constant evocations of *El Libertador* in books, speeches and ceremonies came across as an important Latin American demonstration of the spirit of cultural cooperation across the Americas, which no doubt paved the way for the agreements and investments that would quickly make Mexico's film industry one of the most productive and modern in the world and establish its position as the clear Spanish-language market leader for years to come. Interestingly, the film saw significantly greater publicity in New York's anglophone press than it did in the Spanish-language press of Los Angeles.

MEXICAN CINEMA TAKES ON THE NAZIS

Good neighbour agreements between Hollywood and the Mexican film industry permitted the Mexican industry's expansion and domination of the Spanish-language market beginning in 1943 and led to the establishment of the high-tech Churubusco Studios, in partnership with RKO, in 1945. A number of other factors also contributed to Mexico's favourable market position during this period, many of which had to do with the Mexican film industry's maturation. It could now count on major stars as box-office draws: Cantinflas, Jorge Negrete, María Félix, Dolores del Río (who returned to work in her native Mexico after a successful career in Hollywood, debuting on the Mexican screen in Emilio Fernández's *Flor silvestre* in 1943), among many others. Its studios had also assumed a more cosmopolitan perspective, taking into account the particular interests of foreign audiences in producing films such as *Simón Bolívar*, *Doña Bárbara* and *Konga roja*, which introduced a new rising star, the Cuban *rumbera* María Antonieta Pons. In addition, as mentioned previously, the decline of the Argentine industry due to its tense relations with the USA, along with the weakness of the Spanish industry in Latin America due to its diplomatic and economic isolation, made room for Mexican imports in many nations. Latin American audiences began to grow accustomed to certain attributes of Mexican cinema: its stars, its genres, its themes, its music. 'Mexican films that aimed ... to exalt nationalism and panamericanism ... were accepted because the population was willing to accept them' (Peredo Castro, *Cine y propaganda*, p. 467).

But Mexican film-makers – perhaps after noting the success of *Simón Bolívar*, perhaps as a result of the negotiations that had been going on since months prior to its release with representatives of the USA interested in supporting the Mexican film industry both to bolster panamericanist propaganda, as well as to squeeze out Argentina, which resulted in the June 1942 agreement that would bring US investment and technical aid to the Mexican industry (ibid., pp. 143–68) – soon began to participate in one way or another, not only in panamericanism, but also in war propaganda.

On the other hand, it seems that audiences and even critics had little capacity for reading between the lines and teasing out Mexican films' hidden politics. War themes, whether embedded inexplicably in rural melodramas, or featured prominently, attracted little attention even among Spanish-speaking audiences in the USA, many of whose family members were undoubtedly fighting for the USA in the war (ibid., pp. 226–7).

Emilio 'el Indio' Fernández learned the ropes of the film business acting in minor roles beginning in the late 1920s in Hollywood, where he viewed footage of Sergei Eisenstein's well-known film project in Mexico that is today known as *¡Que viva México!* (1932), and is said to have been the nude model for the Oscar statuette. In the early 1930s, he returned to Mexico, where he acted and sometimes danced (e.g., *Allá en el Rancho Grande*) in various early films. In 1942, he debuted as a director with the film *La isla de la pasión*. He would later go on to win three Ariel awards for best director, three more for best film, as well as a best picture award at the Cannes festival in 1946 for his fourth film, *María Candelaria* (1944). Movies such as *Flor silvestre*, which marked Dolores del Río's highly touted debut in Mexican film, *Enamorada* (1946) and *Salón México* (1949), to name a few, are considered some of Mexico's greatest all-time classics, and were among the industry's most widely distributed and acclaimed during the golden years. A survey of Mexican film specialists carried out in 1994 by the magazine *Somos* lists six of his films among the top thirty Mexican films of all time (quoted in Maza and Soto). To European audiences, he was undoubtedly the best-known Mexican director of the era as his films, following the success of *María Candelaria*, produced in collaboration with a fairly consistent team of technicians and some of Mexico's most admired actors, came to be seen as the product of his own special style and were thought to be exemplary of the 'Mexican cinema school' (Tuñón, 'Emilio Fernández', p. 179), examined in greater detail here in Chapter 7.

But Fernández's second film, following up on the respectful reception of *La isla de la pasión*, was a curious work titled *Soy puro mexicano* (1942). This adventure film stars Pedro Armendáriz – who was already known to Mexican audiences for his appearances in such films as *Jalisco nunca pierde*, *El charro negro* (Raúl de Anda, 1940) and *Simón Bolívar*, but who would become one of the most distinguished actors of Mexican film's golden age through his work in Fernández films such as *María Candelaria*, *Enamorada* and *Maclovia* (1948) – as a Mexican bandit who escapes from jail to a ranch that turns out to be, farfetched as it seems, a haven for axis spies from Germany, Italy and Japan. The film is ostensibly an allegory of national alliances in wartime, with the axis spies cast, of course, as villains, and a Texan dancer and her Mexican boyfriend as good guys, along with Armendáriz, who is an outlaw, but by no means a real 'bad guy', much less a danger to the nation, and with its propagandistic overtones quite obvious. The film scored minor success in Mexico and saw some international distribution, where it raised few eyebrows. Indeed, its odd reception in the USA is emblematic of how much it seems that even the most evident 'subliminal' ideological messages were unable to interfere with the experience that was Mexican cinema to its audiences abroad: an emotionally stirring but always entertainingly fun experience.

It premiered pretty uneventfully in Mexico in November of 1942, overshadowed that year by the growing success of Cantinflas, who starred in the megahit *Los tres mosqueteros*; the pretentious new genre of literary superproductions such as *El conde de Montecristo* (Chano Urueta) and *Historia de un gran amor*; the international blockbuster *Simón Bolívar*; a handful of successful religious-themed movies including *La virgen morena* and *La virgen que forjó patria* (Julio Bracho), the latter of which marked Mexican-born Hollywood star Ramón Novarro's Mexican screen debut; and Mexico's first colour feature *Así se quiere en Jalisco*. While some were aware that Mexico was negotiating with US emissaries as part of a wartime political alliance that would involve Mexican film production, the film itself was not criticised for its rather transparent ideological underpinnings – for the most part.

The movie's theme song, 'Soy puro mexicano', composed by Manuel Esperón, with lyrics by Ernesto Cortázar, interpreted in the film by the great Mexican crooner Pedro Vargas, with its patriotic lyrics ('I'm a pure-blooded Mexican/born in this land/in this beautiful territory/that is my fair nation', reproduced in Peredo Castro, *Cine y propaganda*, p. 215) would seem to be a typical *ranchera* song, except that a few little panamericanist and antifascist touches are added here and there ('Viva Mexico! Viva America!'; 'Viva democracy!'), leading Salvador Novo to joke (or perhaps repeat a joke) that the song was actually written by Nelson Rockefeller (quoted in ibid., p. 216). The line 'Viva America! Oh beautiful land blessed by God!' again, as mentioned above in the case of *La virgen morena*, alludes to the shared religious ideals of many Latin Americans.

Soy puro mexicano garnered more attention in the USA, where the film was a hit upon its release in April of 1943 – with *Cinema Reporter* enigmatically announcing its 'great success in California' well over a week before its US premiere (3 April 1943, p. 31). On the eve of its debut, Los Angeles journal *La Opinión* announced its arrival, calling it a 'Mexicanist film' [*película mexicanista*] and construing from Mexico City reviews that 'it promises magnificent fun' (11 April 1943, p. 3). A subsequent announcement of the extension of its run to a second week calls the film 'patriotic', but gives no further hints of its topical plot (21 April 1943, p. 4). A *Los Angeles Times* review also skirts the propagandistic nature of the plot, focusing on its protagonist, a 'jaunty country *caballero*' who 'ends by turning true patriot and killing or capturing the bad boys'. The bad boys are apparently involved in 'fifth column activity', but the review has nothing more to say about them, never revealing their national origin, nor even implying what trouble they might have in mind hiding out in rural Mexico; a reader of the article might assume that they are antirevolutionary Mexican traitors of some kind (13 April 1943, p. 13). Regardless of how Mexican audiences in Los Angeles may have interpreted its plot, *Soy puro mexicano* was a resounding hit there, exceeding box-office records previously set there by *¡Ay, Jalisco, no te rajes!* by some 30 per cent, and earning the privilege of a wider distribution, with English-language subtitles (*El Cine Gráfico*, 25 April 1943, p. 14; 6 June 1943, p. 2). It played for two weeks in New York, an excellent run, but without generating an interest among critics in its unusual plotline (*New York Times*, 11 June 1943, p. 23). Other films that even more explicitly introduced war propaganda were even lower profile, although *El escuadrón 201* (Jaime Salvador, 1945), a movie commemorating Mexico's participation on the Pacific front, had a gala premiere in New York hosted by the Mexican consul (*Cinema Reporter*, 27 April 1946, p. 62), and Fernández would occasionally introduce similar themes into his film plots, as he did in *Salón México*, one of whose protagonists is a returning fighter pilot from Squadron 201. Interestingly, there is no evidence of *El escuadrón 201* making any impact at all, or indeed of even being released, outside Mexico.

In sum, what the evidence suggests is that even in New York, where *Simón Bolívar* generated significant press as part of the wave of panamericanist fervour of the period, Mexican films with more explicit references to the war in Europe generated little interest. Why focus on the jaunty *caballero* hero and not the Nazi spies, and why fuss over a national hero of Colombia or Venezuela and not Mexico's own World War II heroes? It would seem that Mexico's filmgoing public in the USA, whether Mexican or Anglo, was seeking something in particular from Mexican films, something more related to smiling, swarthy *charros* in wide sombreros or larger-than-life figures of Latin American history – or urban vagabonds like Cantinflas or long-suffering mothers like Sara García or indigenous maidens of exotic Xochimilco like Dolores del Río in *María Candelaria* or dashing revolutionary generals like Pedro Armendáriz in *Enamorada* or Latin American religious icons like the Virgin of Guadalupe: in other words, audiences sought out authentically Mexican or Latin American themes, stories and characters, not improbable plots related to distant wars in Europe or Asia. As Mexican golden age film director Alejandro Galindo notes,

> the image that the US war films and documentaries painted of the world and offered to Latin American audiences ... exhibited a very significant contrast with the spectacle offered by Mexican cinema. While the former spoke of death and destruction in a struggle over ideas and interests that Latin Americans scarcely comprehended, Mexican movies were the only ones that sang of loves and passions that were understandable to them. (Quoted in De los Reyes, p. 182)

Nor did audiences in the USA seem to care much about the sometimes negative perspective presented of the country in Mexican films such as *Konga roja* – or later popular films such as *Campeón sin corona* (Alejandro Galindo, 1946) or *Los tres García*. Mexican film had indeed become, by 1943 when it assumed its leadership position in Spanish-language markets in Latin America, 'our cinema' by knowing what to offer its audiences, and by assuming its own particular Mexican (and Latin American) style.

THE IMPOSITION OF MEXICAN FILM

As mentioned previously, the USA in the mid-1940s, still decades from having homegrown Spanish-language media networks, was the Mexican film industry's most profitable foreign market, one in which distributors began bragging as early as 1937 that 'Mexican movies are imposing themselves' (*Filmográfico*, April–May 1937, p. 9). Within a few years, Texas and California each boasted hundreds of Spanish-language movie theatres, with many more running in Colorado, New York and Florida, as well as agricultural states such as Nebraska, Wyoming and South Dakota (Agrasánchez, p. 11). By the 40s, Mexican film journals including the long-running and influential *Cinema Reporter*, which had by that time established its own offices in Los Angeles (*Cinema Reporter*, 5 June 1942, p. 1), were 'widely read by movie fans and could be bought in any city with a substantial Hispanic population north of the Río Grande' (Agrasánchez, p. 40). The Bracero Program, launched in 1942, was soon bringing tens of thousands of Mexicans to the USA every year. Throughout the country – in Texas, California, Colorado, Arizona, New Mexico, Nebraska, Kansas, New York, Utah, Illinois, Minnesota, Missouri, Wyoming and South Dakota, among others – there was a massive market expansion, with hundreds of new Spanish-language movie theatres opening, in the mid-40s (Agrasánchez, pp. 169–86).

For *braceros* and other recent immigrants, Mexican film represented a sort of 'cultural nourishment' in the face of the relentless pressure to assimilate (David Maciel, quoted in Agrasánchez, p. 14). Meanwhile, in cosmopolitan New York, audiences of different Latin American national heritages enjoyed 'the illusion of a unified Latin American culture' that many Mexican films represented through their subject matter, their actors, their music, thinking of them as Latin American rather than Mexican (Agrasánchez, p. 94) – and ignoring the fact that Mexicans alone were determining what defined what was virtually the only Latin American cultural product (Argentina's market share in the USA was negligible) that reached the international masses through visual media.

By the late 1940s, demand for Mexican movies in the USA exceeded supply, forcing exhibitors to rerelease older films (Saragoza, 'Mexican Cinema', p. 27), and inviting a market for piracy. By 1948, marketable hits from years back, such as *La virgen morena*, *La zandunga* (Fernando de Fuentes, 1938) and *La llorona*, were reportedly circulating on a black market (*Cinema Reporter*, 22 May 1948, p. 31).

Meanwhile, an interesting phenomenon emerged in Mexican film as comic actor Tin Tan (Germán Valdés) rose to stardom with such films as *Calabacitas tiernas* and *El rey del barrio* (Gilberto Martínez Solares, 1950), in which the Mexican actor adopted various traits and mannerisms (e.g., modes of dress, speech) of *pachucos*, a distinctly Mexican American archetype, effectively producing perhaps the first important cultural influence exercised by Mexican Americans on Mexican culture – as critic David Maciel puts it, 'Mexican film goes *bracero*' ('Los desarraigados', p. 181; see also Durán). Tin Tan's films, hugely popular in Mexico, were also inevitably successful in Mexican American markets in the USA, providing a uniquely transnational point of identification for many Mexican Americans.

US MARKETS INTO THE 1950S

By the early 1950s, Mexican films were showing in at least 683 different theatres in 443 US cities and towns nationwide (Agrasánchez, p. 8), with new cinemas continuing to open throughout the decade in Texas, California, New Mexico, Ohio, Florida, Utah, Illinois, Louisiana, Alabama, Arkansas, Michigan, Wisconsin, Missouri, Minnesota and Idaho (*Cinema Reporter*, 13 July 1955, p. 27; Agrasánchez, pp. 169–86). Mexican films were being marketed not just to Spanish-speaking audiences, as distributors and exhibitors brought acclaimed features such as *Río Escondido* (Emilio Fernández, 1948) and *Angelitos negros* to English-speaking audiences in major markets such as New York and Los Angeles (*Los Angeles Times*, 1 October 1950, p. E3).

However, in 1952, the suspension of programming at two major Spanish-language movie houses in Los Angeles, the Maya and the California, was cause for alarm, the first sign of the industry's decline, even as films such as *Aventurera* and *Los olvidados* continued to bring in large crowds in southern California and the USA continued to be one of Mexico's top export markets; the Teatro California would begin showing Mexican films again only a few months later (*El Cine Gráfico*, 24 February 1952, p. 8, section 2, p. 26; 4 May 1952, pp. 6, 8; 1 June 1952, p. 4). Mexican films continued to break box-office records as well, with, for example, distributors claiming that Cantinflas's *Caballero a la medida* had earned more than any other Mexican film ever in a single movie house, in this case Los Angeles's exalted Teatro California (*El Cine Gráfico*, 12 February 1956, p. 11; *Cinema Reporter*, 15 February 1956, p. 32), and films such as the Pedro Infante and Miroslava comedy *Escuela de vagabundos* (Rogelio González, 1955) experiencing extended runs of up to twenty-two weeks (*Cinema Reporter*, 29 February 1956, p. 23). In late 1956, Cantinflas's *Abajo el telón* set another record, becoming the first film ever to have an extended three-week run at Los Angeles's Million Dollar Theater (*Cinema Reporter*, 14 November 1956, p. 21). Even as the golden age was on the verge of fizzling out by the mid-1950s, Mexican cinema continued to make an important impact on Spanish-speaking audiences, especially Mexican American ones, in the USA.

WETBACKS IN MEXICAN FILM

One of the last big hit films of the golden age was the controversial *Espaldas mojadas*. Winner of four Ariel awards (a pair of supporting actor awards for Eulalio González and Carolina Barret, an original story award for Alejandro Galindo, as well as a special award for 'film of greatest national interest'), the film's release had actually been delayed for several years. A cautionary tale on emigration to the USA that presented frank if excessively didactic portrayals of discrimination and hardships experienced by Mexicans in the US southwest, it was deemed upon completion in 1953 too critical of the USA and canned for two years. It was released only in the summer of 1955 after having been amended at the request of the US State Department with a warning:

> Our intention is to warn our compatriots of the problems associated with trying to leave the country illegally, which carries with it the risk of awkward and painful situations that could even cause difficulties for the good relations that fortunately exist between our two nations. (Quoted in Noble, p. 152, translation hers)

It would seem that the State Department was less concerned with promulgating the image of racist and abusive treatment of Mexicans in the USA than it was with simply discouraging Mexicans from crossing the border. Its release in mid-1955 came on the tail of Operation Wetback, which saw the deportation of tens of thousands of Mexicans from the USA.

A scene from Alejandro Galindo's controversial *Espaldas mojadas* (1955)

While the Mexican film industry had produced a handful of minor films representing Mexican emigrants in the USA, going as far back as Conteras Torres's *El hombre sin patria* of 1922, it has been criticised for its promotion of stereotypes, casting emigrants as *pochos*, a insulting term used in Mexico to describe emigrants as traitors who abandon Mexico and allow themselves to be absorbed, although always only partially, into US culture (Maciel, 'Los desarraigados', p. 166). Films such as *Soy mexicano de acá de este lado* (Miguel Contreras Torres, 1945), *Pito Pérez se va de bracero* (Alfonso Patiño Gómez, 1947), *Primero soy mexicano* (Joaquín Pardavé, 1950) and *Acá las tortas* (Juan Bustillo Oro, 1951) fall in this category of positing emigration as antithetical to patriotism (ibid., pp. 182–4). *Espaldas mojadas*, although a cautionary tale on emigration, presented a more realistic view, indeed reflecting a thematic thread explored in some of Galindo's earlier work, including especially *Campeón sin corona*, regarding the psychological consequences of the power differential between the two nations. Galindo, who had spent time in Hollywood in the 1920s and left disillusioned (Meyer, vol. 1, p. 100), once commented that 'gringos are not to my liking' (ibid., p. 96).

Espaldas mojadas exerted a strong appeal in US markets. Indeed, while the film was a hit in Mexico, running five weeks and coming in as the fifth-biggest box-office hit of 1955 (*Cinema Reporter,* 29 February 1956, p. 23), its success in Mexico paled in comparison to its triumph in California when it arrived there in mid-1956, breaking box-office records at Los Angeles's Teatro California (*Cinema Reporter*, 20 June 1956, p. 25; Agrasánchez, p. 67). Even in the face of Operation Wetback, hundreds of thousands of Mexican migrant workers were coming to the USA every year both through the Bracero Program and in its shadows, with the mid-1950s representing the apex of migrant influxes; recent migrants, of course, would have been especially interested in the subject matter of *Espaldas mojadas* (Agrasánchez, p. 10), which was not the first Mexican film to treat emigration to the USA, but was the best-quality film dedicated to the topic to date, and would be by far the most successful (Noble, pp. 151–2; Aviña, pp. 61–3). Chicano film critic David Maciel calls it 'the single best Mexican commercial production on the subject' of emigration ('Braceros', p. 371). It experienced an impressively long run in the Los Angeles area, playing in the city's first run Spanish-language theatres for most of May, and running in the suburbs through at least late June (*La Opinión*, 5 May 1956, p. 4; 5 June 1956, p. 4; 17 June 1956: section 2, p. 6).

This film follows the plights of emigrants in their struggles to cross the border, their difficulties in finding work, their exploitation by abusive and racist employers, their constant fears of getting caught by authorities and the many obstacles they encounter in their attempts to find happiness and prosperity in *el norte*. More than the escapist comedies of Cantinflas, the purely entertaining *caberetera* musicals, the feel-good *ranchera* pictures, or even the more artistically ambitious nationalist melodramas of 'el Indio' Fernández – all of which evoked nostalgia for the homeland, *Espaldas mojadas* interpellated Mexican American audiences directly. Interestingly, while *Espaldas mojadas* garnered minimal attention in other external markets, it was a critical success and audience favourite in the Soviet Union, where it played in Moscow and Minsk, as well as the Kazakhstan cities of Karaganda and Kokchetav, where the negative portrayal of the USA was undoubtedly appreciated by communist authorities (*El Cine Gráfico*, 17 March 1957, p. 6).

If for other Latin Americans outside Mexico – including Puerto Ricans and other 'Latinos' living in the USA – Mexican film was embraced with ambivalence, and ultimately exercised a watered-down version of cultural imperialism that consolidated Mexico's market-leadership position, for Mexican Americans, more than for any other public, including that composed of Mexicans living in Mexico, Mexican golden age cinema was an anti-imperialist cultural product that reasserted Mexican culture's legitimate place in the cultural landscape of the US southwest. From the earliest silent imports to the gala premiere of *Santa* to the enormous success of *Rancho Grande* to the extensive market expansion in the 1940s and 50s across US territory to, finally, the elevation of undocumented immigrants to the role of protagonists in one of the last blockbusters of Mexican golden age cinema in the US southwest, Mexican golden age film's 'imposition' in the USA represented an important affirmation of Mexican culture.

MEXICAN GOLDEN AGE CINEMA AND THE ROOTS OF CHICANO CULTURE

The impact of Mexican golden age film on Mexican American culture in the USA cannot be underestimated. Critics have argued persuasively that Mexican film realised important functions for Mexicans living in the USA, providing cultural connections to their homeland, informing them of what they were missing back 'home' and offering a cultural antidote to prejudice and discrimination:

> cinema helped to maintain Mexican culture, values and traditions, including the Spanish language, in force within the Chicano community. This is important as it contributed to counteracting the powerful processes of assimilation and the negation of everything Mexican advanced by the US education and cultural system. (Maciel, 'Los desarraigados', pp. 165–6)

It also 'offered the Chicano community a positive and very necessary escape due to the difficult, often oppressive, world in which they lived' (ibid., p. 177). In a sense, Mexican film offered 'a form of resistance to the hegemonic cultural and ideological currents in the US' (Saragoza, 'Cinematic Orphans', p. 127).

Nonetheless, it cannot be assumed that audiences were homogeneous, even in cities like Los Angeles where the vast majority of patrons were Mexican Americans. One could think of there being two extremes with regard to the attitudes of Mexicans in the USA towards Mexican golden age cinema:

> Those who adhered to the Spanish language and identified with Mexico and its cultural symbols were often lined up culturally against those who espoused an American cultural outlook. In this period, these differences were nourished to some extent by the polarization created by two hegemonic cultures that stressed conformity through appeals of patriotism. Within the context of Chicano communities, Mexican cinema, therefore, represented a point of reference in distinguishing the 'boundaries' between distinct groups of people of Mexican descent. (Saragoza, 'Mexican Cinema', p. 26)

While those who identified more as Mexicans than as 'Americans' would have been more likely to go to see Mexican movies, the duelling forces of the two powerful ideological forces of US and Mexican nationalism on Mexican Americans cannot be underestimated – so that even among those who identified as Mexicans, there were undoubtedly degrees of identification that were stronger in some than in others.

What is especially interesting regarding the reception of Mexican golden age cinema in the USA, above all in Los Angeles and the southwest, is how this process of identification played out. Going to see Mexican movies was not a process of passively receiving cultural information and unconsciously absorbing values and lifestyles; it was a highly participatory experience. In San Antonio, the informal atmosphere of many theatres often 'encouraged audiences to "stomp and whistle" during the film's climactic moments' earning them moniker of 'stomp and whistle theaters' (Agrasánchez, p. 120). Mexican films were often tear-jerkers that piqued viewers' emotions, provoking laughter and tears, pity and rancour, joy and outrage, often in rapid succession. Anglophone critics were often taken aback at the pleasure Spanish-speaking audiences took in participatory viewing, as is the case with this

New York Times review of the Sara García vehicle, *Mi madrecita* (Francisco Elías, 1940):

> From a cold-blooded, critical point of view the waste of acting talent is *Mi madrecita* is something fearful. But judging from the way Harlem audiences are weeping through most of this highly sentimental film and cheering and laughing at the happy ending, it is just what they like. (24 September 1940, quoted in Agrasánchez, p. 82)

They also made great use of music, introducing new songs, but also bringing back old favourites, with all the emotional connections they might evoke; Agrasánchez opines that 'the populace took pleasure in seeing an idealized version of their sentimentality projected onto the silver screen and endowed with flavorsome tunes' (p. 164). However, in many theatres, music was not limited to the movie soundtrack: 'in the Mexican theaters of LA films were incorporated into larger variety show formats in which programs of Mexican singers, musicians, dancers, and comedians preceded and followed film screenings' (Marez, p. 72). Musical stars, many of whom were active in the Mexican film industry, including actor-singers (Jorge Negrete, Pedro Infante, Libertad Lamarque), as well as stars best known as singers but who also appeared often in Mexican films (Toña la Negra, Pedro Vargas), others most appreciated for their dancing (María Antonieta Pons, Tongolele) or their comic acting (Cantinflas, Tin Tan), or even dramatic actors (David Silva, Lupita Tovar) frequently toured the southwest, making appearances most especially in Los Angeles. Going to the movies constituted a major outing that involved audiences much more actively than did conventional moviegoing in the anglophone USA.

Movie theatres were a social gathering place in which families and communities socialised and bonded. This highly participatory aspect of filmgoing in the USA ties in with Spanish-language film journalism's role not to provide objective criticism, but to foment Mexican golden age cinema's community-building power. This social aspect of film fandom is illustrated in the Denise Chávez novel, *Loving Pedro Infante*, whose protagonists are members of a small-town Pedro Infante fan club. Interestingly, as Chávez constructs fan culture in her novel, at the level of the spectator, participatory film viewing was not at all uncritical as might be inferred from the attitudes of journalists. Indeed, the novel plays out the conflictive cultural forces at work among Mexican American women, who were drawn to Mexican film, but not to all of the values it seemed to promote. However, their 'transnational border feminism' (Heredia) by no means drew them away from Mexican golden age film.

The long-term influence of Mexican golden age film on Mexican American culture in the USA is, of course, well documented. Amalia Mesa-Bains lists Mexican golden age movie iconography as one of the key elements of the Chicano *rasquache* aesthetic seen in painting, conceptual art, theatre, performance art, poetry, etc. (p. 159), and it is indeed important to her own work (pp. 164–5), most notably in her Day of the Dead-style altar, *An Ofrenda for Dolores del Río* (1984), which includes imagery of the Mexican actress from both her Hollywood and her Mexican periods, and presents her as an emblematic figure of Mexican American culture, along with, for example, Frida Kahlo and Sor Juana Inés de la Cruz. According to the artist, 'Historical works such as the Dolores del Río altar contextualize a domestic icon of the cinema within the

Hollywood/Mexicana dual worlds and act as well for my personal narrative of life events' (ibid., p. 165). Ramón García likewise notes the importance of Mexican film iconography in major works of Chicano literature, including titles not only by Denise Chávez, but also Sandra Cisneros and Ana Castillo, while film critic Rosa Linda Fregoso signals the importance of Mexican comedians Cantinflas and Tin Tan for Chicano film production, including most notably *Born in East LA* (Cheech Marin, 1987).

The rise of Mexico's great culture industry of cinema during its golden age thus had an impact whose repercussions went beyond the Mexican American enclaves of the US southwest. As minority cultures were accommodated into the US mainstream in school curricula, museums, media and so on, and as crossover works such as the films of Cheech and Chong earned mainstream success, the long-term impact of Mexican golden age cinema extended its reach. Even back in the day, the collaborations in Hollywood of Emilio Fernández (with John Ford for *The Fugitive*, or with RKO Studios for *La perla*, both in 1947) and Gabriel Figueroa (credits include *The Night of the Iguana* in 1964, *Two Mules for Sister Sara* in 1970) or of Mexican actors trained in the golden age studios (Pedro Armendáriz in films such as John Wayne's *The Conquerer* in 1956 and *To Russia with Love* in 1963; Katy Jurado, memorably, in *High Noon* in 1952 and *Pat Garrett and Billy the Kid* in 1973) – or Artie Shaw and his orchestra's US hit version of 'Frenesí', composed by Mexican Alberto Domínguez and popularised in Mexico through the film *Al son de la marimba* (Juan Bustillo Oro, 1941) or Bing Crosby's (or Elvis Presley's) recording of 'Allá en el Rancho Grande' – point to the impact of Mexican golden age cinema on US culture. While in the USA,Mexico cultural connections followed both migratory routes and political alliances, Mexican golden age cinema's arrival in Spain, a nation with which Mexico had severed diplomatic relations after the Spanish civil war of 1936–39, followed more complicated routes, but made inroads that dramatically challenged existing cultural hierarchies in the Spanish-speaking world.

6

Panhispanic Romances in Times of Rupture: Spanish–Mexican Cinema

Inmaculada Álvarez and Maricruz Castro Ricalde

PANHISPANISM

In 1939, with the end of the Spanish civil war and the establishment of the dictatorship of General Francisco Franco, Spain and Mexico's diplomatic relations would rupture as the Mexican government rejected the legitimacy of Franco's regime. Mexico became a nation of refuge for thousands of exiled Spaniards fleeing postwar repression in their homeland. However, despite this break in political relations, which would continue until the consolidation of Spain's transition to democracy in 1977, the two nations were able to maintain unofficial cultural connections through cinematic connections, which 'created bonds that made up for the absence of formal diplomatic relations' (Lida, p.14). Prominent in these exchanges was an exaltation of national archetypes in films whose plots underscored a Spanish–Mexican fraternity through amorous encounters between characters from the two nations. This common imaginary, which critics have called 'operation panhispanic' (Gubern; Elena, 'Medio siglo'), determined filmic narratives that created a nationally inscribed romance between gendered national archetypes, whose most emblematic protagonists were the Mexican macho, embodied in the figure of the *charro*, often played by the popular singer and actor Jorge Negrete, and the Spanish *gitana* [gypsy woman] and flamenco dancer – as well as the more modern figure of the seductive Mexican 'devourer of men' seen in the provocative characters played by María Félix. In the background of these love stories, the films often promoted shared national values such as honour, passion, courage and courtesy, but at the same time served to redefine the power dynamic between the two nations. Indeed, Negrete was a figure central to Mexico's conquest of the Spanish market and as such his virility, marked by an 'indomitable independence' and a 'proud and invincible individuality' (*Cinema Reporter*, 24 February 1948, p. 6), put the *charro*, the emblematic Mexican, in the role of conquerer of the Spanish market, and of the hearts of Spanish fans. While some Spanish critics attempted to spin Mexico's success as a force meant to unite 'all peoples of Hispanity', product of a 'friendly invasion' (ibid.), others recall how Mexican cinema 'conquered our screens' (*Cinema Reporter*, 4 January 1956, p. 13).

This transnational form of representation of Mexican and Spanish cultures took shape at a time when Mexico's industry was seeking to develop export markets, especially those in which it had a chance of competing meaningfully with Hollywood. This expansionist desire was also attractive for the growing, but relatively small,

Spanish industry – and for the Franco regime, which wished to repair its reputation abroad. The fusion of Mexican and Spanish national archetypes would serve to create a 'panhispanic cinematography' that would benefit the commercial and the political interests of countries. Interestingly, this alliance was only made possible by the relative strength of the Mexican film industry as an international enterprise; the fact that it ultimately represents a rescue of the diminished and demoralised industry of Spain by an ex-colony newly empowered through entertainment technology puts an unusual postcolonial spin on a project that superficially would seem to be merely about commonality and collaboration.

This chapter analyses the cinematic representation of this cultural bond between Mexico and Spain through collaborative production projects, focusing primarily on the period from the late 1940s to the late 50s, which is when this tendency is most evident. In particular, 1948 was a landmark year for collaborative filmic endeavours between the two nations in which two events stood out for consolidating both the new collaborative spirit between the two industries, and its power dynamic. The first was the gala premiere of *Enamorada*, starring María Félix and Pedro Armendáriz, in Madrid and Barcelona in 1948, for which the film was designated of 'national interest', a special status given by the Spanish government during the Franco years to productions exalting the values of the regime (*Cinema Reporter*, 3 April 1948, p. 10; 24 April 1948, p. 18; 22 May 1948, p. 16). The Franco regime's official endorsement of a foreign film – a Mexican film set in a small Mexican town during the Mexican revolution, a clearly nationalist work of a country with which Spain had no diplomatic relations – was extraordinary, and demonstrates the growing cultural importance of Mexican cinema in late 1940s Spain. That same year, Jorge Negrete also visited Spain to film *Jalisco canta en Sevilla*, the first of a series of Mexican–Spanish co-productions, part of a collaborative project launched in Spain as part of the publicity surrounding an international Spanish-language film exhibition. The megastar Negrete's arrival generated, as had the arrival of Félix soon after the premiere of *Enamorada*, an unprecedented level of excitement among Spanish movie fans.

The cycle could be said to close with the Spanish premiere of *Faustina* (José Luis Sáenz de Heredia, 1957), the final feature that the legendary María Félix would film in Spain (a final co-production, *Sonatas*, Juan Antonio Bardem 1959, was filmed mostly in Mexico), a work selected to represent Spanish cinema at the Cannes festival in that year (*Cine Asesor*, 23 May 1957), following on the heels of the release of a pair of co-productions: *Dos charros y una gitana* (also known as *Dos novias para un torero*: Antonio Román, 1956), starring Spanish folkloric actress Paquita Rico and Mexican bullfighter Manuel Capetillo, and *La Faraona* (René Cardona, 1956), in which Spanish actress Lola Flores played her career-defining role of a Spanish gypsy who falls for a Mexican *charro* (Joaquín Cordero). None of these films ultimately generated anywhere near the buzz of 1948. By the latter half of the 1950s, this period of cooperation was already quickly fading out as the Spanish government signed, beginning in 1953, notably the year of Negrete's unfortunate death, treaties with the USA and the Vatican, which opened the door for Spain's admission to the United Nations in 1955. With this international legitimisation, the Franco regime no longer needed to rely on cinematic panhispanism. In reality, this cinema never became as popular as other Mexican golden age genres, such as *ranchera* comedies, Emilio

Fernández's nationalist dramas, or, notably, the *rumbera* musicals that had successfully promoted Mexican co-productions with Cuba. While the panhispanist genre continued on into the early 1960s, it would soon be extinguished entirely. However, its promotion in Spain in the 40s and 50s, along with the popularity of Mexican golden age cinema production in general among Spanish audiences, allowed Mexican culture to assume a powerful presence there, even as it earned Mexico a new imposing status, replacing 'la madre patria' [the motherland] as the leading centre of cultural production in the Spanish-speaking world.

CULTURAL BRIDGES: MEXICAN CINEMA'S INFLUENCE IN SPAIN PRIOR TO 1948

'Both peoples love horses, bulls, friendly get togethers and music; differences are secondary because they also share joyfulness, language and religion,' writes Julia Tuñón as an explanation for the affinity that made cinematic connections between Mexico and Spain so easy back in the day ('La imagen', p. 208). Prior to 1948, the year that with the extended visits of Félix and Negrete, along with an international Spanish-language film festival in Madrid, initiated the period of cinematic co-production between the two nations, Mexican film, as well as its folkloric music, was already quite popular in Spain. In fact, during Spain's post-civil war years, with the nation submerged in poverty and increasingly isolated internationally, Mexico became the country whose music most filled the Spanish airwaves, with the *boleros*, *rancheras* and *huapangos* of Agustín Lara, Pedro Vargas and Trío Calaveras among the favourites there. Additionally, beginning in 1940, Mexico's movies achieved an impressive level of popularity, especially as it became evident that the Mexican industry was coming to rival Hollywood there, while dwarfing activity in Spain's own studios. This scenario of cultural links contrasted with the official absence of political relations between the two nations, beginning with Mexican president Lázaro Cárdenas's official rejection of the Franco dictatorship in 1939. As Mexican film historian Tuñón affirms, 'the cinematic exchange strengthened the affective ties and comprehension between the two nations' at a time when international politics kept them at ideological odds ('Relaciones', p. 128).

Cultural exchanges had for centuries been dominated by flows from Spain to the Americas, as was the case with the wild popularity of Spanish *zarzuela* musical theatre in Mexico in the late nineteenth and early twentieth centuries. However, with the rise of new technologies for transmitting culture, flows began to shift. In Spain, Mexican composer Agustín Lara's songs played constantly on the radio by the 1930s and today remain an integral part of the Spanish musical tradition. Lara's lyrics play out Hispano-Mexican bonds as is the case with his celebrated 'Madrid, Madrid ... in Mexico We Often Think of You' or other songs such as 'Valencia' or 'Granada'. By 1950, Lara was known as 'the most popular Mexican in Spain' and 'the sentimental bridge, made of music and celluloid, between Mexico and Spain' (*Primer Plano*, 22 January 1950). Lara's popularity was such that in 1954 the Franco government invited him to Madrid for a special tribute, something unheard of at the time considering the ongoing diplomatic tensions between the two nations. Music, especially songs rooted in popular folklore that were featured on the radio, were an essential part of Spanish everyday life during a time when cinema was submitted to strict censorship and other forms of entertainment such as theatre had become scarce due to the postwar crisis. The radio was a mainstay in Spanish homes until television started to take over everyday family life in the late 1950s.

Along with music (and bullfighting: including the significant symbolic rivalry between the Spaniard Manolete and the Mexican Carlos Arruza), cinema also became increasingly important to Spanish everyday life and, with the aggressive marketing of Mexican films in Spain that began in the early 40s, Spanish audiences became devoted fans of some of Mexican cinema's biggest stars. However, it should be noted that, prior to the end of Spain's civil war of 1936–39, there had been very little presence of Spanish cinema in Mexico, or vice versa. In the former case, imports were scarce and consisted essentially of folkloric musicals such as *Morena clara* (Florián Rey, 1936) and *Carmen, la de Triana* (Florián Rey, 1938), which were both hits in 1938 (García Riera, 'El cine español', p. 15). Although Spain's industry was poised to become the leading Spanish-language movie producer in the mid-1930s – in 1935 Spain produced forty-four films, compared to only twenty-six in Mexico and thirteen in Argentina – production dropped to almost nothing during the civil war, with only four feature films coming out in 1938 (Peredo Castro, *Cine y propaganda*, p. 477). Meanwhile, among the few Mexican films playing in Spain in those years, *Chucho el Roto* and *Prisionero 13* (Fernando de Fuentes, 1933) stand out. Mexico's *Mundo Cinematográfico* attributed their success to their 'authentically Mexican character and development' foreshadowing the much grander triumph of later Mexican films such as those of the *ranchera* comedy genre – but the fledgling Mexican industry was not able to build on this early attention as the Spanish market closed completely to Mexican imports during the war (*Mundo Cinematográfico*, July–August 1937, p. 4) preventing Mexico from riding out the international success of *Rancho Grande* there until several years later.

In Mexico, as in the rest of Latin America, Spanish cinema never recovered the little market share it had begun to conquer prior to the war. From 1939 to 1942, only eleven Spanish films played in Mexico, and most of those were filmed prior to 1940 (García Riera, 'El cine español', p. 15). Mexican cinema, in contrast, quickly came to occupy an important place in Spain with an average of twenty-eight films launched there annually during the 40s – although it began losing significant market share to Hollywood beginning in the latter half of the decade. Among the factors that explain the meagre presence of Spanish cinema in Mexico is the import of Hollywood movies that saturated Mexico's market and left little room for other imports, while Mexico itself was producing so many quality films in those years that competitors from Spain and Argentina found it difficult to make headway. Differences in dialect and accent also made it difficult for Mexican audiences to identify with Spanish film, especially in light of Mexican foreign policy that portrayed Spain as a repressive state and, essentially, a political enemy. The Spanish market, in contrast, became an important one for Mexican film-makers beginning in 1940, with the belated release there of *Allá in el Rancho Grande* (ibid., p. 19).

Rancho Grande was a huge hit upon its belated postwar Spanish release in 1940, eventually closing only after a record seventeen-week run (*Cinema Reporter*, 19 July 1940, p. 1; 2 March 1946, p. 16). Its success was followed by a slew of late 30s *ranchera* comedies, which Spanish audiences eagerly welcomed, along with other genres such as Cantinflas's urban comedies and romantic dramas including, notably, *El peñón de las ánimas* (Miguel Zacarías, 1943), featuring the already popular *ranchera* singer Negrete and introducing a new Mexican actress, María Félix, who would also quickly become a fan favourite. Mexican cinema's run of success in 1940s Spain inspired the same kind of enthusiastic response in the Mexican press as did Mexico's triumphs in other Spanish-speaking nations. However, its rhetoric of 'conquering markets' and exercising a 'spiritual influence' (*Cinema Reporter*, April 1942, p. 21) take on political overtones in Spain that they do not elsewhere in Latin America, including Argentina, whose political conflicts in the early 1940s were more with the USA than with Mexico.

Meanwhile, by 1941, Spanish news service NODO, whose programmes were shown prior to all feature films in Spanish cinemas, was reporting constantly on Mexican stars, such as *Rancho Grande*'s Tito Guízar. The first important Spanish movie magazines (*Primer Plano, Radio Cinema*) included regular sections featuring news about Mexican cinema, along with numerous features on Mexican stars and films. They also covered the premieres of Spanish cinema in Mexico, with the 'scandalous success' of *Locura de amor* (Juan de Orduña, 1948) standing in contrast to the critical and box-office failure of many other films (*Primer Plano*, 3 April 1949), while Spanish audiences and critics could not seem to get enough of their Mexican favourites: 'a constellation of stars that shine with their own light, beginning with Dolores del Río and ending with Jorge Negrete' (ibid., n. p.). Negrete's popularity in Spain took root from the arrival of his first film hits in the early 1940s: *¡Ay, Jalisco, no te rajes!*, *Así se quiere en Jalisco*, *El peñón de las ánimas* – although the films themselves were not necessarily as successful as Negrete's music (*Cinema Reporter*, 2 March 1946, p. 16). Other favourites in the early 1940s include *ranchera* comedies such as *¡Ora, Ponciano!*, *Jalisco nunca pierde* and *Huapango* (Juan Bustillo Oro, 1938) (*Cinema Reporter*, 28 February 1948, p. 6; 11 August 1954, p. 21). While some films that adhered to these early formulas achieved only 'moderate success' or flopped (*Cinema Reporter*, 2 March 1946, p. 16), Mexico also followed up with newer films of appeal to Spanish audiences, such as *Allá en el trópico* (Fernando de Fuentes, 1940), *Al son de la marimba* and Negrete's early non-*ranchera* films, such as *Historia de un gran amor*. The lag between production and exhibition in Spain, partly attributable to the civil war, may be partly to blame for the failure of some genres, whose relevance may have diminished in comparison with the timeless quality of the *ranchera* films. *El capitán Buen Revés* (Juan Bustillo Oro, 1936) and *¡Qué viene mi marido!* (Chano Urueta, 1940), for example, were released in Madrid only in 1947.

This latter film, an historical drama, broke with the *ranchera* musical formula and invited interest in Spain as its screenplay was based on a novel by nineteenth-century Spanish author Pedro Antonio de Alarcón. While some other films that varied too much from the expected folkloric genres failed – including, notably, the family melodrama *Cuando los hijos se van*, which had been a big hit in other foreign markets (ibid.) – Cantinflas's urban comedies, which began showing in Spain in 1943, became enormous favourites of Spanish audiences (ibid.; *Cinema Reporter*, 2 June 1945, p. 31; 28 February 1948, p. 6). Spanish director Antonio Román attributes a general lack of knowledge in Spain about the range of Mexican cinema to these long delays in distribution, as well as to the excessive focus in the press on just a few stars such as Negrete and Cantinflas (*El Cine Gráfico*, 6 January 1948, p. 22). Thus, even as it conquered an ever larger market share, beyond formulaic folkloric films and the star vehicles of Negrete, Félix and Cantinflas, much Mexican cinema was poorly received in Spain, with complaints of poor quality common: 'Low quality Mexican movies are arriving in Spain in great quantities. The worst is that the public is getting tired of them, and by the time good ones start arriving it will be too late' (*El Cine Gráfico*, 6 July 1947, p. 7).

However, beginning as early as 1939, Spaniards had begun to refer to the Mexican industry as 'the other Spanish cinema'. There are two main reasons why this came about. First, the end of the civil war in Spain resulted in an exodus of Spanish republicans to Mexico thanks to Mexican president Lázaro Cárdenas's open door policy for Spanish political exiles. Many of these exiles were cultural workers of one kind or another who were able to settle easily into Mexico's various cultural enterprises, including its film industry, bringing with them their own homegrown Spanish perspectives and, in the end, exerting a notable degree of influence on Mexican film production styles and techniques (the most obvious case being that of director Luis Buñuel, although his arrival in Mexico came several years later). Second, also in 1939, Mexico officially broke off diplomatic and political relations with the new Franco government, removing its ambassador to Madrid. This rupture reduced economic exchange to a minimum, a consequence that was especially damaging to Spanish industries, the majority of which had been decimated by the war. In the context of the film industry, in the first years of the Franco regime, it was much easier for Mexican cinema to gain market share in Spain than vice versa.

In this 'other Spanish cinema' that was produced in Mexico in the 1940s, just as in Mexican cinema production in general at the time, there was a visible presence of Spanish actors, mainly in secondary roles, but occasionally in leads, and many of the films in which they acted were set in Spain. Their themes ranged from popular folklore: *La morena de mi copla* (Fernando Rivero, 1946) to adaptations of Spanish literary classics: *Pepita Jiménez* (Emilio Fernández, 1946) to romantic comedies: *Dos mexicanos en Sevilla* (Carlos Orellana, 1942) or *El verdugo de Sevilla* (Fernando Soler, 1942), playing out what appears to be an affective link between the two countries, a tendency that would become more pronounced in later co-productions. While the precise inspirations behind these films are not clear, critics such as Pérez Monfort and García Riera have speculated that the presence of so many Spanish artists and intellectuals in Mexico at the time, along with a conservative 'Hispanist will' in both industries, may have been the catalyst for the trend. This mutual Hispanism implied a representation, following Díaz López, of 'shared traditions, combinations of folklores to reflect an historical fraternity' ('Buscar y amar', p. 125).

A film within this tendency that particularly stands out is *En tiempos de la Inquisición* (Juan Bustillo Oro, 1946), in which Negrete plays the role of a Spanish nobleman in love with a Moorish princess. This Mexican cinema, injected as it was with a significant Spanish flavour, became quite popular in Spain in the 1940s despite the diplomatic rupture between the two countries. Spanish film producer and administrator Enrique Domínguez Rodiño affirmed with enthusiasm:

I don't miss a single Mexican movie. I like them; they are exciting and fun. Seeing and enjoying them I feel more profoundly Spanish. And the same thing happens with our audiences. The influence that Mexican cinema is having on the Spanish spirit is extraordinary. (*El Cine Gráfico*, 6 January 1948, p. 32)

In the end, the consolidation of this multinational Hispanism as a thematic axis in many films of both countries served both the Mexican film industry's economic motivations, as well as Spain's political objectives of promoting a prominent and favourable image for the country among Latin American filmgoers, despite its poor standing in terms of international political relations.

Notwithstanding the Spanish government's apparent desire to forge more congenial cultural relations with Latin America, its deep involvement with the movie business in Spain, from production to distribution, did not always facilitate these goals. Beginning in 1946, Spanish dubbing was obligatory for all foreign-language pictures, with the aim of controlling and censoring dialogues, especially in the case of Hollywood films – a policy known as 'linguistic censorship'. Some Spanish-language films would be dubbed as well, including, for example, the Dolores del Río hit *La otra* (Roberto Gavaldón, 1946), arousing outrage in Latin America for the Spanish authorities' contention that 'in Spain they don't understand the idiom of the Mexicans' and because this disguised censorship 'completely changes the plot of the movies', a story covered as far away as Bogotá (*Magazin Dominical*, 17 January 1954, p. 24). It should be noted that even the films of Mexico's most beloved actors in Spain, such as Negrete and Félix, were subject to censorship. In contrast, in Mexican productions, the 'lisp' characteristic of Spanish pronunciation (i.e., the 'z' and soft 'c' are pronounced as 'Θ') was proscribed at a time when Mexican-accented Spanish tacitly became the international standard for much of Latin America – with a curious exception being the role of Jesus Christ, interpreted by Spanish actors with their Spanish accent intact in films such as *Jesús de Nazareth* (José Díaz Morales, 1942), *María Magdalena, pecadora de Magdala* (Miguel Contreras Torres, 1946) or *El mártir del calvario* (Miguel Morayta, 1952) (García Riera, 'El cine español', p. 22).

The Franco regime's code of film censorship took into account political, religious, moral and sexual content. While film content was often questioned elsewhere (including, for example, Cuba, Colombia and Venezuela), Spain's censors interfered much more actively with distribution than those anywhere else in the Spanish-speaking world. While some Mexican films were either cut or banned entirely, the consequences for Spanish producers were much greater. For fear of the censors, Spanish movie production of the era was often seen as dull with regard to themes and characters, with mediocre scripts based on insubstantial stories about local customs and the like. As García Riera affirms, 'there was a prudishness in Spanish cinema that made Mexican censorship look like a marvel of tolerance in comparison' (ibid., p. 18), and this lack of creative freedom significantly hindered Spain's chances at making inroads into Latin American markets. This censorship notably prohibited the exhibition of Mexico's highly popular *rumbera* genre for what censors judged as its immorality and indecency. While Mexico was a country that maintained a certain separation between church and state, Franco's Catholic Spain proclaimed itself the 'the West's spiritual reserve', in the words of Spanish fascist leader José Antonio Primo de

Rivera, although this difference in moral values would not impede the fusion of national imaginaries through co-productions.

Spain's movie production would remain largely mediocre and inconsequential until 1951, with the release of the critically acclaimed neo-realist production *Surcos* (José Antonio Nieves Conde), known in its Mexican release as *Bajo el cielo de Madrid*. It might be added that this was the same year that exiled Spanish director Luis Buñuel, making his third Mexican film, was celebrated with a Best Director award at Cannes for *Los olvidados*, which in Mexico swept up eleven different Ariel prizes including Best Picture, Best Cinematographer (Gabriel Figueroa) and Best Screenplay (Buñuel in collaboration with Spanish exile Luis Alcoriza), a major surprise considering Buñuel's outsider status within the Mexican machine – despite the fact that he had obtained Mexican citizenship in 1949. The prudish strictures of Francoist moral codes produced saccharine romances and historical dramas nicknamed 'cardboard stones' for the makeshift nature of the studio sets on which they were filmed, or propaganda films such as *Raza* (José Luis Sáenz de Heredia, 1942), an epic film biography of Francisco Franco that was banned in Mexico. This style of movie production, disdained by international critics, did not have much of an entry point into the Mexican market. For example, while Spanish studios released forty-two films in 1947, only six made it to Mexican screens and only one of those, *El Clavo* (Rafael Gil, 1944), won any critical acceptance in the face of tepid popular reception (*El Cine Gráfico*, 4 January 1948, pp. 7, 12; 14 February 1948, p. 4).

At the end of World War II in 1945, with the return of competition from reviving movie industries elsewhere in Europe, Mexico responded immediately. Its studios sent producers and distributors to Spain to actively promote Mexican film and to foster co-productions. Mexico-based actors Sara García, Juan José Martínez Casado, María Antonieta Pons and Rosario 'Charito' Granados, and directors Roberto Rodríguez, José Díaz Morales, Roberto Gavaldón, Raúl de Anda and Ramón Pereda were among those who travelled to Spain in 1947 and 1948 – along with the highly publicised and eagerly awaited visits of Negrete and Félix (*El Cine Gráfico*, 6 July 1947, p. 3; 20 July 1947, p. 4; 17 August 1947, p. 5; 14 March 1948, p. 6; 25 April 1948, p. 5; 6 June 1948, p. 2). Mexican studios also began producing Spanish-themed films such as *Pepita Jiménez* and *Una gitana en Jalisco* (José Díaz Morales, 1947), designed to help the Mexican industry better penetrate the Spanish market. This latter film, though not a big hit, likely served as a loose early model for constructing plots and thematics for future co-productions, with its many musical numbers and romantic plotline ending in the happy uniting of a Mexican man and Spanish woman. Meanwhile, Mexican studios hoped to promote other stars – aside from the reliable Félix, Negrete and Cantinflas – in Spain, including Dolores del Río, Arturo de Córdova, Sofía Álvarez and Fernando Soto 'Mantequilla' (*El Cine Gráfico*, 13 June 1947, p. 6). Several del Río vehicles of the postwar years – *La malquerida* (Emilio Fernández, 1949), *Deseada* (Roberto Gavaldón, 1951) and *Doña Perfecta* (Alejandro Galindo, 1951) – bore some connection to Spain: adaptations of Spanish literary works in the first and last cases, and a co-starring role with Jorge Mistral, who was to become Spain's most popular leading man in Mexican cinema, in the second.

As early as 1946, there was buzz in Mexico about possible co-productions and exchanges of artists, and *Cinema Reporter* soon announced that a first-class theatre in

Madrid, the Gran Vía, would be dedicated exclusively to the launching of Mexican movies (2 March 1946, p. 16). A week later word arrived in Mexico that there would now be two premiere theatres for Mexican films in Madrid, along with another eight neighbourhood second-run houses dedicated to Mexican imports (*Cinema Reporter*, 9 March 1946, p. 33). Around the same time as this was going on, it was announced that *María Candelaria* and two other Mexican films would be competing in Cannes, and that a private screening of this film for the Spanish press generated rave reviews (*Cinema Reporter*, 23 March 1946, pp. 30, 32). It would open in Spain at the end of March of 1946 and be a major box-office and critical success (*Cinema Reporter*, 30 March 1946, p. 34).

María Candelaria defined a new kind of Mexican cinema, no longer 'folkloric' in the style of *Rancho Grande*, but still idiosyncratically Mexican. Emilio Fernández's films, which were soon to be launched one after another in Spain and all over Europe throughout the late 1940s and into the early 50s, portrayed Mexico's indigenous and rural communities, its urban underbelly, its revolutionary struggles, often with traditional music (*rancheras, boleros, huapangos, corridos*) playing in the background. By the end of the 40s, the Mexican press would report that the opinion of Spanish directors was unanimous in its praises of Fernández's work (*El Cine Gráfico*, 6 January 1948, pp. 20–1). However, for the most part, the Spanish filmgoing public did not buy in, greatly preferring Cantinflas's gags, Negrete's hacienda romances and María Félix's subtly sexy shenanigans. *Cámara* attempted to explain the phenomenon of audiences that accepted, without hesitation, low-budget films with plots and themes that had been repeated many times before, surmising that modest producers with 'their unpretentious regionalist movies' had crossed national boundaries and broken the ice of 'those phantasmagoric "foreign markets"'; they had turned characters of Mexican folklore into the diplomatic ambassadors of Mexican cinema. While Spanish intellectuals fretted over the,

> overabundance and monotony of the typically Mexican themes, the regional folklore, this cinema, on its own and without any fanfare, won the hearts of our audiences, of those great masses, who almost never opine, but who are the ones that fill the movie houses, or leave them empty. (*Cámara*, 26 December 1947, p. 19)

The ever-growing popularity of Félix and Negrete, the new international cachet earned for Mexican cinema with the critical attention obtained by Fernández, what seemed to be a growing interest in both Mexico and Spain for a thawing of cultural relations after the initial rupture caused by the civil war and the establishment of the Franco dictatorship, and the need of both nations' film industries to reach out more effectively to external markets in the changing postwar environment together set the stage for the cinematic collaborations that were to come.

A NEW ERA OF CO-PRODUCTIONS

Beginning with the advent of sound cinema, Spanish-language producers, including principally those of Spain, Mexico, Argentina and – to a much lesser extent – Cuba, developed movie genres for national popular consumption, with archetypical or historical characters that brought to life national imaginaries, inviting audiences to identify through them with their national communities. These 'national genres', such as the folkloric comedy known as the *españolada* in Spain, the Mexican *ranchera* comedy, or the Argentine tango film, sought to visualise national values, while uniting them with musical folkloric traditions (D'Lugo, 'Gardel', p. 149). In May 1944, the Spanish movie magazine *Primer Plano* published an article affirming that: 'the portrayal of our personality in the cinema must show the world the cultural traits and temperaments that constitute what differentiates us as a race' (n. p.). The Spanish 'race' appears to be imagined here as something more cultural or affective than physical, an idea that would influence how the fusion of Mexicanness and Spanishness played out in Spanish–Mexican co-productions that sought to represent a transnational Hispanic 'race'.

As indicated above, Mexican films were becoming increasingly popular: 'with only very rare exceptions, their plots feature what Spaniards most love, music and songs; besides that, the acting and arguments are really pleasing to them' (*El Cine Gráfico*, 24 August 1947, p. 11). Very soon extended visits of Negrete and Félix in 1948 – symbolising a new international connection made feasible by the inauguration of air travel between the two nations in January of 1948 (*El Cine Gráfico*, 25 January 1948, p. 6) – along with the staging of the Hispanoamerican Cinema Congress, featuring the best in recent film production from Spain, Mexico, Argentina and Cuba, marked the beginning of a new era of transatlantic cinematic cooperation.

The collaborative productions that would proliferate beginning at this time would exalt the similarities in archetypes and national values: honour, bravery, decency, passion – commonplaces in Mexico and Spain's own national imaginaries – represented by national icons of masculinity: the Mexican *charro*, the Spanish bullfighter, or of feminine beauty: the Mexican *china poblana*, the Andalusian *gitana*; the definitive scenario pitted the macho against the passionate but virtuous woman in a context of honour and courage in a shared Mexican and Spanish cultural space.

These were themes and characters that were well established in the above-mentioned national genres and whose clichés and stars were now being joined in Hispano-Mexican co-productions to create a sentiment of 'racial unity', a fraternity between the two Spanish-speaking peoples (Santaolalla, p. 59). The invocation of a common history and of blood ties would become part of the era's thinking; however, a third element would link the two peoples: mutual affection. If the first elements form part of an historical heritage, the latter appeals to a present-day will, to the desire to launch common business ventures.

This new economically motivated structure of feeling can be seen in the premiere of *Enamorada*, featuring María Félix, at the Avenida de Madrid movie house in April of 1948. Its elegant invitations read:

> it is not expressive affinity, but, simply, sentimental identity that makes possible the miracle of what is Spanish-Mexican and what is Mexican-Spanish. Mexicans are a people enamoured with Spain, with the love of a valiant son and of a beloved sister in the immense family of Hispanity. (Cited in *El Cine Gráfico*, 24 April 1948, p. 5)

This type of rhetoric can be seen as well in the speech that inaugurated the above-mentioned international film congress, as delivered by the Spanish Minister of

National Education, Ernesto Giménez Caballero: 'I thank you, esteemed representatives of Mexico and Argentina, with the words that a member of a family uses to thank others of the same lineage' (*Primer Plano*, May 1950). It is in this way that 'Hispanic romance' became defining paradigms in Spanish–Mexican co-productions, through the affective relationship between the *charro* and the *gitana* – or, in a more modern variation, the Spanish gentleman and the Mexican devourer of men. Some researchers interpret this romance of a united Hispanic race as a 'metaphor of Spain's "motherhood" in relation to her American "children"' (Santaolalla, p. 59) since, while Mexico sought in these collaborative projects a means of broadening its markets, Spain pursued more political and social objectives: some degree of international acceptance of the Franco government and recognition of its national values as universal Hispanic values, in this case implicitly present in Mexican culture. However, the popular success of the beloved Mexican stars, Negrete and Félix in particular, exceeded the objectives of Spanish institutions. The argument of Mexican culture being derivative of the culture of the motherland is hard to support given the evidence at hand; indeed, it would be much easier to make a case for saying that Negrete and Félix achieved something of a conquest of the Spanish public by the Mexican cinema industry – that is, the imposition of Mexican cinema in Spain.

For the masses of Mexican spectators, the triumph of their idols in Europe would confirm the ideas of postrevolutionary nationalism, even when its ambassadors come from an untouchable elite. Far from provoking rejection or antipathy, the displays of wealth and extravagance on the part of celluloid stars reaffirmed the representations of this 'new' Mexico, thriving, animated by the confrontations realised earlier in the century. Félix and Negrete condensed – in their physical appearance, in the characters they played in their films, in their way of speaking, singing, moving – the proud archetypes of *mestizaje*. For the first time in five centuries of history, Mexicans were arriving in the *madre patria* not in the role of poor and submissive children, but as equals if not as adults who are more successful and prosperous than their own progenitors.

Félix, for three years, would live in the two most luxurious hotels in Madrid, the Ritz and the Palace. She would travel with her entourage of assistants: hairdresser, makeup artist, secretary, seamstress and tailor (Félix, p. 66). Even Negrete, less accustomed to the high life than Félix, stayed at the Palace. Félix's exhibition of splendour and the superstar treatment given to Negrete produced an image of glamour rivalling the aura of Hollywood stars, and only strengthened the admiration for the Mexicans on the part of their Spanish fans, who were suffering the consequences of the nation's most severe economic crisis of the century.

JORGE NEGRETE AND PANHISPANIC MASCULINITY

Notwithstanding the star images of Félix and Negrete, which ensured that the new joint cinematic ventures would generate excitement, the most enduring representations of these nations in their filmic co-productions of the late 1940s and early to mid-50s were much less ostentatious and magnificent, but instead turned to down to earth, if colourful, archetypes of popular culture. These movies built on the successful model of Fernando de Fuentes's original 1936 version of *Allá en el Rancho Grande*, whose late 1940s remake, featuring Negrete, would show in previews at the 1948 Madrid competition, thus coinciding with the launch of cooperative production efforts between the two nations. This event, highly publicised in both countries, also coincided with Negrete's (and Félix's) extended stay in Spain during which he performed in concert to sold-out shows in Madrid, while also filming several of the first films produced in the spirit of 'panhispanism', starting with the Spanish–Mexican co-production *Jalisco canta en Sevilla*, which would be followed with the Mexican film *Una gallega en México* (Julián Soler, 1949) – which ironically featured Argentine comic actress Niní Marshall in the starring role as a Spanish immigrant living in Mexico – and the Spanish production *Teatro Apolo* (Rafael Gil, 1950).

Negrete was the embodiment of what was sold as the prototype of Mexicanness: the *charro*. From the time of the triumph of *Rancho Grande*, the *charro*-cowboy with his particular aesthetic is the character that represents the national archetype of masculinity, more so than other common film representations such as the revolutionary insurgent or the family patriarch, a tendency especially pronounced for Spanish audiences. The *charro* represents a range of putative national values: 'fatherland, family, virility, morality, respect for the Catholic religion and traditions' (Pérez Montfort, ' El hispanismo', p. 43), a construction of traditional Mexican values that coincided to a great degree with values promoted for Franco's Spain of the 1940s, which may explain the success of this genre of Mexican film in Spain along with the consolidation of Negrete as icon of Hispanic (not only Mexican) masculinity.

In the co-productions launched through Negrete's high-profile visit to Spain, *churros* abounded, as did Andalusian/gypsy folklorism as symbol of Spanish culture, along with bullfighting themes common to both Spanish and Mexican cinematic traditions. Popular culture, above all, was what seemed to link the two nations. In *Jalisco canta en Sevilla*, Negrete's *charro* character feels right at home on an Andalusian ranch (owned by a former bullfighter who had spent ample time in Mexico), where he sings, 'Long live Mexican soil, which could well be here.' Mexico's *ranchera* comedy films were admired from the institutions of Franco's government, as is made evident in the book *Amor a Méjico a través de su cine* (Loving Mexico Through Its Cinema) – which, it should be noted, spells Mexico with a 'j' as was traditional of the linguistic 'purism' of the Franco era, arrogantly ignoring Mexico's cultural autonomy, seen in its employment of the 'x' in proud reference to the Mexica peoples – that is, Mexico's indigenous roots – published by Spanish film-maker and fascist ideologue Ernesto Giménez Caballero in 1948: 'in Mexican movies today, Spain sees its own genuine, viril and enduring drama of honour brought to life in the *charro*', an always armed and often belligerent figure on horseback presented as the epitome of manliness, recalling the historical icon of the Spanish conquistador (quoted in ibid., p. 44).

No Mexican actor better assumed the role of the proud and viril *charro* than Negrete, who from his earliest releases in Spain in the early 1940s made a huge impression. When *Me he de comer esa tuna* (Miguel Zacarías, p. 1945) premiered there in 1947, distributors initially requested an unheard of 5,000 lobby cards, which they thought to be a conservative estimate of what they would ultimately need (*El Cine Gráfico*, 20 July 1947, p. 4). His trip to Spain in 1948 was a major media event, drawing

Jorge Negrete upon his
arrival in Madrid in 1948

throngs of supporters to greet him upon his arrival and wherever he went, large
numbers of enamoured women – not to mention admiring men. The idealisation of
Negrete in the 1940s and 50s as a model of Hispanic masculinity was captured in
Giménez Caballero's book, whose second chapter is dedicated to the Mexican star and
emphasises his seductive image: 'the many Spanish female fans of Jorge Negrete are
not the only ones who flock to the cinemas to see him; men, young and old alike, also
go as they can't explain how this figure attracts women with a legendary halo' (p. 52).

The release of the first Spanish–Mexican co-production, *Jalisco canta en Sevilla*,
marked the definitive consecration of Negrete in Spain. Not only did his music fill the
radio waves, but his extended visit to Madrid in mid-1948 (just in time for the
Hispanoamerican Film Awards) had earned him the adoration of his Spanish fans, an
affection enhanced by the news disseminated a few months prior to his arrival that he
had family living there (*Cinema Reporter*, 7 February 1948, p. 20). His popularity kept
his name in the headlines constantly for the several months that he spent there. The
NODO government newsreels likewise followed his moves regularly. Upon his arrival
at the Madrid train station on 31 May 1948, he was eagerly welcomed by a multitude
of admirers, in one of the few spontaneous popular manifestations in public spaces
that the Franco regime would allow. Women threw themselves at him, grabbing at his
clothes, truly exceptional behaviour at the time in a country marked by an
ultraconservative Catholic regime of social control. The following day, after another
similar scene, Negrete made a declaration, a phrase that would frequently be quoted
and would define his image in Spain: 'Are there no longer any machos in Spain?' That
phrase, along with his supposed rebuff to Spanish folkloric actress Carmen Sevilla, his
co-star in *Jalisco canta en Sevilla*, symbolised a rivalry of masculinities, Mexican and
Spanish, in which the Mexian variety was defiantly dominant.

It was well known that Negrete opposed the Franco regime. In a 1946 Mexican
newspaper interview, the Mexican star, then the Secretary of the National Association

of Actors (ANDA) in Mexico, had sworn he would not travel to Spain as long as Franco remained in power as he had an 'aversion to dictators' (D. Negrete, p. 278). Nevertheless, he gave in, taking the opportunity to consolidate his reputation not only as movie and music star, but as the epitome of Mexican, and by extension 'Hispanic', macho masculinity. His films established, through music and folklore, a sort of masculine fraternity that superseded ideological differences. The closeness that his particular style of masculinity promoted between Mexican and Spanish culture was reinforced by his own declarations made while filming *Jalisco canta en Sevilla*. Spanish film magazine *Primer Plano* quoted Negrete's first phrases upon arriving in Madrid: 'God bless my homeland, which is this one! Long live Spain!' (June 1948, n. p.), and soon afterwards the same journal published additional declarations that Negrete made at a press conference: 'In Mexico we adore Spain, we are impassioned, expansive, violent, as is the style here, and this does not come from our indigenous heritage, it comes from the Spanish' (ibid.). In a similar vein, according to *Radiocinema*, Negrete stated that 'our blood, language and religion, along with our temperament and character are part of our Spanish heritage' (June 1948), adding that 'Spaniards and Mexicans alike feel at home in either of the two nations' (ibid.). These phrases show that Negrete complied, consciously or not, in his own public relations discourse, with the Spanish government's rhetoric of promoting the idea of a common 'Spanish race' that united Spain and Mexico. Negrete's image was thus ideologically 'cleansed' in Spain so as to better construct the Hispanic leading man that Spain needed for these transnational productions. Negrete would later be quoted as saying, 'Andalusia is not so different from Jalisco: the landscapes, types of people, colour' (*Cinema Reporter*, 23 October 1948, p. 24). Negrete's *charro* archetype, then, easily allowed for the translation of the Mexican macho cliché (Díaz López, 'Jalisco') into a concept of use to the Spanish nationalist ideology of the era, in which his machismo became not only Mexican but Hispanic. The Franquist ideology expressed in Giménez Caballero's book takes advantage of the popular admiration for Negrete and, obliterating Mexico's rejection of the dictatorship, deploys his image to reinforce the values imposed by the regime (*Radiocinema*, June 1948, n. p.).

Negrete's various remarks were uttered within a context of a bitter polemic that had arisen in Mexico where the press accused him of being 'an anti-Mexican renegade' and of rejecting president Miguel Alemán (Serna, p. 13). He was maligned for his antinationalist attitudes and his unconditional surrender to the *madre patria*, whose government Mexico continued to condemn as fascistic. In the avalanche of Negrete interviews and commentaries published in those months, journals in both countries chose to focus on whatever was most controversial: sexuality and nationalism, it would seem, were in Spain and Mexico, respectively, two of the most delicate topics of discussion at mid-century.

These two concepts were, of course, the foundational concepts of Negrete's image. Negrete, already a superstar as Mexico's most popular *charro*, became an icon of not just Mexican, but Hispanic masculinity in a way that not only helped promote the idea of a transnational Hispanic market, but also emphasised an image of masculinity that was attuned to the conservative values of Franco's Spain. In Spain, Negrete is portrayed as exhibiting 'deep human values, religion, a precise concept of duty and high moral virtues: those of being a good son, a good husband, a good father and a good citizen' (*Radiocinema*, 6 June 1948*)*. In order to highlight Negrete's role as an imaginary link bonding a common Spanish and Mexican set of values, in the majority of the co-productions, his Mexican character had a Spanish father or grandfather, as was the case in both *Jalisco canta en Sevilla* and *Teatro Apolo*, in which, moreover, he sang Spanish *zarzuelas*, earning him an award from the Film Critics Circle of Madrid. The quintessential Mexican *charro* had played a Spanish character in an earlier Mexican film, *En tiempos de la Inquisición*, and the Spanish–Mexican co-productions built on this existing association, tweaking Negrete's very Mexican image by emphasising his Spanish heritage, thereby transforming it from a nationalist symbol into more panhispanic archetype.

In the romantic movies that were typical of Mexican–Spanish co-productions of the era, hybrids combining key elements of *ranchera* comedies and *españoladas*, Negrete's characters were inevitably accompanied by Spanish female counterparts, invariably sensual yet morally righteous women with strong characters, but who submitted readily when in love, a dynamic reflected in the Negrete song, 'Agua del pozo' from the film *Jalisco canta en Sevilla*: 'Don't dare to mock a macho man who gives you his affection'. Spanish audiences had responded positively to María Félix's assertiveness, and it might be said that her character type was reworked in these films in roles of strong-willed and beautiful (but in these Spanish reworkings always virtuous) Spanish women played by such actresses as Carmen Sevilla, who co-starred opposite Negrete in *Jalisco canta en Sevilla*; Lola Flores, whose first co-production was *¡Ay, pena, penita, pena!* (Miguel Morayta, 1953); and Paquita Rico of the co-production *Dos novias para un torero*. A formula quickly developed in which the *gitana* and *charro* meet, are attracted (although their pride or other plot complications keep them at a distance) and, finally, confess their mutual love in a final scene full of folkloric clichés.

The Spanish premiere of *Jalisco canta en Sevilla* generated the same kind of excitement that his trip to Spain had several months earlier. One Spanish reviewer wrote:

> For the first time a movie has been made in Spain in which Spanish and Mexican actors have intervened, in close brotherhood, led by the magnificent Jorge Negrete and our lovely and talented Carmen Sevilla. They have thus created a Hispano-Mexican cinematic jewel, an emblem of well-deserved pride for Spanish-language cinema with captivating Mexican songs and joyous Andalucian melodies. (*Primer Plano*, 29 May 1949)

While the transnational Hispanic brotherhood theme circulated in the press back in Mexico as well, observers there were also mindful of what the success of this collaborative endeavour meant for the Mexican industry. In an article focusing on Mexican cinema's inroads into markets beyond Latin America made possible by prizes and critical acclaim in France, Italy, the USA and Spain, *Cinema Reporter* boasts: 'Since some time ago, Mexican cinema has imposed itself worlwide through its quality' (10 August 1949, p. 31), a claim that the Spanish industry could not make. Thus, it was clear that in Negrete's romantic bonding with Sevilla, it was the Mexican who won the Andalusian beauty, a Mexican whose presence in Spain had implied from his controversial arrival a national emasculation.

However, despite all the fanfare, while Negrete was at the height of his popularity at mid-century, none of his Spanish films would be as popular as his emblematically Mexican films, from his early hits, to the iconic colour superproduction *Allá en el Rancho Grande,* or the instant classic *Dos tipos de cuidado*, in which he co-starred with another Mexican megastar, Pedro Infante, nor would Negrete film again in Spain. These films, like other Negrete vehicles, were box-office hits, but did not generate a great pro-Hispanic buzz abroad, and Negrete's Hispanic connection was soon forgotten by many fans, who would become more interested in his marriage to María Félix (in 1952), his union activities in Mexico, or his always popular Mexican *ranchera* films, such as *Tal para cual* (Rogelio González, 1953).

However, Mexico did make inroads in Spain and elsewhere in Europe in the late 1940s, although not through the work of Negrete, nor as a result of these highly touted transnational collaborations. Mexico's push for new market share in Spain happened to coincide with its promotion of another genre of emblematically Mexican films no longer rooted in popular music and folklore, but in the indigenist and revolutionary aesthetic established in the oeuvre of Emilio Fernández and introduced to Europe with the triumph of *María Candelaria* in Cannes in 1946. At the 1948 Spanish-language film exhibition in Madrid, four Mexican films, *Río Escondido* with María Félix, *La otra* with Dolores del Río, *La barraca* (Roberto Gavaldón 1945) and *Crepúsculo* were honoured – and heavily publicised, earning Mexican cinema a new artsy image in Spain (*Cinema Reporter*, 27 November 1948, p. 45). Soon the premieres of films like Emilio Fernández's *La perla* were major events in Spain's largest cities (*Cinema Reporter*, 10 October 1949, p. 24). And, as previously noted, with the gala premiere of the Emilo Fernández film, *Enamorada*, also in 1948, another category of Mexican star, not associated with *ranchera* musicals, made its mark in Spain.

LA DOÑA IN SPAIN

María Félix became an icon of Mexican feminine beauty and power through hit films such as *Doña Bárbara, La mujer sin alma* (Fernando de Fuentes, 1943), *Amok* and *La devoradora* (Fernando de Fuentes, 1946). The 'devourer of men' character originated in *Doña Bárbara*, the film that made her an international superstar, and Mexican studios quickly capitalised on her success, reworking this character again and again in her later film roles, just as she adapted it in the construction of her own often extravagant public image. Spanish audiences were fascinated with the lack of conformity to gender norms, or to moral codes, on the part of many of the characters Félix played. For example, two years prior to *Enamorada*'s gala release, Félix broke box-office records with *La monja alférez* (Emilio Gómez Muriel, 1944), in which she played a colonial-era Spanish nun who cross-dresses and lives as a man. Another Félix vehicle, *La mujer de todos* (Julio Bracho, 1946), was launched with great fanfare despite its racy plot in which Félix plays a promiscuous seductress (*Cinema Reporter*, 15 November 1947).

Félix's popularity did not guarantee distribution of her sometimes controversial films in Spain: *La mujer de todos* was mutilated by censors, and *Amok*, in which she plays a woman whose manipulations and demands drive her lover to ruin, and *La*

María Félix wowed Spanish
fans in *La monja alférez*
(1944)

devoradora, in which a similar character drives her various lovers to suicide and
murder, were withheld completely. Interestingly, several of these films that served
both to introduce her to Spanish audiences and to challenge, and emphatically so, the
conservative views of female sexuality promoted by the Franco regime were co-written
by Spaniards in exile, including Antonio Momplet (*La mujer de todos*) and, perhaps
more controversially, Max Aub and Eduardo Ugarte (*La monja alférez*), both of whom
had been politically active as antifascists prior to their exile. However, given the
ubiquitous presence of Spanish political exiles in Mexican golden age cinema, the
participation of a few in these films is perhaps inevitable. Another civil war exile,
Paulino Masip, co-wrote the screenplay for the wholesome *Jalisco canta en Sevilla* – as
well as Félix's racy *La devoradora*.

Félix visited Spain in 1948 not only to promote her Mexican films there, but also to
act with Spanish director Rafael Gil in a series of pictures designed to build on her
trademark character, including *Mare nostrum*, *Una mujer cualquiera* (1949) and *La noche
del sábado* (1950); she would also star in the Franco-Spanish co-production *La corona
negra* (1951) under the directorship of Argentine Luis Saslavsky, the Franco-Italo-
Spanish film *Messalina* (Carmine Gallone, 1951) and the previously mentioned
Faustina (as well as several other European productions arranged independently of her
Spain-based endeavours). During the same period, she starred in the Mexican
production of *Doña Diabla*, based on the dramatic work of Spaniard Luis Fernández
Ardavín, and the Spanish–Mexican co-production *Camelia* (Roberto Gavaldón, 1954),
in which her diva character plays with the heartstrings of a Spanish bullfighter played
by Spanish leading man Jorge Mistral. *Faustina* and the co-production *Sonatas* – filmed
mainly in Mexico – would mark her last excursions into Spanish cinema.

While it would seem from the general popularity of her films that Spanish audiences loved the headstrong, seductive, domineering and often brutally manipulative women she portrayed, the films that accompanied her arrival in Spain, both Emilio Fernández films with high production values and a polished aesthetic, presented characters that were more virtuous and respectable than the roles that made her famous, while still maintaining the aura of feminine strength, independence and allure she always exuded. In *Río Escondido*, the Félix vehicle presented in the 1948 festival, she played a schoolteacher, wilful, honest and patriotic, while her character in *Enamorada*, Beatriz Peñafield, remained a strong and sensuous woman – in an emblematic scene, after the revolutionary general played by Pedro Armendáriz whistles at her, she boldly slaps him across the face – but one who exhibited a more virtuous sex appeal than that seen in the manipulative title character of *Doña Bárbara*, a fiery but unquestionably honourable sexuality (similar to that of the soon to become emblematic Spanish *gitana* archetype). Thus it was *Enamorada* that premiered as a film 'of national interest', rather than some of her earlier Fernando de Fuentes films such as *Doña Bárbara*, *La mujer sin alma* or *La devoradora*.

Enamorada was just the third foreign film given this honour and, following the overwhelming box-office success of its predecessors, the Hollywood films *The Devil and Daniel Webster* (William Dieterle, 1941) and *The Song of Bernadette* (Henry King, 1943), it opened simultaneously in an astounding 3,000 cinemas all over Spain (*El Cine Gráfico*, 7 March 1948, p. 10), without, to some critics' amazement, having been altered at all by censors (*El Cine Gráfico*, 4 April 1948, p. 5). Premiering only weeks before her much anticipated arrival in Spain in early May of 1948, the film was a huge hit. There had been buzz about her trip for nearly a year; and the preproduction of *Mare nostrum* had begun long before filming began as director Rafael Gil had confirmed her participation a year ahead of time.

Meanwhile, in the first months of 1948 in Mexico, Félix underwent a period of severe criticism in the Mexican press. Not even her unquestioned beauty could save what was judged her atrocious acting in *La diosa arrodillada* (*El Cine Gráfico*, 6 January 1948, p. 12). Praise was often tinged with insults; in a review of *Que Dios me perdone* (Tito Davison, 1948), the assessment was: 'we have been able to appreciate that this is the first time in her artistic career that María Félix has managed to act before the camera' (*El Cine Gráfico*, 4 April 1948, p. 4). While these films had not yet arrived in Spain, Spaniards following news about La Doña, as she had been known ever since *Doña Bárbara*, were confronted with controversies from Félix's personal life. Félix was often celebrated in Spain as 'María Bonita', the title of the song dedicated to her by her husband since 1943, the equally beloved Agustín Lara. Spaniards eagerly anticipated not only her much hyped visit to Spain in 1948, but that of her husband, who was to accompany her – until word leaked out that the two were divorcing. In addition, just before travelling to Madrid, she had filmed *Maclovia* in the area of Lake Pátzcuaro, in Michoacán. Her eccentricities were widely discussed: she ordered a hydroplane to deliver her an electric refrigerator so that she could enjoy 'her fresh juices, her American fruits, her special dishes and waiters from the Philippines in white gloves as she had during the filming in Cholula of *Enamorada*' (*El Cine Gráfico*, 7 March 1948, p. 4).

Félix was conscious of the antagonism of the Mexican press, which she refered to as 'journalistic rabble', yet observed that the more they attacked her, the greater her celebrity (Félix, p. 76). It was soon rumoured that she would be paid a sum that would have been inconceivable to Mexican producers for acting in her first Spanish picture (*El Cine Gráfico*, 9 May 1948, p. 4), and that those funds were not being obtained honourably – a story that would be kept out of the Spanish press. In Mexico, the rumour was that Spanish columnists simply could not repeat what the Mexican press was printing about her because of censorship, since gossip about her included taboo themes of adultery, infidelity and cohabitation with Spanish film producer Césareo González. Félix's version was that:

> the Mexican press soon rushed to invent a romance. They said it was my fault that Césareo had left his wife and children in misery, just like the middle-aged men I ruined in my movies. In that way they took advantage of the public's tendency to confuse my real life with my screen image as a vampiress. (Félix, p. 65)

In Spain, however, the press showed her nothing but love. In return, Félix did her part to play up her affection for Spain, declaring: 'Spain has made a magnificent impression on me; it captivates me so much with its natural beauty as well as the friendliness of its people and the sympathy that one breathes in here' (*Primer Plano*, 24 April 1949), adding on another occasion that 'Madrid is the cleanest city I've ever seen, and is just beautiful' (23 July 1949). That summer, she made a show, which the press was happy to cover, of lighting a candle to the Virgin of Fatima for the Spanish national soccer team (ibid.).

Her first Spanish co-production, *Mare nostrum*, was a box-office disappointment despite the praise of Spanish critics, such as this one: 'There is not a single metre of celuloide that does not serve as an accessory to exalt the dazzling beauty and supersensitive art of that splendid woman who knows how to conquer and influence us' (*El Cine Gráfico*, 2 January 1949, p. 4). However, the film did succeed in symbolically uniting Spain and Mexico through the participation of the latter nation's greatest star in a film made in Spain: 'It puts a Mexican star in the Spanish cinematic sky, thus inaugurating a promising bond. The director uses the beauty and poise of María Félix, who fills every angle of the film with light' (*Primer Plano*, 29 May 1949). Moreover, her co-star was one of Spanish cinema's most beloved leading men, Fernando Rey. However, her privileged status with Spanish critics did not last long, as just a few months later, a review of her next film *Una mujer cualquiera* complained that Félix 'is absolutely inexpressive'(*Primer Plano*, 21 August 1949).

She went on to make *La noche del sábado*, followed by *La corona negra*, a Franco-Spanish co-production, filmed in Morocco and Rome, directed by Argentine Luis Saslavsky, and co-starring Italian actors Rossano Brazzi and Vittorio Gassman. This latter film fared particularly poorly, flopping at its Madrid premiere, and again in Argentina (Urrero). In the end, none of her Spanish films count among Félix's most memorable. Once again the Spanish film industry had hoped to use Félix in order to demonstrate a transnational will that would earn it greater approval in markets where its reputation had been damaged by the civil war and its repressive aftermath, an effect achieved more from the international publicity surrounding Félix's work in Spain than from the films themselves, which were equally disappointing in their reception in Latin America.

María Félix plays a Spanish woman in the French production, *La bella Otero* (1954)

Interestingly, Félix's film that was most applauded among those made in Europe was the 1954 French *La bella Otero* (Richard Pottier), in which she dresses in flamenco garb and dances with castanets. NODO ran features on her that year, comparing her Spanish look with that of Spanish star Lola Flores in her folkloric flamenco movies. By that time Félix had suffered the loss of Jorge Negrete, to whom she'd been married from late 1952 until his sudden death in late 1953. If her participation in mediocre co-productions did not consolidate that connection between her Mexican image and the one developed by Spain's own larger than life Lola Flores, a panhispanic temperamental seductress, her marriage to the deeply 'panhispanified' Negrete and her new flamenca look may have done the trick.

Her best-known Spanish counterpart indeed was Lola Flores, who would soon earn the nickname of 'la Faraona' [the female pharaoh] after starring in the Mexican film of that title, under the direction of René Cardona, in 1956. In the Franco years, the *gitana* archetype that Flores came to personify was deployed in Spanish cinema to represent a deeply embedded essence of national culture, a 'metaphor for Spanishness in the same way that the *charro* is for Mexicanness' (Santaolalla, p. 67). The *gitana* in the Spanish movies of the era is not so much a racial as a temperamental referent; for example, in the Mexican–Spanish co-production *Gitana tenías que ser* (Rafael Baledón, 1953), Carmen Sevilla is a young *gitana* whose non-gypsy-like traits such as her light-toned skin are emphasised, while the film also plays up more cultural aspects such as flamenco dance and fiestas. In this film, interestingly, the *gitana*, in the final scene, ends up dressed in the traditional Mexican costume of the *china poblana*. While this *gitana*-ness that symbolises Spanish femininity through traits of seductiveness and arrogance might well have been made prominent in Spanish film as a response to the popularity of María Félix's distinctive image, the former clearly lacks the blatantly wicked qualities of Félix's trademark characters.

And it must be noted that Félix's image in conservative Catholic Spain, with its assiduous censorship, was toned down, at least superficially, as can be seen in the posters advertising her Spanish films, where Félix never shows even a hint of cleavage, instead being dressed always in clothing that avoids sensuality. This occurs with the publicity for *Mare nostrum* and *La noche del sábado*, and even more so with *La corona negra*, a French-Spanish co-production whose French promotional materials feature the star in a sexy dress, an image excluded from Spanish publicity, which substitutes a close-up of the actress's face. The Mexican lobby card offers four separate images of her, one in which she clutches a pair of scissors that she appears poised to thrust into Rossano Brazzi's throat, accompanied by a provocative caption, absent in the Spanish version, that reads 'The whole world at her feet, but she could not be happy at any price'.

Both Félix and Negrete suffered censorship in Spain. For example, *La posesión* (Julio Bracho, 1950) starred Negrete as a *charro* who abandons his fiancée for the daughter of another rancher, an image that deviated from one the Franco regime supported of the actor (Carmona, p. 183). In the production of Félix's *Messalina* in Italy, the original script's erotic tone was muted to avoid censorship in Spain. Years later, another Félix film, *La estrella vacía* (Emilio Gómez Muriel, 1960) was censored outright, preventing its release in Spain, due to María Félix's representation of a frivolous and liberal actress who resorts to anything, including abortion, to obtain the fame she desires (ibid., p. 184). La Doña could be strong and seductive, but needed in Spain to be a model more in synch with the Catholic values of Franco's Spain whose official femininity was that exhibited by the women's wing of the Spanish Phalanx, the ultraconservative party responsible for the regime's ideological doctrine, which adopted as icons of Spanish womanhood Queen Isabel la Católica and Santa Teresa (Martín Gaite, p. 10).

In both her Spanish and her Mexican films, Félix is confident, tough and demanding, as well as seductive. She represents, in some ways, an inversion of gender roles, which is sometimes made palpable through transvestism (*Doña Bárbara*, *La monja alférez*), functioning as confrontation towards patriarchal power (Pizarro, p. 8), an inversion that Enrique Krauze evokes in the title to his prologue to Félix's autobiography, *Todas mis guerras* (All My Wars), which quotes Félix's own self-assessment: 'A woman with the heart of a man.' This paradox of feminine seduction fused with manly attitudes would be stressed in the magnetism of her physique and her personality, both onscreen and off. Thus her 56 cm (22 in) waist was accompanied by the voice 'of a sergeant', preferable, according to Félix, to possessing a more feminine voice 'like a whistle'. Her virile demeanour was accented by her habit of wearing trousers: 'but I wear them on the outside, not on the inside', she clarified for Elena Poniatowska in an interview (Poniatowska, p. 155). The fascination produced by Félix, then, derives from the contradictions generated through this mix of femininity and masculinity, and through a physically 'Mexican' type that rejects the stereotypes of the humble indigenous woman and the self-sacrificing mother, substituting poses of haughtiness and aristocracy. In many ways, her bad girl, gender-bending image was not the good fit for the goals of Hispanism that Negrete clearly was, nor could her films' representations of romance evoke the transnational unity allegorised in the charro–gitana romance genre as they rarely ended happily.

Félix's Spanish films featured her in roles of seductive, wilful, strong, ambitious and dominant women, a paradigm of femininity that these productions helped transform into one that could be more broadly Hispanic (her characters were often European, not Mexican), and which could, with minor alterations, be reformulated as the hot-blooded *gitana* archetype or even the powerful figure of Queen Isabel la Católica, with the caveat that these Hispanised versions of the arquetype needed to be less devious and more righteous than the typical characters represented by Félix. For example, another Spanish actress whose image echoes that of Félix to some degree is Sara Montiel, who was often cast, like Félix, as a great seductress, although never as dominating or as blatantly immoral in her motivations as those played by the Mexican diva. A variation different from the *gitana* archetype, Montiel's characters are more modern, and their behaviour, which pushed the envelope by portraying liberal (for some, libertine) sexual conduct, led inevitably to a tragic ending in which she was 'punished', as occurred in films such as *El último cuplé* (Juan de Orduña, 1957) and *La violetera* (Luis César Amadori, 1958) – as was also often the case with Félix, as well, in classic films such as *Doña Bárbara* and *La devoradora*. Montiel even went so far as to imitate Félix's arched eyebrow for a photograph in a pose 'typical of Félix': arched eyebrow, long black hair, arm on her hip illustrating an article on her trip to the Americas in 1950 in which she confesses to being 'in love with Mexico' (*Primer Plano*, 8 October 1950), where she would make a splash starring alongside Miroslava Stern and Katy Jurado as a pregnant dancer and murderess in the sordid *Cárcel de mujeres* (Miguel Delgado, 1951).

In the case of her Spanish films, the tendency is similar: in *Mare nostrum*, she plays a Mata Hari-like character, a femme fatale who ends up condemned to death; in *Una mujer cualquiera*, she is a prostitute accused of murder, who seduces her accuser. In *La noche del sábado*, she is led by her own father into a career as a streetwalker and, later, a fancy courtesan, who finds by chance, two decades later, the daughter she had spurned. She then becomes an errant murderess after losing her memory in *La corona negra*, and an actress who manipulates wealthy men to maintain her lavish lifestyle and heroine addiction, and whose love for bullfighter (Jorge Mistral) is only realised when she is on her death bed in *Camelia*. Unfortunately, none of these characters is as memorable as that of La Cucaracha, the hard-drinking female Mexican revolutionary she plays in the Mexican film of the same title (Ismael Rodríguez, 1959); it is through her Mexican films: *Doña Bárbara*, *La devoradora*, *La Cucaracha* that she built her legend.

Félix herself avowed that at some moments she thought that these characters were based on her own life. For example, she (jokingly?) identified with her role in *Mare nostrum*: 'In the final scene, when the firing squad was about to shoot me and the jailer asked me what my last wish would be, I responded "Have them bring me my jewels and my mirror!"' (Félix, p. 70). It could easily be argued that audiences were influenced more by the liberating aspect of these revised femininities that entertained and startled them for ninety minutes, than by the lessons supposedly taught in the predictably tragic last ten minutes when she is punished, and traditional gender hierarchies are restored. If Félix's films, especially those produced in conservative Spain, were 'coded', to use Stuart Hall's term, to make her the villain, her Spanish fans would appear to have decoded them in accordance with their own criteria, as, no matter what moral norms she transgressed, they continued to adore her.

The popular success of María Félix in Spain was similar in many ways to that of Negrete. The NODO announced with great fanfare, that 'upon their arrival in Spain, Negrete and María Félix received a popular welcome that shows their personal attractiveness and the success of Mexican cinema in Spain'. Interestingly, this newsreel shows Negrete's cacophonous arrival at the Madrid train station full of crazed fans, while Félix's reception occurs at the airport where government authorities present her with an enormous bouquet of flowers as the diva looks off towards her multitude of admirers in the distance: the male idol of the masses versus the diva attended to by politicians. Just as with the model of masculinity constructed through the figure of Negrete, a series of feminine values were communicated through the iconic female figure of Félix and the strong, seductive female Spanish characters that seemed to follow from Félix's archetype. In Mexican–Spanish co-productions, Spanish women played by actresses such as Flores, Sevilla or Rico would seduce Mexican men – or Spanish gentleman would fall for the bold but irresistible Mexican characters played by Félix. Panhispanic romance was the real protagonist of these films through which the Spanish press constructed an image of the admired and idolised Mexican actress: 'the beautiful diva of legend' (*La Vanguardia*, 31 July 1952, p. 2).

However, it is important to note that the female star protagonising this panhispanism was not one known for her portrayal of meek or otherwise helpless damsels such as Dolores del Río (of *María Candelaria*) or María Elena Márquez (of *Doña Bárbara*), or long-suffering mothers such as Sara García (of *Cuando los hijos se van*), but the assertive and imperious devourer of men. As in the case of Negrete's Mexican macho, the presence of Félix's man-eater in Spain signified a new spirit of cultural cooperation between the two nations, but also the 'conquest' of the Spanish market by the more powerful Mexican industry.

THE FALL OF HISPANO-MEXICAN CINEMATIC PANHISPANISM

By the early 1950s, competition from the USA, France and Italy, and from Spain itself were leading to a decline in the popularity of Mexican film in Spain. The 'folkloric character' of certain Mexican films that had so captivated Spanish audiences a few years earlier (*Cinema Reporter*, 16 August 1947, p. 9) was losing its charm as critics began complaining of too much 'mexicanada': 'movies of horrendous quality, stupid *charro* films that rather than being vehicles of propaganda for Mexico's beauty and life in that great nation, denigrate and ridicule the existence of the Mexican people'

(*Cinema Reporter*, 4 October 1952, p. 5). One critic claimed that of the twenty-nine Mexican films released in Spain in 1952, only two or three were of decent quality (*Cinema Reporter*, 24 January 1953). Mexican imports were falling, and most Mexican films played only in 'second-rate cinemas or neighbourhood movie houses of the poorest sectors' (*Cinema Reporter,* 11 August 1954, p. 21). While *El derecho de nacer*, starring Spanish-born Mexican cinema idol Jorge Mistral, was a major hit in Spain, Mexican film had lost the cachet it had obtained in the late 40s. Changing attitudes can be seen in the news reports mentioned earlier, which were circulating around Latin America, that Spain had begun dubbing Mexican films (*Magazin Dominical*, 17 January 1954, p. 24) – although, ironically, one of the films purportedly dubbed was the US–Mexico co-production *Furia roja* (Steve Sekely and Víctor Urruchúa, 1951), a film that featured performances by Emilia Guiú, Sara Montiel and Gustavo Rojo, Spanish actors who routinely employed Mexican accents in the many Mexican movies in which they acted. By 1954 and 1955, only seventeen and fifteen Mexican films, respectively, were being distributed in Spain, while critics nostalgically recalled the era of *Allá en el Rancho Grande* and bemoaned the decadence of Mexico's film production (*Cinema Reporter*, 4 January 1956, p. 13).

Meanwhile, there is little evidence to show that Mexican–Spanish co-productions achieved sufficient success to significantly boost Spain's reputation abroad. For example, the 1949 Mexican film, *Una gallega en México*, while neither a co-production nor a romance, shared the objective of the Negrete and Félix films of building affective connections between Spain and Latin America through popular movies. Its reception in Latin America, however, was typically cool, with one Colombian critic complaining that the film includes so many cultural references outside the plot: bullfights, soccer matches, music performances, that 'it has everything except cinema', and when lead actors Niní Marshall – an Argentine playing a Spanish woman – and her Mexican co-star Joaquín Pardavé 'do some foolish things', 'nobody pays attention to them'. The critic, however, admits that the public seemed to enjoy themselves (*Cromos*, 29 April 1950, p. 26). Félix's *Camelia*, however, was better received, playing for several weeks in Bogotá, with critics lauding both La Doña's performance and that of Jorge Mistral, and expressing appreciation for the addition of bullfighting scenes, this time better integrated into the plot (*El Tiempo*, 12 September 1954, p. 12).

Camelia, filmed in Mexico, but with financing from both countries, undoubtedly was more controversial in Spain, and not only for its scandalous plot. Mistral had gone to Mexico in 1949 to get married, with Spanish journals insisting that 'his trip is exclusively to get married and afterwards he will return immediately to Spain'. This initial report chose to represent this event as one of panhispanic unity, adding an anecdote about 'an excited woman who hugged him and exclaimed "Long live Spain!"' (*Primer Plano,* 18 December 1949). However, a few months later, the same journal published another article under the title 'Will Jorge Mistral Stay in Mexico?' that acknowledged that 'Jorge does not wish to return to Madrid because they have offered him contracts. It will be a bad thing for him to stay in Mexico; it will carry negative consequences for him' (5 February 1950). Mistral indeed remained in Mexico, becoming one of the Mexican industry's biggest romantic leads of the 1950s – and a *persona non grata* for the Spanish cultural administration and the officialist press.

In any case, with the international acceptance of Franco's Spain seen by the mid-1950s in the nation's integration into the United Nations, and the signing of a bilateral agreement with the USA, Spain entered a new era in both politics and cultural production. While the Mexican government would not relent in its rejection of the Spanish dictatorship until its demise with Franco's death, Spain's new status elsewhere would produce transformations in its popular culture and its needs. Cinematic Hispanism ceased to be a priority for the industries of both nations. By the late 1950s, Mexico's hopes faded for establishing a solid transnational Hispanic market as competition from Hollywood, from Europe and from television sent producers scrambling to try and keep the golden age's magic alive, even if only for domestic audiences. It was thus that what energy remained for co-productions began to diverge from the folkloric themes that had once been their driving force.

This decadence of the Mexican–Spanish romantic comedy genre coincided roughly with another Mexican–Spanish co-production of greater significance for international film history: Luis Buñuel's *Viridiana* (1961), winner of the Palme d'Or at the Cannes Film Festival – although the exhibition of the film would be prohibited in Spain for another sixteen years, until after Franco's death. The film, which starred Mexican actress Silvia Pinal and Spanish star Fernando Rey, was a great critical success, and is today considered by many to be one of Buñuel's greatest works. Rather than a formulaic romantic comedy, the movie tells the story of a nun who leaves the convent after being drugged and nearly raped by her uncle, who then commits suicide. When she inherits his house, ex-nun Viridiana opens it up to the homeless and infirm, setting the stage for a series of ironic clashes and conflicts. Although Buñuel's mockery of Catholic symbols such as the last supper would prevent such a collaboration from being repeated, it did show that it was possible to make a different kind of collaborative cinema between the two nations.

CONCLUSION

This chapter has shown how Mexican golden age cinema helped to bring together two countries whose political relations had been severed. Although the Mexican government remained steadfast in its rejection of the Franco dictatorship for its duration, the two nations remained culturally linked, and cinema was the medium that, along with radio, most strongly bonded the Mexican and Spanish peoples during the nearly forty years of diplomatic rupture. A key year in fomenting cultural ties was 1948, with the staging of the Congress of Hispanoamerican Cinema, the extended visits of Mexican megastars Jorge Negrete and María Félix to Spain and the launching of a series of cinematic co-productions helping to begin mending relations between the two nations at the symbolic level.

These collaborations were meant to help both nations. Mexico used them to firm up its leadership position in Spanish-language film production by enhancing its place in the profitable Spanish market; Spain, meanwhile, hoped to bolster its much weaker film industry while also improving its image abroad in a time of diplomatic isolation. From these mutual interests, a cinematic genre emerged that portrayed a panhispanic unity in alignment with established stylistic patterns of Mexican cinema – most notably through use of well-known elements from the *ranchera* comedy model – but always kept in check by the conservative ideology of the Franco regime. These Hispano-Mexican folkloric comedies integrated national stereotypes of Spain and Mexico and juxtaposed emblematic musical genres of the two nations in romantic plots that used affective relations of *charros* and *gitanas* to allegorise transnational unity. During the same period, María Félix's romantic dramas performed a somewhat different transnational allegory as she played the seductive devourer of men, symbolically asserting Mexico's dominant role in Spanish-language cultural production. She and Negrete, working alongside Spanish stars such as Lola Flores and Jorge Mistral, became idols of Spanish popular culture in the 1940s and 50s. Negrete became a model of Hispanic macho masculinity, and Félix in turn would be a model for the woman of the Spanish 'race': 'demanding, strong, tough and, at the same time, seductive' (Pizarro, p. 194). These two icons provided vehicles for the fusion of clichés that represented the two nations.

While in Mexico, critics saw these productions as 'excessively insipid' (*Radiocinema,* February 1949, n. p.) and their popular success was always eclipsed by the best of Mexican cinema, along with increasingly overwhelming competition from Hollywood, in Spain the Hispano-Mexican co-productions and their stars made their impact. The success of this cinema of panhispanic romance lay precisely in its ability to maintain a popular sentimental bond between two countries whose political relations were broken. The already established popularity of Negrete and Félix in Spain, which only grew with their extended visits in 1948, made it easy for their well-known images, polished in alignment with the ideologies of the Franco regime and its conservative censors, to contribute to a cultural rapprochement between the two countries, establishing an influential 'celluloid bond' (Tuñón, 'Relaciones', p. 159).

At the same time, these films allowed Spanish audiences to create a sort of parenthesis within the rigid moral control of the dictatorship. Negrete provoked among Spanish audiences, female and male alike, used to an everyday masculinity diminished by a repressive state, a fascination with his prodigious hypervirility, just as María Félix upset reigning models of passive and chaste femininity not only with the haughtiness and strength of the characters she played, but also with the range of social transgressions presented in her films. Always punished in the final scenes, she nonetheless played out through these roles the possibility of other ways of being.

In addition, while these cinematic collaborations may have succeeded with some viewers in establishing bonds capable of suturing the rupture between the two nations – although cultural dialogues are one thing, and legal pronouncements, geographical barriers and political frontiers are another – they also performed a sort of neo-colonialism, in reverse. The long-ago conquered territory, once dominated for three centuries by the other nation, inverts the power dynamic of their relationship through the interventions of charismatic movie stars. For nearly a decade, with 1948 as a paradigmatic inaugural moment, the press on both sides of the Atlantic fomented an image of wealth, cosmopolitanism and progress being delivered to the Old World, concretely to Spain, by the glamorous and imposing machine that was Mexican golden age cinema.

The panhispanism of this decade of cooperation was imposed in Spain as a political necessity, but it also functioned commercially and culturally – although it should be noted that even at the peak of cooperation in the early 1950s, Spain never became a top export market for Mexican films, with at least ten Latin American countries (including small ones like Guatemala, Panama and Costa Rica) importing more Mexican product than Spain (*El Cine Gráfico*, 4 May 1952, p. 6). However, there is no denying that these Hispano-Mexican productions reinforced cultural bonds in a way that facilitated the acceptance of Mexican golden age cinema in Spain, and thereby guaranteed the influence of Mexican popular culture on its Spanish audiences. Félix and Negrete, along with Cantinflas and many other figures and archetypes of Mexican cinema, ultimately 'imposed themselves' into the history of Spanish popular culture, just as they had done in so many Latin American countries, as well as more distant lands, where their impact came most unexpectedly.

7

'Vedro Nebo' in Far-off Lands: Mexican Golden Age Cinema's Unexpected Triumph in Tito's Yugoslavia

Dubravka Sužnjević and Robert McKee Irwin

MEXICAN GOLDEN AGE CINEMA IN YUGOSLAVIA

This chapter examines Mexican cinema's startling – and virtually unknown in Mexico – triumph in Yugoslavia in the early 1950s. While Yugoslavian fervour for Mexican revolutionary melodrama was short-lived, its influence was not. One of 'el Indio' Fernández's later films, *Un día de vida* (1950), largely forgotten in Mexico, became a megahit in Yugoslavia and is, indeed, remembered in the region as one of world cinema's all-time classic films. Aside from a universal appeal for various melodramatic plot devices – an unrealisable mutual love, the suffering of a mother faced with the imminent death of her beloved son, sacrifice for the noble cause of revolution, eternal bonds of male friendship – the Yugoslavs also loved the melodramatic *ranchera* music that accompanied them, leading to a boom in homegrown mariachi bands that translated Mexico's classics to Serbo-Croation. Thus, 'Cielito lindo' became an instant Yugoslav hit as 'Vedro nebo', as Yugoslav musicians dressed up as *charros* and paid homage to Jalisco, film distributors renewed the rights again and again to show *Un día de vida* in theatres and on television, and moviegoers wrote fan mail to Columba Domínguez. Mexican golden age film's impact in Yugoslavia is one of its most impressive and unexplored achievements.

MEXICAN GOLDEN AGE CINEMA IN EUROPE

As early as 1938, Mexican cinema was earning praises in Europe. Along with megahit *Allá en el Rancho Grande*, Mexican studios sent *¡Ora Ponciano!* and *Noches de gloria* (Rolando Aguilar, 1938) to the Venice Film Festival where *Rancho Grande* won a 'Special Recommendation' award for its overall artistic contribution, most especially the cinematography of Gabriel Figueroa (*Cinema Reporter*, 16 December 1938, p. 1). These apparently were Mexican cinema's first screenings in Europe (*Cinema Reporter*, 16 July 1938, p. 1). With the advent of World War II, there would be few openings for Mexican cinema in most of Europe for many years to come, with a few exceptions – one being a wartime cooperative effort on the part of Mexico, which shipped a handful of movies to Great Britain's Ministry of Foreign Affairs in early 1944 to be shown in places such as hospitals and arms factories (*El Cine Gráfico*, 30 January 1944, p. 16). Spain, of course, was a special case (treated in the previous chapter), and it might be mentioned that in Lisbon, ¡Ora Ponciano! became 'the sensation of the moment' in early 1942 (Cinema Reporter, April 1942, p. 27).

As we have seen, Mexican cinema suddenly came to the attention of European critics upon sharing the grand prize of the first postwar film festival in Cannes in 1946. María Candelaria won not only for best film, but for the cinematography of Gabriel Figueroa, who won again for his work on this film at the Locarno International Film Festival the following year. Emilio Fernández's success in general can be attributed to some degree to enthusiasm for his work among French critics (Cinema Reporter, 23 November 1946, p. 29) such as Georges Sadoul and Raymond Borde – although more recent critics charge that their praise for Fernández's films is based on misreadings that reflect 'the imposition of Euro-American paradigms and aesthetic theories upon non-European cultural practices' (Tierney, pp. 54–5).

These prizes coincided with new distribution deals struck between Mexican studios and Spanish distributors to promote Mexican films throughout Europe (Cinema Reporter, 2 March 1946, p. 16; 27 July 1946, p. 33). In the same period, Mexico, likewise, set its sights on separate deals on anglophone markets, including England (Cinema Reporter, 26 April 1947, p. 32). Soon Mexican studios were sending what they considered their best films: most anything by Emilio Fernández and his team, as well as those films that did best in Mexico's own Ariel awards, including quadruple winner Campeón sin corona, which was soon screening in France (Cinema Reporter, 3 July 1948, p. 27), where six films were imported in 1948, followed by another seven in 1949 (Ramsaye, 1949–50, p. 694; Ivers and Aaronson, p. 724).

Mexico's first European awards also coincided with the highly publicised career launch of the Czechoslovakia-born actress Miroslava Stern in Mexico, where she would quickly become a major star (see, for example, Cinema Reporter, 22 November 1947), which undoubtedly helped to open the doors for Mexican film distribution in Eastern Europe, although the first films to arrive would not be Miroslava's light romantic films or melodramas, but the kind of artsy nationalistic cinema that Europe expected to see building off of the success of María Candelaria. Thus, among the first Mexican films to open in Prague were La perla, La barraca and Río Escondido (Cinema Reporter, 12 June 1948, p. 28).

By the early 1950s, Ninón Sevilla had become a well-known star in France, where at least one critic, after seeing her in Fernández's Víctimas del pecado, claimed she was more talented than Italian diva Silvana Mangano (Cinema Reporter, 9 February 1952, p. 23). A few years later, reports arrived in Mexico City claiming that a Paris theatre was playing only Mexican fare (Cinema Reporter, 3 November 1954, p. 18), this around the time that María Félix had gone to France to star in a series of movies, including, most notably Jean Renoir's French Can-Can (1954). Meanwhile Italy – where Columba Domínguez had been brought in to film L'edera (Augusto Genina) in 1950 – was importing as many as fourteen Mexican films a year (Ivers and Aaronson, p. 732; see also Kann, p. 788; Aaronson, 1953–54, p. 928; Aaronson, 1955, p. 968) and films such as Angelitos negros were earning praises (but not awards) at the Venice Film Festival (Cinema Reporter, 22 June 1955, p. 26). In England, the mid-1950s saw a new enthusiasm for Mexican film as critic Betsy Ross began to promote it in journals and

Emilio Fernández's *Un día de vida* (1950) was a surprise hit in Yugoslavia

claimed to be writing a book on its history (*Cinema Reporter*, 15 December 1954, p. 25; 25 May 1955, p. 16). Mexican studios report having exported forty-four films to France, forty to Italy, fourteen to Germany, ten to England, nine to Portugal, seven to Belgium, six to Czechoslovakia, four to Switzerland, two to Norway and one to Russia in 1950 and 1951 (*El Cine Gráfico*, 4 May 1952, p. 6). By mid-decade, Eastern Europe appears to have been an especially fruitful market for Mexico's European distributors, with various Fernández classics making the rounds in Czechoslovakia, Russia, Hungary and Bulgaria (*Cinema Reporter*, 10 July 1954, p. 27; 17 November 1954, p. 27; 15 December 1954, p. 24; 29 June 1955, p. 13; 7 September 1955, p. 17). Interestingly, there is no discussion in Mexico of the sensation that *Un día de vida* and other films from the era roused in Yugoslavia.

ONE DAY IN LIFE

Un día de vida was produced in 1950, pretty much at the tail end of the series of major critical successes for Emilio Fernández and his production team, which included cinematographer Gabriel Figueroa, screenwriter Mauricio Magdaleno and editor Gloria Schoemann, along with many of Mexico's greatest actors of the era: Dolores del Río, Pedro Armendáriz, María Félix, Columba Domínguez, Marga López, Carlos López Moctezuma and Roberto Cañedo, to name a few. Following *María Candelaria*'s Cannes prize in 1946, Fernández would see his films nominated annually for Mexico's Ariel award for best picture for five straight years (nominations in 1946 for *Las abandonadas* and 1950 for *Pueblerina*, and a triumvirate of wins in 1947, 1948 and 1949 for *Enamorada La perla* and *Río Escondido*, respectively), and parallel success in the Best Director category (nominations all five years, and wins 1947–49 for the same films). By the time *Un día de vida* was released in late 1950, Fernández's films were no longer achieving the same level of acclaim that they had during the apex of his team's success – what Dolores Tierney calls his personal 'golden age', 1943–50 (p. 66) – and none would be nominated for an Ariel for best film or best director for nearly twenty-five years – although his frequent collaborator, Figueroa, who won four straight Ariels for Fernández films from 1947 to 1950, continued his winning record for Luis Buñuel's *Los olvidados* (1950) in 1951, Robert Gavaldón's *El rebozo de Soledad* (1952) in 1953 and Fernández's *El niño y la niebla* (1953) in 1954; and the team's editor, Gloria Schoemann, would pick up – in addition to her 1947 win for *Enamorada* – Ariels in 1954 and 1955 for the Fernández films *El niño y la niebla* and *La rebelión de los colgados* (1954).

Un día de vida featured a first-rate crew, including Fernández, Figueroa, Magdaleno – whose lone Ariel came for the Fernández film *Río Escondido* – and Schoemann, and a talented cast, including that year's Ariel winner for best actor, Roberto Cañedo (for *Pueblerina*), 1949 best supporting actress (and Fernández's wife) Columba Domínguez (for the Fernández film *Maclovia*), future Ariel winner Rosaura Revueltas (for Roberto Gavaldón's *Rebozo de Soledad* in 1952) and Fernando Fernández (Emilio Fernández's cousin/stepbrother, an accomplished popular crooner). While Revueltas, in the role of Mamá Juanita, would be nominated for an Ariel in 1951, this would be the film's only nomination, and it would pass quickly from view, garnering only minimal attention in Mexico, and even less in Latin American export markets. For example, although it did receive at least one positive review in Colombia where it enjoyed a brief run (*Sábado*, 15 September 1951, p. 16), its opening in Venezuela generated no press at all (*Mi Film*, 8 September 1951, p. 27), and it was never even released in some smaller markets. In Peru, distributors were optimistic, launching it simultaneously in ten theatres in Lima; however: 'attendance was so poor as to not warrant mention'; it closed after only two days and it was reported from Lima that 'this movie can be considered the worst produced this year' (24 February 1952, p. 8). The film quickly fell into oblivion in Mexico and is rarely mentioned in Mexican film histories.

Un día de vida is a revolutionary melodrama – that is, a film that treats the historical context of the Mexican revolution through a sentimental plot advanced by a series of melodramatic devices. Its protagonist is Belén Martí (Domínguez), a Cuban journalist who travels alone to Mexico hoping to 'write about its great matters, and to get to know the Revolution and its men' (Fernández and Magdaleno, *Un día de vida*, p. 3). She identifies with an idea of Mexico's revolutionary spirit, and wishes to approach a world that she idealises. As a foreigner, her role is always that of outside observer, admirer, and maybe it is for this reason that a non-Mexican public might identify with it more than would a national audience. It might also explain why Yugoslavs fell in love, as we shall see later, not with Revueltas, whose performance is the only one in the film to earn an award nomination in Mexico, nor with handsome leading man Roberto Cañedo, the revolutionary hero, but with Columba Domínguez.

The popularity of 'el Indio' Fernández's films is a product not so much of their ability to represent Mexican reality as their tendency towards its idealisation – aligned as it were with the expectations of international critics of prestige cinema (that is, European art film). The cinematography of Gabriel Figueroa, influenced undoubtedly by the vision of the great Russian director Sergei Eisenstein, who, like Belén Martí, travelled to Mexico in search of revolutionary fervour, portrays a Mexico of ancient

Yugoslavian playbill of *Un día de vida* with Columba Domínguez and Roberto Cañedo

processions, solitary agaves, majestic palms, grave Indians, exotic rites and citizens who are both humble and proud (see Sánchez, *El Arte de Gabriel Figueroa*). Especially striking in *Un día de vida* are the broad skyscapes that serve as backdrops to geometrically positioned actors, which together form compositions representing Mexico in highly dramatic and aesthetically polished terms: clean lines, marked contrasts of dark and light shades, extreme angles.

The film's protagonist evokes the memory of José Martí and all he symbolises: Latin American unity, the 'natural man' and the spirit of anti-imperialism. As is typical in Fernández films, this one is awash in national symbols. One of the first scenes takes place at Hotel Iturbide, a name and site that evoke historical class conflict in Mexico (Agustín de Iturbide was the conservative leader who led Mexico to its ultimate independence from Spain in 1821, but with the objective of ensuring the continuation of monarchy rule: he was named Mexico's first emperor, and Hotel Iturbide had, in fact, been Emperor Agustín I's royal palace), a theme that is underlined in the dialogue between Martí and the hotel manager, who explains to her with great pride that Iturbide is a hotel 'of lineage' (Fernández and Magdaleno, *Un día de vida*, p. 3); later she visits la Villa de Guadalupe in order to see the famous image of the Virgin of Guadalupe, for her the symbolic mother 'of all of us who speak the same language in America' (ibid., p. 7); finally, much of the action of the film takes place in a small town located in view of the pyramids of Teotihuacan, symbol of the glory of the ancient inhabitants of the region and the profundity and complexity of the culture of the nation and of the entire hemisphere.

Upon arriving in Mexico, Martí hears the news that an officer in the revolutionary army, Coronel Lucio Reyes, has been sentenced to death by firing squad for treason for having led an armed protest against the assassination of Emiliano Zapata in 1919 by forces supported by President Venustiano Carranza, a revolutionary leader who had broken in 1914 with the more radical (and charismatically popular) Pancho Villa and Zapata. To Martí, Reyes is an authentic hero of the revolution, and is poised to become, like Zapata, one of its martyrs. She tells herself, 'I must see him, because whoever dies in that way, for an ideal, holds the secret of his people' (ibid., p. 12). She attempts to visit him at the barracks where he is being held prisoner but is not granted entry. However, they do allow her to send the prisoner the gift of a box of Cuban cigars. Upon receiving them, Coronel Reyes, played by Roberto Cañedo (who, in a later Fernández film, *La rosa blanca* [1955], would play the role of José Martí himself), waxes nostalgic, recalling the great affection that has always existed between Cuba and Mexico, and calls up a pair of great icons of Mexican–Cuban fraternity. He speaks of the Cuban poet José María Heredia, who, he remembers, 'was governor of Mexico State and died here in the capital' (ibid., 16), and of José Martí, who 'lived his best years' in Mexico, where he dedicated verses to Rosario de la Peña (the great muse of nineteenth-century Mexican poetry), and married in Mexico – and whose sister at one time had been courted by Venustiano Carranza, the man who had pronounced Reyes's death sentence (ibid.).

If Zapata represents a first moment of revolutionary idealism that is associated with Heredia and Martí, Carranza belongs to a second more complex epoch in which the revolution is put into practice, but not necessarily according to the ideals of those who launched it and who fought most ardently for it. The idealist Reyes will not live to see the postrevolution, but his best friend, General Felipe Gómez (Fernando Fernández), will. The pragmatic Gómez receives the order to execute the death sentence of his boyhood friend.

Belén Martí, fascinated by the figure of Reyes, tries once more to get to know him, not directly, but now by seeking out an interview with his mother, who is known as Mamá Juanita (Rosaura Revueltas). She travels to the village of Cieneguilla, located near the Teotihuacan pyramids; there she meets Mamá Juanita, who invites her to spend the night at her house because she is convinced that her son will return the following day, as is his custom for his mother's saint's day. It turns out that the whole town has conspired to hide from Juanita the news that her son is to be put to death. Martí, who is made quite uncomfortable by the fact that she knows Reyes's fate, prefers not to stay, but Juanita, who has taken to the young reporter, insists: 'How often I have dreamed that Lucio would bring home such a fiancée or wife ... intelligent and lovely, like you!' (ibid., p. 31).

As is evident, the film is a melodrama, a genre, as Jesús Martín Barbero has shown, that is fundamental to Mexican golden age cinema and to Latin American popular culture in general for its longstanding mass appeal (pp. 151–62, 226–30). The film's characters and events evoke notions of patriotism, sacrifice, love and family bonds on the one hand or, on the other hand, obedience and ambition (in the case of Gómez) – and inspire pronounced emotional reactions. Through the curiosity and sentiments of Belén Martí, the friendship of Reyes and Gómez, and the maternal devotion of Mamá Juanita, the revolutionary war becomes a personal drama, and the audience –

especially an audience predisposed to enjoy melodrama, as was the case with Mexican and Latin American audiences of the era – suffers the same anxiety felt by Martí at being confronted with the situation of this mother who at some moment will have to learn of the imminent death of her beloved and noble son.

The following day, a band plays the traditional Mexican birthday song, 'Las mañanitas', while the whole village prepares for the party. But, Lucio has not arrived, and Belén can barely hide the apprehension she feels for Juanita, to whom someone will soon have to reveal the truth. Mamá Juanita, with a grave expression, says to Belén: 'I still have not lost hope that he will come' (Fernández and Magdaleno, *Un día de vida*, p. 38). 'Las mañanitas', traditionally a song of celebration, is resignified in this context as a lugubrious ballad. But suddenly, everything changes: Lucio Reyes arrives at his mother's house, accompanied by Felipe Gómez, who, of course, knew of the family rite of the annual visit and was unable to deny this final moment of pleasure to his friend or to his friend's mother, whom he has loved as well since he was a boy. So 'Las mañanitas' is sung yet again and, according to the tradition, Felipe is the one who sings it. The party turns festive, but Belén's anguish only intensifies; she refuses to eat and leaves the scene so that she can cry away from Mamá Juanita's sight.

Lucio, fascinated with the lovely young Cuban and obsessed with the image of José Martí that her name evokes, appears to be falling in love with her – and she with him, her martyr hero of the revolutionary cause she so admires. As the party goes on, Belén begs both Felipe and Lucio to come up with some plan of escape, but Lucio fears implicating the townspeople as accomplices and is resigned to assume his role as martyr. And while Mamá Juanita enjoys her saint's day party as she would any other year, Belén cannot help thinking of what will happen the next day.

But when the party is over, Juanita reveals to Felipe that despite all his efforts, she knows the truth: 'I found out as soon as he was sentenced to death' (ibid., p. 58). The film ends with the inevitable execution of Reyes at the orders of Gómez, with Martí present as witness along with other admirers. In the final scene, Mamá Juanita appears to claim the body of her son: 'Over this portrait of *mater dolorosa* with her son in her arms – while the other two [Belén, Felipe] approach, appears the word: END, followed by a final fade out' (ibid., p. 65).

MEXICAN MOVIES IN YUGOSLAVIA

The triumph of this film in Yugoslavia – greater than that of others by the same production team, which had obtained much greater critical and popular success in their principle markets of Mexico and Latin America with a dozen earlier films released between 1943 and 1949 – can be attributed to the historical moment. The late 1940s and early 50s was a time of great tension between the governments of Tito and Stalin in which the Soviets expelled Yugoslavia from the Communist Information Bureau (see Mazzini; Mijatović, p. 2). The ensuing anti-Soviet propaganda disseminated throughout Yugoslavia turned the public away from Soviet cinema, and as early as 1949, it was reported that 'Soviet Russia today has reduced imports [to Yugoslavia] to a trickle' (Ivers and Aaronson, p. 744). According to Slovenian writer Miha Mazzini,

Another Mexican hit in
Yugoslavia: *Camelia* (1954)
starring María Félix and Jorge
Mistral

> Yugoslav authorities had to look somewhere else for film entertainment. They found a
> suitable country in Mexico: it was far away, the chances of Mexican tanks appearing on
> Yugoslav borders were slight and, best of all, in Mexican films they always talked about
> revolution in the highest terms. (n. p.)

One of the first Mexican film hits in Yugoslavia was *Un día de vida*, which arrived in
Yugoslav cinemas towards the end of 1952, two years after its premiere in Mexico.
'Never before had a film provoked so many tears,' declared Yugoslav writer Aleksandar
Vučo in a review, noting that the film was showing to sell-out crowds in three cinemas
around Belgrade (*Borba*, 21 December 1952). The film became an all-time classic in
film history for Yugoslavs – rivalled only by the Esther Williams classic, *Bathing Beauty*
(George Sidney, 1944) – and, according to a 1997 article by Vladimir Lazarević from
the Serbian journal *Politika Ekspres*, *Un día de vida* is 'the most watched film in
Yugoslavia in the last fifty years', if not of all time (14 September 1997), a claim that
has been repeated often in (ex)Yugoslavia. In 1953, noting that *Un día de vida* had been
the most popular film of the previous year, critic Stevan Petrović added that the
number of tickets sold in Belgrade (over 200,000) was roughly equal to the city's
population at the time (quoted in Mijatović, p. 3, translation hers) – although there
were undoubtedly many repeat viewers. Radoslav Zelenović, General Manager of the

Film Archive of the Republic of Serbia, avows that while running a movie programme on Yugoslav television, he received more request letters from viewers for *Un día de vida* than for any other film (ibid.). Mazzini asserts,

> Emilio Fernández's *Un día de vida* became so immensely popular that the old people in the former republics of Yugoslavia even today regard it as surely one of the most well-known films in the world ever made; although, in truth, it is probably unknown in every other country. (n. p.)

Yugoslav distributors renewed the rights for the film three times, and it was relaunched every two or three years for two decades. A faded poster advertising the film was on display as recently as a few years ago in an old Sarajevo movie house. Musicologist Brana Mijatović observes that a Google search for *Jedan dan života*, the film's title in Serbo-Croatian, generates numerous hits in discussion forums and torrent requests, while similar searches in Spanish or English yield nothing substantial (p. 3). Indeed, clips of *Un día de vida* posted on YouTube have Serbo-Croation subtitles. While *Un día de vida*'s screenplay (a Fernández collaboration with Mauricio Magdaleno) is preserved only in a very rough manuscript form in Mexico's Cineteca Nacional, in Yugoslavia a translation was published in 1953, as was that of another popular Fernández film starring Pedro Armendáriz, Dolores de Río and Yugoslav favourite Columba Domínguez, *La malquerida* (this one another Fernández–Magdaleno collaboration, based on a play by Spanish playwright Jacinto Benavente), both as part of the Filmska Biblioteka 'Ars' series 'Memorable Films'.

The success of *Un día de vida* had repercussions that went beyond the context of cinema. Mexican music, especially of the *ranchera* genre, became quite popular – not through the importation of Mexican albums, but through the formation of Yugoslavian mariachi bands and Mexican-style trios. The classic song of the genre, representing what musicologist Mijatović refers to as Yugoslavia's 'Mexican craze' (p. 1), is 'Mama Huanita' (better known in Mexico as 'Las mañanitas', Mexico's birthday celebration song), 'a song every mother loved to hear on the radio for her birthday' (Mazzini), evoking the emotional final encounter between mother and son in the movie. Mazzini describes the panorama of what he calls 'Yu-Mex' artists: 'The most charming Mexicans were Nikola Karović and Slavko Perović; while the most determined was Ljubomir Milić. Ana Milosavljević was the queen and the dark voice of Nevenka Arsova her first companion'. (n. p) Mazzini has a website that serves as, in his words, 'a small homage to hundreds of performers who covered themselves with sombreros to become Slavic Mexicans' (ibid.) and where one can listen to various examples of these songs, including, for example, Arsova's version of the classic 'Paloma negra' and Trío Tividi's 'Ay Jalisco' ('Ay Jalisco, no te rajes').

While, occasionally, these groups retained Mexican lyrics, more often they translated them into Serbo-Croatian; thus, 'Cielito lindo' becomes 'Vedro nebo'. However, few songs were direct translations. As one of the genre's most successful artists Slavko Perović admits, 'I don't speak Spanish, nor did my colleagues who sang Mexican songs; so I wrote the lyrics for these songs according to the melody' (interview with Sužnjević), although musicologist Mijatović's analysis shows that their lyrics also reflected a particular idealised vision of Mexico, undoubtedly inspired from the most popular Mexican films of the era, including *Un día de vida* as well as others that portrayed Mexico as an idyllic, proud, simple, honest and spirited nation. Indeed, his method for composing lyrics to songs such as 'Mama Huanita' was to make cassette recordings of the songs while watching the films, and then to use the recordings to come up with lyrics.

Perović and Karović's version of 'Como México no hay dos' [There's no place like Mexico], known in Yugoslavia as 'Moj Meksiko' ['My Mexico'] roughly follows the theme of the original Spanish lyrics, whose narrative voice recounts how, while travelling all over the world, he can find no place that compares to Mexico. While the Mexican original compares Mexico to California, with 'its orange trees and sighs made of grapes/its colourful apples/San Francisco, Hollywood and its artists/it was nearly our nation' (translated by Mijatović, pp. 6–8), evoking Mexico's troubled past with the USA, to which it had ceded California in the war of 1846–48, the Serbo-Croatian makes comparisons with other Latin American places ('Paraguay, Chile, La Paz'), and European locations, such as Paris and Naples, which would serve as more relevant references for Yugoslavs.

Mijatović argues that these songs often invent a nostalgia for an idealised image of Mexico appropriated by Yugoslavians as somehow their own. In 'Moj Meksiko', the narrative voice declares: 'But my Mexico has always been my most favourite warm corner [of the world ...]/My wonderful homeland is a true paradise' (translation in Mijatović, pp. 7–8). These songs also paint a vision of Mexico reminiscent of many of cinematographer Gabriel Figueroa's most characteristic aestheticised images, popularised in Yugoslavia in *Un día de vida*, *El rebozo de Soledad*, *La malquerida* and other favourites. The original composition 'Sombrero', composed by Nikica Kalogjera in 1959, for example, presents a series of iconic images: 'Around you are cacti agave/Great blue skies/Tall dry grass, like swords, like rapiers', featuring, of course, that of the wide-brimmed Mexican sombrero (translated in ibid., pp. 8–9), all of which call to mind some of the most celebrated images of Figueroa's award-winning work. Perović, who composed lyrics for nearly fifty Mexican songs, admitted that he adapted his lyrics to reflect the preferences of Yugoslav audiences – although it would seem that lyrics were meant more precisely to conform to Yugoslav fantasies about Mexico. Thus, Mexican composer Felipe Valdés Leal's 'Entre copa y copa' [With each additional drink] whose original lyrics open 'With each additional drink my life ends/Crying drunk over your lost love', in Perović's version puts aside the alcoholic excess and begins instead with an evocation of a gorgeous Figueroa skyscape: 'As night falls and the sun sets' (interview with Sužnjević).

This was not a minor fad. Mazzini's site lists, in addition to the previously mentioned artists: Trio Paloma (sometimes billed as Kvartet Paloma), Rade Marić, Miroslava Mrđa, Trio Tenori, Manjifiko, Jôzica Svete, Peter Ambrož, Predrag Gojković, Đorđe Masalović and Nikola Karović. It has been reported that Trio Paloma earned Yugoslavia's first gold record with a *ranchera* album, selling 100,000 records 'at a time when in the whole Yugoslavia there was a total of 60,000 gramophones' (Mirijana Maljokovic, quoted in and translated by Mijatović, p. 5) – although another account claims that it was Predag Cune Gojković who achieved that milestone (*Duga*, 22 July 1962, p. 34). In 1961, Gojković, in an interview in which he was called 'the first baritone of Mexican songs in Yugoslavia', the rising star, beloved for his rendition of

'Mama Huanita', ranked Mexican *ranchera* singer Lola Beltrán third among the top five greatest pop/jazz musicians of the day (*Duga*, 11 June 1961, p. 34), and he soon began recording Mexican compositions such as Lara's 'Granada' and 'Bésame mucho', and Alberto Domínguez's 'Perfidia' (*Duga*, 22 July 1962, p. 34). In addition, Yugoslav musicians began gaining international fans for their interpretations of Mexican songs, as can be seen in a Hungarian tour by several Yugoslav artists in which Dragan Tokovićs interpretation of Lara's 'Granada' earned one of the biggest ovations (*Duga*, 17 December 1961, p. 34) and, in the in early 1962 participation of Milija Spasojević's musical ensemble, featuring Gojković, in an international competition in Milan in which they won second prize for the song 'Halisko' ('Ay Jalisco no te rajes') (see http://www.balkanmedia.com/magazin/303/predrag_gojković_cune_kafu_mi_draga_ispeci.html).

Slavko Perović was perhaps the artist most associated with the rise of Mexican folk music in Yugoslavia. By 1966, he had recorded five hit albums of mostly Mexican songs, and planned on recording more (*TV Novosti*, 9 September 1966). Perović claims that the Vokalni Trio Jovanović–Đukić–Tomljanović launched the Mexican music trend in 1953 (interview with Sužnjević) – although it seems their first actual recording of Mexican music did not come out until 1958 (http://discogs.com) – followed soon after by Gojković, with his memorable 'Halisko'. He credits Ivo Robić with the early popularisation of 'Mama Huanita' and identifies another important early act as Trio TiViDi, who specialised almost exclusively in Mexican songs during their six years as a group from 1958 to 1964, touring with the Meksikanski Orkestar Nikica Kalogjera (Efendić), and popularising such Mexican classics as 'Vedro nebo', José Alfredo Jiménez's 'Cuatro caminos' ('Cetiri staze') and Tomás Méndez's 'Cucurrucucú paloma'. Perović himself began recording in 1963, sometimes in collaboration with Trio Paloma. His first three albums went gold; as he puts it, 'it was an incredible trend', of which he acknowledges being leader. Soon Mexican-inspired songs, such as 'Sombrero', composed by Nikica Kalogjera, began to appear; as another Yugoslav composer, Đorđe Novković, told Perović: 'Upon hearing Perović with his violins, trumpets and Mexican songs, I began to compose that type of thing for Mišo Kovač' (interview with Sužnjević). According to Perović, in the 1960s, many of the most popular groups – typically trios – dressed in mariachi garb and 'the influence of Mexican music was so great in our country that every singer sang at least one of those songs' (ibid.). In 1969, Perović was awarded a gold record for having sold a million copies (cumulative total of his various albums from 1963 to 1969) of his mostly Mexican music. Majatović dates the Mexican craze from the late 1950s to the early 70s – although Perović continued to earn gold records for his Mexican recordings into the 80s, as occurred with a collaborative album he made with Nikola Karović in 1980 (interview with Sužnjević). Tito himself was seduced by Mexican culture, as can be seen in several photos of celebrations in which he sports Mexican sombreros (see Irwin, 'Mexican Golden Age', p. 161).

MEXICAN GOLDEN AGE FILM'S LONG-TERM IMPACT

If Tito resented Soviet political or military interventions, Yugoslavians, who adored him, saw Soviet cultural production as an unwanted imposition but, following Tito's politics, were not willing to simply substitute new cultural alliances with the USA by importing more product from Hollywood, whose market penetration had dropped from prewar levels of 65 per cent to only 40 per cent by the early 1950s (Ramsaye, *1937–38*; p. 1143; Kann, p. x). Mexican culture, well known as 'revolutionary', but closely allied neither with the Soviet Union nor the USA in Cold War politics, provided a unique point of identification for Yugoslavia, a perspective located outside the overbearing context of the Cold War. Mexico, indeed, like Yugoslavia, smaller and poorer than the imperial giants of the era, asserted its cultural autonomy from the shadows of Cold War empire. While Yugoslavia's cultural and political contacts with Mexico were minimal, it is not difficult to imagine the two nations sharing a certain cultural empathy.

The first round of Mexican films exhibited generated a great deal of excitement, with features such as *La malquerida*, starring Dolores del Río, Pedro Armendáriz, Columba Domínguez and Roberto Cañedo, and the early Cantinflas hit *Los tres mosqueteros* earning critical admiration for their 'quality, originality and artistic freshness' and especially for breaking from Hollywood formulas to establish a true 'national style' of their own (*Borba*, 16 November 1952); these, indeed, were the first Mexican films to arrive in Yugoslavia, about a month before *Un día de vida* would cause a sensation. Mexican cinema was all the rage for a period, with films like *El rebozo de Soledad* earning raves – in this case for Figueroa's cinematography and the performances of film's leading actors Pedro Armendáriz, Arturo de Córdova and Estela Inda, as well as its screenplay, written by novelist José Revueltas in collaboration with director Roberto Gavaldón (*Borba*, 20 August 1953).

While a few of the films were comedies, most of the best received were, like *Un día de vida*, nationalist melodramas, produced with great attention to a cinematographic aesthetic that idealised Mexican landscapes, faces and physiognomies. Yugoslavian audiences responded, according to an early critic, to 'the immediacy of the experience, the enhanced sentimentality, Mexican folk songs and the sporadic accentuation of the exotic through an unusual visual technique' (Petrović, quoted in and translated by Mijatović, p. 4). Another Yugoslav film critic interpreted *Un día de vida*'s success in 1952 in the following way:

> Through *Un día de vida*, Mexico gave itself, told everything about itself. It told its history and foretold its future. It has shown us its heart. We saw it and felt it. That is the first time when seeing Mexico I thought of Yugoslavia. Maybe it was a subconscious feeling of connectedness, maybe a similarity in the hearts and characters: their songs and dances, their country, their people looked similar to ours. (Voja Rehar, quoted in Mijatović, p. 4)

Yugoslavs' taste for melodrama can also be seen in the popular success of *El derecho de nacer*, a film utterly lacking in Fernández and Figueroa's artistic pretensions, based on a popular Cuban radio soap opera (*Filmski Svet*, 1956). Fernández's films in general were critical favourites, with some of his earlier films, such as *María Candelaria* and *Enamorada*, continuing to earn praises (*Filmski Svet*, 1955), along with those of Roberto Gavaldón, including *La escondida* (1956) (*Filmski Svet*, 20 December 1956). Columba Domínguez, in particular, established as an exotic object of Yugoslav desire, had become Mexican cinema's most memorable star: 'Columba Domínguez and her extraordinary beauty are explained by the presence of indigenous blood. Columba heightens it even more with her particular hairstyle, typical of the indigenous peoples of central Mexico' (*Filmski Svet*, 1955). As mentioned earlier, Mijatović argues that the most popular Mexican songs of the 'Mexican craze' tended to idealise Mexico through stereotypes: 'Mexico – idealized, simplified, stereotyped – began functioning as an object of desire, or more precisely, a symbolic geographical space where the contradictions between the real hardships and an imaginary easy lifestyle coexisted in an uncomplicated relationship' (p. 5). Yugoslav mariachi music and the films like *Un día de vida* that gave rise to them evoked a 'longing for Mexico as an imagined homeland' for a nation battered by World War II, which underwent great hardships in trying to rebuild under the leadership of a new regime and its sometimes harshly imposed ideology (ibid.).

But by the mid-1950s, even as Mexican music was just catching on, critics were beginning to tire of Mexican cinema. As early as 1953, Yugoslav critics were expressing disappointment in Mexico's submissions to Cannes, including Luis Buñuel's *Él* (1953) and Emilio Fernández's *La red* (1953) (*Ilustrovani List Duga*, 14 June 1953). A critic of a lesser Fernández melodrama, *Siempre tuya* (1952), starring Jorge Negrete and Gloria Marín, complained of being fed up with what had become the director's tiresome style (*Borba*, August 1954). Eventually Yugoslavs, having seen the best of Mexican cinema, were sent older hits that were of lesser artistic quality, such as *Konga roja*, a drama set in the context of banana plantations, starring Pedro Armendáriz and *rumbera* María Antonieta Pons, which premiered simultaneously in ten theatres in Belgrade, but was written off by critics as 'nonsense' (*Borba*, 16 August 1956). *Cantando nace el amor* (Miguel Delgado, 1954) was reviewed under the headline, 'In Bad Taste' (*Borba*, 10 October 1956), and while critics appreciated Libertad Lamarque's musical performances in a biopic about the great Mexican *bolero* composer, María Grever, it again used a sarcastic headline above the film's title, *Cuando me vaya* (Tito Davison, 1954), whose English translation is 'When I Leave': 'Get Out As Soon As Possible' (*Borba*, 29 March 1957). By this time appreciation for Mexican cinema had fizzled. It is impossible to say whether this was because audience tastes were changing, quality was dropping off as the golden age came to an end, or simply because Mexican film was a fad in the early 1950s that simply couldn't be sustained in a country so otherwise disconnected from Latin American culture – although this latter explanation would seem to be belied by the lasting success of Mexican music there.

However, nostalgia for the golden age of Mexican cinema would keep *Un día de vida* playing intermittently for years, and would also inspire the organisation of Mexican film retrospectives, including a 1963 event that brought back classics such as *Los olvidados*, *Maclovia* and *El rebozo de Soledad*, and more praises for old favourites Gabriel Figueroa, Luis Buñuel, Emilio Fernández, Roberto Gavaldón, María Félix, Pedro Armendáriz, Columba Domínguez, Dolores del Río, Cantinflas and Estela Inda (*Politika*, 25 March 1963). This festival created a great deal of buzz by bringing to Yugoslavia the 1933 version of Sergei Eisenstein's Mexico project, released as *Thunder Over Mexico* (*Politika*, 30 March 1963; 2 April 1963) and, a few months later, Roberto Gavaldón's remarkable *Macario* (1960) opened in Belgrade after having won a handful of international awards and earned nominations for the Palme d'Or in Cannes and the

Best Foreign Film Oscar in the USA (*Politika*, 20 June 1963), but by that time Mexico was producing mainly B movies, and would not have any other follow-ups for Yugoslavian fans. A 1974 festival that attempted to bring contemporary Mexican films – by the same old 1950s directors, none of whom had produced a critically acclaimed film in years – such as *María* and *La choca* (Emilio Fernández, 1974) did not generate the same degree of excitement (*Politika*, 30 September 1974).

MAMA HUANITA

Balkan Mexicanist fervour was renewed in 1997 when actress Columba Domínguez, whom the Yugoslav press erroneously claimed had won an Ariel for *Un día de vida* (*Filmski Svet*, 1955) – actually she had not even been nominated – and who continued receiving letters from Yugoslav admirers for decades (interview with Sužnjević), was invited to Belgrade for a homage. There she attended a gala screening of *Un día de vida* at the Yugoslavian Film Archive that was preceded by a live performance of 'Mama Huanita' by Slavko Perović, whose popularity continues to this day, as is evidenced by his release of a new CD of his Mexican (and Greek) hits in 2007, inevitably titled *Jedan dan života*, followed up by the 2009 reissue of fifty-six of his original recordings from 1963 to 1969. The Serbians (Yugoslavia was in the process of gradual disintegration at the time, and by 1997 Slovenia, Croatia, Bosnia and Macedonia had already seceded from the union) also staged a grand reception in her honour at the Serbian Ministry of Culture and a lavish dinner attended by crown prince Tomislav Karadjordjević. Domínguez was treated as if she were one of the greatest stars of national cinema. This time the accompanying film festival brought back the old Fernández favourites such as *Maclovia*, *La malquerida*, *Río Escondido* and *Pueblerina*, all of which featured performances by Domínguez, pairing them with a newly popular (and broadly defined) Mexican cinema, including *Como agua para chocolate* (Alfonso Arau, 1992) alongside *My Family* (known in Mexico as *Mi familia*), the 1995 film directed by Chicano Gregory Nava (*Borba*, 9 September 1997).

Contemporary critics looking back see the furore over *Un día de vida* as something of a zeitgeist. The Yugoslav public, 'educated with postwar melodramas and the heroic characters of wars and revolutions suddenly found all of this in one movie' (*Politika Ekspres,* 14 September 1997). *Un día de vida* was remembered not just as a huge movie hit and beloved old film, but as an important cultural influence, with one critic affirming that '*Un día de vida* codified a matrix' that made possible the embracing of Mexican culture by Yugoslavians in the 1950s, and their continued love affair with Latin America, as is seen in their fervent ardour for telenovelas (*Politika*, 13 September 1997): 'all this madness for Latin American telenovelas would not have reached its currently enormous proportions if more than four decades ago a marvellous Mexican film, *Un día de vida*, had not conquered our land' (*Borba*, 13 September 1997). Apparently, Coraima Torres, star of the Venezuelan telenovela *Kassandra* (1992), which had been a huge hit in Yugoslavia (and most of the world), who had recently caused much excitement upon a visit to Belgrade, was the relevant point of comparison: Domínguez was remembered for having been the Coraima Torres of the 1950s (*Borba*, 9 September 1997).

And 'Mama Huanita' was just as important as the film that transformed Mexico's generic birthday song into a Yugoslavian homage to mothers: 'the popular song "Mama Huanita" from the 1950s influenced the emotional life of Yugoslavians' (*Politika Ekspres*, 13 September 1997). A day later, the same critic, Vladimir Lazarević adds: 'The song "Mama Huanita" was in constant rotation on radio programmes, which is how a love for … Mexican music was awakened, a love that lasted for decades'; 'Mama Huanita' can also be seen as a 'precursor to the rage of Latin American culture' in the region (*Politika Ekspres*, 14 September 1997).

Nostalgia for the Mexican craze of the 1950s lives on. Indeed, Mijatović argues that demand for Mexican favourites resurged in the 90s as 'many people in former Yugoslav republics experienced something referred to locally as Yugo-nostalgia', of which a key element has to do with music:

> Music from the 1960s and 1970s especially became popular again, and through it, several mariachi songs … through their overt sentimentalism, evoke a rememberance of a past time, including 'Mama Huanita' … These songs now form a standard repertoire for many singers and cover bands. (p. 11)

Indeed, the same year as Columba Domínguez's grand homage, across the border in Croatia, a new mariachi band, Los Caballeros, formed, garnering enough critical success to be invited twice (in 2000 and 2002) to perform at the annual International Mariachi and Charrería Festival in Guadalajara ('Mariachi Los Caballeros'); and the influence of Mexican melodrama that was seen as early as the 1950s in Yugoslav film (Pavćić) would continue to have echoes decades later, for example in the 1986 film *Srećna nova '49* (Stole Popov), which features a scene with a young boy singing 'La Malagueña', a song Yugoslavs knew as it was featured prominently in a version by Trío Calaveras in the Fernández film *Enamorada*.

Mexican cinema's appeal to Yugoslavs was multifaceted: it offered a visual representation of an exotic, picturesque and fundamentally revolutionary culture, along with the exaltation of universal values (patriotism, motherly love and international fraternity); likewise, its stylistic conventions (melodrama, as well as the prominent role many films assigned to cinematography and to music) were apparently in synch with Yugoslavs' own cultural idiosyncrasies (Panjeta). Due to an improvised south–south affinity felt by Yugoslavs for Mexican cultural production in the face of more powerful imperialistic cultural forces, *Un día de vida* not only exceeded the acclaim that *María Candelaria* had experienced in France and other European countries a few years before, but also exercised an astounding cultural influence in Yugoslavia, where 'Yu-Mex' music continued to be popular for decades, and is one of the most remarkable examples of just how powerful a cultural machine Mexican golden age cinema had come to be by the early 1950s.

Epilogue

Robert McKee Irwin and Maricruz Castro Ricalde

By the late 1950s, Mexico's cinema industry was in decline, although exports continued to be strong to some of its most reliable markets into the 60s. Its studios would soon fade out completely from the world stage, reducing production to reptetitive low-budget *churros* hardly of export quality. For years, Mexican studios continued operating, but producing only low-budget films geared towards less-educated and not very demanding domestic audiences. Among its most prominent genres were wrestling adventures starring superhero El Santo; semi-pornographic *fichera* films set in bordellos; drug-trafficking adventures, some based on notorious *narcocorridos*; comedies starring locally popular entertainers such as La India María; family-oriented melodramas featuring still active but faded golden age stars such as Libertad Lamarque and Arturo de Córdova; and dramas starring luminaries of popular music such as Enrique Guzmán and Lola Beltrán. While, elsewhere in Latin America, a 'new' Latin American cinema gained the attention of intellectuals and critics (if not audiences) around the world by rejecting the commercialism and frivolity of the classic cinema of Hollywood and Mexico, Mexican producers continued to put out the movies that seemed to be the most commercially viable, with less and less attention paid to artistic or technical quality.

While other countries (Cuba, Argentina, Chile, Bolivia, Brazil) are more readily associated with the more socially conscious, intellectually challenging and artistically inspired cinema that today is most associated with Latin American film production of the 1960s and 70s, a few Mexican cinematic entrepreneurs scraped together funding to produce what today would be considered independent-style features during those years, some of which have obtained some critical acclaim, most notably the films of Arturo Ripstein (*El lugar sin límites*, 1978), Paul Leduc (*Reed, México Insurgente*, 1973), Felipe Cazals (*Canoa*, 1976), Jaime Humberto Hermosillo (*María de mi corazón*, 1979) and Jorge Fons (*Los albañiles*, 1976). However, very few of these films obtained significant distribution or attention abroad.

It was only with the foundation of Mexico's Institute of Cinematography (IMCINE) in 1983 and the general trend of globalisation that facilitated international collaboration in film production that Mexican film producers began to find the means to make movies that once again brought Mexican films to significant numbers of international screens. By the eary 1990s, works such as *Cabeza de Vaca* (Nicolás Echevarría, 1991), *Como agua para chocolate*, *Danzón* (María Novaro, 1991) and *Cronos* (Guillermo del Toro, 1993) were setting the stage for the even greater success that

Mexican cinema lost its lustre in the 1960s

Mexican-made movies (nowadays mostly co-productions, with funding from Mexico as well as Spain, the USA or elsewhere) would realise a decade later, with the release of *Amores perros* (Alejandro González Inárritu, 2000), *Y tu mamá también* (Alfonso Cuarón, 2001), *El crimen del padre Amaro* (Carlos Carrera, 2002), *El laberinto del fauno* (Guillermo del Toro, 2006), *Rudo y cursi* (Carlos Cuarón, 2008) and *Biutiful* (Alejandro González Iñárritu, 2010).

Bibliography

Aaronson, Charles, *1953–54 International Motion Picture Almanac* (New York: Quigley, 1953).
—— , *1955 International Motion Picture Almanac* (New York: Quigley, 1954).
Agramonte, Arturo y Luciano Castillo, *Ramón Peón: el hombre de los glóbulos negros* (Havana: Editorial de Ciencias Sociales, 2003).
Agrasánchez, Rogelio, *Mexican Movies in the United States: A History of the Films, Theaters and Audiences, 1920–1960* (Jefferson, NC: McFarland, 2006).
Almendros, Néstor, *Días de una cámara* (Barcelona: Seix Barral, 1993).
Alvaray, Luisela, 'Melodrama and the Emergence of Venezuelan Cinema', Darlene Sadlier (ed.), *Latin American Melodrama* (Urbana: University of Illinois Press, 2009).
Arango, Adriana, et al., *¡Acción!: cine en Colombia* (Bogotá: Museo Nacional de Colombia, 2008).
Ardila, Omar, 'Cine del sur: entre el asombro y la aventura', *La Hojarrasca* 24, www.escritoresyperiodistas.com/NUMERO24/omar.htm. Accessed 7 July 2010.
Argente, Héctor, 'El génesis de la lágrima', *Somos*, Special issue: *La novia de América: Libertad Lamarque*, vol. 10 no. 190, December 1999, pp. 32–41.
—— , 'Un maya en el cine gaucho', *Somos*, Special issue: *La voz de rostro inolvidable: Arturo de Córdova*, vol. 10 no. 180, February 1999, pp. 70–3.
Ávila Camacho, *Informes presidenciales, en Cámara de Diputados: LX Legislatura* [1941–46], Mexico City, 2006, http://www.diputados.gob.mx/cedia/sia/re/RE-ISS-09-06-09.pdf. Accessed 4 September 2010.
Aviña, Rafael, *Una mirada insólita: temas y géneros del cine mexicano* (Mexico City: Océano/Cineteca Nacional, 2004).
Ayala Blanco, Jorge, *La aventura del cine mexicano* (Mexico City: Era, 1968).
Beer, Amy Barnes, 'From the Bronx to Brooklyn: Spanish-Language Movie Theaters and Their Audiences in New York City', doctoral dissertation, Northwestern University, Evanston, IL, 2001.
Benjamin, Walter, 'The Work of Art in the Age of Mechanical Reproduction', [1935], http://walterbenjamin.ominiverdi.org/wp-content/workart.pdf. Accessed 4 September 2010.
Bernal Ramírez, Manuel, 'Libertad en el teatro musical', *Samos*, 1 December 1999, pp. 68–71.
Briggs, Asa and Peter Burke, *De Gutenburg a internet: una historia social de los medios de comunicación* [2002] (Mexico City: Taurus, 2008).
Burton Carvajal, Julianne, '*Araya* Across Time and Space: Competing Canons of National (Venezuelan) and International film Histories', Chon Noriega (ed.), *Visible Nations: Latin American Cinema and Video* (Minneapolis: University of Minnesota Press, 2000), pp. 51–81.

——, Patricia Torres and Ángel Miquel (eds), *Horizontes del segundo siglo: investigación y pedagogía del cine mexicano, latinoamericano y chicano* (Guadalajara/Mexico City: Universidad de Guadalajara/Instituto Mexicano de Cinematografía, 1998).

Camarena, Amelia, 'A México le debo todo lo que soy', *Somos*, Special issue: 'Las rumberas del cine mexicano', no. 189, September 1999, pp. 56–9.

Carmona, Luis Miguel and Bienvenido Llopis, *La censura franquista en el cine de papel* (Madrid: Cacitel/Ministerio de Cultura, 2009).

Castro Ricalde, Maricruz, 'Cuba exotizada y la construcción cinematográfica de la nación mexicana', *Razón y Palabra* no. 71, 2010, http://www.www.razonypalabra.org.mx/N/N71/TEXTOS/CASTRO_REVISADO.pdf. Accessed 4 September 2010.

——, 'Del panamericanismo al nacionalismo: relaciones cinematográficas entre México y Cuba', *Brújula. Revista interdisciplinaria sobre estudios latinamericanos* vol. 8 no. 1, 2010, pp. 41–57.

——, 'El género y los estudios cinematográficos en México', *Ciencia Ergo Sum* vol. 16 no. 1, March–June 2009, pp. 64–70.

——, '*La Rosa Blanca* (1954) y la nación como concepto fracturado', Alberto del Castillo and Alba González Reyes (eds), *Estudios Históricos sobre Cultura Visual. Nuevas Perspectivas de Investigación* (Morelia: El Colegio de México, Instituto de Investigaciones Dr José María Luis Mora, forthcoming).

——, 'We Are Rumberas, But Decent', unpublished manuscript.

—— and Robert McKee Irwin, '*La Rosa Blanca* (1954): La disputa por José Martí', *El cine mexicano* se impone. *Mercados transnacionales y penetración cultural en la edad dorada* (México: UNAM, 2011), pp. 243–61.

Chanan, Michael, *Cuban Cinema* (Minneapolis: University of Minnesota Press, 2004).

Contreras Soto, Eduardo, 'Ponce y Pomar: esos danzoneros', *Tierra Adentro: Vereda Tropical* vol. 143–4, March 2007, pp. 5–11.

Dávalos Orozco, *Albores del cine mexicano* (Mexico City: Clío, 1996).

DeFleur, Melvin, *Teorías de la comunicación masiva* (Buenos Aires: Paidós, 1976).

De Francisco, Isabel, *La mujer en el cine español* (Madrid: Arkadin, 2010).

De la Mora, Sergio, *Cinemachismo: Masculinities and Sexuality in Mexican Film* (Austin: University of Texas Press, 2006).

De la Vega Alfaro, Eduardo, *Alberto Gout* (Mexico City: Cineteca Nacional, 1988).

——, *El cine de Juan Orol* (Mexico City: Filmoteca de la Universidad Nacional Autónoma de México, 1984).

——, '*Contrabando*: primera incursión del cine sonoro mexicano en el tema fronterizo', Ignacio Durán, Iván Trujillo and Mónica Verea (eds), *México-Estados Unidos: encuentros y desencuentros en el cine* (Mexico City: Universidad Nacional Autónoma de México/Instituto mexicano de Cinematografía, 1996), pp. 147–64.

——, 'The Decline of the Golden Age and the Making of the Crisis', Joanne Hershfield and David Maciel (eds), *Mexico's Cinema: A Century of Film and Filmmakers* (Wilmington, DE: Scholarly Resources, 1999), pp. 165–91.

——, *La industria cinematográfica mexicana: perfil histórico-social* (Guadalajara: Universidad de Guadalajara, 1991).

——, 'Origin, Development and Crisis of the Sound Cinema', Paulo Antonio Paranaguá (ed.), *Mexican Cinema* (London/Mexico City: BFI/Instituto Mexicano de Cinematografía, 1995), pp. 79–93.

——— and Alberto Elena (eds), *Abismos de la pasión: relaciones cinematográficas hispanoamericanas*, Special issue of *Cuadernos de la Filmoteca* no. 13, 2009.

De los Reyes, Aurelio, *Medio siglo de cine mexicano (1896–1947)* (Mexico City: Trillas, 1987).

Dever, Susan, *Celluloid Nationalism and Other Melodramas* (Albany: State University of New York Press, 2003).

Díaz López, Marina, 'Buscar y amar los lugares comunes', Eduardo de la Vega Alfaro and Alberto Elena (eds), *Abismos de la pasión: relaciones cinematográficas hispanoamericanas*, Special issue of *Cuadernos de la Filmoteca* no. 13, 2009, pp. 125–46.

——— , 'Jalisco nunca pierde: raíces y composición de la comedia ranchera como género popular mexicano', *Archivos de la Filmoteca* no. 31, 1999, pp. 45–58.

——— , 'Las vías de la hispanidad en una coproducción hispano-mexicana de 1948 *Jalisco canta en Sevilla*', *Cuadernos de la Academia* no. 5, May 1999, pp. 159–76.

D'Lugo, Marvin, 'Aural Identity, Genealogies of Sound Technologies, and Hispanic Transnationality on Screen', Nataša Ďurovičová and Kathleen Newman (eds), *World Cinemas, Transnational Perspectives* (New York: Routledge, 2010), pp. 160–85.

——— , 'Gardel, el film hispano y la construcción de la identidad auditiva', Nancy Berthier and Jean-Claude Seguin (eds), *Cine, nación y nacionalidades en España* (Madrid: Casa de Velázquez, 2008), pp. 147–63.

Douglas, María Eulalia, *La tienda negra: el cine en Cuba (1897–1990)* (Havana: Cinemateca de Cuba, 1996).

Durán, Ignacio, Iván Trujillo and Mónica Verea (eds), *México-Estados Unidos: encuentros y desencuentros en el cine* (Mexico City: Universidad Nacional Autónoma de México/Instituto Mexicano de Cinematografía, 1996).

Durán, Javier, 'Nation and Translation: The Pachuco in Mexican Popular Culture: Germán Valdez's Tin Tan', *Journal of the Midwest Modern Language Association* vol. 35 no. 2, 2002, pp. 41–9.

Efendić, Nadir, 'Trio TiViDi', http://www.barikada.com/vremeplov/kao_nekad_u_8/2004-12-02_trio_tividi_-_biografija.php. Accessed 4 September 2010.

Elena, Alberto, 'El cinema latinoamericano en España: materiales para una historia desde la recepción', *El ojo que piensa*, no. 1, August 2003, http://www.scribd.com/doc/6887290/El-cine-latinoamericano-en-Espana. Accessed 20 November 2010.

——— , 'Medio siglo de coproducciones hispano-mexicanas', Eduardo de la Vega Alfaro and Alberto Elena (eds), *Abismos de la pasión: relaciones cinematográficas hispanoamericanas*, Special issue of *Cuadernos de la Filmoteca* no. 13, 2009, pp. 279–304.

——— and Paulo Antonio Paranaguá, 'Mitologías latinoamericanas', *Archivos de la Filmoteca* no. 31, 1999, pp. 5–7.

España, Claudio, 'El cine sonoro y su expansión', Jorge Miguel Couselo, et al., *Historia del cine argentino* (Buenos Aires: Centro Editor de América Latina, 1984), pp. 47–89.

Falicov, Tamara, 'Hollywood's Rogue Neighbor: The Argentine Film Industry During the Good Neighbor Policy, 1939–1945', *The Americas* vol. 2 no. 63, October 2006, pp. 245–60.

Fein, Seth, 'From Collaboration to Containment: Hollywood and the International Political Economy of Mexican Cinema After the Second World War', Joanne Hershfield and David Maciel (eds), *Mexico's Cinema: A Century of Film and Filmmakers* (Wilmington, DE: Scholarly Resources, 1999), pp. 123–63.

——— , 'Myths of Cultural Imperialism and Nationalism in Golden Age Mexican Cinema', Gilberto Joseph, Anne Rubenstein and Eric Zolov (eds), *Fragments of a Golden Age: The Politics of Culture in Mexico Since 1940* (Durham, NC: Duke University Press, 2001), pp. 159–98.

Félix, María, *Todas mis guerras* (Mexico City: Clío, 1993).

Fernández, Emilio and Mauricio Magdaleno, *Un día de vida*, unpublished screenplay manuscript, Mexico City, 1949.

—— , *Jedan dan života* (Belgrade: Filmska Biblioteka 'Ars', 1953).

—— , adaptation of play by Jacinto Benavente, *La malkerida* (Belgrade: Filmska Biblioteka 'Ars', 1953).

Fernández L'Hoeste, Héctor, 'Imperialismo cultural', Mónica Szurmuk and Robert McKee Irwin, *Diccionario de estudios culturales latinoamericanos* (Mexico City: Siglo XXI/Instituto Mora, 2009), pp. 150–4.

Flores y Escalante, Jesús and Pablo Dueñas, 'La dama del tango', *Somos*, 1 December 1999, pp. 56–67.

Fraser, Nicholas and Marysa Navarro, *The Real Life of Eva Perón* (New York: W. W. Norton, 1996).

Fregoso, Rosa Linda, 'El espacio simbólico de México en el cine chicano', Ignacio Durán, Iván Trujillo and Mónica Verea (eds), *México-Estados Unidos: encuentros y desencuentros en el cine* (Mexico City: Universidad Nacional Autónoma de México/Instituto Mexicano de Cinematografía, 1996), pp. 189–96.

Gallegos C., José Luis, 'Libertad Lamarque: mi nombre y el de Eva Perón, unidos a la historia de Argentina, Parte I', *Excélsior*, 3 March 1997, p. 1E.

—— , 'Libertad Lamarque participó en la primera película que Luis Buñuel dirigió en México, *Gran casino*, en 1946, Parte II', *Excélsior*, 4 March 1997, pp. 1E–2E.

García, Gustavo, *Pedro Armendáriz: el mejor actor del mundo* (Mexico City: Clío, 1997).

—— and Rafael Aviña, *Época de oro del cine mexicano* (Mexico City: Clío, 1997).

García Canclini, Néstor, *Consumers and Citizens: Globalization and Multicultural Conflicts* [1995], trans. George Yúdice (Minneapolis: University of Minnesota Press, 2001).

—— , 'El consumo cultural y su estudio en México: una propuesta teórica', Néstor García Canclini (ed.), *El consumo cultural en México* (Mexico City: Consejo Nacional para la Cultura y las Artes, 1993), pp. 15–42.

—— (ed.), *Los nuevos espectadores: cine, televisión y video en México* (Mexico City: Instituto Mexicano de Cinematografía/Consejo Nacional de la Cultural y las Artes, 1994).

García Fernández, Emilio, 'Cinematografías de la semejanza', *Revista Virtual del Instituto Cervantes* 2007.

García Riera, Emilio, 'El cine en México: algunos antecedentes', *Televisión, cine, historietas y publicidad en México* (Mexico City: Universidad Nacional Autónoma de México, 1978), pp. 23–9.

—— , 'El cine español de la postguerra visto desde el exilio mexicano', Eduardo de la Vega Alfaro and Alberto Elena (eds), *Abismos de la pasión: relaciones cinematográficas hispanoamericanas*, Special issue of *Cuadernos de la Filmoteca* no. 13, 2009, pp. 15–24.

—— , *Historia documental del cine mexicano*, 18 Vol. [1969–71] (Guadalajara: Universidad de Guadalajara, 1992–97).

—— , 'The Impact of *Rancho Grande*', Paulo Antonio Paranaguá (ed.), *Mexican Cinema* (London/Mexico City: BFI/Instituto Mexicano de Cinematografía, 1995), pp. 128–32.

—— and Javier González Rubio, *El cine de Katy Jurado* (Guadalajara: Universidad de Guadalajara, 1999).

García Saucedo, Jaime, *Diccionario de literatura colombiana en el cine* (Bogotá: Panamericana, 2003).

Gilard, Jacques (ed.), *Gabriel García Márquez: obra periodística*, 3 Vol. (Barcelona: Bruguera, 1981–82).

Giménez Caballero, Ernesto, *Amor a Méjico a través de su cine* (Madrid: Seminario de Problemas Hispanoamericanos, 1948).

Granados, Pável, 'Todo lo que cante se llenará de sol: Toña la Negra y las diosas tropicales de la radio', *Tierra Adentro: Vereda Tropical* vol. 143–4, March 2007, pp. 21–31.

Gubern, Román, 'La exogamia pasional hispanoamericana ilustrada por el cine durante el franquismo', Eduardo de la Vega Alfaro and Alberto Elena (eds), *Abismos de la pasión: relaciones cinematográficas hispanoamericanas*, Special issue of *Cuadernos de la Filmoteca* no. 13, 2009, pp. 89–100.

Guevara, Alfredo, 'Realidades y perspectivas de un nuevo cine', *Cine Cubano* vol. 1 no. 5, 1960, pp. 3–10.

Guía Cinematográfica 1955 (Havana: Centro Católico de Orientación Cinematográfica, 1957).

Guía Cinematográfica 1956–1957 (Havana: Centro Católico de Orientación Cinematográfica, 1957).

Habra, Hedy, 'La deconstrucción del tejido mítico franquista', *Espéculo* no. 28, 2004, pp. 1–13.

Hall, Stuart, 'Encoding/Decoding', in Stuart Hall, Dorothy Hobson, Andrew Love and Paul Willis (eds), *Culture, Media, Language* (London: Hutchinson, 1980), pp. 128–38.

Hamelink, Cees, *La aldea transnacional* (Barcelona: Gustavo Gil, 1981).

Hennebelle, Guy, *Los cinemas nacionales contra el imperialismo de Hollywood* (Valencia: Fernando Torres, 1977).

Heredia, Juanita, 'From Golden Age Mexican Cinema to Transnational Border Feminism: The Community of Spectators in *Loving Pedro Infante*', *Aztlán* vol. 33 no. 2, 2008, pp. 37–59.

Hernández, Tulio, 'Cronología', José Miguel Acosta et al., *Panorama historic del cine en Venezuela 1896–1993* (Caracas: Fundación Cinemateca Nacional, 1997), pp. 15–18.

Hershfield, Joanne and David Maciel (eds), *Mexico's Cinema: A Century of Film and Filmmakers* (Wilmington, DE: Scholarly Resources, 1999).

Heuer, Federico, *La industria cinematográfica mexicana* (Mexico City: Policromía, 1964).

Hjort, Mette, 'On the Plurality of Cinematic Transnationalism', Nataša Ďurovičová and Kathleen Newman (eds), *World Cinemas, Transnational Perspectives* (New York: Routledge, 2010), pp. 12–33.

Irwin, Robert McKee, *Mexican Masculinities* (Minneapolis: University of Minnesota Press, 2003).

—— , 'Memín Pinguín, Rumba and Racism: Afro Mexicans in Classic Comics and Film', Caroline Levander and Robert Levine (eds), *Hemispheric American Studies* (New Brunswick: Rutgers University Press, 2007), pp. 249–65.

—— , 'Mexican Golden Age Cinema in Tito's Yugoslavia', *Global South* vol. 4 no. 1, 2010, pp. 149–64.

Ivers, James and Charles Aaronson, *1950–51 International Motion Picture Almanac* (New York: Quigley, 1950).

Izaguirre, Rodolfo, *Acechos de la imaginación* (Caracas: Monte Ávila, 1993).

—— , 'Del infortunio recurrente al acto promisor: 1940–1958', José Miguel Acosta et al., *Panorama histórico del cine en Venezuela 1896–1993* (Caracas: Fundación Cinemateca Nacional, 1997), pp. 115–28.

Joseph, Gilbert, Anne Rubenstein and Eric Zolov, 'Assembling the Fragments: Writing a Cultural History of Mexico Since 1940', *Fragments of a Golden Age: The Politics of Culture in Mexico Since 1940* (Durham, NC: Duke University Press, 2001), pp. 3–22.

Kann, Red, *1951–52 International Motion Picture Almanac* (New York: Quigley, 1951).

King, John, *Magical Reels* [1990] (London: Verso, 2000).

——, Ana López and Manuel Alvarado (eds), *Mediating Two Worlds: Cinematic Encounters in the Americas* (London: BFI, 1993).

Krauze, Enrique, 'Prólogo: Una mujer con corazón de hombre', in María Félix, *Todas mis guerras*, vol. I (Mexico City: Clío, 1993), pp. 16–23.

Kriger, Clara, *Cine y peronismo: el estado en escena* (Buenos Aires: Siglo XXI, 2009).

Lam, Rafael, 'Famosos en la música en el Hotel Nacional de Cuba', *Visiones Alternativas*, http://www.visionesalternativas.com.mx/index.php?option=com_deeppockets&task=contShow&id=95649&Itemid=. Accessed 20 November 2010.

Lamarque, Libertad, *Libertad Lamarque* (Buenos Aires: Joaquín Vergara, 1986).

Lida, Clara (ed.), *México y España en el primer franquismo, 1939–1950: rupturas formales, relaciones oficiosas* (Mexico City: El Colegio de México, 2001).

López, Ana, 'Are All Latins from Manhattan?: Hollywood, Ethnography and Cultural Colonialism', John King, Ana López and Manuel Alvarado (eds), *Mediating Two Worlds: Cinematic Encounters in the Americas* (London: BFI, 1993), pp. 67–80.

——, 'A Cinema for the Continent', Chon Noriega and Steven Ricci (eds), *The Mexican Cinema Project* (Los Angeles: UCLA Film and Television Archive, 1994), pp. 7–12.

——, 'Crossing Nations and Genres: Traveling Filmmakers', Chon Noriega (ed.), *Visible Nations: Latin American Cinema and Video* (Minneapolis: University of Minnesota Press, 2000), pp. 33–50.

——, 'Historia nacional, historia transnacional', Julianne Burton Carvajal, Patricia Torres and Ángel Miquel (eds), *Horizontes del segundo siglo: investigación y pedagogía del cine mexicano, latinoamericano y chicano* (Guadalajara/Mexico City: Universidad de Guadalajara/Instituto Mexicano de Cinematografía, 1998), pp. 75–81.

——, 'Of Rhythms and Borders', Celeste Fraser Delgado and José Esteban Muñoz (eds), *Everynight Life: Culture and Dance in Latin/o America* (Durham, NC: Duke University Press, 1997), pp. 310–44.

——, 'Tears and Desire: Women and Melodrama in "Old" Mexican Cinema', John King, Ana López and Manuel Alvarado (eds), *Mediating Two Worlds: Cinematic Encounters in the Americas* (London: BFI, 1993), pp. 147–63.

Maciel, David, 'Braceros, Mojados, and Alambristas: Mexican Immigration to the United States in Contemporary Cinema', *Hispanic Journal of Behavioral Sciences* vol. 8 no. 4, 1986, pp. 369–85.

——, 'Los desarraigados: los chicanos vistos por el cine mexicano', Ignacio Durán, Iván Trujillo and Mónica Verea (eds), *México-Estados Unidos: encuentros y desencuentros en el cine* (Mexico City: Universidad Nacional Autónoma de México/Instituto mexicano de Cinematografía, 1996), pp. 165–88.

Mahieu, José Agustín, 'Diálogo cultural entre España e Iberoamérica', *Cuadernos Hispanoamericanos* no. 390, 1982, pp. 667–76.

Maltby, Richard, 'Introduction: "The Americanisation of the World"', Richard Maltby and Melvyn Stokes (eds), *Hollywood Abroad: Audiences and Cultural Exchange* (London: BFI, 2004), pp. 1–20.

—— and Melvyn Stokes (eds), *Hollywood Abroad: Audiences and Cultural Exchange* (London: BFI, 2004).

Marez, Curtis, 'Subaltern Soundtracks: Mexican Immigrants and the Making of Hollywood Cinema', *Aztlán* vol. 29 no. 1, 2004, pp. 57–82

'Mariachi Los Caballeros', http://www.los-caballeros.com/. Accessed 12 February 2009.

Marrosu, Ambretta, 'Los modelos de la supervivencia', José Miguel Acosta et al. *Panorama histórico del cine en Venezuela 1896–1993* (Caracas: Fundación Cinemateca Nacional, 1997), pp. 21–50.

——, 'Notas comparativas entre dos Canaimas', *Una Documenta* vol. 3 no. 2, 1984, pp. 19–24.

Martín Barbero, Jesús, *De los medios a las mediaciones* [1987] (Bogotá: Convenio Andrés Bello, 2003).

Martín Gaite, Carmen, *Usos amorosos en la posguerra española* (Barcelona: Anagrama, 1994).

Martínez, Gastón, *El tango en México*, vol. II, CD liner notes (Mexico City: Secretaría de Educación Pública/DGCP/Museo Nacional de Culturas Populares, 1984).

Martínez Pardo, Hernando, *Historia del cine colombiano* (Bogotá: América Latina, 1978).

Maza, Maximiliano and Tania Soto, *Más de cine años de cine mexicano*, http://cinemexicano. mty.itesm.mx/front.html. Accessed 4 September 2010.

Mazzini, Miha, 'Yu-Mex', http://www.mihamazzini.com/ovitki/default.html. Accessed 24 September 2009.

Mesa-Bains, Amalia, '"Domesticana": The Sensibility of Chicana Rasquache', *Aztlán* vol. 24 no. 2, 1999, pp. 157–67.

Meyer, Eugenia (ed.), *Cuadernos de la Cineteca: Testimonios para la historia del cine mexicano*, vols 1, 2, 6 (Mexico City: Cineteca Nacional, 1975).

Mijatović, Brana. 'Nostalgia for an Imagined Homeland: Mariachi Music in Former Yugoslavia', unpublished manuscript (2010).

Miller, Toby, Nitin Govil, John McMurria, Richard Maxwell and Tim Wang, *Global Hollywood 2* (London: BFI, 2005).

Miranda, Olivia and Marcia Castillo, *Mirta Aguirre: crónicas de cine* (Havana: Letras Cubanas, 1988).

Monsiváis, Carlos, *Aires de familia: cultura y sociedad en América Latina* (Barcelona: Anagrama, 2000).

——, *Escenas de pudor y liviandad* [1988] (Mexico City: Grijalbo, 1994).

——, 'Mythologies', Paulo Antonio Paranaguá (ed.), *Mexican Cinema* (London/Mexico City: BFI/Instituto Mexicano de Cinematografía, 1995), pp. 117–27.

——, 'Vino todo el público y no cupo en la pantalla: notas sobre el público del cine en México', Carlos Monsiváis and Carlos Bonfil, *A través del espejo: el cine mexicano y su público* (Mexico City: Ediciones El Milagro/Instituto Mexicano de Cinematografía, 1994), pp. 49–97.

—— and Carlos Bonfil, *A través del espejo: el cine mexicano y su público* (Mexico City: Ediciones El Milagro/Instituto Mexicano de Cinematografía, 1994).

Mora, Carlos, *Mexican Cinema: Reflections of a Society 1896–1988* [1982] (Berkeley: University of California Press, 1989).

Moragas, Miguel de, *Teorías de la comunicación* (Barcelona: Gustavo Gil, 1981).

Muñoz Castillo, Fernando, *Las reinas del trópico* (Mexico City: Grupo Azabache, 1993).

Negrete, Diana, *Jorge Negrete: biografía autorizada* (Mexico City: Diana, 1987).

Negrete, Jorge, 'Carta a Juan Domingo Perón' [1948], Enrique Serna, *Jorge El Bueno: La vida de Jorge Negrete* (Mexico City: Clío, 1993), p. 48.

Noble, Andrea, *Mexican National Cinema* (New York: Routledge, 2005).

Noguer, Eduardo, *Historia del cine cubano: cien años 1897–1998* (Miami: Universal, 2002).

Noriega, Chon and Steven Ricci (eds), *The Mexican Cinema Project* (Los Angeles: UCLA Film and Television Archive, 1994).

Normland, John, *Teatro mexicano contemporáneo, 1900–1950* (Mexico City: Instituto Nacional de Bellas Artes, 1967).

Ocasio, Rafael, 'La apropiación de María Félix del icónico personaje en *Doña Bárbara* de Rómulo Gallegos', *Romance Quarterly* vol. 57 no. 4, 2010, pp. 273–85.

Ossa Coó, Carlos, *Historia del cine chileno* (Santiago: Quimantú, 1971).

Paladino, Diana, 'Libertad Lamarque, la reina de la lágrima', *Archivos de la Filmoteca* vol. 31, 1999, pp. 61–75.

Panjeta, Lejla, 'Telenovelas in Bosnia and Herzegovina', conference paper, First World Summit on Telenovela Industry, Miami, 2003.

Paranaguá, Paulo Antonio (ed.), *Le Cinéma Cubain* (Paris: Centre Georges Pompidou, 1990).

—— , 'María Félix: imagen, mito y enigma', *Archivos de la Filmoteca* no. 31, 1999, pp. 68–79.

—— (ed.), *Mexican Cinema*, trans. Ana López (London/Mexico City: BFI/Instituto Mexicano de Cinematografía, 1995).

—— , 'Ten Reasons to Love or Hate Mexican Cinema', Paulo Antonio Paranaguá (ed.), *Mexican Cinema* (London/Mexico City: BFI/Instituto Mexicano de Cinematografía, 1995), pp. 1–13.

—— , *Tradición y modernidad en el cine de América Latina* (Madrid: Fondo de Cultura Económica, 2003).

Pavčić, Jurica, '"Lemons in Siberia": A New Approach to the Study of Yugoslav Cinema of the 1950s', *New Review of Film and Television Studies* vol. 6 no. 1, 2008, pp. 19–39.

Peña, Mauricio, 'La rumba hecha mujer', *Somos*, Special issue: 'Las rumberas del cine mexicano', no. 189, September 1999, pp. 14–24.

Peredo Castro, Francisco, *Alejandro Galindo, un alma rebelde en el cine mexicano* (Mexico City: Instituto Mexicano de Cinematografía/Consejo Nacional para la Cultural y las Artes, 2000).

—— , *Cine y propaganda para Latinoamérica: México y Estados Unidos en la encrucijada de los años cuarenta* (Mexico City: Universidad Nacional Autónoma de México, 2004).

Pérez Llahi, Marcos Adrián, 'Los arrabales de la periferia: albores del sonoro en las cinematografías marginales de América Latina', Ana Laura Lusnich (ed.), *Civilización y barbarie: en el cine argentino y latinoamericano* (Buenos Aires: Biblos, 2005), pp. 175–81.

Pérez Monfort, Ricardo, 'El hispanismo conservador en el cine mexicano de los años 40', Eduardo de la Vega Alfaro and Alberto Elena (eds), *Abismos de la pasión: relaciones cinematográficas hispanoamericanas*, Special issue of *Cuadernos de la Filmoteca* no. 13, 2009, pp. 37–52.

—— , 'Un nacionalismo sin nación aparente: la fabricación de lo "típico" mexicano 1920–1950', *Política y Cultura* no. 12, 1999, pp. 177–93.

Pérez Perucha, Julio, *Antología crítica del cine español* (Madrid: Filmoteca Española, 1998).

Pérez Turrent, Tomás, 'Luis Buñuel in Mexico', Paulo Antonio Paranaguá (ed.), *Mexican Cinema* (London/Mexico City: BFI/Instituto Mexicano de Cinematografía, 1995), pp. 202–8.

Piñera, Walfredo, 'Le cinéma parlant pré-revolutionnaire', Paulo Antonio Paranaguá (ed.), *Le Cinéma Cubain* (Paris: Centre Georges Pompidou, 1990), pp. 63–77.

Pizarro, Ana, 'Divas de los cincuenta: María Félix', *Alpha* no. 28, July 2009, pp. 183–96.

Podalsky, Laura, 'Negotiating Differences: National Cinemas and Co-productions in Prerevolutionary Cuba', *The Velvet Light Trap* no. 34, 1994, pp. 59–70.

Poniatowska, Elena, 'María Félix', *Todo México I* [1990] (Mexico City: Diana, 1991), pp. 155–81.

Poinsset, Joel Roberts, *Notes on Mexico* (Philadelphia: H. C. Carey and I. Lea, 1824).

Pribham, E. Deirdre, 'Spectatorship and Subjectivity', Toby Miller and Robert Stam (eds), *A Companion to Film Theory* (Malden, MA: Blackwell, 1999), pp. 146–64.

Ramón, David, 'Biografía: una vida tranquilamente intensa', *Somos*, Special issue: *La voz de rostro inolvidable: Arturo de Córdova* vol. 10 no. 180, February 1999, pp. 12–18.

Ramsaye, Terry, *1937–38 International Motion Picture Almanac* (New York: Quigley, 1937).

——, *1939–40 International Motion Picture Almanac* (New York: Quigley, 1939).

——, *1947–48 International Motion Picture Almanac* (New York: Quigley, 1947).

——, *1949–50 International Motion Picture Almanac* (New York: Quigley, 1949).

Rangel, Ricardo and Rafael Portas (eds), *Enciclopedia cinematográfica mexicana 1897–1955* (Mexico City: Publicaciones Cinematográficas, 1955).

Rodríguez, América, 'Creating and Audience and Remapping a Nation: A Brief History of US Spanish Language Broadcasting 1930–1980', *Quarterly Review of Film and Video* vol. 16 no. 3, 1997, pp. 357–74.

Roffé, Alfredo, 'Políticas y espectáculo cinematográfico en Venezuela', José Miguel Acosta et al., *Panorama histórico del cine en Venezuela 1896–1993* (Caracas: Fundación Cinemateca Nacional, 1997), pp. 245–68.

Rosales, Hernán, 'Historia de las más famosas canciones mexicanas' [1937], *Históricas: Boletín del Instituto de Investigaciones Históricas* no. 82, May–August 2008, pp. 24–32.

Salcedo Silva, Hernán, *Crónicas del cine colombiano 1897–1950* (Bogotá: Carlos Valencia, 1981).

Samper, Juana, *María Félix, María bonita, María del alma* (Bogotá: Panamericana, 2005).

Sánchez, Alberto Ruy (ed.), *Hojas de cine: testimonios y documentos del nuevo cine latinoamericano* (Mexico City: Secretaría de Educación Pública, 1988).

—— (ed.), *El Arte de Gabriel Figueroa* [1988], *Artes de México* no. 2, March 2006.

Santamaría Delgado, Carolina, 'Bolero y radiodifusión: cosmpolitanismo y diferenciación social en Medellín, 1930–1950', *Signo y Pensamiento* no. 52, June 2008, http://www.scielo.unal.edu.co/scielo.php?script=sci_arttext&pid=S0120-48232008000100003&lng=en&nrm=iso

Santaolalla, Isabel, *Los 'otros': etnicidad y raza en el cine español* (Madrid: Prensa Universitaria, 2005).

Saragoza, Alex, 'Cinematic Orphans: Mexican Immigrants in the United States Since the 1950s', Chon Noriega (ed.), *Chicanos and Film: Essays on Chicano Representation and Resistance* (New York: Garland, 1992), pp. 127–42.

——, 'Mexican Cinema in Cold War America, 1940–1958: An Inquiry Into the Interface Between Mexico and Mexicans in the United States', Chicano Political Economy Collective, Working Paper Series (Berkeley: Chicano Studies Library, 1983).

Schiller, Herbert, *Cultura S.A.: la apropiación corporative de la expresión pública* (Guadalajara: Universidad de Guadalajara, 1993).

Serna, Enrique, *Jorge El Bueno: la vida de Jorge Negrete* (Mexico City: Clío, 1993).

Sidorkovs, Nicolás, *Los cines de Caracas en el tiempo de los cines* (Caracas: Armitano, 1994).

Soto Ávila, Antonio, *La época de oro del cine mexicano en Maracaibo* (Maracaibo: Universidad de Zulia/Editorial Kuruvindi/CONAC/SERBILUZ-CIDHIZ, 2005).

Suárez, Juana, Ramiro Arbeláez and Laura Chesak, '*Garras de oro* (The Dawn of Justice – Alborada de Justicia): The Intriguing Orphan of Colombian Silent Films', *The Moving Image* vol. 9 no. 1, 2009, pp. 54–82.

Sunkel, Guillermo, 'Introducción: el consumo cultural en la investigación en comunicación-cultural en América Latina', Guillermo Sunkel (ed.), *El consumo cultural en América Latina: construcción teórica y líneas de investigación*, 2nd edn (Bogotá: Convenio Andrés Bello, 2006), pp. 15–44.

Sužnjević, Dubravka, interview with Columba Domínguez, Mexico City, October 2009.

——, interview with Slavko Perović, Belgrade, 13 January 2010.

Szurmuk, Mónica, interview with Nuria Madrid de Sumel, Buenos Aires, 2 December 2008.

Terrón Montero, José, *La prensa en España durante el régimen de Franco* (Madrid: CIS, 1981).

Tierney, Dolores, *Emilio Fernández: Pictures in the Margins* (Manchester: Manchester University Press, 2007).

Tirado, Ricardo, *Memoria y notas del cine venezolano (1897–1959)* (Caracas: Fundación Neumann, 1987).

Tranche, Rafael, 'Iberoamérica en las imágenes del NODO', *Secuencias* no. 6, April 1997, pp. 76–8.

Tuñón, Julia, 'Emilio Fernández: A View Behind the Bars', Paulo Antonio Paranaguá (ed.), *Mexican Cinema* (London/Mexico City: BFI/Instituto Mexicano de Cinematografía, 1995), pp. 179–92.

—— , *Historia de un sueño: el Hollywood tapatío* (Mexico City/Guadalajara: Universidad Nacional Autónoma de México/Universidad de Guadalajara, 1986).

—— , 'La imagen de los españoles en el cine mexicano de la edad de oro', *Archivos de la Filmoteca* no. 31, 1999, pp. 199–211.

—— , *Mujeres de luz y sombra en el cine mexicano: la construcción de una image, 1939–1952* (Mexico City: El Colegio de México/Instituto Mexicano de Cinematografía, 1998).

—— , 'Relaciones de celuloide: el Primer Certamen Cinematográfico Hispanoamericano (Madrid 1948)', Clara Lida (ed.), *México y España en el primer franquismo, 1939–1950: rupturas formales, relaciones oficiosas* (Mexico City: El Colegio de México, 2001), pp. 121–61.

—— , *Los rostros de un mito: personajes femeninos en las películas de Emilio el 'Indio' Fernández* (Mexico City: Arte e Imagen, 2000).

Urrero, Guzmán, '"La corona negra" (1955), de Luis Saslavsky', *Cine y Letras*, 10 October 2010, http://www.guzmanurrero.es/index.php/Clasicos-del-cine/qla-corona-negraq-1951-de-luis-saslavsky.html. Accessed 29 November 2010.

Valbuena, Ángel, 'Hacia la cooperación cintematográfica hispano-mexicana', *Cuadernos Hispanoamericanos* no. 4, July 1948, pp. 196–7.

Valdés, Marta (ed.), *Libertad Lamarque: archivo de la palabra* (Mexico City: Instituto Mora, 1976).

Valdés Peña, José Antonio, 'Feliz centenario, maestro Buñuel', *Buñuel: una mirada del siglo XX* (Mexico City: Consejo Nacional para la Cultura y las Artes/Cineteca Nacional, 2000), pp. 9–16.

Valdés Rodríguez, José Manuel, *Ojeada al cine cubano* (Havana: Universidad de la Habana, 1963).

Vega, Sara, et al., *Historia de un gran amor: relaciones cinematográficas entre Cuba y México, 1897–2005* (Havana/Guadalajara: Instituto Cubano de Arte e Industria Cinematográficos/Universidad de Guadalajara, 2007).

Velázquez, Valentina, 'Foreign Women in Mexican Literature and Film: Identity, Culture, and Nationalism', doctoral dissertation, University of California, Davis, 2010.

Vélez-Serna, María Antonia, 'The Construction of Popular Taste According to Colombian Filmmakers in the 1940s', *Particip@tions* vol. 5 no. 1, May 2008, http://www.participations.org/Volume%205/Issue%201%20-%20special/5_01_velezserna.htm. Accessed 4 September 2010.

Verdugo Fuentes, Waldemar, 'La más alta estrella de cine que Cuba aporta al mundo: elogio a Ninón', *Artes e Historia*, 1994, http://waldemarverdugo.blogspot.com. Accessed 15 January 2009.

Viñas, Moisés, *Índice general del cine mexicano* (Mexico City: Instituto Mexicano de Cinematografía, 2005).

Vincenot, Emmanuel, 'Histoire du Cinéma à Cuba : des origines à l'avènement de la révolution', doctoral dissertation, Université de Bourgougne, 2005.

Wortman, Ana, 'Audience', Robert McKee Irwin and Mónica Szurmuk (eds), *Latin American Cultural Studies Dictionary* (Gainesville: University Press of Florida, 2012), pp. 28–34.

Zúñiga, Félix, 'La vida no le debe nada', *Somos*. Special issue: *La novia de América: Libertad Lamarque* vol. 10 no. 190, December 1999, pp. 6–19.

FILMOGRAPHY

Álvarez Correa, Emilio, *Sendero de luz* (Bogotá: Ducrane Films, 1945).

Benacerraf, Margot, *Araya* (Caracas/Paris: Caroní Films/Films de l'Archer, 1959).

Brückner, Hans, *Golpe de gracia* (Bogotá: Ducrane Films, 1944).

Bracho, Julio, *Cantaclaro* (Mexico City: Producciones Interamericanas, 1946).

Buñuel, Luis, *Gran casino*, with Jorge Negrete, Libertad Lamarque (Mexico City: Películas Anáhuac, 1947).

Bustillo Oro, Juan, *Canaima*, with Jorge Negrete, Gloria Marín (Mexico City: Filmex, 1945).

Calvo Olmedo, Máximo, *Flores del valle* (Cali: Calvo Film Company, 1941).

Chalbaud, Ramón, *Caín adolescente* (Caracas: Allegro Films, 1959).

Christensen, Carlos Hugo, *La balandra Isabel llegó esta tarde*, with Arturo de Córdova (Caracas: Bolívar Films, 1950).

Contreras Torres, Miguel, *Simón Bolívar*, with Julián Soler (Mexico City: Producciones Grovas, 1942).

Crevenna, Alfredo, *Pueblo, canto y esperanza*, with Roberto Cañedo, Columba Domínguez (Mexico City: Alianza Cinematográfica Mexicana, 1956).

De Anda, Raúl, *La reina del trópico*, with María Antonieta Pons (Mexico City: Producciones Raúl de Anda, 1946).

Fernández, Emilio 'el Indio', *Un día de vida*, with Columba Domínguez, Roberto Cañedo, Fernando Fernández, Rosaura Revueltas (Mexico City: Cabrera Films, 1950).

—— , *Enamorada*, with María Félix, Pedro Armendáriz (Mexico City: Panamerican Films, 1946).

—— , *María Candelaria*, with Dolores del Río, Pedro Armendáriz (Mexico City: Films Mundiales, 1943).

—— , *La rosa blanca*, with Roberto Cañedo (Mexico City/Havana: Películas Antillas, 1954).

—— , *Soy puro mexicano*, with Pedro Armendáriz (Mexico City: Producciones Raúl de Anda, 1942).

Fernández Bustamante, Alfredo, *María la O* (Mexico City/Havana: Producciones Amador, 1948).

Fuentes, Fernando de, *Allá en el Rancho Grande*, with Tito Guízar (Mexico City: Alfonso Rivas Bustamante/Fernando de Fuentes, 1936).

—— , *Allá en el Rancho Grande*, with Jorge Negrete (Mexico City: Producciones Grovas, 1949).

—— , *Doña Bárbara*, with María Félix (Mexico City: Clasa Films, 1943).

—— , *Jalisco canta en Sevilla*, with Jorge Negrete, Carmen Sevilla (Mexico City/Madrid: Producciones Diana/Chamartín Producciones, 1949).

Galindo, Alejandro, *Espaldas mojadas*, with David Silva (Mexico City: Ata Films/Atlas Films, 1955).

Gil, Rafael, *Mare nostrum* (Madrid/Rome: Suevia Films/Scalera Film, 1948).

Gómez Muriel, Emilio, *Llamas contra el viento* (Mexico City: Producciones Rosas Priego, 1956).

Gómez Urquiza, Zacarías, *El derecho de nacer*, with Jorge Mistral, Gloria Marín (Mexico City: Galindo Hermanos, 1952).

Martínez Solares, Gilberto, *La trepadora* (Mexico City: Clasa Films, 1944).

Méndez Bernal, Alberto, *Contrabando* (Ensenada: Alberto Méndez Bernal, 1933).

Moreno, Antonio, *Santa*, with Lupita Tovar, Juan José Martínez Casado (Mexico City: Compañía Nacional Productora de Películas, 1931).

Orol, Juan, *Embrujo antillano*, with María Antonieta Pons (Mexico City/Havana: Hispano Continental Films, 1947).

Peón, Ramón, *El romance del palmar*, with Rita Montaner (Havana: Pecusa, 1938).

—— , *Sucedió en la Habana*, with Rita Montaner (Havana: Pecusa, 1938).

Saa Silva, Roberto, *Allá en el trapiche* (Bogotá: Ducrane Films, 1943).

Soffici, Mario, *La cabalgata del circo*, with Libertad Lamarque, Hugo del Carril (Buenos Aires: Estudios San Miguel, 1944).

Soria, Gabriel, *La virgen morena* (Mexico City: Alberto Santander/Gabriel Soria, 1942).

Zacarías, Miguel, *La vorágine*, with Armando Calvo, Alicia Caro (Mexico City: Producciones Diana, 1949).

JOURNALS

ABC (Madrid)
Anuario Cinematográfico (Buenos Aires)
Bohemia (Havana)
Borba (Belgrade)
Cámara (Madrid)
Carteles (Havana)
Chic (Havana)
Cine (Buenos Aires)
Cine Argentino (Buenos Aires)
Cine Cubano (Havana)
El Cine Gráfico (Mexico City)
Cine Guía (Havana)
Cinema (Havana)
Cine Mundial (Mexico City)
Cinema Reporter (Mexico City)
Cine-Noticias (Bogotá)
El Crisol (Havana)
Cromos (Bogotá)
Diario de la Marina (Havana)
Dominical (Bogotá)
Duga (Belgrade)
Écran (Santiago de Chile)
El Espectador (Bogotá)
Esto (Mexico City)
Excélsior (Mexico City)
Filmográfico (Mexico City)
Filmski Svet (Belgrade)
Heraldo del Cinematografista (Buenos Aires)

Hoy (Havana)
Ilustrovani List Duga (Belgrade)
Informaciones (Madrid)
Los Angeles Times
Magazin Dominical (Bogotá)
Mi Film (Caracas)
El Mundo (Havana)
Mundo Cinematográfico (Mexico City)
El Mundo Gráfico (Madrid)
New York Times
Novedades (Buenos Aires)
La Opinión (Los Angeles)
El País (Havana)
Politika (Belgrade)
Politika Ekspres (Belgrade)
Primer Plano (Madrid)
Radiocinema (Madrid)
Sábado (Bogotá)
Sintonía (Buenos Aires)
El Tiempo (Bogotá)
El Universal Gráfico (Mexico City)
La Vanguardia (Madrid)

Index

Note: Page numbers in **bold** indicate detailed analysis. Those in *italic* refer to illustrations. *n* = endnote.

LIST OF ILLUSTRATIONS

While considerable effort has been made to correctly identify the copyright holders, this has not been possible in all cases. We apologise for any apparent negligence and any omissions or corrections brought to our attention will be remedied in any future editions.